Energy Policy Analysis

Energy Policy Analysis

A Conceptual Framework

Michael S. Hamilton

M.E.Sharpe
Armonk, New York
London, England

—For Carol—

Library of Congress Cataloging-in-Publication Data

Hamilton, Michael S.
  Energy policy analysis : a conceptual framework / by Michael S. Hamilton.
     p. cm.
  Includes bibliographical references and index.
  ISBN 978-0-7656-2381-2 (hardcover : alk. paper)—ISBN 978-0-7656-2382-9 (pbk. : alk. paper)
   1. Energy policy—United States. 2. Power resources—United States. 3. Renewable energy sources—United
States. I. Title.

HD9502.U52H35 2012
333.790973—dc23   2012014910

Printed in the United States of America

The paper used in this publication meets the minimum requirements of
American National Standard for Information Sciences
Permanence of Paper for Printed Library Materials,
ANSI Z 39.48-1984.

⊗

| IBT (c) | 10 | 9 | 8 | 7 | 6 | 5 | 4 | 3 | 2 | 1 |
| IBT (p) | 10 | 9 | 8 | 7 | 6 | 5 | 4 | 3 | 2 | 1 |

Contents

~~~~~~~~~~~~~~~~~~~~

Preface

Most of us recall a small number of people who had great influence upon our development, usually at critical times in our lives. I was fortunate to encounter Robert M. Lawrence in and outside classrooms at Colorado State University near a crossroads in life, while deciding what future path to take. An extraordinary scholar and classroom instructor, Professor Lawrence has an unusual and marvelous capacity for translating very complex ideas into plain language. This greatly affected both my intellectual development and my teaching style. Although he might be surprised to learn some of the things we discussed in his classes remain with me after all these years, from him I learned to set high standards for myself and that some things are worth more thought than others. Consequently, I have been thinking about the subject of this book for more than thirty years, and have attempted to present the subject with clarity and precision.

Nonetheless, responsibility for the content and views expressed in this book is solely mine and does not necessarily represent those of any person or organization with which I have been previously or currently may be affiliated.

Energy Policy Analysis is designed for use in social science or engineering courses concerned with the analysis, formulation, and implementation of national energy policy. This includes undergraduate and graduate courses in public policy analysis, energy policy, natural resources policy, environmental policy, national security policy, and energy and the environment. It is amenable to being used with a supplementary text focused on technical aspects of energy technologies or one with more historical content, such as Roy Nersesian's *Energy for the 21st Century*, 2nd ed. (M.E. Sharpe 2010). The book is cross-disciplinary, informed by the literatures of engineering and the social sciences, especially political science, public policy analysis, public administration, national security studies, international relations, and economics. It provides a straightforward and timely framework for analyzing alternatives and making national energy policy decisions for any national government.

I wish to express my appreciation to a group of extraordinarily creative students at the University of Southern Maine who explored with me the subject of this book during an undergraduate seminar in spring 2009: Dan Boyden, Sarah Busch, Sarah Dietz, Moriah Duval, Maggie Guzman, Shannon Keeler, Scott Kingsbury, Alex Lehnen, Chester Lunt, Caleb Moffitt, Kent Murdick, and Ashley Sevigney. Their research and observations during application of the conceptual framework confirmed its decision-making utility.

Finally, I could not possibly publish this book without acknowledging the highly professional, expeditious, and meticulous manner in which the folks at M.E. Sharpe handled it from start to finish. Although I believe he will not approve of my saying it here, I must acknowledge I count myself especially fortunate to have stumbled on Harry Briggs, who must certainly be the most patient and encouraging editor an author could ever hope to find on this planet. Without fanfare or unnecessary drama, Harry earned my everlasting gratitude by nursing this project along through a most difficult gestation over a period of three years, in a most gracious and supportive manner. Without Harry, I can truthfully say this book would never have been completed. Thank you, Harry.

Michael S. Hamilton

Energy Policy Analysis

1

A Framework for Analysis of Energy Choices

No president since Jimmy Carter in the late 1970s has advanced a coherent national energy policy (USDOE 1979; Executive Office of the President 1977), and Congress failed to approve most of his proposals. What should our national energy policy be? This book provides an analytical framework for answering this important and timely question. With energy prices higher now than in the 1970s, and with the nuclear industry vigorously promoting nuclear electric generation as a panacea for global climate change, even in the absence of a viable technology for permanent high-level radioactive waste management, this seems like an auspicious time for a new look at energy policy analysis. Historically there have been three approaches evident in the development of proposals for national energy policy in the United States: supply expansion, demand suppression, and cost analysis.

SUPPLY EXPANSION

Proponents of supply expansion have focused on energy conversion and distribution for the answers to the energy problem. This approach is based on the observation that there is no physical shortage of energy in the world. It advances the proposition that there is more energy in the world than we could ever possibly use, so the problem is not really a shortage, but barriers between us and the use of various energy sources.

Identification of these barriers usually has centered on one or more of the following: technical, geographical, economic, political, or environmental barriers to energy resource conversion and distribution.

Technical Barriers

Engineering feasibility of a technology defines technical barriers to use of various sources of energy. For example, we have created thermonuclear weapons based on nuclear fusion processes, but have as yet been unable to engineer adequate control over such processes and sustain them for sufficient periods of time to make fusion useful for generating electricity. Such technology might provide very substantial energy supplies and has been researched for some time, at considerable expense, but holds little promise for utilization in the foreseeable future due to technical difficulties. Expenditure of funds by government for continued basic research will be necessary to overcome these technical barriers, as there is no near-term prospect of profits from commercialization of fusion technology to encourage such investments by the private sector. Overcoming technical barriers may require large investments that ultimately increase the market price of some technologies if and when they become commercially available. Also, the lack of a proven technology for permanent management of high-level radioactive waste has not prevented increased use of nuclear fission to generate electricity, and such waste continues to accumulate in temporary storage. Apparently conversion and distribution are more sensitive to technical barriers than is waste management in the nuclear fuel cycle.

Geographical Barriers

Energy resources are not evenly distributed throughout the world; they are often found at consid-erable distances from large population concentrations where their utilization is most desirable. The location where energy resources are found is often a barrier to their use. North Sea British oil and North Slope Alaskan oil could not be used before new pipeline and drilling technolo-gies were developed, illustrating a common association between geographical and technical barriers. Tidal power and ocean thermal gradient technology may eventually provide energy supplies to some coastal and island areas, but not to interior areas of large continents (e.g., South Dakota). High-temperature geothermal resources are relatively rare and local in nature, although development of low-temperature geothermal resources using chemical technology is becoming more common with engineering advances. Overcoming geographical barriers may involve substantial expenditures to develop new technology or to move an energy resource from its origins to where it is utilized.

Economic Barriers

Market prices of some energy technologies are sometimes too expensive to compete effectively with resources in use at a particular point in time. Technologies have long been available to extract liquid hydrocarbons from oil shale and coal, but at greater expense than importing petroleum to the United States from the Middle East. Electricity can be generated using nuclear fission processes, but at much greater total expense than with coal or oil. Economic barriers may be particularly sensitive to technological developments, decreasing as new inventions in nuclear reactor tech-nology become available, for example, or increasing with policy changes such as more stringent requirements for reactor safety.

Political Barriers

Policy changes are produced by political behavior of individuals and groups affecting both inter-national relations and domestic activities, which may increase or decrease access to some energy supplies. U.S. support for Israel led to reduced access to imports of Middle Eastern oil during the oil embargo of 1973. Combative relations with Libya and Iraq have at other times impeded imports of oil from those countries. Political barriers are partly emotional in nature and may in some cases be more intractable and difficult to overcome than some technical barriers.

Environmental Barriers

Development, transportation, or use of some energy resources in some locations may entail un-acceptable disruption of the environment, contrary to widely held values of the populace. The combustion of coal without stringent air pollution controls has stimulated several national policy changes in the United States, and its continued use without some associated carbon sequestration may stimulate more changes out of concern for global climate change. Development of hydro-electric facilities has been excluded from some unique scenic areas, and the use of nuclear fission from others. Environmental barriers are political in nature, and their erection or modification may affect the market price of an energy technology, so they are often related to economic barriers and may be quite difficult to overcome without technological change.

These five barriers to supply expansion sometimes work in combination, with complex interrelationships that may be cumulative. For example, environmental, political, and economic barriers may combine to make oil shale development undesirable. Alternatively, these barriers may sometimes conflict with each other, necessitating trade-offs of one for another. Technical barriers to use of a potentially environmentally benign nuclear fusion technology may be most difficult to overcome. Or an economically attractive coal combustion technology may be environmentally undesirable.

The current so-called energy crisis seems to be due to a flaw in the armor of a great nation. Actually it is not a one-time crisis, but a recurring problem. After all, the first American "energy crisis" was the subject of a White House Conference in 1908 (White 1908) due to the perceived profligate waste of coal and natural gas resources that were then being used faster than new reserves were being found. High oil prices in early 2008 were reason for concern, but did not threaten the demise of the nation. In the short term, the U.S. energy policy problem appears to be principally a foreign policy problem, political in nature, based on U.S. relationships with Israel and several other Middle Eastern nations. Failure of the United States to balance its support for Israel with its need for Middle Eastern oil has created a host of difficulties for national energy policy. The energy policy problem in the United States is secondarily an economic problem, because our appetite for imported oil has made our economy vulnerable to disruption. Americans are not used to paying the full price for energy production and utilization, and do not care for rapid price increases for anything. Thirdly, the U.S. energy policy problem is an environmental problem, because many of the least expensive and most used resources have significant detrimental effects on the human environment.

Thus, those who approach energy policy from the supply side of the problem see it as policy designed to remove or overcome these barriers to expanded energy conversion and distribution. They seek to remove political, economic, and environmental barriers to increased energy consumption, rather than to suppress demand or make decisions based on cost analysis. Presidents Nixon, Reagan, and George W. Bush emphasized supply expansion. Recent proposals to open the Arctic National Wildlife Refuge and the outer continental shelf to increase drilling for oil and natural gas and to reduce safety requirements for new nuclear plants are manifestations of this approach. Significant barriers inhibiting the use of various energy sources will be identified in the course of this book.

DEMAND SUPPRESSION

Persons emphasizing demand suppression have focused on reducing energy consumption in their energy policy proposals. This approach is critical of consumerism and advances the proposition that our energy problems are attributable to human nature, which is viewed as inherently self-centered. Those who favor demand suppression maintain most people crave an ever higher standard of living, no matter how well off they may be. They suggest human beings have an insatiable appetite for material goods: cars, homes, boats, expensive clothing, and restaurant meals.

Most goods and services are produced through expenditure of energy during production and transportation to point of sale. Even the few notable exceptions are vulnerable: a scenic view is an aesthetic enjoyment, yet manufacture of a camera and transportation to a scenic location require use of energy; knowledge for the sake of knowledge entails travel to a library or use of the Internet for research, which also requires use of energy.

To most people in the United States and the world, America means *more:* affluence, expansion of frontiers, a rising gross domestic product (GDP), and a higher standard of living; that is, the United States is associated with *growth*, and growth is perceived as inherently good. Thorstein

Veblen characterized the American spirit as one of "conspicuous consumption" (1953), and his theory seems more applicable today than ever before. Among most Americans, forced change of lifestyles is perceived as categorically un-American. Consequently, the use of coercion to force lifestyle changes is not considered an acceptable policy solution in the United States. It would be easier to harness the sun than to change American lifestyles drastically, although small changes do occur, if slowly and noisily. When oil prices increase rapidly, many complaints are heard, Congressional investigations are initiated, hearings are held, and emergency measures are considered. Yet when prices decline even a bit, Americans get back into their SUVs and drive to the shopping mall.

Those who approach energy policy from the demand side maintain we must either cope with materialism by increasing supplies—the feasibility of which they view with great skepticism—or else change our lifestyles in order to reduce demand and conserve domestic energy resources for use in future periods. They tend to propose that people should make individual sacrifices, like putting on a sweater and turning down the thermostat, using less lighting, riding a bicycle, bus, or train to work instead of driving a car, staying at home on vacations and driving less generally, and refraining from purchase of energy-wasting home appliances and gadgets. President Jimmy Carter emphasized demand suppression measures in two major energy policy proposals (1977; USDOE 1979), neither of which was embraced with much enthusiasm by the U.S. Congress.

Many of these proposals are strikingly similar to wartime rationing of goods, and might have significant impacts on manufacturing, utility, and tourism portions of the national economy. Growth in consumption of energy-saving devices since the late 1970s has to some extent reduced these effects. More significantly, many Americans simply refuse to cut back or will do so only temporarily while demanding relief in the form of policy change. U.S. energy policy proposals since the 1970s have included a bewildering mixture of proposals to both remove barriers and change lifestyles. Perhaps this explains why we have such a shambles of energy policy: the choices are too numerous, demanding, and unpleasant to be considered legitimate by many citizens.

COST ANALYSIS

In a seminal article shortly after the oil embargo of 1973, Robert M. Lawrence suggested that national energy policy choices in the United States were constrained by three primary costs of continued high energy use: higher energy prices, greater environmental degradation, and increased security risk (1975). Seldom explicit but nonetheless implicit in previous energy policy proposals have been unsystematic comparisons of the costs of each available energy alternative. Unsystematic comparisons of the mix of different kinds of costs for each available energy resource have determined, and perhaps will continue to determine, policy choices in the United States about which energy technologies will be used and which deemphasized in the future.

A conceptual framework is presented here for analysis of various conventional and renewable energy fuel technologies in terms of their respective dollar costs, environmental costs, and national security costs to the nation. The objective of this analysis is to examine alternative national energy policy choices in a systematic fashion and specify the outlines of a coherent national energy policy. This conceptual framework may be used to evaluate energy policy choices for any nation-state in the world and with some modifications might be applied to subnational state energy policy decision making. The focus here is on analysis of technological options for formulating a coherent national energy policy for the United States.

Dollar Costs

An economic factor, the dollar costs to a society for utilizing each energy fuel technology is based on physical attributes of the fuel and the technologies used in each of several phases of a fuel cycle. Due to market forces and changes in technology, dollar costs may vary at different points in time. A fuel cycle includes discovery and exploration to verify the extent of a fuel resource, development, transportation, utilization, and final dispensation of waste by-products. Several fuels may be utilized with more than one technology, and each technology entails different dollar costs. The dollar costs for some energy fuel technologies may change over time based on discovery of previously unknown or unverified reserves, invention and utilization of new technologies, or changes in tax policies or those designed to manage and sustain the human environment. The dollar costs of a particular technology may be determined to some extent by the level of national security costs and environmental costs deemed acceptable by policy makers.

Dollar costs include the market price paid by consumers plus subsidies paid by taxpayers in a society to obtain the goods or services desired. Sharp increases in market price due to supply short-ages, collusion among suppliers, or other factors may have an adverse effect on local or national economies by shifting expenditures away from other goods and services and slowing activity in those sectors, as happened during the oil embargo of 1973 and after hurricanes destroyed some refinery capacity in the Gulf of Mexico in 2005.

Dollars paid by consumers of imported energy resources also may add up to a substantial drain on capital available for investment in the United States. It has been said that the flow of dollars from the United States to some countries such as Saudi Arabia to purchase oil constitutes the largest transfer of wealth from one country to another in the history of the world (Pickens 2008).

> Of America's $0.9 trillion oil bill in 2008, $388 billion went abroad. Some of this money paid for state-sponsored violence, weapons of mass destruction, and terrorism. This wealth transfer also worsens U.S. trade deficits, weakens the dollar, and boosts oil prices even higher as sellers try to protect their purchasing power. It's equivalent to a roughly two percent tax on the whole economy, without the revenues. Since 1975, America's oil imports have sucked well over $3 trillion of cash out of other expenditures and investments. (Lovins and Rocky Mountain Institute 2011, 3)

To the extent such transfers of wealth make investment capital scarcer in the United States and cause interest rates to rise, they slow growth in the U.S. economy and contribute to higher prices, unemployment, and increased government expenditures for social services.

Costs additional to market prices may be imposed on taxpayers to provide research and development of new fuels or technologies, or tax expenditures to encourage production of a particular resource. Development of several designs for nuclear fission reactors to generate electricity was largely funded by the U.S. Congress in the 1950s and 1960s, and exploration for new oil reserves was subsidized by an "oil depletion allowance" provided to the oil industry for many years through the U.S. tax code. Long-term management of high-level radioactive waste created by generation of electricity in commercial nuclear reactors continues to be subsidized by the U.S. government and its taxpayers.

The market cost to consumers for all energy consumed in 2009 is estimated at a bit over $1 trillion during a recession, and at $1.4 trillion in 2008 (USEIA 2011a, Table 3.5). Total federal energy-specific subsidies and supports for all forms of energy are estimated at a bit less than $14.8 billion for fiscal year (FY) 2010, which included most of calendar year 2007 and part of calendar year 2008, including $17.9 billion for electricity production (USEIA 2011b, xiii, xiv). It is often difficult to obtain empirical data to quantify the value of some taxpayer costs, which must nonetheless be identified and taken into consideration in a comprehensive cost analysis. Federal subsidies change somewhat from year to year with fluctuations in the economy and enactment of new legislation, and many studies present only aggregate data for multiple years (Environmental Law Institute 2009). In most cases, cost analysis relies most heavily on market prices to consumers, which cover most but not all significant dollar costs for utilizing a fuel technology.

National Security Costs

A political factor, the national security costs of an energy fuel technology are also based on the physical attributes of the fuel and the technologies used in several phases of a fuel cycle. As is the case with dollar costs, national security costs may vary at different times due to changes in technologies and relations between nation-states. National security costs are determined by application of accepted concepts of what is necessary to sustain the national security of any nation-state in the contemporary world. National security is defined as the "integrity of the national territory and of its institutions" (Morgenthau 1960, 562). Fundamentally this includes two attributes of sovereignty: continued *survival* of a nation and its institutions in their physical existence and social well-being; and *freedom of action* of a nation's government in the pursuit of its national interests in the conduct of foreign affairs—the freedom to choose between alternative foreign policies without interference by others. Threats to the survival of a nation include armed invasion by another nation-state and the acquisition of nuclear weapons and delivery capability by a hostile state or terrorist organization. Threats to freedom of action in foreign affairs include dependence of a nation-state on energy resources that must be imported from other nation-states hostile to some preferred foreign policy of the importing country, and reluctance of a nation-state to engage in activities that may directly or indirectly cause the extinction of another nation-state. Thus, national security costs are viewed as significant threats to the physical existence and well-being of a nation-state, including those threats that may interfere with or constrain choices between alternative foreign policies toward other nation-states.

Dependence of the United States on oil resources that must be imported from nation-states in the Middle East who are hostile toward U.S. foreign policy in support of Israel threatened U.S. freedom of action in its foreign affairs during the Arab oil embargo of 1973, when Organization of Arab Petroleum Exporting Countries (OAPEC) reduced sales of oil to the United States in retaliation for U.S. support of Israel during and after the war of 1967 (Halabi 2009; Nersesian 2010, 150–151; Geller 1993; U.S. Congress 1975). Although the effects of the embargo were relatively short-lived, due to "leakage" of oil supplies to the United States from international oil markets in Europe and elsewhere, they did produce significant disruption of the U.S. economy for some period, rendering U.S. foreign policy makers more sensitive to the views of OAPEC members than they had been previously and stimulating expansion of the Strategic Oil Reserve in the United States (Barton et al. 2004, 153; Davis 1993; Kalt 1981). The exact degree to which U.S. support of Israel has been reduced or has shifted in subsequent years is undetermined, but there has certainly been an increase in concern for the views of OAPEC countries toward U.S. foreign policy.

Similarly, continued large-scale use of carbon fuels such as coal promises to affect adversely through sea-level rise nation-states with large populations living in deltaic regions, such as the Philippines, Indonesia, Bangladesh, Vietnam, China, and Egypt, and may cause the extinction of several low-lying island nation-states in the world, such as the Maldives, the Marshall Islands, Tuvalu, and Kiribati (Henley 2008; O'Carroll 2008; Nicholls et al. 2007, 315–356). According to the International Organization for Migration, as many as 200 million refugees could be displaced by climate change by 2050 in the South Pacific and Indian Ocean regions (MacFarquhar 2009). The impact on nearby nation-states of an influx of so many persons seems likely to destabilize some governments in these regions, including Bangladesh and perhaps Australia.

Recognition that environmental factors such as climate change may have national security costs and entail issues requiring particular attention by the U.S. Department of Defense is found in the most recent *Quadrennial Defense Review*:

> Assessments conducted by the intelligence community indicate that climate change could have significant geopolitical impacts around the world, contributing to poverty, environmental degradation, and the further weakening of fragile governments. Climate change will contribute to food and water scarcity, will increase the spread of disease, and may spur or exacerbate mass migration.
>
> As climate science advances, the Department will regularly reevaluate climate change risks and opportunities in order to develop policies and plans to manage its effects on the Department's operating environment, missions, and facilities. Managing the national security effects of climate change will require DOD to work collaboratively, through a whole-of-government approach, with both traditional allies and new partners. (USDOD 2010, 85, 86–87)

Moreover, as Admiral Michael G. Mullen, chair of the Joint Chiefs of Staff, wrote in 2011 in *Joint Force Quarterly*,

> The impending scarcity of resources compounded by an influx of refugees if coastal lands disappear not only could produce a humanitarian crisis, but also could generate conditions that could lead to failed states and make populations more vulnerable to radicalization. These troubling challenges highlight the systemic implications—and multiple-order effects—inherent in energy security and climate change. (2–3)

Consequently, it seems appropriate to include environmental factors such as climate change as national security costs in a conceptual framework for evaluation of energy policy choices.

After a ten-year drought, severe wildlife decline, killer heat waves in the south, and monsoon flooding in the north, Australia's agricultural economy collapsed in 2009; its tourist economy may be next, and there is widespread belief it may be one of the early casualties of climate change (Cart 2009). Large, continental nation-states such as the United States have not until recently perceived the difficulties of small island states as sufficiently important to warrant changes in domestic energy policy, but actions that affect key allies like Indonesia, Australia, and Egypt, or key rivals such as China, may reasonably be expected to have some impact on U.S. foreign policy and national security. Although the moral argument has never been a particularly strong force in international relations, to the extent other nation-states may be reluctant to contribute to the extinction of "endangered nation-states," large-scale reliance on fossil fuels may threaten their freedom of action in foreign affairs and may limit their choices in use of energy technologies for domestic purposes.

Historically, discussions of "energy security" have been couched largely in terms of concern for oil prices, with only occasional mention of possible supply disruptions (Barton et al. 2004; Copaken 2003; USGAO 1993). These discussions were shaped historically by the Organization of Petroleum Exporting Countries (OPEC) cartel strategy of influencing the international price of crude oil through curtailments and expansions of supply, and have only peripherally touched on the possibility of the use of violence to resolve imbalances in the global distribution of natural resources or of supply and demand.

Recently, a new literature of "resource scarcity" has begun to develop around the concept of uneven distribution of natural resources in the world (Ophuls and Boyan 1992), raising the prospect of "resource wars" both within nation-states (e.g., civil wars) and between nation-states over access to scarce natural resources such as oil (Lahiri-Dutt 2006; Klare 1995, 2004; Butts 1994). Some have asserted that such wars would be more common and more likely in the future between developing countries rather than large powers and that they may exacerbate existing conflicts and civil strife within states based on other factors rather than providing stimulus for new interstate conflicts (Homer-Dixon 1993, 1999; Homer-Dixon and Percival 1996). Others have approached the same issue from a different direction, noting that about a quarter of the roughly fifty wars and armed conflicts active in 2001 had strong natural resource dimensions and asserting that "abundant natural resources help fuel conflicts"; it has also been noted that "Where resource wealth is a factor in conflicts, it is primarily non-renewable resources such as fuels and minerals that are at issue. . . . On the other hand, where resource scarcity is a factor, it concerns principally resources that cannot be looted and traded, such as farmland and water" (Renner 2002, 6, 9). Still other participants in policy-making discussions have taken a broader view in identifying environmental threats to U.S. national security (Butts 1994).

Under what circumstances might continued reliance on fossil fuels by one nation-state be considered aggression against other more vulnerable nation-states due to the effects of global climate change? Although small nation-states have little ability to threaten the continued existence of large powers like the United States, trade and security relations with some large nation-states may be adversely affected if significant portions of their populations are perceived to be impacted by continued emissions of atmospheric carbon and global climate change, especially if those nation-states have taken action to reduce their emissions more than others. Moreover, no nation-state today is beyond the reach of acts of terrorism that may inflict unacceptable damage on domestic populations or economies. The extent to which U.S. concern for future relations with affected and endangered nation-states might moderate consumption of fossil fuels is not yet evident. No increase in U.S. foreign assistance to endangered nation-states or significant reduction in consumption of fossil fuels is yet discernible.

Because international relations between nation-states may change over time due to numerous factors within and beyond the control of human beings, preferences for particular foreign policies and national security costs may also change over time. National security costs for some energy fuel sources may change based on invention and utilization of new energy technologies, defensive military technologies or strategies, regime change, or changes in foreign policy preferences of relevant nation-states.

Environmental Costs

A political factor, the environmental costs of each energy fuel technology are based on physical attributes of the fuel and the technologies used in several phases of a fuel cycle. Like dollar costs, environmental costs may vary at different times due to changes in technologies and market conditions. Environmental costs are losses by destruction or impairment of some desirable attribute of the human environment and biosphere. Congress recognized the profound impact of human activities on the natural environment, particularly the influences of population growth, high-density urbanization, industrial expansion, resource exploitation, new technological advances, and the critical importance of restoring and maintaining environmental quality when it enacted the National Environmental Policy Act, requiring the national government to use all practicable means and measures to create and maintain conditions under which humans and nature can exist in productive harmony (42 U.S. Code §4331). Assessing environmental costs during analysis of energy policy options is consistent with this mandate.

Some environmental costs can be easily quantified in terms of the dollars required to mitigate harmful impacts of human activity. Examples are capital and operating expenditures for air and water pollution control equipment at fossil-fueled electric generating stations, or cleanup costs for hazardous waste sites on the Superfund National Priorities List. Examination of such environmental costs reveals an important relationship between them and dollar costs in this analytical framework: some environmental costs can effectively be converted to dollar costs. However, it is specifically recognized in long-standing U.S. national environmental policy that environmental costs must be identified and included in any reasonable analysis for decision making, even if not currently quantifiable (42 U.S. Code §4332[B]). These might include the value of a scenic view of the Grand Canyon as mitigating against hydroelectric development at that location. Many economists maintain such values can be estimated in dollar terms using various methods (e.g., replacement costs, willingness to pay) that produce different values for the same resource. Often no consensus on the resulting value is apparent. They continue to argue over an appropriate way to estimate such values that might be politically acceptable to the entire nation.

Although national security costs and environmental costs may sometimes be expressed in terms of dollars, neither is always amenable to expression in terms of quantifiable units. Consequently, some national security costs and environmental costs may also be expressed as positive or negative effects. This may be troublesome to some economists, but by now the difficulties of including unquantifiable amenities in analytical frameworks should at least be familiar, if not completely satisfying. Excluding significant unquantifiable values from the analytical framework is deemed by the author to be intellectually dishonest and a greater evil than complicating the analysis by including them.

ANALYTICAL FRAMEWORK

From the foregoing discussion it should be evident that analyzing and formulating national energy policy are not merely domestic, internal policy matters, but overlap large areas of international relations, foreign policy, and defense policy. As others have often observed, domestic and foreign policies are intertwined and interact in complex ways.

The analytical framework presented here allows examination of issues and problems associated with implementation of U.S. energy policies in the context of major social goals (e.g., growth, equity), with treatment of conflicts and trade-offs between energy development and other social values (e.g., health and safety; cultural, historical and aesthetic values). These are salient political issues today for policy makers formulating national energy policy and decision makers implementing it. Rather than producing a single optimum energy technology choice, it should be expected that the mix of energy technologies with the lowest overall costs in these three categories (dollar costs, environmental costs, and national security costs) would produce the most viable national energy policy.

PREVIOUS ENERGY POLICY STUDIES

Most of the extant book literature on energy policy was written in the 1970s and 1980s, including a book by the Ford Foundation (1974), on which President Jimmy Carter's two major national energy policy proposals were based. Other sources include an "unfinished business" text written by the Ford Foundation at the end of the Carter administration (1979) and several other texts written by academics (Rosenbaum 1987; Kash and Rycroft 1984; Zinberg 1983; Daneke and Lagassa 1980), proponents of economic development (Schurr et al. 1979; Stobaugh and Yergin 1979), and proponents of environmental protection (Commoner 1979; Lovins 1979). The world has changed since then and these books are all seriously out of date today. Energy prices, technologies, U.S. international relations, environmental knowledge, and government policies have changed in the interim.

As oil prices declined, only a few texts on energy policy were published in the 1990s and since 2000. Most of these are also dated (Davis 1993; Lee 1990; Munasinghe 1990). Some are highly technical and suitable only for a graduate audience in econometrics or computer modeling (Munasinghe and Meier 1993). Some focus on economic analysis of various fuels without significant treatment of environmental or national security issues (Banks 2007; Geller 2003), thereby limiting their utility for policy decision making. Others provide detailed information about energy technologies but lack an explicit conceptual framework for analyzing energy policy choices (Nersesian 2010). The need for an operational analytical framework is evident in publication by the Congressional Research Service of *Energy Policy: Conceptual Framework and Continuing Issues* (Bamberger 2006). However, at fifteen pages, there are more conclusions than analysis there.

Although Davis (1993) purports to advance a conceptual framework for analysis of energy policy choices based on three sets of independent variables—physical characteristics of the fuel, market forces, and a vague notion of "the general political environment"—the analytical framework is weak. It relies in part on a fuzzy description of history ("era in which a particular form of energy first emerges") as shaping "the general political environment" without explaining how one might operationalize this variable for analytical purposes. Plus times have changed: policies governing hydropower and coal are no longer dominated by the progressive and labor politics of the eras in which they were first widely utilized. The Davis text devotes full chapters to coal, oil, natural gas, electricity, and nuclear energy, but deals with all renewables, conservation, and synthetic fuels in a single chapter. The text is quite out of date and does not lend itself readily to analyzing energy alternatives or making national policy decisions today.

A recent text providing a more inclusive approach to both conventional and alternative energy technologies (Cipiti 2007) examines a number of transportation and power generation technologies "from different *perspectives*" (emphasis added), including their environmental impact, economics, size of domestic resource base, public acceptance, and reliability. However, presentation of these "perspectives" is more intuitive than conceptually well-explicated, and surveying more than a dozen energy fuel technologies in terms of each of five "perspectives" in 180 pages produced a text that is more descriptive than analytical, and not well-developed for decision making among energy policy choices.

For example, although utilization of domestic energy resources in preference to foreign sources may in some cases be reasonable, by relying on the size of domestic resource base as a decision-making variable without much explanation, Cipiti introduces a rather isolationist (or even jingoistic) emotional flavor into policy making toward U.S. allies like Canada, who may have significant resources (e.g., tar sands) that can produce oil for use in the United States at reasonable prices, with arguably acceptable environmental and national security costs. Cipiti's use of a "public acceptance" variable unsupported by substantial empirical evidence is also somewhat problematical. Evaluation of several energy fuels (e.g., wind, nuclear) in terms of their reliability of supply while failing to evaluate the related electric utility delivery system in terms of its questionable reliability is a serious shortcoming. And Cipiti's failure to evaluate the trade-offs between reliability and price of several energy sources renders the text seriously flawed. Some energy sources can be made more reliable by requiring investments in additional technology that makes them more expensive (e.g., load shedding equipment for electric transmission and distribution systems).

Some recent texts have focused on less environmentally disruptive renewable resources like solar, hydro, and wind to the exclusion of more conventional and widely used energy sources like coal, oil, and nuclear technologies (Simon 2007; Mallon 2006; Komor 2004; Geller 2003). These texts usually begin from an assumed premise that the use of fossil fuels and nuclear technologies is unsustainable and undesirable, emphasize a "crisis" approach, and advocate mitigating or removing "entrenched advantages" held by conventional technologies to speed a shift to renewable sources (Geller 2003, Ch. 1).

Consequently, these books generally provide only an implicit decision-making framework for choosing between energy policy options; they often provide only the most cursory analysis of conventional fuels and technologies, if they provide any at all. For example, although Simon (2007) discusses the technical, political, economic, and social feasibility of several renewable technologies, he does not provide comparable treatment of conventional energy technologies or an explicit conceptual framework for analyzing alternative national energy policy decisions.

Although such advocacy pieces have their uses in a classroom, they must be used with additional texts, making course adoption expensive. And restricting available energy supply options to renewables without providing a sound conceptual basis for doing so fails to recognize substantial existing investments ("sunk costs") in conventional energy sources that must be taken into consideration if a desired shift to renewables might be accomplished without severe economic dislocation—a concern most American politicians and government decision makers find of signal importance.

Unlike the foregoing texts, this book presents an explicit, well-developed conceptual framework for analysis of energy technologies in terms of their respective dollar costs, environmental costs, and national security costs, thereby extending the literature of energy policy analysis. Components of this conceptual framework are applied to various conventional and renewable energy fuel technologies and alternative national energy policy choices in the following chapters.

REFERENCES

Bamberger, Robert. 2006. *Energy Policy: Conceptual Framework and Continuing Issues*. Washington, DC: U.S. Government Printing Office.

Banks, Ferdinand E. 2007. *The Political Economy of World Energy*. Hackensack, NJ: World Scientific.

Barton, Barry, Catherine Redgwell, Anita Ronne, and Donald N. Zillman. 2004. *Energy Security: Managing Risk in a Dynamic Legal and Regulatory Environment*. Oxford: Oxford University Press.

Butts, Kent Hughes. 1994. *Environmental Security: A DOD Partnership for Peace*. Carlisle, PA: U.S. Army War College.

Cart, Julie. 2009. "The Writing on the Wall; Drought, Fire, Killer Heat and Suicides—Scientists Say Climate Change Fears Have Become Reality in Australia." *Los Angeles Times*, April 9.

Carter, Jimmy, Executive Office of the President. 1977. *The National Energy Plan*. Washington, DC: U.S. Government Printing Office.

Cipiti, Ben. 2007. *The Energy Construct: Achieving a Clean, Domestic, and Economical Energy Future*. North Charleston, SC: BookSurge.

Commoner, Barry. 1979. *The Politics of Energy*. New York: Knopf.

Copaken, Robert R. 2003. *The Arab Oil Weapon of 1973–74 as a Double-edged Sword: Its Implications for Future Energy Security*. Durham, UK: University of Durham, Institute for Middle Eastern and Islamic Studies.

Daneke, Greg, and George Lagassa. 1980. *Energy Policy and Public Administration*. Lexington, MA: D.C. Heath.

Davis, David H. 1993. *Energy Politics*, 4th ed. New York: St. Martin's Press.

Environmental Law Institute. 2009. *Estimating U.S. Government Subsidies to Energy Sources: 2002–2008.* Washington, DC: Environmental Law Institute.

Executive Office of the President. 1977. *The National Energy Plan.* Washington, DC: U.S. Government Printing Office.

Ford Foundation. 1974. *A Time to Choose: America's Energy Future.* Cambridge, MA: Ballinger.

———. 1979. *Energy: The Next Twenty Years.* Cambridge, MA: Ballinger.

Geller, Howard S. 1993. *Twenty Years After the Embargo: U. S. Oil Import Dependence and How It Can be Reduced.* Washington, DC: American Council for an Energy-Efficient Economy.

———. 2003. *Energy Revolution: Policies for a Sustainable Future.* Washington, DC: Island Press.

Halabi, Yakub. 2009. *U.S. Foreign Policy in the Middle East: From Crises to Change.* Farnham, UK: Ashgate.

Henley, Jon. 2008. "The Last Days of Paradise." *Guardian,* November 11.

Homer-Dixon, Thomas F. 1993. *Environmental Scarcity and Global Security.* New York: Foreign Policy Association.

———. 1999. *Environment, Scarcity, and Violence.* Princeton, NJ: Princeton University Press.

Homer-Dixon, Thomas F., and Valerie Percival. 1996. *Environmental Scarcity and Violent Conflict: Briefing Book.* Washington, DC: American Association for the Advancement of Science.

Kalt, Joseph P. 1981. *The Economics and Politics of Oil Price Regulation: Federal Policy in the Post-Embargo Era.* Cambridge: MIT Press.

Kash, Don, and Robert Rycroft. 1984. *U.S. Energy Policy: Crisis and Complacency.* Norman: University of Oklahoma Press.

Klare, Michael T. 1995. *Rogue States and Nuclear Outlaws: America's Search for a New Foreign Policy.* New York: Hill & Wang.

———. 2004. *Blood and Oil: The Dangers and Consequences of America's Growing Petroleum Dependency.* New York: Metropolitan Books.

Komor, Paul. 2004. *Renewable Energy Policy.* New York: iUniverse.

Lahiri-Dutt, Kuntala. 2006. "'May God Give Us Chaos, So That We Can Plunder': A Critique of 'Resources Curse' and Conflict Theories." *Development* 49(3):14–21.

Lawrence, Robert M. 1975. "Higher Prices, Insecurity, and Degradation: Tradeoffs in U.S. Energy Policy." *American Behavioral Scientist* (September/October): 8–36.

Lee, Thomas. 1990. *Energy Aftermath.* Boston: Harvard Business School Press.

Lovins, Amory. 1979. *Soft Energy Paths: Toward a Durable Peace.* New York: Harper and Row.

Lovins, Amory, and Rocky Mountain Institute. 2011. *Reinventing Fire.* White River Junction, VT: Chelsea Green.

MacFarquhar, Neil. 2009. "Refugees Join List of Climate-Change Issues." *New York Times,* May 29.

Mallon, Karl, ed. 2006. *Renewable Energy Policy and Politics.* London: Earthscan.

Morgenthau, Hans J. 1960. *Politics Among Nations.* New York: Alfred A. Knopf.

Mullen, M.G. 2011. "From the Chairman." *Joint Force Quarterly* 60 (1st quarter). www.ndu.edu/press/from-the-chairman-60.html.

Munasinghe, Mohan. 1990. *Energy Analysis and Policy.* Boston: Butterworths.

Munasinghe, Mohan, and Peter Meier. 1993. *Energy Policy Analysis and Modeling.* New York: Cambridge University Press.

Nersesian, Roy L. 2010. *Energy for the 21st Century,* 2nd ed., Armonk, NY: M.E. Sharpe.

Nicholls, R.J., P.P. Wong, V.R. Burkett, J.O. Codignotto, J.E. Hay, R.F. McLean, S. Ragoonaden, and C.D. Woodroffe. 2007. "Coastal Systems and Low-Lying Areas. Climate Change 2007: Impacts, Adaptation and Vulnerability." In *Contribution of Working Group II to the Fourth Assessment Report of the Intergovernmental Panel on Climate Change,* ed. M.L. Parry, O.F. Canziani, J.P. Palutikof, P.J. van der Linden, and C.E. Hanson. Cambridge, UK: Cambridge University Press.

O'Carroll, Eoin. 2008. "Faced with Rising Sea Levels, the Maldives Seek New Homeland." *Christian Science Monitor,* November 11.

Ophuls, William, and A. Stephen Boyan. 1992. *Ecology and the Politics of Scarcity Revisited.* New York: W.H. Freeman.

Pickens, T. Boone. 2008. "America Is Addicted to Foreign Oil." PickensPlan.com. http://media.pickensplan.com/pdf/pickensplan.pdf.

Renner, Michael. 2002. *The Anatomy of Resource Wars.* Washington, DC: Worldwatch Institute.

Rosenbaum, Walter. 1987. *Energy, Politics and Public Policy,* 2nd ed. Washington, DC: CQ Press.

Schurr, Sam H., and National Energy Strategies Project. 1979. *Energy in America's Future*. Baltimore, MD: Resources for the Future.

Simon, Christopher. 2007. *Alternative Energy: Political, Economic, and Social Feasibility*. Lanham, MD: Rowman and Littlefield.

Stobaugh, Robert, and Daniel Yergin, eds. 1979. *Energy Future*. New York: Random House.

U.S. Congress. Committee on International Relations. 1975. *Oil Fields as Military Objectives: A Feasibility Study*. Report prepared by the Congressional Research Service, 94th Cong., 1st sess., August 21. Washington, DC: U.S. Government Printing Office.

U.S. Department of Defense (USDOD). 2010. *Quadrennial Defense Review*. Washington, DC: U.S. Department of Defense.

U.S. Department of Energy (USDOE). 1979. *National Energy Plan II*. Washington, DC: U.S. Government Printing Office.

U.S. Energy Information Administration (USEIA). 2011a. *Annual Energy Review 2010*. Washington, DC: U.S. Government Printing Office.

———. 2011b. *Direct Federal Financial Interventions and Subsidies in Energy Markets 2010*. Washington, DC: U.S. Government Printing Office.

U.S. General Accounting Office (USGAO). 1993. *Energy Security and Policy Analysis of the Pricing of Crude Oil and Petroleum Products*. Washington, DC: U.S. General Accounting Office.

Veblen, Thorstein. 1953. *Theory of the Leisure Class*. New York: New American Library.

White, I.C. 1908. "The Waste of Our Fuel Resources." In *White House Conference on the Conservation of Natural Resources*, chair J. Horace McFarland. Philadelphia: American Civic Association.

Zinberg, Dorothy S., ed. 1983. *Uncertain Power: The Struggle for a National Energy Policy*. New York: Pergamon.

2

Coal

~~~~~~~~~~~~~~~~~~~~~~~~

Domestic reserves of coal in the United States are plentiful. As of January 1, 2010, remaining U.S. recoverable coal reserves were estimated at over 259 billion short tons (a short ton equals 2,000 pounds), from a demonstrated base of 484 billion short tons of reserves that may support economic mining using current technologies, depending on market price (USEIA 2011a, Table 15). For comparison, U.S. coal consumption was about 1.05 billion short tons in 2010 (Table 26). At current rates of consumption, the United States had 246 to 460 years of coal remaining. In the United States, about 68.7 percent of coal was produced from surface mines in 2010 (Table 2). Surface mines typically recover 90 to 95 percent of available coal, while underground mines recover 50 to 60 percent (Christman et al. 1980, 87).

The coal fuel cycle includes exploration, mining, processing, transportation, combustion, and disposal of waste by-products, as illustrated in Figure 2.1.

COAL EXPLORATION

In the United States, where coal has been used since the early 1700s in Virginia, most exposed outcrop seams of coal have been discovered and exploited, so exploration tends to require more sophisticated technologies involving remote sensing or satellite imagery of geologic formations, or drilling to verify suspected resources not yet proven. Consequently, the most significant environmental costs from coal exploration often attend the construction of new roads in roadless areas, and core drilling for samples. Regions where coal is found in the United States are illustrated in Figure 2.2.

A coal exploration program occurs in stages, designed to give a geologist enough reliable data to characterize the reserve and a mining engineer enough data to produce a plan for development of a mine, extraction of the coal, and reclamation of the site. The initial stage of

Figure 2.1 **The Coal Fuel Cycle**

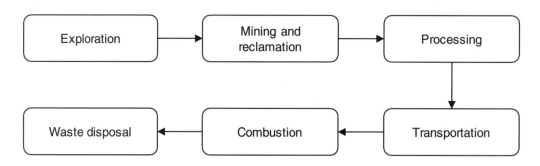

Figure 2.2 **US Coal Reserves, Locations**

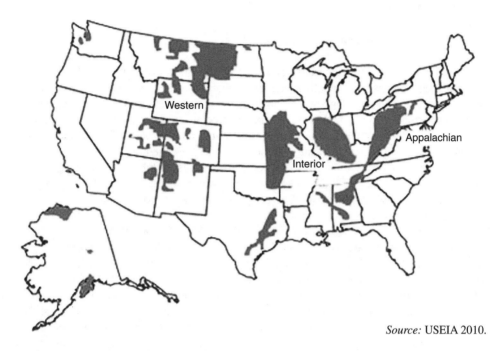

Source: USEIA 2010.

exploration consists of gathering available information about an area from library sources, state and local government agencies, previous mining activities, and oil, gas, and water well records. This information will be used to prepare databases and preliminary maps of the area showing seam depth, thickness, and structure. Reports and maps available on the Internet or digital analysis of satellite imagery may be used (Upadhyay 2000). The second stage of coal exploration is a site visit by field geologists. They verify data gathered during the first stage and supplement it with measurements of any outcrops, samples from exposed coal seams, and other physical evidence. The field team checks access to possible drill sites, local laws and regulations concerning drilling, and ability of local infrastructure to support a drilling effort (e.g., roads, accommodations, fuel).

After completion of the second stage and reevaluation of a location's potential, core drilling and logging of boreholes provide detailed measurements of coal reserves and information on the depth, structure, thickness, and quality of coal, the most important and costly stage of exploration. Spacing of drill holes depends on the complexity of local geology, but for measured reserves is typically 0.5 miles (Christman et al. 1980, 73). Drill hole cores provide detailed information on mine roof and floor materials, as well as coal samples for quality analysis. A small percentage of drill holes are cored top to bottom to provide detailed geochemical information on overburden material. Core drilling is significantly more expensive than normal drilling, so methods have been developed to provide the same information without coring, through use of various well log tools, and digital down-hole data logging is increasingly common. Geophysical logs can provide measurements of material density, clay content, and coal quality. After the drilling and logging program is completed, detailed maps of coal structure, thickness, quality, and depth of burial are produced (Upadhyay 2000). This data is easily converted to maps and reports (Hamilton 2005, 222–23). With this information, it is possible to decide whether the prospect area provides sufficient economic potential to justify proceeding with development planning and feasibility studies (Christman et al. 1980, 73).

Environmental Costs of Coal Exploration

Exploration for coal produces environmental effects on roadless areas not regularly visited by humans. Off-road vehicles are generally used for reconnaissance, and their use intrudes into wildlife habitats, damaging or destroying low-growing vegetation and creating zones of erosion along ruts. Loss of vegetation combined with reduced natural percolation rates due to soil compaction tends to increase soil erosion rates. Increased soil erosion increases sediment loads in local streams, degrading water quality and increasing sedimentation of lakes and ponds.

Exploration activity involving off-road vehicle travel also inhibits regrowth of vegetation. Soil compaction reduces the ability of soil to absorb water, which further inhibits plant growth by destroying microorganisms in soil. Where vegetation is destroyed by vehicle use, revegetation will take anywhere from one growing season in wet climates (Christman et al. 1980) to ten years in arid locations like the western United States (OSM 1979; USBLM 1975).

Long-term or concentrated off-road vehicle use can drive wildlife from its normal ranges and disrupt breeding and nesting habits of small mammals and birds (USBLM 1975). Off-road vehicle travel may also damage or destroy archeological or historic sites (U.S. Advisory Council on Historic Preservation 1978). In some terrain, road construction is a necessary part of exploration to provide access to drill sites for large equipment. During road construction, all vegetation is removed. Bulldozing and grading create cut-banks and deposits of surplus soil and other disturbed material. This surface disturbance increases erosion and sedimentation. Increased suspended sediments in streams adversely affect aquatic organisms (Christman et al. 1980). Roadways concentrate runoff and are susceptible to landslides and slope instabilities (USGS 1979). Large-scale surface disturbance by road construction reduces biological productivity, eliminates terrestrial habitats, and disturbs the wildlife community by intruding into little used areas. Travel on unpaved roads produces visible dust that may adversely affect the health of any nearby residents, degrade the esthetic quality of an area, and adversely affect existing land uses (USBLM 1975). Dust deposits on vegetation reduce both its productivity and palatability as forage for wildlife and farm animals (OSM 1979).

Exploration drill holes may penetrate several aquifers and result in leakage between aquifers and to the surface with possible degradation of water quality (USGS 1979). Drilling activities can have detrimental impacts on surface water and groundwater, resulting in harm to aquatic organisms, vegetation, and humans. Lowering the groundwater level in an aquifer can result in increased pumping costs at nearby wells or can cause wells to go dry. Open holes present a danger to domestic and wild animals, as well as humans. Improperly plugged drill holes allow surface water to enter an aquifer. This may be detrimental to groundwater, depending on the quality and degree of contamination of surface water.

In situations where coal deposits are near the surface, pits are sometimes excavated to obtain bulk samples for laboratory analysis. Heavy equipment is used to remove overburden and expose the coal, producing considerable surface disturbance. Vegetation is lost and soils are rearranged, similar to strip mining operations but on a smaller scale. Where pits are excavated to provide coal samples, wildlife and domestic stock may be endangered by slope instabilities and potential landslides unless pits are backfilled promptly (USGS 1979). Other impacts from exploration drilling include noise, damage to archeological and historical sites, and possible contamination by drilling muds and fluids (USBLM 1975).

Coal Mining Methods

There are two basic methods of mining a coal reserve: underground mining and surface mining. The choice of mining method depends primarily on depth of burial and thickness of the coal seam. Seams relatively close to the surface, at depths less than approximately 180 feet, are usually surface mined. Coals that occur at depths of 180 to 300 feet are usually deep mined, although in some cases surface mining techniques can be used. For example, some western U.S. coals that occur at depths in excess of 200 feet are mined by open pit methods, due to thickness of the seam (sixty to ninety feet). Coals occurring below 300 feet are usually deep mined (Christman et al. 1980, 74).

Coal is mined only where technically feasible and economically justifiable. Evaluation of technical and economic feasibility of a potential mine requires consideration of many factors: regional geologic conditions; overburden (e.g., rock and soil) characteristics; coal seam continuity, thickness, structure, quality, and depth; strength of materials above and below the seam for roof and floor conditions; topography (especially altitude and slope); climate; land ownership as it affects the availability of land for mining and access; surface drainage patterns; groundwater conditions; availability of labor and materials; coal purchaser requirements in terms of tonnage, quality, and destination; and capital investment requirements (Christman et al. 1980, 74).

From about 1945 to 1960, use of coal for rail and water transportation and for space heating declined, while overall demand increased for electricity generation. Today, demand for coal is driven by the electric power generating sector, which accounts for 90 percent of coal consumption. As demand increased, capital-intensive surface coal mining grew at the expense of labor-intensive underground coal mining; accelerated use of surface mining technology in large-scale area mines shifted production from eastern coalfields to the western United States; underground mining shifted from conventional room and pillar mining to longwall mining, further displacing labor; and improvements in mining equipment durability and capability increased productivity and helped keep coal mining costs low (Bonskowski, Watson, and Freme 2006, 1–6). In the 1990s, growth in total coal demand slowed to a little over 1 billion tons per year and coal prices decreased by 45 percent in real dollar terms, as average mine size continued to increase; production was increasingly concentrated among fewer, larger companies; "high-grading" of reserve properties forced the closure of less competitive properties; and productivity continued to increase (Bonskowski 2000, 1).

UNDERGROUND MINING

When coal occurs at depths too great for economic surface mining methods, a tunnel entry to the seam is driven horizontally into the hillside (drift mine), at an angle to intercept the seam (slope mine), or vertically to reach the coal at depth (shaft mine). In deep underground mines, machinery, miners, and coal are transported by rail cars, conveyors, or elevator hoists. Deep mining involves removing the coal seam without removing the overburden. In many instances, the mine roof is permitted to collapse after coal is removed, which may result in some subsidence, or differential lowering of the land surface due to downward movement of overburden to occupy mined-out spaces (Christman et al. 1980, 74–75). Underground mining methods are separated into two categories: room and pillar, and longwall. Each accounted for about half of underground coal production in the United States in 2007 (Weir International Inc. 2008).

Room and Pillar

In the room and pillar method, pillars of coal, typically fifty-foot squares, are left in place to support the roof while rooms of coal are mined. In order that the work can proceed without interruption, at least five rooms are mined at one time, to accommodate the following five different operations of conventional room and pillar mining:

1. Undercutting: a slot is cut at the bottom of the coal face to facilitate breaking of the coal when it is blasted.
2. Drilling: a series of holes is drilled in the face for the placement of explosives.
3. Blasting (shooting): explosives are placed in the drill holes and detonated to fracture the coal and break it away from the face.
4. Loading and hauling: the broken coal is loaded on shuttle cars to be moved from the face to the main haulage way for transport to the surface.
5. Roof bolting: the roof in front of the face is drilled and bolts are driven upward into the overlying beds to prevent spalling, or flaking off of roof material. (OSM 1979)

Pillars left behind account for the low recovery rate (50 to 60 percent) of this mining method. As operations retreat, coal in pillars can be extracted, allowing the roof to collapse into abandoned rooms, but this was not common practice until recent years (Christman et al. 1980, 76).

Continuous mining differs from conventional room and pillar mining in that cutting, drilling, shooting, and loading operations are all performed by one machine, a "continuous miner." This machine uses a rotating drum with hardened teeth to rip coal from the face. It loads coal on a conveyor that transports it to shuttle cars or carries it out of the mine. A roof bolter may be mounted on a continuous miner, but more often mining temporarily ceases as the continuous miner advances while a separate roof bolter operates to keep the roof from collapsing (Christman et al. 1980, 76).

Longwall

Longwall mining is similar to continuous mining in that coal is ripped from the face and loaded on a conveyor. A longwall miner travels along the coal face (850 to 1,000 feet), and a conveyor transports coal to an entry where it is loaded on shuttle cars or larger conveyors for removal from the mine. The primary difference between room and pillar mining and longwall mining is that in longwalling, the roof is temporarily supported by hydraulic lifts that advance automatically as mining progresses, allowing the unsupported roof to collapse behind the active area. This provides a controlled method of roof collapse and is particularly useful in mines with poor roof conditions. Longwall mining on a fairly short face (200 feet or less) is sometimes called shortwalling (Christman et al. 1980, 76).

Environmental Costs of Underground Mining

The environmental costs of deep mining are mostly limited to the area around tunnel openings, ventilation shafts, and spoil piles, unless the hydrologic balance is disturbed and groundwater is contaminated or diverted from existing wells. Mine tunnels, bore holes, subsidence fractures, and other openings may provide cross connections between underground aquifers, allowing flows between previously separate water supplies (Christman et al. 1980, 98). Subsidence occurs as a result of long-wall mining or collapse of cavity or tunnel roofs, sometimes many years after mining has ceased. Exposure to respirable coal dust has long been recognized as the cause of pneumoconiosis, or black lung disease, which reduces lung capacity and may result in death by suffocation (Dvorak 1977). This is a much greater risk to workers in underground mines than in surface mines, but not a significant risk to the general public.

SURFACE MINING

The process of removing earth, rock, and other material, collectively known as overburden, to expose an underlying mineral deposit is surface mining. Large earthmoving equipment is used to remove or strip away overburden and expose the coal seam. Topsoil must first be removed and stored for later reuse. To remove overburden, blasting or ripping may be required, depending on the material involved. Overburden material is then loaded and hauled to a disposal site. Because overburden handling is a major cost item in surface mining, it is common to use the spoil from a fresh cut to refill nearby older workings, thereby avoiding handling the same material twice and saving on costs of fuel and maintenance of equipment. In some instances, overburden handling is a single operation. For instance, a dragline removes material from a fresh cut and deposits it as fill in older cuts in a single movement. In other cases, overburden material is loaded on trucks by front-end loaders and hauled to a dumping site where it is spread and graded by bulldozers. An alternative method uses self-loading scrapers that haul the material and spread it (Christman et al. 1980, 77).

After overburden has been removed, the coal seam is cleaned to remove any remaining material that would contaminate the coal. Coal is then broken up, loaded, and hauled to a preparation plant or shipping site. If necessary, the coal is drilled and blasted before loading. After the overburden or spoil has been used to refill an area, it is graded and recontoured, topsoil is redistributed, and vegetation is planted to hold surface soil together and reduce erosion of spoil.

Strip mining is a specific kind of surface mining in which overburden is removed in strips, one cut at a time. Three types of strip mining methods are used to mine coal: area, contour, and mountaintop removal. The choice of method depends primarily on topography and coal seam structure (OSM 1979).

Area Mining

In area mining, overburden is removed in long cuts to expose the coal. The spoil from the first cut is deposited in an area outside the planned mining area; spoil from subsequent cuts is deposited as fill in the previous cut after coal has been removed. This method is most suitable for areas with flat terrain. Many separate operations are involved in this type of mining, and a wide range of equipment options is available, such as dragline, truck and shovel, front-end loader, and bucket wheel excavator (Christman et al. 1980, 78).

In the western states, coal seams are commonly ten to twenty feet thick, with up to 100-foot seams in the Powder River Basin of Wyoming; in the Midwest coal seams are typically three to seven feet thick and seventy-five to 100 feet below the surface. Because of the large size of area mines and their relatively unrestricted sites, enormous equipment may be used to remove overburden and reconstruct the land. The life of some area mines may be more than fifty years (OSM 1987, 4).

Contour Mining

The contour mining method consists of removing overburden from the seam in a pattern following the contours along a ridge or around a hillside. This method is most commonly used in areas with rolling to steep terrain. It was once common to deposit the spoil on the downslope side of the bench thus created, but this method of spoil disposal consumed much additional land and created severe landslide and erosion problems. To alleviate these problems, a variety of methods were devised to use freshly cut overburden to refill mined-out areas. These haul-back or lateral movement methods generally consist of an initial cut with the spoil deposited downslope or at some other site and spoil from the second cut refilling the first. A ridge of undisturbed natural material fifteen to twenty feet wide is often intentionally left at the outer edge of the mined area. This barrier adds stability to the reclaimed slope by preventing spoil from slumping or sliding downhill (OSM 1987, 5).

When an operation reaches a predetermined stripping ratio (tons of overburden per tons of coal), it is not profitable to continue contour mining. Depending on equipment available, it may not be technically feasible to exceed a certain height of highwall. At this point, it may be possible to produce more coal with the augering method, in which spiral drills bore tunnels into a highwall from the bench roughly horizontally up to 200 feet into a seam to extract coal without removing the overburden (Christman et al. 1980, 78).

Mountaintop Mining

Mountaintop mining combines area and contour strip mining methods. In areas with rolling or steep terrain and a coal seam occurring near the top of a ridge or hill, the entire mountaintop is removed in a series of parallel cuts. Overburden is deposited in nearby "valley fills," in steep terrain where there are limited disposal alternatives. This method usually leaves ridge and hill tops as flattened plateaus (Christman et al. 1980, 79).

Spoil is placed at the head of a narrow, steep-sided valley or hollow. In preparation for filling this area, vegetation and soil are removed and a rock drain constructed down the middle of the area to be filled, where a natural drainage course previously existed. When the fill is completed, this underdrain will form a continuous water runoff system from the upper end of the valley to the lower end of the fill. Typical head-of-hollow fills are graded and terraced to create permanently stable slopes (OSM 1987, 5). In the United States, mountaintop coal mining operations are concentrated in eastern Kentucky, southern West Virginia, western Virginia, and Tennessee (USEPA 2005). When the ratio of tons of overburden removed to tons of coal recovered exceeds an economically defined limit, the mine operator has three alternatives: (1) if conditions are favorable, continue mining the seam with underground methods; (2) continue mining with auger mining; or (3) close down the mining operation.

Environmental Costs of Surface Mining

Surface mining of coal destroys the genetic soil profile, degrades air quality, eliminates existing vegetation, displaces or destroys wildlife and habitat, alters current land uses, and to some extent permanently changes the general topography of the area mined (Hamilton 2005; OSM 1979).

During mining, the land surface—often hundreds of acres—is dedicated to mining activities until it can be reshaped and reclaimed.

Soils

The community of microorganisms and nutrient cycling processes are upset by movement, storage, and redistribution of soil. Generally, soil disturbance and associated compaction result in conditions conducive to erosion. Soil removal from the area to be surface mined alters or destroys many natural soil characteristics and may reduce its productivity for agriculture or biodiversity. Soil structure may be disturbed by pulverization or aggregate breakdown. In arid areas like Montana, it may take 150 to 200 years for biological productivity to recover (USGS 1979).

Air Quality

Removal of vegetative cover and activities associated with construction of haul roads, stockpiling of topsoil, displacement of overburden, and hauling of spoil and coal increase the quantity of dust around mining operations (Axtell 1978), especially in the western United States due to arid climate and persistent winds. Dust degrades air quality in the immediate area, can have adverse impacts on vegetative life, and may constitute a health and safety hazard for mine workers and nearby residents (Murray 1978). Small dust particles less than ten microns, and especially those less than two microns, are considered most dangerous to public health; they can be transported up to twenty kilometers (about 12.4 miles) from mining operations (Dvorak 1977). The amount of fugitive dust resulting from surface mining 100,000 tons of coal has been estimated at twenty-two tons, 80 percent of which would settle within mine boundaries. Fifteen percent, or 3.3 tons, would be dust of respirable size and might be carried further from the mine (Christman et al. 1980, 117).

Health effects on miners also include on-the-job accidents and exposure to high levels of noise from use of some types of equipment (Christman et al. 1980, 117, 123). Noise from equipment and vibration from blasting may also have detrimental effects on some nearby structures off the mine site, thereby affecting the general public. Although these effects are regulated, noise, vibration, and structural damage due to blasting continue to impose costs on some coal mining operations in the United States today.

Water Quality

Surface mining can adversely impact the hydrology of any region. Deterioration of stream quality can result from acid mine drainage; addition of heavy metals, toxic trace elements, and radioactivity; high content of dissolved solids in mine drainage water; and increased sediment loads discharged to streams. Waste piles and coal storage piles can yield sediment to streams, and leached water from these piles can be acidic and contain toxic trace elements. Surface waters may be rendered unfit for agriculture, human consumption, bathing, or other household uses. Controlling these impacts requires careful management of surface water flows into and out of mining operations (OSM 1979).

Flood events can cause severe damage to improperly constructed or located coal haul roads, housing, coal crushing and washing plant facilities, waste and coal storage piles, settling basin dams, surface water diversion structures, and the mine itself. Besides the danger to life and property, large amounts of sediment and poor quality water may have detrimental effects many miles downstream from a mine site after a flood.

Groundwater supplies may be adversely affected by surface mining (Dunrud 1976). These impacts include drainage of usable water from shallow aquifers, causing loss of potable well-water supplies; lowering of water levels in adjacent areas and changes in flow directions within aquifers; contamination of usable aquifers below mining operations due to infiltration or percolation of poor-quality mine water; and increased infiltration of precipitation on spoil piles. Where coal or carbonaceous shales are present, increased infiltration may result in increased runoff of poor-quality water and erosion from spoil piles; recharge of poor-quality water to shallow groundwater aquifers; or flow of poor-quality water to nearby streams. This may contaminate both groundwater and nearby streams for long periods. Lakes formed in abandoned surface mining operations are more likely to be acidic if there is coal or carbonaceous shale present in spoil piles, especially if these materials are near the surface and contain pyrites (OSM 1979).

Wildlife and Vegetation

Surface mining of coal causes direct and indirect damage to wildlife. The impact on wildlife stems primarily from disturbing, removing, and redistributing the land surface. Some impacts are short-term and confined to the mine site; others may have far-reaching, long-term effects. The most direct effect on wildlife is destruction or displacement of species in areas of excavation and spoil piling. Mobile wildlife species like game animals, birds, and predators leave these areas. More sedentary animals like invertebrates, many reptiles, burrowing rodents, and small mammals may be directly destroyed. If streams, lakes, ponds, or marshes are filled or drained, fish, aquatic invertebrates, and amphibians are destroyed. Food supplies for predators are reduced by destruction of these land and water species. Animal populations displaced or destroyed may eventually be replaced from populations in surrounding ranges, provided the habitat is eventually restored (OSM 1979). An exception could be extinction of resident endangered species.

Many wildlife species are highly dependent on vegetation growing in natural drainages. This vegetation provides essential food, nesting sites, and cover for escape from predators. Any activity that destroys this vegetation near ponds, reservoirs, marshes, and wetlands reduces the quality and quantity of habitat essential for waterfowl, shore birds, and many terrestrial species. The commonly used head-of-hollow fill method for disposing of excess overburden is of particular significance to wildlife habitat in some locations. Narrow, steep-sided, V-shaped hollows near ridge tops are frequently inhabited by rare or endangered animal and plant species. Extensive placement of spoil in these narrow valleys eliminates important habitat for a wide variety of species, some of which may be rendered extinct (OSM 1979).

Broad and long-lasting impacts on wildlife are caused by habitat impairment. The habitat requirements of many animal species do not permit them to adjust to changes created by land disturbance. These changes reduce living space. The degree to which a species or an individual animal tolerates human competition for space varies. Some species tolerate very little disturbance. In instances where a particularly critical habitat is restricted, such as a lake, pond, or primary breeding area, a species could be eliminated. Large mammals and other animals displaced from their home ranges may be forced to use adjacent areas already stocked to carrying capacity (OSM 1979). Overcrowding usually results in degradation of remaining habitat, lowered carrying capacity, reduced reproductive success, increased interspecies and intraspecies competition, and potentially greater losses to wildlife populations than the number of originally displaced animals.

Loss of Topsoil

Removal of soil and rock overburden covering the coal resource, if improperly done, causes burial and loss of topsoil, exposes parent material, and creates vast, infertile wastelands. Pit and spoil areas are not capable of providing food and cover for most species of wildlife. Without rehabilitation, these areas must weather for some period, which may take a few years or many decades, before vegetation is reestablished and they become suitable habitat. With rehabilitation, impacts on some species are less severe. Complete restoration of natural biotic communities is unlikely to occur, but reclamation of land and rehabilitation efforts geared to wildlife needs mitigate the damage of surface mining. Rehabilitation not geared to the needs of wildlife species or improper management of other land uses after reclamation can preclude reestablishment of many members of the original fauna (OSM 1979).

Aquatic Habitats

Severe degradation of aquatic habitats often results from surface mining and may be apparent to some degree many miles downstream from a mining site. Sediment contamination of surface water is common with surface mining. Sediment yields may increase 1,000 times over their former levels as a direct result of strip mining. In some circumstances, especially those involving disturbance of unconsolidated soils, approximately one acre-foot of sediment may be produced annually for every eighty acres of disturbed land (OSM 1979).

The effects of sediment on aquatic wildlife vary with the species and amount of contamination. High sediment loads can kill fish directly, bury spawning beds, alter temperature gradients, fill in pools, spread stream flows over wider, shallower areas, and reduce production of aquatic organisms used as food by other species. These changes destroy the habitat of some valued species and may enhance habitat for less desirable species. Current conditions are already marginal for some freshwater fish in the United States. Sedimentation of these waters can result in their elimination. The heaviest sediment pollution of a drainage normally comes within five to twenty-five years after mining. In some areas, unrevegetated spoil piles continue to erode even fifty to sixty-five years after mining (OSM 1979).

The presence of acid-forming materials exposed as a result of surface mining can affect wildlife by eliminating habitat and by causing direct destruction of some species. Lesser concentrations can suppress productivity, growth rate, and reproduction of many aquatic species. Acids, dilute concentrations of heavy metals, and high alkalinity can cause severe wildlife damage in some areas. The duration of acidic waste pollution can be long-term. Estimates of the time required to leach exposed acidic materials in the eastern United States range from 800 to 3,000 years (OSM 1979).

Land Use

Surface mining operations and coal transportation facilities are fully dedicated to coal production for the life of a mine. Mining activities incorporating little or no planning to establish postmining land use objectives usually result in reclamation of disturbed lands to a land use condition not equal to the original use. Existing land uses such as livestock grazing and crop and timber production are temporarily eliminated from the mining area. High-value, intensive land use areas like urban and transportation systems are not usually affected by mining operations. If mineral values are sufficient, these improvements may be removed to an adjacent area (OSM 1979).

Topography

Where thick seams are removed, such as in Wyoming, enough overburden may not be available to replace coal that was removed, and some permanent alteration of the surface contour results.

Surface mining operations have produced cliff-like highwalls as high as 200 feet in the United States. Such highwalls may be created at the end of a surface mining operation where stripping becomes uneconomical or where a mine reaches the boundary of a current lease or mineral ownership. These highwalls are hazards to people, wildlife, and domestic livestock. They may impede normal wildlife migration routes. Steep slopes also merit special attention because of the significance of impacts associated with them when mined. While impacts from contour mining on steep slopes are of the same type as all mining, the severity of these impacts increases as the degree of slope increases. This is due to increased difficulties in dealing with problems of erosion and land stability on steeper slopes (OSM 1979).

Geologic and Historic Resources

Adverse impacts on geological features of human interest may occur in a surface mine area. Geomorphic and geophysical features and outstanding scenic resources may be sacrificed by indiscriminate mining. Paleontological, cultural, and other historic values may be endangered due to disruptive activities of blasting and excavating coal. Stripping of overburden eliminates and destroys archeological and historic features unless they are removed beforehand. Extraction of coal by surface mining disrupts virtually all esthetic elements of the landscape (OSM 1979).

Socioeconomic Impacts

Due to intensive mechanization, surface mines may require fewer workers than underground mines with equivalent production. The influence on human populations of surface mining is therefore not generally as significant as with underground mines. In low-population areas, however, local populations cannot provide needed labor so there is migration to the area because new jobs are available at a mine. Unless adequate advance planning is done by government and mine operators, new populations may cause overcrowded schools and hospitals and make demands on other public services that cannot easily be met. Some social instability may be created in nearby communities by coal mining.

Many impacts can be minimized but may not be eliminated entirely by use of best mining practices either voluntarily or to comply with government regulatory programs. Financial incentives to minimize costs of production may limit use of best mining practices in the absence of effective regulation. Some temporary destruction of the land surface is an environmental price we pay for utilization of coal resources. The scale of disturbance, its duration, and the quality of reclamation are largely determined by management of the operation during mining (Hamilton 2005).

Beneficial Effects

Surface mining may have beneficial impacts on some wildlife. Where large, continuous tracts of forest, bush land, sagebrush, or grasslands are broken up during mining, increased edge and openings are created. Preferred food and cover plants can be established in these openings to benefit a wide variety of wildlife. Under certain conditions, creation of small lakes in the mined area may also be beneficial. These lakes and ponds may become important water sources for a variety of wildlife inhabiting adjacent areas, provided water quality is good. Many lakes formed in mine pits are initially of poor quality as aquatic habitat after mining, due to lack of structure, aquatic vegetation, and food species. They may require habitat enhancement and management to be of significant value to wildlife (OSM 1979).

COAL SEAM FIRES

Fires sometimes occur in coal beds underground. When coal beds are exposed, the fire risk is increased. Coal seam fires cause serious hazards to health, safety, and the environment, including smoke and toxic fumes; reigniting grass, brush, or forest fires; and subsidence of surface infrastructure such as roads, pipelines, electric lines, bridge supports, buildings, and homes. Almost all fires in solid coal are ignited by surface fires caused by lightning or people clearing land with fire or burning trash or brush in the presence of outcrop deposits of coal or peat. Coal seam fires may continue to burn for decades until the fuel source is exhausted, a permanent groundwater table is encountered, the depth of the burn becomes greater than the ground's capacity to subside and vent, or humans intervene. Coal seam fires are particularly insidious because they continue to smolder underground after surface fires have been extinguished, before flaring up and restarting forest and brush fires nearby. Because they burn underground, coal seam fires are unlikely to be extinguished by rain (Whitehouse and Mulyana 2004, 95). Coal refuse dumps are susceptible to spontaneous combustion and represent a significant potential source of air pollution. In 1978 the Environmental Protection Agency (EPA) reported there were 250 million metric tons of burning coal refuse in the United States, in addition to fires in abandoned mines and along outcrops of exposed coal (Chalekode and Blackwood 1978). These fires emit various pyrolysis and combustion air pollutants that may contribute to deterioration of air quality in the vicinity of coal-cleaning plants.

PROCESSING COAL

Coal cleaning, or washing, removes slate, clay, carbonaceous shales, pyrite, and rock aggregate from the coal product to meet specifications of purchasers. The many processes for cleaning coal produce toxic wastes, fugitive dust, and noise. Coal preparation plants, with associated raw coal storage and waste disposal areas, are typically situated at the mine site and considered part of the mine area.

When the cleaning process is completed, waste or refuse material is disposed of in solid and liquid forms. Solid waste, or gob, is piled in spoil banks or waste piles near the preparation plant. Because storage of waste requires large areas of land, a preferred disposal method is to return this waste to the mine for permanent burial, isolating it from surface water and groundwater. Gob piles can have many detrimental effects. Depending on the method used to pile and contain the waste, the refuse may be unstable and subject to slope failures and landslides (Nunenkamp 1976). In 1972 a coal mine waste dam failed near Buffalo Creek, Virginia, releasing water and debris that killed 125 persons. The U.S. Army Corps of Engineers inspected many similar dams and found 50 to 60 percent to be potentially hazardous (Dvorak 1977). Runoff from gob piles is a source of significant acid drainage (Martin 1974). Liquid waste, or slurry, contains high proportions of suspended sediments consisting of fine coal particles, heavy metals, and other trace elements and contaminants. Slurry is generally pumped to a series of ponds where sediments settle out by gravity and water is clarified before discharge to streams or rivers. These ponds must be cleaned out periodically to maintain sufficient depth to be effective (Hamilton 2005, 158).

Waste material discarded at prep plants may contain over 80 percent marketable coal fines, and more than 20 percent of the coal extracted from a mine may be lost unless a fine coal recovery system is included in the preparation plant. Fine coal particulates of less than two millimeters contain the same heat value as larger pieces of coal and are highly combustible. Consequently, coal fines are routinely recovered and sold as part of the product shipped from mines in the United States (Hamilton 2005, 158, 144). Both waste piles and sediment ponds are sources of airborne fugitive dust, particularly in dry regions. Coal cleaning also generates dust in and around the plant during transport, storage, transfer, and processing. Airborne emissions from thermal dryers include combustion products from coal-fired furnaces, particulates, and heavy metals (Nunenkamp 1976). Emissions can adversely impact visibility in the immediate vicinity of the dryer and may negatively affect local flora and fauna with particulate deposition.

Land areas occupied by the preparation plant and associated disposal areas entail loss of wildlife habitat. With low pH conditions common at these sites, plant growth is inhibited and sometimes limited to acid-tolerant species. If the water table is lowered by diversion of water for processing activities, nearby ponds and streams may dry up, causing a further loss of habitat. The discharge or runoff of acid waters from coal-washing plants has impacts similar to those of acid mine drainage (Christman et al. 1980). Noise in coal preparation plants results from use of heavy industrial machinery that must be quieted to some extent or contained inside buildings to meet existing standards governing allowable noise levels in industrial environments (Christman et al. 1980).

COAL TRANSPORTATION

Transporting coal from a mine to the point of combustion requires trucks, barges, trains, and pipelines utilized in various combinations, with attendant safety, environmental, and social impacts. Foremost are consumption of diesel and gasoline fuels, air pollution, and deaths and injuries from transportation accidents. The principal environmental impacts of coal transportation are ambient air quality deterioration resulting from loading and unloading operations and fugitive particulate emissions during rail, barge, and truck transport. Water quality deterioration is of concern for slurry pipeline and barge operations. Social impacts stem primarily from increased congestion in rail, barge, and truck operation.

Rail

Of the billion tons of coal shipped annually to utilities and other industrial users, more than half is transported by rail. A typical coal unit train consists of approximately a hundred 100-ton coal cars and five 3,000-horsepower diesel locomotives (Rifas and White 1976). Fugitive dust release is unavoidable in transporting coal by rail. Although hoppers can be covered to dampen dust release, the usual practice is to carry loads uncovered. A variety of light oil coatings may be sprayed on coal after loading to prevent loss of fine coal particulates during transport. The principal emissions that result from combustion of diesel fuel in locomotives are particulate matter, sulfur oxides, carbon monoxide, hydrocarbons, nitrogen oxides, aldehydes, and organic acids. These must be controlled pursuant to applicable air quality standards for mobile sources. Rail transport has the added problems of noise and vibration, accidents with vehicles at rail crossings, excessive wear of rail and roadbed due to the weight of unit trains, and congestion of the rail network. Of these effects, the most serious and most quantifiable is accidents at grade crossings. It has been estimated that approximately 0.79 deaths and 8.8 injuries result from every million tons of coal transported by rail (Christman et al. 1980, 191).

Barge

Transportation of coal by water has long taken advantage of the nation's 29,000 miles of navigable waterways, including the inland Mississippi system, the Gulf and Atlantic Intracoastal system, and the Great Lakes. Coal traffic accounts for over 20 percent of all waterborne shipments. When geography permits, transportation by water is more efficient than rail transport at about one-third the cost of comparable rail transport.

Most coal in river traffic is shipped in open hopper barges with a capacity of 1,000 to 1,500 tons. The barges are usually lashed together to form a tow of as many as thirty-six barges. Diesel-propelled towboats of up to 10,000 horsepower are used to push the load. For oceangoing and Great Lakes operation, self-propelled bulk cargo carriers averaging 20,000-ton capacity are used instead of barge and towboat configurations (Christman et al. 1980, 188; Witten and Desai 1978).

In addition to the chronic problem of fugitive dust, principal air pollution emissions from river vessels include sulfur dioxide, carbon monoxide, hydrocarbons, and nitrogen oxides. Accidental discharge of coal loads to water is also of concern, and coal barge traffic must share responsibility for shore erosion as a result of passing wakes. However, the most serious problem resulting from coal barge traffic is the increase in congestion of inland waterway systems, especially on the Mississippi River, where locks and dams have been operating at or above capacity for many years. Barge transportation is in general more energy-efficient than rail transport (Christman et al. 1980, 191).

Trucks

In surface mining operations, coal is loaded onto trucks at the coal face and carried to storage piles or conveyor belts for subsequent rail or barge transport. Small mines (surface or underground) without loading facilities may also use trucks to carry coal to central receiving areas where the output of several mines is combined, but the economic range of coal trucks is approximately 150 miles. The high coal volume required by large industrial plants limits truck use to mine-mouth power plant operation. Highway limitations prohibit trucks from exceeding forty tons gross weight. The largest coal trucks in highway use weigh approximately ten tons and have a thirty-ton carrying capacity. Truck transportation of coal can result in severe road degradation. Damage from one 55,000-pound (27.5 ton) truck has been shown to be equivalent to the wear produced by 2,500 automobiles (Christman et al. 1980, 193). Principal air emissions from these large trucks include carbon monoxide, hydrocarbons, nitrogen oxides, aldehydes, sulfur oxides, and particulate matter. Noise, congestion, and safety are also problems with truck transport.

It is often most economical to take advantage of more than one mode to transport coal from mine to end user. For example, the Burlington Northern Railroad operates a transshipment terminal in Havanna, Illinois, where 5 million tons of coal from Decker, Montana, are first carried by rail and then transferred to barges on the Illinois River for subsequent delivery to three Commonwealth Edison utility plants in the Chicago area (Christman et al. 1980, 195).

COAL STORAGE

Mine operators generally minimize the amount of coal stockpiled at mine sites because unshipped coal does not recover the costs of extracting it from the ground and because stockpiles are prone to spontaneous combustion. Temporary stockpiles at preparation plants and shipping docks are generally minimized as coal is transported from the mine to purchasers as rapidly as possible. At industrial locations that use coal, a steady flow of fuel into boilers tends to keep operating costs low, so to meet fluctuations in demand and possible delays in shipping, extra coal is kept on-site in stockpiles. Daily and hourly fluctuations in consumption are met by a small storage pile near the boiler, and a larger intermediate stockpile is maintained on-site to handle holidays or transportation difficulties. A seasonal reserve is often built up during summer months to handle higher winter consumption levels for heating, except at electric generating stations in southern climates where peak demand may be experienced during summer for air conditioning. Electric utilities, coke production plants, other industrial boilers, producers, and distributors together stockpiled a year-end total in 2010 of almost 233.6 million tons at thousands of locations nationwide (USEIA 2011a, Table 27).

Coal storage stockpiles are potential sources of water pollution from precipitation runoff, and air pollution from coal fires and fugitive dust. Moisture and air in contact with coal cause oxidation of pyrites and marcasite to sulfuric acid, and rain washes some of this acid into surface and groundwater (Christman et al. 1980). Concentrated "slugs" of acid drainage may be released immediately after rainfall. Sulfuric acid produced by weathering of high-sulfur coals reduces the pH of streams, and the resulting increased acidity stresses aquatic organisms. Runoff contains fine coal particles, various minerals, and trace elements, increasing suspended sediments in receiving streams and aquifers and altering their chemistry. Fugitive dust of fine coal particulates may be blown from coal stockpiles whenever a breeze blows. Fires in stockpiles provide uncontrolled emissions of smoke, particulates, and regulated pollutants such as sulfur dioxide, nitrogen oxides, and carbon monoxide, which are hazardous to human health. If smoke containing high concentrations of sulfur dioxide comes in contact with nearby vegetation, it may be visibly harmed by acid deposition.

COAL COMBUSTION

Coal-fired electricity generating plants accounted for about 30.4 percent of summer installed generating capacity at 1,445 generating units and generated about 44.7 percent of the electricity produced in the United States during 2010 (USEIA 2011d, Table 1.1.A, Table 2.1.A). Each power plant requires dedication of several hundred to a few thousand acres of land to a single industrial use for the boiler and generator, coal storage and handling facilities, water storage and purification, pollution control equipment, and solid waste handling and storage facilities, access to which must be limited for safety reasons.

At a typical coal-fired electric generating unit, crushed coal is first pulverized to a powder about the consistency of a fine face powder. A mixture of finely pulverized coal and air is blown into a combustion chamber at the base of a boiler and ignited as it passes through a burner flame, as illustrated in Figure 2.3. Above the combustion zone of the boiler, water is pumped through banks of metal tubes, which transfer heat from burning gases to the water, which leaves the boiler as superheated steam, which turns a turbine and drives an electrical generator. Lower-pressure steam leaving the turbine is fed into a cooling system that extracts residual heat and recycles condensed water back to the boiler for reuse, yielding an overall system efficiency of 36 to 40 percent (Perry 1973).

Environmental Costs of Coal Combustion

Environmental costs of coal combustion include deterioration of air quality in the form of airborne particulates, sulfur oxides, nitrogen oxides, lead, unburned hydrocarbons, carbon monoxide, carbon

Figure 2.3   **Coal-Fired Power Plant**

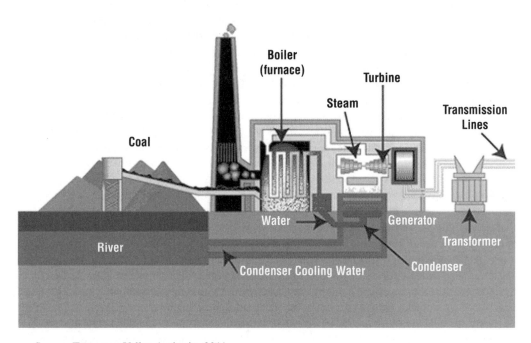

Source: Tennessee Valley Authority 2011.

dioxide, ozone, and trace elements such as mercury, asbestos and beryllium; degradation of water quality; concentrations of hazardous solid waste; depletion of natural resources; and consumption of capital and energy.

REGULATORY CONTROLS

Before national legislation addressing air pollution was enacted in 1955, regulation of air contaminants was the responsibility of state and local governments (Davies and Davies 1975). Prior to enactment of the Clean Air Act of 1970, there were no legally enforceable national requirements for air pollution control at coal-fired power plants in the United States (Kneese and Schultz 1975). Few coal-fired generating units built before 1970 utilized such equipment, and uncontrolled air emissions were the norm. The Clean Air Act of 1970 established for the first time meaningful sanctions for violation of national primary and secondary ambient air quality standards designed to protect public health and property; the act also established performance standards for new stationary sources (84 Statutes at Large §§ 1679–1686). These provisions effectively required owners of coal-fired generating units constructed thereafter to include the capital and operating costs of air pollution control equipment in their investment plans. More stringent requirements were imposed by provisions in the Clean Air Act Amendments of 1977, designed to prevent further deterioration of air quality in pristine areas (91 Statutes at Large §§ 731–740), and the Clean Air Act Amendments of 1990, regulating the precursors of acid rain (104 Statutes at Large §§ 2584–2645; 42 U.S. Code §§ 7401–7671q). Consequently, all generating units in the United States built since 1978 and many of those built earlier are equipped to handle combustion by-products with exhaust stack gas cleaning equipment.

Similarly, discharge of pollutants to the nation's waterways without a permit is prohibited by the Clean Water Act (33 U.S. Code §§ 1251–1387), and permits are required for storage structures such as impoundments that constitute a potential for discharges (§ 1342). These permits must specify limits for each pollutant or combination of pollutants discharged (§ 1316). If discharged into publicly owned treatment works, these discharges must meet pretreatment standards for the applicable industrial category of point source (§ 1317). Solid waste materials and sludge from air pollution control facilities (42 U.S. Code 6903[26A]–[27]) are regulated under the Resource Conservation and Recovery Act (42 U.S. Code 6901–6992k) and must be disposed of in a permitted sanitary landfill designed to isolate waste materials from surface and ground waters, as distinct from an open dump (42 U.S. Code 6945). Most coal-fired electric generating plants have on-site solid waste handling and disposal systems, cooling systems, and water treatment equipment.

Air Pollution Control

Use of air pollution controls at coal-fired bulk electric power generating plants is basically a strategy of converting a health-impairing air pollution problem into a potentially health-threatening solid waste disposal problem, which must be managed carefully to prevent harm to the general public. Coal combustion concentrates lead, mercury, sulfur, and other impurities found in the fuel by a factor of about ten, producing a contaminated ash that is either retained within the boiler (bottom ash) or carried out with exhaust gases (fly ash). Depending on the type of furnace used, most of this is fly ash, which in turn constitutes most of the particulate matter emitted to the atmosphere in exhaust gases by such facilities. Fly ash is removed from exhaust gases in the form of particulate matter by air pollution control equipment such as electrostatic precipitators (dry scrubbers), venturi or bed scrubbers (wet scrubbers), or fabric filters (baghouses). Electrostatic precipitators use an electrical charge to ionize particulate matter in exhaust gases and deposit them on metal plates, which are periodically rapped to dislodge accumulated particulates into a collection area below. Although they are less effective on units burning low-sulfur coal, electrostatic precipitators have demonstrated particulate removal efficiencies of 99 to 99.8 percent with moderate power consumption at units burning medium- to high-sulfur coals.

Venturi scrubbers use high-pressure sprays of atomized water to remove particulates from exhaust gases. Fixed or moving bed scrubbers percolate flue gases through liquid in a bed of small spheres, capturing particulates in a scrubbing liquor that is filtered to remove them and recycled in the scrubber. Baghouses capture particulates by filtering flue gases through long, narrow fabric bags woven of synthetic or glass fiber, analogous to household vacuum cleaner bags. The bags are cleaned periodically by isolating them from the exhaust flow, shaking them or using a high-pressure pulse of air counter to the direction of gas flow, and particulates are recovered in a hopper below. Particulate collection efficiencies for all these methods range from 95 to over 99 percent (Christman et al. 1980, 219–222). About 396 (25 percent) of the 1,579 fossil-fueled electric generating units in the United States continued to operate without collecting particulates in 2006 (USEIA 2011d, Table 3.10).

Sulfur oxides, principally SO_2, are removed from exhaust gases using wet or dry scrubbers containing a chemical sorbent like lime or limestone. The resulting slurry or solid waste, which may contain trace amounts of inorganic pollutants present in fly ash, is discarded in licensed sanitary landfills. Wet lime or limestone scrubbers have demonstrated SO_2 removal efficiencies of 80 to 90 percent, but dry scrubbers are effective only where low-sulfur coal is used and SO_2 removal of less than 80 percent is required (Christman et al. 1980, 223–224). Only 432 (27.4 percent) of the 1,579 fossil-fueled electric generating units in the United States used flue gas desulfurization scrubbers in 2010 (USEIA 2011d, Table 3.10).

Nitrogen oxide emissions from coal-fired boilers are generally reduced by modifying combustion conditions in the boiler to reduce peak temperatures and oxygen available during combustion. A 20 to 50 percent reduction in nitrogen oxide emissions has been demonstrated using combustion modification techniques, usually by installing more efficient burners and control equipment (Christman et al. 1980, 225). Controlling NO_x emissions is generally considered less demanding than controlling SO_2 emissions, so when a generating unit is shut down for retrofit with SO_2 control equipment, NO_x emissions controls are often installed at the same time.

Particulate matter and sulfur residues recovered from air pollution control equipment are often stored in large detention ponds at the power plant site before disposal in sanitary landfills or returned to the mine site for disposal in mine pits. Ash and particulate storage ponds pose a significant risk of breaching and contaminating substantial areas of land and surface waters unless carefully maintained, as was graphically illustrated on December 22, 2008, when an ash pond at the Tennessee Valley Authority's Kingston Fossil Plant spilled over 1 billion gallons of sludge, inundating more than 300 acres and many residences along the Emory River in Tennessee (Fausset 2009; Dewan 2008, 1).

Thus, in addition to converting an air pollution health problem into a solid waste management problem, the use of air pollution control equipment at coal-fired power plants involves converting environmental costs into dollar costs for equipment, labor, and maintenance that are paid by consumers of electricity.

Thermal Pollution

Performance standards for power plants prohibit the discharge of heat to natural bodies of water pursuant to the Clean Water Act (33 U.S. Code § 1316), due to the adverse impact on organisms in aquatic ecosystems. Conventional cooling systems to control thermal pollution are of three basic types: once-through cooling systems, cooling ponds or lakes, and cooling towers.

Once-Through Cooling

After superheated steam is used to turn turbines and generate electricity, the steam is cooled by passing it over a bank of tubes through which cold water is circulated, and heat transferred to the cooling water is discharged back into its source (e.g., river, lake, ocean). The two sets of pipes, one containing steam and the other cooling water, are separate except for the heat transfer, so water from one does not mix with water in the other. Steam water, after cooling, is recirculated to the boiler for reheat and reuse (Christman et al. 1980, 226). Only the cooling water is discharged to the environment. Once common due to its low cost, once-through cooling is rarely used on new generating units due to the need to control thermal pollution.

Cooling Ponds or Lakes

In this method, heated cooling water is discharged to artificial ponds or lakes constructed on the power plant site for this purpose, with size of the pond determined by capacity of the generating units using it. A surface area of one to two acres per megawatt of generating capacity is typical (Christman et al. 1980, 226), and no discharge to natural water bodies is allowed. This method of cooling is common in areas where land is relatively inexpensive.

Cooling Towers

Cooling towers discharge waste heat from turbine-cooling water to the atmosphere through a variety of means. Wet cooling towers allow hot water to cascade through numerous layers of fill material in walled structures, while circulating cooler air through the water either using fans or naturally. Heat is exhausted at the top of the tower. Natural draft towers may be 350 to 550 feet tall and mechanical draft towers are typically fifty to sixty-five feet tall (Christman et al. 1980, 227). Cooling towers may produce a plume of wet air that, under unfavorable meteorological conditions, may create a ground fog, reducing visibility nearby and creating a driving hazard at night, so wet-dry towers heat the plume and partially cool incoming water in an attempt to reduce this effect. Dry cooling towers circulate water through a closed system comparable to a radiator on an automobile, transferring heat to air via radiation and convection to avoid this problem; this type of tower is rare in the United States (Christman et al. 1980, 227).

Every electric power generating plant has an industrial water treatment plant to treat incoming water before it is introduced into equipment; various agents are used to minimize corrosion, buildup of mineral scale, and organic materials. Small quantities of waste, some of which is chemical waste, are generated from routine operation and maintenance of electric generator cooling systems and water treatment plants. These include ash transport water, metal cleaning waste, boiler blowdown (e.g., cleaning water used to remove particles of corrosion and scale), cooling tower blowdown, construction site and material storage runoff, and several low-volume waste streams (e.g., scrubber waste water, water treatment plant waste, in-plant drainage systems) (Christman et al. 1980, 228). Consequently, chemical effluent limitations for the utility industry restrict the discharge of acidity, polychlorinated biphenyls (PCBs), total suspended solids, oil, grease, chlorine, copper, iron, zinc, chromate, and phosphorous under the Clean Water Act (33 U.S. Code § 1316). These environmental costs are converted to dollar costs as a matter of regulatory policy. Yet other unpriced environmental costs of utilizing coal total $180 to $530 billion per year, enough to double or triple the dollar costs of coal if they were included in our electric bills (Epstein et al. 2011).

COSTS OF COAL UTILIZATION

Dollar Costs

U.S. consumption of coal was about 1.048 billion short tons in 2010, up from about 997.5 million short tons in 2009 (USEIA 2011b, Table 7.1). The market cost to consumers for coal energy in calendar year 2009 was estimated at a bit over $45.8 billion, and a little over $49.4 billion in 2008 (Table 3.5). Federal subsidies and tax expenditures for coal were estimated at almost $1.36 billion for FY2010 (USEIA 2011c, xiii), including $1.2 billion for electricity production (xviii). Efforts to develop synthetic liquid fuels from coal received no subsidies in FY2010, a drastic reduction from over $3 billion in subsidies and tax expenditures from FY2007 (xiv).

Coal has been described as a "sick industry" in relative decline during the twentieth century through the mid-1970s (Davis 1993, Ch. 2), beset by persistent labor and environmental problems as it shifted production from underground mines to surface mines and later shifted its underground mines from pick and shovel to longwall operations. The resulting price instability had long made it difficult for any but the largest operations to survive. One result was a long-term trend toward consolidation of the industry into fewer, ever-larger firms, a trend that continues today. The delivered price of coal varies according to the distance from the mine to the boiler in which it is burned, and the adequacy of rail and barge facilities. For example, the delivered price per ton of coal to electric generating stations in northern New England, New Jersey, and southern California makes it prohibitively expensive in those states, because there are no nearby mines. Correspondingly, the delivered price of coal to power plants in Montana, Wyoming, and North Dakota is among the lowest in the nation because there are large mines in those states; and the price is also low in Nebraska and Iowa because there is excellent railway infrastructure to them from large mines in nearby states (USEIA 2011a, Table 34).

The price of coal also varies due to sulfur and Btu content. Coal with high Btu content is more expensive because it has high heat content. High-sulfur coal is less expensive but its use requires more capital investment in air pollution control equipment. The advantage enjoyed by low-sulfur coal may be offset by higher transportation costs to the point of utilization today, and in future by increased regulation of toxic air pollutants like mercury, lead, and other heavy metals, which will require additional capital investment in air pollution control equipment for the burning of even low-sulfur coal. Coal will become less attractive in general as compared to other fuels as we move toward regulation of greenhouse gases like carbon emissions, because that will make coal more expensive relative to other fossil and nonfossil fuels. A variety of "clean coal technologies" are available today, but using them makes it more expensive to produce electricity. Although coal at one time was widely used in rail transportation, it was displaced by development of large diesel locomotives, and it may find a similar fate when we begin to get serious about reducing the impact of carbon emissions on global climate change.

Historically, planning lead times for development and construction of coal-fired generating plants have been much longer than for all other technologies except nuclear plants. A 1980 study of new power-generating stations in the southwestern United States found planning lead times reported by electric utilities then typically ran six to eleven years for coal-fired plants, three to six years for natural gas combustion turbines, three to seven years for combined cycle units, and ten to fourteen years for nuclear units (Hamilton and Wengert 1980, 69). Long lead times to construct coal-fired plants increase the financial costs of borrowing capital in the form of interest paid, as compared to shorter lead times. The longer the period after money is borrowed before revenue is produced by a new facility, the more expensive is capital construction.

In July 2011, the EPA finalized the Cross-State Air Pollution Rule (CSAPR), which requires twenty-seven states in the eastern United States to significantly improve air quality by reducing power plant emissions that contribute to ozone or fine particle pollution in other states. Carried long distances across the country by wind and weather, power plant emissions of sulfur dioxide and nitrogen oxide continually travel across state lines, reacting in the atmosphere and contributing to harmful levels of ground-level ozone and fine particulate soot, which are scientifically linked to widespread illnesses and premature deaths and prevent many cities and communities from enjoying healthy air quality.

Emission reductions were scheduled to take effect starting January 1, 2012, for sulfur dioxide and annual nitrogen oxide reductions, and May 1, 2012, for ozone season nitrogen oxide reductions. By 2014, the CSAPR, combined with other final state and EPA actions, will reduce power plant sulfur dioxide emissions by 73 percent and nitrogen oxide emissions by 54 percent from 2005 levels in the CSAPR region (USEPA 2011b).

According to the EPA, the CSAPR rule will protect over 240 million Americans living in the eastern half of the country, resulting in up to $280 billion in annual benefits, which would far outweigh the $800 million projected to be spent annually on the rule in 2014 and roughly $1.6 billion per year in capital investments already under way as a result of the earlier Clean Air Interstate Rule. EPA expects pollution reductions to occur quickly without large expenditures by the power industry. Many power plants covered by the rule have already made substantial investments in clean air technologies to reduce sulfur dioxide and nitrogen oxide emissions. In states where investments in control technology are required, health and environmental benefits will be substantial (USEPA 2011b).

In December 2011, EPA issued its final mercury and air toxics standards (MATS), which will require about 40 percent of all coal-fired power plants in the United States to install pollution control equipment to curb emissions of heavy metals, including mercury, arsenic, chromium, and nickel, and acid gases, including hydrochloric acid, hydrofluoric acid, and cyanide, within three years.

EPA also revised the new source performance standards (NSPS) that new coal- and oil-fired power plants must meet for particulate matter, sulfur dioxide, and nitrogen oxides (USEPA 2011a). Under this rule, all power plants will have to limit their toxic emissions, preventing 90 percent of the mercury in coal burned from being emitted into the air. The standards set work practices, instead of numerical limits, to limit emissions of organic air toxics, including dioxin and furans, from existing and new coal- and oil-fired power plants. The work practice standards essentially require for each unit an annual performance test that includes inspection, adjustment, maintenance, and repairs to ensure optimal combustion. Revisions to the NSPS for fossil fuel–fired units include revised numerical emission limits for particulate matter, sulfur dioxide, and nitrogen oxides.

EPA claims the standards can be met with a "range of widely available and economically feasible technologies, practices and compliance strategies available to power plants to meet the emission limits, including wet and dry scrubbers, dry sorbent injection systems, activated carbon injection systems, and fabric filters" (USEPA 2011a). All coal- and oil-fired electric generating units with a capacity of twenty-five megawatt (MWe) or more will be required to comply with MATS within four years. EPA maintains that "power plants are the largest remaining source of several toxic air pollutants," including arsenic, cyanide, and dioxin, and are responsible for half the mercury and over 75 percent of acid gas emissions in the United States. More than half of all coal-fired power plants already installed pollution control technologies that will help them meet these standards. The new standards will ensure that remaining plants—about 40 percent of all coal-fired power plants—take similar steps to decrease dangerous pollutants (USEPA 2011a).

The EPA estimates that generating units having 4,700 MWe of coal-fired capacity would be required to retire from service, representing less than one-half of 1 percent, of all coal plants. EPA maintains the standard will save lives and create 9,000 jobs as plants invest billions of dollars to install pollution controls. The agency also emphasizes public health benefits, stating the rule could prevent 17,000 premature deaths from toxic emissions. Projected annual private costs to the power sector of the final air toxics rule are $9.6 billion in 2015 (in 2007 dollars) (USEPA 2011a). Combined, the two new rules are estimated to prevent up to 46,000 premature deaths, 540,000 asthma attacks in children, and 24,500 emergency room visits and hospital admissions. The two programs are an investment in public health that will provide a total of up to $380 billion in return to American families in the form of longer, healthier lives and reduced health-care costs. EPA estimates that electricity rates are projected to stay "well within normal historical fluctuations." The standards will result in relatively small changes—about 3 percent—in the average retail price of electricity, primarily due to increased demand for natural gas, the agency says (USEPA 2011b).

National Security Costs

Of the 1.05 billion tons of coal of all types (steam, metallurgical) consumed in the United States in 2010 (USEIA 2011a, Table 26), only about 19.4 million tons (1.8 percent) were imported (USEIA 2011e, Table 4), mostly from Columbia, South America. This includes coal imported to Puerto Rico and the Virgin Islands from sources nearby, to minimize transportation costs. The imported

Figure 2.4 **The Costs of Utilizing Coal Technologies**

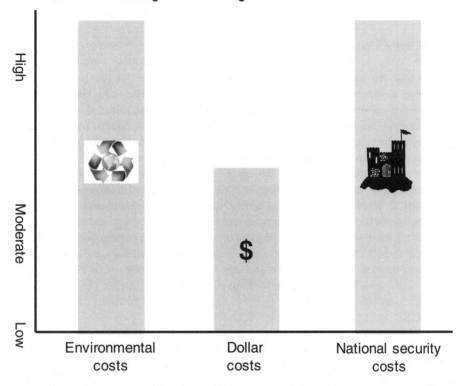

portion could easily have been produced in the United States, which has substantial additional production capacity. Coal exports were 81.7 million tons in 2010, mostly to Europe and Canada (USEIA 2011e, Table 4). Because most coal used in the United States is produced at dispersed locations within the United States, it would be unimaginably difficult for any terrorist organization or foreign government to cut off or significantly reduce supplies of this fuel for utilization within the country. The prospect of such actions would encourage greater stockpiling of coal than is currently typical, at acceptable cost to most users. Seasonal stockpiling of substantial quantities of coal is common practice today, and stockpiling by electric utilities and others increases noticeably during labor negotiations with coal miners.

However, combustion of fossil fuels is the greatest source of carbon emissions in the United States contributing to global climate change. Of 5,937 million metric tons of greenhouse gas emissions in the United States in 2010, fossil fuels contributed 5,633 million metric tons (94.9 percent), of which coal contributed 1,985 million metric tons, or about 33.4 percent of the total (USEIA 2011b, Table 11.2).

To the extent that other nations may be concerned about or affected by climate change and perceive those effects to be caused in large part by the United States, our relationships with some countries may in the future be adversely affected by utilization of such large quantities of coal, so it cannot be said that the national security costs of coal utilization are nil. There are some national security costs of utilizing coal, but their significance for U.S. energy policy is determined by which countries are affected, how much, and whether we care about their concerns. At the current time, the national security costs of utilizing this resource are mistakenly considered by many analysts to be low, but they may be expected to increase in the future, as different countries are affected and make their concerns known to the United States through diplomatic channels or in the international arena, as described in Chapter 1.

SUMMARY OF COSTS

The costs of utilizing coal technologies are summarized in Figure 2.4 (see page 37). The environmental costs to American society of using coal must be described as high because of the loss of productivity on destroyed and unreclaimed mined lands, contaminated water supplies, air pollution from coal combustion, and the impacts of global climate change. Some environmental costs of using coal are converted to dollar costs in the form of pollution control technologies and activities, but others remain unpaid, especially for carbon emissions.

The dollar costs of utilizing coal are moderate, as compared to other energy fuels, but do not yet reflect the full costs of controlling carbon emissions or reclaiming abandoned mined lands. The national security costs of utilizing coal are certainly high and getting higher as other nation-states begin to comprehend the impacts of American reliance on this fuel on global climate change, and especially the effects of sea-level rise on island states and those with large populations in low-lying deltaic regions. Increasing numbers of "climate change refugees" will increase instability, conflict, and resentment toward the United States and other developed countries by putting pressure on neighboring countries who receive them for housing, food, and public services.

REFERENCES

Axtell, K. 1978. *Survey of Fugitive Dust from Coal Mines*. Washington, DC: U.S. Environmental Protection Agency.
Bonskowski, Richard. 2000. *The U.S. Coal Industry in the 1990's: Low Prices and Record Production*. Washington, DC: U.S. Energy Information Administration. ftp://ftp.eia.doe.gov/pub/coal/coalfeat.pdf.
Bonskowski, Richard, William Watson, and Fred Freme. 2006. *Coal Production in the United States: An Historical Overview*. Washington, DC: U.S. Energy Information Administration. www.eia.doe.gov/cneaf/coal/page/coal_production_review.pdf.
Chalekode, P.K., and T.R. Blackwood. 1978. *Source Assessment: Coal Refuse Piles, Abandoned Mines, and Outcrops, State-of-the-Art*. Cincinnati, OH: U.S. Environmental Protection Agency.
Christman, R.C., J. Haslbeck, B. Sedlik, W. Murray, and W. Wilson. 1980. *Activities, Effects and Impacts of the Coal Fuel Cycle for a 1,000-MWe Electric Power Generating Plant*. Washington, DC: U.S. Nuclear Regulatory Commission.
Clean Air Act. 42 U.S. Code §§ 7401-7671q.
Clean Water Act. 33 U.S. Code §§ 1251-1387.
Davies, J. Clarence, and Barbara S. Davies. 1975. *The Politics of Pollution*, 2nd ed. Indianapolis: Pegasus.
Davis, David H. 1993. *Energy Politics*, 4th ed. New York: St. Martin's Press.
Dewan, Shaila. 2008. "Coal Ash Spill Revives Issue of Its Hazards." *New York Times*, December 24.
Dunrud, C.R. 1976. "Some Engineering Geologic Factors Controlling Coal Mine Subsidence in Utah and Colorado." U.S. Geological Survey Professional Paper 969. Washington, DC: U.S. Government Printing Office.
Dvorak, Anthony J. 1977. *The Environmental Effects of Using Coal for Generating Electricity*. Argonne, IL: Argonne National Laboratory.
Epstein, Paul R., Jonathan Buonocore, Kevin Eckerle, Michael Hendryx, Benjamin M. Stout III, Richard Heinberg, and Richard W. Clapp. 2011. "Full Cost Accounting for the Life Cycle of Coal." *Annals of the New York Academy of Sciences* 1219: 73–98.
Fausset, Richard. 2009. "Residents Fear Repercussions of Massive Tennessee Coal Ash Spill." *Chicago Tribune*, January 1.
Hamilton, Michael S. 2005. *Mining Environmental Policy: Comparing Indonesia and the USA*. Burlington, VT: Ashgate.
Hamilton, Michael S., and Norman I. Wengert. 1980. *Environmental, Legal and Political Constraints on*

Power Plant Siting in the Southwestern United States. Fort Collins: Colorado State University Experiment Station.

Kneese, Allen, and Charles Schultze. 1975. *Pollution, Prices and Public Policy.* Washington, DC: Brookings Institution Press.

Martin, J.F. 1974. *Quality of Effluents from Coal Refuse Piles.* Washington, DC: U.S. Environmental Protection Agency.

Murray, F.X. 1978. *Where We Agree: Report of the National Coal Policy Project.* Boulder, CO: Westview Press.

Nunenkamp, David C. 1976. *Coal Preparation and Environmental Engineering Manual.* Research Triangle Park, NC: U.S. Environmental Protection Agency.

Perry, John H. 1973. *Chemical Engineers Handbook.* New York: McGraw-Hill.

Rifas, Bertram E., and Sally J. White. 1976. *Coal Transportation Capability of the Existing Rail and Barge Network, 1985 and Beyond.* Palo Alto, CA: Electric Power Research Institute.

Tennessee Valley Authority. 2011. "Coal-Fired Power Plant." www.tva.gov/power/coalart.htm.

Upadhyay, Raja. 2000. "Developments in Coal Exploration." *Pincock Perspectives* (February).

U.S. Advisory Council on Historic Preservation. 1978. *Effects of Strip Mining on National Historic and Natural Sites.* Washington, DC: U.S. Government Printing Office.

U.S. Bureau of Land Management (USBLM). 1975. *Final Environmental Impact Statement on the Proposed Federal Coal Leasing Program.* Washington, DC: U.S. Government Printing Office.

U.S. Energy Information Administration (USEIA). 2010. *U.S. Coal Resource Regions.* Washington, DC: U.S. Energy Information Administration. www.eia.doe.gov/cneaf/coal/reserves/reserves.html.

———. 2011a. *Annual Coal Report.* www.eia.gov/coal/annual/.

———. 2011b. *Annual Energy Review 2010.* Washington, DC: U.S. Government Printing Office.

———. 2011c. *Direct Federal Financial Interventions and Subsidies in Energy Markets 2010.* Washington, DC: U.S. Government Printing Office.

———. 2011d. *Electric Power Annual 2010.* Washington, DC: U.S. Government Printing Office. www.eia.gov/electricity/annual/.

———. 2011e. *Quarterly Coal Report.* http://38.96.246.204/coal/production/quarterly/pdf/t4p01p1.pdf.

U.S. Environmental Protection Agency (USEPA). 2005. *Mountaintop Mining/Valley Fills in Appalachia: Final Programmatic Environmental Impact Statement.* Washington, DC: U.S. Government Printing Office. www.epa.gov/region3/mtntop/eis2005.htm.

———. 2011a. "EPA Issues First National Standards for Mercury Pollution from Power Plants." Press Release, December 21. Washington, DC: U.S. Environmental Protection Agency.

———. 2011b. "EPA Reduces Smokestack Pollution, Protecting Americans' Health from Soot and Smog." Press Release, July 7. Washington, DC: U.S. Environmental Protection Agency.

U.S. Geological Survey (USGS). 1979. *Draft Environmental Statement, Proposed Colstrip Project, Rosebud County, Montana.* Washington, DC: U.S. Government Printing Office.

U.S. Office of Surface Mining Reclamation and Enforcement (OSM). 1979. *Permanent Regulatory Program Implementing Section 501(b) of the Surface Mining Control and Reclamation Act of 1977: Environmental Impact Statement.* Washington, DC: U.S. Department of the Interior.

———. 1987. *Surface Coal Mining Reclamation: 10 Years of Progress, 1977–1987.* Washington, DC: U.S. Government Printing Office.

Weir International Inc. 2008. *United States Longwall Mining Statistics, 1989–2007.* Downers Grove, IL: Weir International Inc. www.weirimc.com/United%20States%20Longwall%20Mining%20Statistics.pdf.

Whitehouse, Alfred, and Asep A.S. Mulyana. 2004. "Coal Fires in Indonesia." *International Journal of Coal Geology* 59: 91–97.

Witten, John M., and Samir A. Desai. 1978. *Water Transportation Requirements for Coal Movement in 1985.* Washington, DC: U.S. Department of Transportation.

3

Nuclear

~~~~~~~~~~~~~~~~~~~~~~~~

From its discovery in 1789 until World War II, uranium was mined mostly for its radium content, which was sought for use as luminous paint for watch dials and other instruments, as well as for health-related applications. The by-product uranium was used mostly as a yellow pigment. In the United States, uranium ore was found in 1871 in gold mines near Central City, Colorado, which produced about fifty tons of high-grade ore between 1871 and 1895. However, most American uranium ore before World War II came from vanadium deposits in the Colorado Plateau of Utah and Colorado (Dahlkamp 1993).

Domestic reserves of uranium are reported by the U.S. government in terms of "maximum-forward cost" estimates that do not include some costs of development, such as sunk costs for exploration and land acquisition, income taxes, profit, and the cost of money. Consequently, this may result in somewhat optimistic estimates of recoverable reserves. As of December 31, 2008, U.S. forward-cost uranium reserves were estimated at about 1,227 million pounds of uranium hexafluoride (U_3O_8) at US$100 per pound, or 539 million pounds of U_3O_8 at US$50 per pound (USEIA 2010d), reflecting the difference in reserves at various market prices. The weighted-average price of uranium purchased by owners and operators of U.S. civilian nuclear power reactors in 2011 was $55.64 per pound of U_3O_8 (USEIA 2012c, Table S1b). U.S. production of uranium concentrate (yellowcake) was 3.99 million pounds in 2011 (USEIA 2012a, Table 3), most in Utah, Nebraska, Texas, and Wyoming.

The nuclear fuel cycle includes exploration, mining, processing, transportation, utilization, decommissioning, and disposal of waste by-products and spent fuel (see Figure 3.1). Human exposure to radiation is associated with each of these activities, and each stage of the nuclear fuel cycle generates radioactive wastes.

URANIUM EXPLORATION

Uranium prospecting is similar to exploration for coal in the United States (see Chapter 2 in this volume), but relies upon some specialized instruments for detecting the presence of radioactive isotopes. Ionization chambers and Geiger counters were first adapted for field use in the 1930s. They were the principal instruments used for uranium prospecting for many years until Geiger counters were replaced by scintillation counters. The use of airborne ionization chambers and Geiger counters to prospect for radioactive minerals began in the 1940s. Airborne gamma-ray spectrometry is now the accepted leading technique for uranium prospecting worldwide.

After a search of available records, site visits by geologists are followed by core drilling and logging of boreholes to determine the amounts of uranium materials that are extractable at specified costs from a deposit. Uranium reserves are the amounts of ore that are estimated to be recoverable at stated costs.

Exploration for uranium produces significant environmental damage similar in quality and scale to that caused by coal exploration as described in detail in Chapter 2. Such damage is particularly

Figure 3.1   **The Nuclear Fuel Cycle**

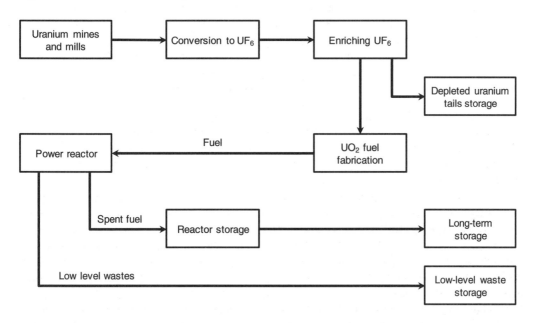

severe in roadless areas. Revegetation of mined lands takes anywhere from one growing season in wet climates to ten years in arid locations like the western United States, where most exploration for uranium occurs. Although large sample pits dug during coal exploration are seldom excavated for uranium ore, other impacts from exploration drilling such as equipment noise and possible contamination by drilling muds and fluids may be severe in uranium exploration.

The principle methods of uranium mining are box cut mining, open pit mining, and in situ leaching. As with coal, the choice of mining method depends primarily on the depth of burial and thickness of the uranium deposit.

UNDERGROUND URANIUM MINING

Although it is seldom used in the United States today, if uranium is buried too far below the surface for open pit mining, an underground mine may be used with tunnels and shafts dug to access and remove uranium ore. There is less waste material removed from underground mines than open pit mines, but underground mining exposes workers to higher levels of radon gas than surface mining.

Other ores, such as copper, gold, and silver, are often mined in association with uranium. Once an ore body has been identified, a shaft is sunk in the vicinity of the ore veins, and crosscuts are driven horizontally to the veins at various levels, usually every 329 to 492 feet (100 to 150 meters). Similar tunnels, known as drifts, are driven along the ore veins from the crosscut. The next step is to drive tunnels through the deposit from level to level. These are known as raises when driven upward and winzes when driven downward. Raises are subsequently used to develop stopes where ore is mined from veins.

A stope, which is the workshop of an underground mine, is an excavation from which ore is extracted. Two methods of stope mining are commonly used. In the cut-and-fill or open stoping method, the space remaining following removal of ore after blasting is filled with waste rock and cement. In the shrinkage method, just enough broken ore is removed via chutes below to allow miners to work from the top of the pile while drilling and blasting for the next layer to be broken off, eventually leaving a large hole.

As with coal, the environmental costs of deep mining uranium include impacts near tunnel openings, ventilation shafts, and spoil piles; cross connections between aquifers, allowing contamination of previously separate water supplies; and surface subsidence as a result of collapse of cavity or tunnel roofs. Because uranium ore emits radon gases and other sources of radiation, it can be more dangerous than other underground mining unless adequate ventilation systems are installed.

OPEN PIT SURFACE MINING

In open pit or surface uranium mining, overburden is removed by drilling, blasting, and ripping to expose an ore body, which is mined by blasting and excavation via loaders and dump trucks, similar to surface coal mining as described in Chapter 2. Uranium ore is then broken up, loaded, and hauled to a milling site. Unlike surface coal mining, there are no national requirements for reclamation of uranium surface mines in the United States, which are regulated only by state laws. Historically, uranium mines have a poor record of preserving topsoil for later distribution during reclamation. Overburden material is usually hauled to a disposal site. Uranium ore is excavated, broken up, and hauled to milling facilities before transport to fabrication facilities. Overburden or spoil is sometimes used to refill a mined area, but often not. After spoil has been graded and recontoured by bulldozers, topsoil may be redistributed and vegetation planted to hold surface soil together and reduce erosion of spoil. In surface uranium mining operations, workers spend much time in climate-controlled, enclosed cabins to limit their exposure to dust and radiation. Water is used to suppress airborne dust.

IN SITU LEACHING

In situ leaching, sometimes referred to as in situ recovery or solution mining, is performed by pumping liquids (weak acid or weak alkaline depending on the calcium concentration in the ore) down through injection wells placed on one side of a deposit of uranium. The liquid flows through the deposit and is pumped up through recovery wells on the opposing side of the deposit, recovering uranium by leaching. In situ leaching is often cost-effective because it avoids excavation costs and may be implemented more quickly than conventional mining. However, it is not suitable for all uranium deposits because the host rock must be permeable to liquids (as is often the case in sandstone), in which case it may be impossible to contain leaching chemicals and prevent them from contaminating nearby groundwater aquifers. Environmental impact studies and monitoring must be performed continuously when evaluating in situ leaching.

MINING HAZARDS

Waste rock is produced during open pit mining when overburden is removed and during underground mining when driving tunnels through non-ore zones. Piles of these tailings often contain elevated concentrations of radioisotopes compared to normal rock. Other waste piles consist of ore of too low a grade for processing. The difference between waste rock and ore depends on technical and economic feasibility criteria, especially the market price of U_3O_8. All these piles threaten people and the environment after shutdown of the mine, due to their release of radon gas and seepage of water containing radioactive and toxic materials. In some cases uranium has been removed from this low-grade ore by heap leaching. This may be done if the uranium content is too low for the ore to be economically processed in a uranium mill. The leaching liquid (often sulfuric acid) is introduced at the top of a tailings pile and percolates down until it reaches a liner below the pile, where it is caught and pumped to a processing plant. This method entails potential for extreme damage to the surrounding environment, especially surface and ground waters, and must be carefully managed and monitored.

Surface mining of uranium entails environmental impacts similar to surface mining of coal, as described extensively in Chapter 2. It affects air quality, water supply and quality, wildlife, vegetation, land use, soils, topography, and geologic and historic resources. As with coal surface mining, what becomes of the land surface after uranium mining is determined by the manner in which mining is conducted and reclamation implemented. Depending on the specific geologic strata and location, uranium is found in ore with a wide variety of other minerals and heavy metals, many of which are carcinogenic or toxic to humans, such as fluorine, lead, mercury, arsenic, cadmium, copper, nickel, and chromium. These materials may contaminate dust and surface water in and near uranium mines, at mills, and in tailings deposits (USBLM 1997; USNRC 1997).

Exposure to air- and water-borne dust and radiation from uranium mill tailings has been associated with high rates of leukemia, lung cancer, bone cancer, spontaneous abortions, premature births, a variety of birth defects including broken chromosomes and mental retardation, impaired kidney function, and chronic diarrhea (Wasserman and Solomon 1982; USNRC 1980, 1981; Jacobs and Dickson 1979; Dreesen 1978; USGAO 1978, 1979). This is a much greater risk to workers in underground mines than in surface mines, but also affects nearby residents. Noise, vibration, and structural damage due to blasting continue to impose costs on some uranium mining operations in the United States today.

From 1944 to 1986, nearly 4 million tons of uranium ore were extracted from Navajo lands under leases with the Navajo Nation. Many Navajo people worked the mines, often living and raising families in close proximity to mines and mills. Today the mines are closed, but a legacy of uranium contamination remains, including over 500 abandoned uranium mines, and homes and drinking water sources with elevated levels of radiation. Potential health effects include lung cancer from inhalation of radioactive particles, bone cancer and impaired kidney function from exposure to radionuclides in drinking water (USEPA 2011a, 2011b). A statistically significant subset of these early miners later developed small-cell carcinoma after exposure to uranium ore (Gottlieb and Husen 1982). Since 1994 the EPA has used its Superfund authority working with the Navajo Nation EPA to assess 250 high-risk sites for further evaluation and has conducted screening-level review and site visits of an additional 452 abandoned uranium mine sites, with more detailed assessments to be completed at up to thirty-five mines, to identify appropriate courses of action for the highest-priority mines. The EPA also completed a removal action to clean up mine waste at Skyline Mine and an interim removal action at the Northeast Church Rock Quivira Mine (USEPA 2011a, 2011b). Due to concerns over such health effects, and especially concern for protecting groundwater drinking water supplies from contamination, the Navajo Nation tribal government in 2005 adopted legislation banning uranium mining and processing on tribal lands in Arizona (Navajo Nation 2005).

Groundwater supplies may be adversely affected by surface mining of uranium as with surface mining of coal. On tailings piles where low-grade uranium or leaching chemicals are present, increased infiltration may contaminate both groundwater and nearby streams for long periods. Lakes formed in abandoned surface mining operations are more likely to be toxic if there are contaminants in tailings piles, especially if these materials are near the surface. As is the case with coal mining, described in Chapter 2, surface mining of uranium causes direct and indirect damage to wildlife and vegetation. Although head-of-hollow fills are used in coal mining, they are rarely used in uranium mining, which often occurs in rolling or relatively flat terrain. However, other impacts on wildlife are encountered due to often arid sites where much uranium mining occurs and species survival is already marginal. In semi-arid areas of the southwestern United States, successful revegetation is unlikely without substantial commitments of effort and water over many years.

The presence of associated minerals exposed as a result of surface mining uranium can affect wildlife by eliminating habitat and by causing direct destruction of some species. Dilute concentrations of radioactive heavy metals can cause severe wildlife damage in some areas. The effects of acidic waste produced by coal mining are less prevalent in uranium mines. Where thick ore bodies are extracted, such as in the Grants mineral belt of New Mexico, enough overburden may not be available to replace uranium that was removed, and some permanent alteration of the surface contour results. Steep slopes are hazards where open pit mines are not properly regraded and reclaimed, and accumulation of contaminated water in the lower reaches of such mines is a significant hazard for wildlife and children.

PROCESSING URANIUM

Providing enriched uranium fuel for nuclear electric power plants involves milling of the uranium ore, conversion of uranium oxide (U_3O_8), often called "yellowcake," to uranium hexafluoride (UF_6), enrichment, fuel fabrication, and transportation of radioactive materials between facilities. Radioactive waste is produced during each of these activities (USEPA 1973a, 1).

Ore Milling and Tailings

Natural uranium ore usually contains about 0.71 percent uranium-235. Mined ore is milled to a concentrate containing about 85 percent U_3O_8. Milling of uranium ore is done to separate uranium yellowcake from extraneous rock. This is accomplished by mechanical crushing of ore so it can be dissolved by a sulfuric acid or sodium carbonate leach or solvent extraction process. Uranium is purified and concentrated in several solvent extraction steps, separated by thickening and centrifuging, and finally calcined and pulverized for packaging in fifty-five gallon drums for shipment (USEPA 1973a).

Radon gas, which is harmful to humans, is released from uranium ore storage piles, ore crushing and grinding ventilation systems, leach tank vents, and tailings retention systems. Dusts containing uranium and uranium daughter products (principally thorium-230 and radium-226) are released from ore piled outside of mills and from ore crushing and grinding ventilation systems, while a dust containing mostly uranium without daughters is released from yellowcake drying and packaging operations. These dusts are discharged to the atmosphere by means of low stacks (USEPA 1975b). There is no identifiable practical method that will prevent the release of radon gas from uranium mills (USEPA 1973b).

Radioactivity associated with uranium mill effluents comes from the natural uranium and its daughter products present in the ore. During milling, most of the natural uranium is separated and concentrated, while most radioactive uranium daughter products remain in uranium-depleted solid residues pumped to a tailings retention system. Liquid and solid wastes from the milling operation contain low-level concentrations of these radioactive materials, and airborne radioactive releases include radon gas, particles of the ore, and uranium oxide (USEPA 1973b).

Uranium discharged to the air as ore dust and as calcinated yellowcake, and radium-226 and thorium-230 discharged to the air as ore dust, are all considered insoluble aerosols. If inhaled, insoluble aerosols tend to remain in the pulmonary region of the lung, so the lung becomes the most important organ when critical radiation dose is calculated (USEPA 1973b).

Extraneous rock is disposed of in a tailings retention system consisting of large "tailings ponds" that must periodically be dredged, with solid materials placed nearby to drain in large "tailings piles." Both ponds and piles provide significant radiological impacts on the environment by continuously discharging radon-222 gas, emitting gamma rays from radon-222 and its daughters during radioactive decay, discharging radium-226 and thorium-230 to the air, and leaching into surface and ground waters (USEPA 1973a, 24). Experience in Grand Junction, Colorado, Salt Lake City, Utah, and Church Rock, New Mexico, has shown that members of the general public received very high levels of radiation exposure to the lung by release of radon from uranium mill tailings piles (Dingmann 2009; Pasternak 2006; USEPA 1973a, 72).

Gaseous and particulate effluents must be controlled at mills in three principal areas: ore crushing areas, fine ore bins, and yellowcake packaging and drying areas. Wet dust control systems are generally used in ore crushing areas and fine ore storage bins. Wet scrubbers and bag filters are used in drying and packaging areas (USEPA 1973a, 14). Waste streams from wet processes involve mechanical separation of solid waste particles from water after chemical treatment to encourage formation of particles. Residual chemicals in the waste stream must then be neutralized through further treatment (USEPA 1973a, 18). The impacts of tailings piles may be controlled by grading them and constructing appropriate drains to divert runoff, covering them with topsoil, and restoring sufficient vegetation to hold the structures together so they do not erode and contaminate water supplies. There is no method to effectively prevent the release of radon gas from uranium tailings ponds (USEPA 1973b).

The liquid effluent from an acid-leach process mill consists of waste solutions from the leaching, grinding, extraction, and washing circuits of the mill. These solutions, which have an initial pH of 1.5 to 2, contain the unreacted portion of sulfuric acid used as the leaching agent in the mill process, sulfates, and some silica as the primary dissolved solids, along with trace quantities of toxic soluble metals and organic solvents. Radioactive products of radon decay may also be present in small concentrations. Since the concentrations of radium-226 and thorium-230 are much higher than applicable standards, considerable effort must be exerted to prevent any release of this material from the site (USEPA 1973b). Waste milling solutions from a mill using the alkaline leach process may have a pH value of about ten and contain sodium, sodium carbonate, sodium bicarbonate, and sulfate as the principal dissolved solids (USNRC 1976). Waste milling solutions are, therefore, discharged with solids into tailings ponds, which are constructed to prevent discharge into the surface water system and to minimize percolation into the ground (USEPA 1973b).

The waste milling solution is used to slurry solid waste tailings to a retention pond system that uses an impervious clay-cored earth dam combined with local topographic features of the area to form an impoundment. The retention system permits evaporation of most of the contained waste liquids and serves as a permanent receptacle for residual solid tailings after the plant closes (USEPA 1973b). Constructing a barrier of material such as clay on top of the pile to prevent radon from escaping into the atmosphere, and covering mill tailings with soil, rocks, or other materials to prevent erosion are common practices (USNRC 2002). Toward the end of the operating lifetime of a retention system, some of the tailings will no longer be under water and will dry out to form a beach. Wind erosion can then carry off tailings material as airborne particulate matter unless control measures are taken to prevent such erosion, and considerable quantities of radon will be emitted (Sears et al. 1975).

Immediately after a retention system is put to use, there will be small losses of radioactive mill waste liquids through and around the dam (USNRC 1976; Humble Oil and Refining Co. 1971). This will be seen as surface water seeping from the foot of the dam. The radiological significance of this seepage will depend on the location of the pond. In arid regions, the seepage may evaporate before leaving the site, leaving the radioactivity entrained and absorbed on soil. Should the tailings pond be located next to a river, leakage might be discharged to the river. Discharge of pond seepage into streams providing insufficient dilution and not under the control of the licensee would not be acceptable. In such cases, a secondary dam may be built below the primary dam to catch seepage, which may then be pumped back into the tailings ponds. It is sometimes stated that this seepage will diminish over a period of about two years because of the sealing effect from accumulation of finer particles between the sandstone grains (Humble Oil and Refining Co. 1971).

Radium-226 is a radionuclide of great concern because levels as high as thirty-two picocuries per liter (pCi/l) have been found in seepage from current operating mills (USEPA 1975a). Assuming a seepage rate of 300 liters per minute, the concentration of radium-226 seeping into a streamflow of 140 liters per second (five cubic feet per second) is approximately one pCi/l. In the applicant's environmental report for the Highland Uranium Mill, a seepage concentration of 350 pCi/l of radium-226 was assumed (Humble Oil and Refining Co. 1971). There is no safe level of radioactivity exposure for human beings (Gofman 1981).

Unless prevented by an impermeable layer of clay or a plastic liner, considerable quantities of mill waste solution may seep downward into the soil beneath an impoundment area. Ordinarily this is not expected to result in off-site releases of radioactive materials because the radionuclides are strongly absorbed onto clay soil particles. They are removed from solution and considered to be permanently retained on the mill site. However, this is a continuing problem requiring monitoring programs to ensure there is no significant movement of contaminated liquids off-site (USEPA 1975b). There are now some 140 million tons of uranium mill tailings scattered around the western United States. Former Commissioner of the U.S. Nuclear Regulatory Commission Victor Gilinsky considered them "the dominant contribution to radiation exposure" of the entire nuclear fuel cycle (Wasserman and Solomon 1982).

For example, in July 1979, at Church Rock, New Mexico, about twenty miles from Gallup, a temporary dam holding an evaporation pond of several hundred million gallons of liquid mill tailings burst, sending 1,100 tons of radioactive mill wastes and 90 million gallons of contaminated liquid pouring into a gulley that ran into the Rio Puerco, and carrying toxic tailings seventy miles downstream into Arizona. It left residues of radioactive uranium, thorium, radium, and polonium, as well as traces of metals such as cadmium, aluminum, magnesium, manganese, molybdenum, nickel, selenium, sodium, vanadium, zinc, iron, and lead and high concentrations of sulfates along its path. The spill degraded the western Rio Puerco as a water source and contaminated livestock in the region (Wasserman and Solomon 1982). The dam had been built by United Nuclear Corporation on unstable ground, its temporary permit had expired, and the U.S. Congress heard testimony to the effect that the entire incident could have been avoided (U.S. Congress 1979).

Conversion

Conversion chemically purifies and converts U_3O_8 to UF_6, a volatile chemical form that is fed into enrichment plants. Gaseous, solid, and liquid wastes are produced by these processes (USEPA 1973a, 77). Gaseous effluents in conversion areas are controlled using a wet scrubber system combined with hydrogen fluoride recovery and a hydrogen burner. Dry bag filter systems are used to control uranium dust in both processes. Dust is deposited in the porous fabric of woven or felted fabric bags, and the pressure increases until the dust is removed by manual or automatic means, such as rapping, shaking gear, or automatic flow reversal mechanisms. Wet solvent extraction systems also require absorption towers for removing oxides of nitrogen. Gaseous effluents escaping from the scrubber and bag filter systems are released to the environment through stacks without further treatment (USEPA 1973a, 15–16).

Processes that produce liquid wastes include high-efficiency centrifuges; chemical treatments for flocculation, precipitation, and neutralization; filtration; and settling basins or ponds. Dissolved waste matter is usually in the form of ions, which may be separated from the waste stream by passing it though beds of small spheres of chemically treated resins on which ions are absorbed. Flocculation and neutralization chemicals may be added to the waste stream, causing dissolved wastes to form particles that may settle out or be separated from water by filters or centrifuges. Settling basins or ponds of about four feet depth may be several acres in size and are preferred because their operation entails little power or maintenance costs. Such structures must be lined with clay soils or artificial liners of plastic or chemically treated fabric to prevent seepage into the ground and contamination of groundwater (USEPA 1973a, 18).

Enrichment

Conversion is followed by isotopic enrichment, in which the uranium-235 concentration of the uranium feed is increased to the design specification (usually 2 to 4 percent uranium-235) of the power reactor. In the United States a gaseous diffusion process is used, where volatile UF_6 is pumped under pressure through a system of numerous (e.g., ~1,700) porous membranes that discriminate against the passage of heavier isotopes of uranium-238, allowing more uranium-235 to pass, thereby producing a fuel with a higher concentration of uranium-235 (USEPA 1973a, 96). This requires compressors driven by electric motors utilizing large quantities of electricity and generating substantial process heat that requires cooling. During enrichment, liquid, gaseous, and airborne material impurities are removed from effluents with cold traps and aluminum traps, descriptions of which are not publicly available (USEPA 1973a, 16) for security reasons. There is only one operating gaseous diffusion plant in the United States, at the Department of Energy's Paducah, Kentucky, site, operated by the U.S. Enrichment Corporation (USEC), which was created as a government corporation by the Energy Act of 1992 and privatized in 1996 (USNRC 2011c).

An alternative enrichment technique requires use of numerous gas centrifuges, a large number of rotating cylinders interconnected to form cascades. UF_6 is placed in a cylinder, which is then rotated at a high speed, creating a strong centrifugal force that draws more of the heavier gas molecules containing the U-238 toward the wall of the cylinder, while lighter gas molecules containing the U-235 tend to collect closer to the center. Slightly enriched U-235 is then extracted and fed into the next higher stage of centrifuges. Two gas centrifuge enrichment plants are currently under construction in the United States, one by USEC at Piketon, Ohio, and another in Lea County, New Mexico (USNRC 2011c). These facilities will require a great deal of electricity to run.

A third alternative separates the U-235 isotope from uranium through photoexcitation by using specially tuned lasers that are able to ionize a specific isotope, changing its properties and allowing it to be separated from the rest of the uranium. A proposal to construct a laser enrichment plant in Wilmington, North Carolina, was pending in the U.S. Nuclear Regulatory Commission (NRC) licensing process as this book went to press (USNRC 2012). Electric utilities have expressed concern about the limited uranium enrichment capacity in the United States and their resulting dependence on foreign sources of enriched uranium fuel (NERC 2009, 369). In each alternative, the greatest portion of uranium becomes a predominantly uranium-238 waste product impoverished in uranium-235 that cannot be released to the environment and is stored in cylinders as UF_6.

Fuel Fabrication

The enriched portion of UF_6 is processed into uranium dioxide (UO_2) pellets, loaded into alloy tubing, and fabricated into individual fuel assemblies that may be inserted into a power reactor (USEPA 1973a, 2). Systems for conversion of UF_6 to UO_2 are equipped with scrubbers and high-efficiency particulate air filters for uranium dust removal, which is recycled into the pellet fabrication process (USEPA 1973a, 17).

Transportation

The principal mode of exposure of a human population to radioactivity in the uranium fuel cycle is from direct radiation resulting from the passage of hundreds of shipments per year of fuel and waste products along rail, truck, and barge shipment routes. There are no planned releases of radioactive materials from transportation activities, so this pathway for radiation exposure is based entirely on the risk of accidents. Effects are long-term radiation exposure to the skeleton and other organs of the body, especially the lungs (USEPA 1973a, 9).

NUCLEAR POWER GENERATION

Nuclear electric generating plants accounted for about 9.7 percent of summer installed generating capacity at 104 generating units (USEIA 2011c, Table 1.1.A) and generated about 19.6 percent of the electricity produced in the United States during 2008 (USEIA 2011d, Table 2.1.A). Like coal-fired generators, each power plant requires dedication of several hundred to a few thousand acres of land to a single large industrial use for one or more reactors and generators, unused fuel handling and storage facilities, spent fuel handling and storage facilities, cooling water storage and purification, and solid waste, low-level, and high-level radioactive waste handling and storage facilities, access to which must be severely restricted for safety and security reasons.

Nuclear power plants rely on heat energy generated from nuclear fission to produce steam that turns a turbine to generate electricity. A nuclear reactor replaces an industrial boiler to produce steam, but the turbine generator and many auxiliary systems are quite similar to those used to generate electricity in conventional fossil-fueled generating units. The principal differences are the nuclear heat source and reactor safety systems.

In the nuclear fission process, the nucleus of a heavy element such as uranium or plutonium splits when bombarded by neutrons in a nuclear reactor. The fission process for uranium atoms yields small amounts of radioactive materials and tremendous amounts of energy in the form of radiation and heat. Because more neutrons are released from uranium fission than are required to initiate it, the nuclear reaction can become self-sustaining—a chain reaction—under controlled conditions, thus producing a tremendous amount of energy (USEIA 2011e). The process is essentially identical to that in a nuclear explosion, except in a nuclear reactor it takes place under controlled conditions at a much slower rate.

In most commercial nuclear power plants, heat energy generated by uranium fuel is transferred to ordinary water that is carried away from the reactor's core either as steam in boiling-water reactors (BWRs) or as superheated water in pressurized-water reactors (PWRs). Boiling-water and pressurized-water reactors are sometimes called light-water reactors (LWRs), because they utilize

Figure 3.2 **Pressurized Water Reactor**

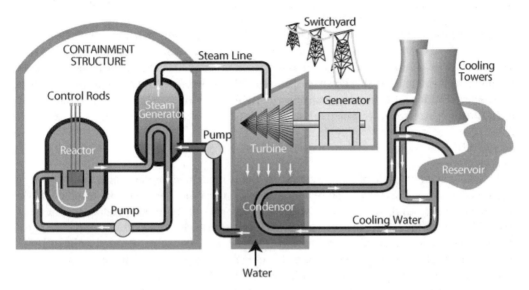

Source: USEIA 2012.
Note: In a typical commercial pressurized light-water reactor the reactor core generates heat, pressurized-water in the primary coolant loop carries the heat to the steam generator, inside the steam generator heat from the primary coolant loop vaporizes the water in a secondary loop producing steam, the steam line directs the steam to the main turbine causing it to turn the turbine generator, which produces electricity. The unused steam is exhausted to the condenser where it is condensed into water. The resulting water is pumped out of the condenser with a series of pumps, reheated, and pumped back to the steam generator. The reactors core contains fuel assemblies which are cooled by water, which is force-circulated by electrically powered pumps. Emergency cooling water is supplied by other pumps, which can be powered by on-site diesel generators. Other safety systems, such as the containment cooling system, also need power.

ordinary water (H_2O) to transfer the heat energy from reactor to turbine in the electricity generation process. In other reactor designs, the heat energy is transferred by heavy water (deuterium), helium gas, or a liquid metal such as lead or sodium (USEIA 2011e).

In a PWR, superheated water in a primary cooling loop flows through a special heat exchanger called a steam generator that is used to boil water and create steam in a secondary loop that turns the turbine-generator. The two-loop design of a PWR keeps radioactivity isolated; only clean steam is circulated through the turbine. This design helps minimize maintenance costs and radiation exposure to plant personnel. In the BWR reactor design, water is boiled inside the reactor core and then sent directly to the turbine-generator to produce electric power. The BWR is a simpler design, but has the disadvantage that the turbine and more of the plant become radioactive over time. In either a boiling-water or pressurized-water installation, steam under high pressure turns a turbine whose shaft is connected to an electric generator (USEIA 2011e).

The fuel core for a nuclear power reactor can have up to 800 fuel assemblies. An assembly consists of a group of sealed fuel rods, each filled with slightly enriched uranium oxide pellets, supported by metal spacer-grids to brace the rods and maintain the proper distances between them. During operation of the reactor, the concentration of U-235 in the fuel is decreased as those atoms undergo nuclear fission to create heat energy. Some U-235 atoms are converted to atoms of fissile Pu-239, some of which will, in turn, undergo fission and produce energy. Others decay into other nonfissionable radioactive elements such as Pu-240 and lead. Products created by nuclear fission reactions are retained within the fuel pellets and become neutron-absorbing products that act to slow the rate of nuclear fission and heat production. As reactor operation continues, a point is reached at which the declining concentration of fissile nuclei in the fuel and the increasing concentration of neutron-absorbing by-products result in lower than optimal heat generation. At this point, a reactor must be shut down temporarily and refueled. The fraction of the reactor's fuel core replaced during refueling is typically one-fourth for a boiling-water reactor and one-third for a pressurized-water reactor (USEIA 2011e).

REACTOR SAFETY

The human mind is capable of infinite creativity. But is it possible for the human mind to invent a technology so complicated and powerful it cannot be controlled by those who invented it? Or by persons other than those who invented it, who are more likely to be operating it on a daily basis? The continuing safety risks of utilizing nuclear fission to generate electric power were aptly illustrated with the core meltdown at Three Mile Island near Harrisburg, Pennsylvania, in 1979, with the core explosions in Ukraine at Chernobyl in 1986, and again with multiple core meltdowns at the Fukushima Daiichi nuclear plant in Japan on March 11, 2011. These three lessons have gradually increased in severity, the first two being discounted by many Americans because there was no loss of life at Three Mile Island and because Chernobyl is located at such a great distance from the United States and utilized a reactor design not used in this country.

Still, Three Mile Island illustrated how mechanical failures could be compounded by failure of plant operators to understand the situation due to poor control room design and deficient training. The result was a "partial" core meltdown (Kemeny 1979) in a 906 megawatt (MWe) pressurized-water reactor that had become operational in 1978, only a year before its demise. This was the first time the term "partial" meltdown was used, apparently as a public relations measure to minimize the apparent severity of a catastrophic situation. In the nuclear industry, a meltdown is a meltdown, partial or otherwise. It involves the distortion of metal fuel-rod assemblies in a reactor core such that control rods cannot be inserted or removed, thus relieving plant operators of most control over reactor core temperatures. This situation creates the possibility of a steam explosion that may disperse highly radioactive materials over a large area and create a mess of destroyed, highly radioactive equipment that is exceedingly difficult to clean up without harm to human life. Three Mile Island stimulated more stringent safety regulation by the U.S. Nuclear Regulatory Commission and cancellation of many orders for nuclear reactors, which the electric utility industry had already begun to abandon due to their exceedingly high capital costs; however, the significance of its warning has diminished over the years as memories have faded.

At Chernobyl, poor design of a 1,000 MWe nuclear reactor and human errors during operation and testing of safety features caused an explosion and fire, releasing into the atmosphere large quantities of radioactive contamination, which eventually spread over much of the western Soviet Union and Europe. The disaster involved one of four 1,000 MWe reactors at the site first operational in 1977, a light-water reactor moderated by a graphite medium, fueled with natural, unenriched uranium dioxide. The resulting contamination of the environment with radioactive plutonium, iodine, strontium, and cesium stimulated evacuation of more than 100,000 people from the affected region during 1986 and relocation of another 200,000 people from Belarus, the Russian Federation, and Ukraine. Over 5 million people continue to live in contaminated areas (IAEA 2011a), and up to 4,000 could eventually die of radiation exposure from the Chernobyl disaster (WHO 2005). Yet lack of American interest in events overseas, coupled with differences in design between the nuclear reactor at Chernobyl and those located in the United States—stressed by the U.S. nuclear industry—resulted in only short-term increased concern over nuclear reactor safety in the United States.

The Fukushima I nuclear disaster was based on a series of equipment failures, reactor core meltdowns, and releases of radioactive materials following the 9.0 magnitude Tōhuku earthquake and tsunami on March 11, 2011, in Japan (DiSavino 2011). The Fukushima I Nuclear Power Plant, operated by the Tokyo Electric Power Company (TEPCO), contained six boiling-water reactors (BWR) designed by General Electric, similar to many in the United States. Its electrical generators had a combined capacity of 4,700 MWe, making Fukushima I one of the twenty-five largest nuclear power stations in the world. Unit 1 was a 439 MWe reactor that began commercial operation in 1971. Units 2, 3, 4 and 5 were all 784 MWe reactors, and Unit 6 had 1,100 MWe of generating capacity.

At the time of the quake, only Units 1, 2, and 3 were operating, and they shut down automatically after the earthquake, while emergency generators started up to run control electronics and water pumps needed to cool reactors. Fuel had previously been removed from Unit 4, and Units 5 and 6 were in cold shutdown for scheduled maintenance (CNN Wire Staff 2011). The plant was protected by a seawall designed to withstand a 5.7-meter (19-foot) tsunami but not the 14-meter (46-foot) maximum wave that arrived about an hour after the earthquake (IAEA 2011b). The entire plant was flooded, including low-lying generators, electrical switchgear in reactor basements, and external pumps for supplying cooling seawater. Diesel fuel tanks for backup generators were swept away. The connection to the electrical grid was broken. All power for cooling was lost and reactors started to overheat.

In the next few days, Units 1, 2, and 3 experienced a full meltdown (IAEA 2011b). Hydrogen explosions destroyed the upper level of buildings housing Units 1, 3, and 4; an explosion damaged the containment of Unit 2; and multiple fires broke out at Unit 4. Fuel rods in all three reactors and in spent fuel storage pools were exposed to air, and temperatures were uncontrolled. With the remnants of its reactor core fallen to the bottom of its damaged reactor vessel, Unit 1 continued to leak cooling water three months after the initial events, and similar conditions were believed to exist at the other two melted-down reactors (CNN Wire Staff 2011).

Despite being shut down, fuel rods stored in pools at Units 5 and 6 began to overheat as water levels dropped. Unit 6 was restarted on March 17, allowing some cooling at Units 5 and 6, which were least damaged. Grid power was restored to parts of the plant on March 20, but machinery for Units 1 through 4, damaged by floods, fires, and explosions, remained inoperable (Makinen and Vartabedian 2011). On May 5, two months after the earthquake, workers were able to enter reactor buildings for the first time (MacKenzie 2011a).

Worldwide measurements of iodine-131 and cesium-137 suggested that releases of those isotopes from Fukushima were of the same magnitude as those from Chernobyl in 1986 (MacKenzie 2011b). Plutonium contamination was detected in soil at two sites in the plant.

Japanese officials initially assessed the accident as Level 4 on the International Nuclear Event Scale, and it was eventually raised to Level 7, the maximum scale value (Shears 2011). Only Chernobyl is rated as high. Experts consider Fukushima the second-largest nuclear disaster after Chernobyl, but more complex because multiple reactors were involved. A workforce in the hundreds or even thousands will take years or decades to clean up the area (Makinen and Vartabedian 2011).

The Fukushima II Nuclear Power Plant, located about seven miles north of Fukushima I, has four BWR of 1,100 MWe each, totaling 4,400 MWe capacity, which automatically shut down immediately after the earthquake. Diesel engines were started to power reactor cooling. While the cooling system for Unit 3 was undamaged, the other reactors were affected. The cooling systems remained operational, but overheated. The cooling systems were repaired and activated in Units 1, 2, and 4 in the days following the emergency shutdown after cooling could resume. By March 15, 2011, all four reactors of Fukushima II had reached cold shutdown (Winter 2011).

The disaster at Fukushima I illustrates how poor design responses to foreseeable natural disasters can produce catastrophic environmental costs, releasing large quantities of radioactive contamination into the atmosphere and ocean and completely destroying valuable generating plant assets. The contrast between the results at Fukushima I and the speed with which cooling water was restored at Fukushima II units is striking, considering both plants are owned and operated by the same utility. Fukushima II incorporated more realistic information about the potential severity of earthquakes and tsunamis into its design, and although it was damaged, it was able to recover without release of nuclear materials or permanent loss of its assets. For example, at Fukushima II, backup generators were located in waterproof buildings instead of in the turbine building as at Fukushima I, and diesel fuel tanks for backup generators were not located where they could be destroyed by a tsunami. Such precautions might have been taken at Fukushima I, but the utility decided it was too expensive to make the necessary changes and therefore suffered the expensive consequences.

Political repercussions from this event began soon after it occurred. On May 30, 2011, German chancellor Angela Merkel abandoned plans laid only nine months earlier to extend the life of Germany's nuclear power stations and ordered instead that they be phased out by 2022 (Cowell 2011). This decision is likely to have a profound effect on the German industrial sector, which uses about half the electricity produced in the country. Earlier in May, Switzerland decided to abandon plans to build new nuclear reactors and will phase out its existing plants when they reach the end of their normal lives (Dempsey and Ewing 2011). Japan has made no announcement about its future plans to construct nuclear plants.

REPROCESSING SPENT FUEL

Less than 1 percent of the uranium is typically burned in a reactor before it is discarded as "spent fuel." This is because of buildup of neutron-absorbing by-products in the fuel from the fission process and because metal cladding on the fuel assembly weakens over time with exposure to radiation. The remaining uranium and newly created fissile plutonium in spent fuel can be reclaimed for future use in reactors or weapons by chemical reprocessing. However, in the United States, the "once-through fuel cycle" is currently preferred in national policy over reprocessing of spent fuel (Andrews 2008).

A Purex solvent extraction process has been used in the United States for many years to recover fissile material from military waste and was seriously considered for reprocessing spent fuel from nuclear electric generating reactors. In this process, spent fuel is chopped into small pieces and dissolved in nitric acid; the uranium, plutonium, and remaining radioactive waste materials are easily separated either for disposal or for shipment and further use as reactor fuel (Bishop and Miraglia 1976, 2–3).

The primary radiological effluents are gaseous fission products and solid materials such as U-235, krypton-85, iodine-129, iodine-131, carbon-14, tritium, and transuranic wastes (Bishop and Miraglia 1976, 2–21). Of these, doses and potential health effects from exposure to krypton-85 are believed to be the most dangerous (USEPA 1973b, 124). Reprocessing spent fuel creates new forms of radioactive waste that require remote handling and geological isolation and that have a larger volume and heat content than spent uranium fuel itself. Reprocessing creates large volumes of low and intermediate waste as well as high-level waste in liquid form and increases the difficulties and dangers of interim waste management (Wohlstetter et al. 1979, 5, 11).

Many countries reprocess spent fuel or contract with France or Great Britain to do it, taking back the resulting plutonium and high-level waste. However, "an increasing backlog of plutonium from reprocessing is developing in many countries" and "it is doubtful that reprocessing makes economic sense in the present environment of cheap uranium" (Vandenbosch and Vandenbosch 2007, 247). Fears about development of a "plutonium economy" that might accelerate proliferation of nuclear weapons materials and technologies, along with the lack of economic incentives for reprocessing spent fuel, led President Jimmy Carter in April 1977 to postpone indefinitely further government support for development of commercial reprocessing technology in the United States (Sailor 1999, 111; Executive Office of the President 1977, 506–507).

DECOMMISSIONING NUCLEAR FACILITIES

Decommissioning nuclear facilities involves removal and disposal of all radioactive components and materials and cleanup of any radioactivity that remains in buildings or on-site. Radioactive surface material accumulated inside pipes and heat exchangers or on floors and walls must be removed. Chemical, physical, electrical, and ultrasonic processes are used to decontaminate equipment and surfaces, and liquid and solid waste materials are collected, packaged, and shipped to licensed low-level radioactive waste disposal sites. Spent fuel, reactor fuel assemblies, reactor vessels, primary heat exchange loops, and equipment that cannot be decontaminated must be secured in wet or dry temporary storage under or above ground while awaiting transport to a permanent high-level radioactive waste repository. Spent fuel may be submerged under about three meters of water for five to ten years in specially designed and structurally reinforced pools to shield radiation and allow further cooling (Ruff 2006, 4). A longer-term temporary alternative is dry cask storage in rugged containers made of steel or steel-reinforced concrete, eighteen or more inches thick, sometimes lined with lead as a radiation shield (USNRC 2002).

Three decommissioning strategies are currently in use in the United States.

1. Immediate dismantlement, or DECON, of equipment, structures, and portions of a facility containing radioactive contaminants shortly after a nuclear facility closes. Normally reactor fuel is removed from such a facility and the remaining structures are allowed to cool as radioactivity decays for many months before the rest of the facility is dismantled.
2. After reactor fuel is removed, a nuclear facility may be maintained and monitored in a condition that allows radioactivity to decay and cool for a period of years in SAFSTOR, or "delayed DECON," after which it is dismantled.
3. In a process referred to as ENTOMB, after reactor fuel is removed, a nuclear facility may be permanently encased on-site in a structurally sound material such as concrete, which is maintained and monitored until radioactivity decays to safe levels.

A combination of the first two strategies may also be used, in which some portions of a facility are dismantled or decontaminated while other parts are left in SAFSTOR. This strategy is often used where multiple generating units built at different times occupy a single site and complete decommissioning of one unit is deemed undesirable until all units have ceased operations (US NRC 2002).

Until the United States builds a permanent radioactive waste repository, high-level radioactive materials will remain at reactor sites nationwide. As of January 2008, hundreds of tons of spent fuel and other high-level radioactive wastes were stored in this manner at twenty-four decommissioned nuclear reactors and 104 operating power plants throughout the United States (USEIA 2011a).

RADIOACTIVE WASTE MANAGEMENT

Radioactive wastes are the leftovers from the use of nuclear materials for the production of electricity, diagnosis and treatment of disease, and other purposes (USNRC 2002). The United States in April 2008 had about 56,000 metric tons of spent fuel and 20,000 canisters of solid defense-related waste; these amounts are expected to increase to 119,000 metric tons by 2035 (Physicians for Social Responsibility 2009, 1; Olesky 2008). Lacking a central repository, spent fuel continues to accumulate in temporary storage at each of the 104 operating reactor sites. In the United States, radioactive materials and the wastes produced from using them are subject to regulatory control by the federal government or federally approved programs in thirty-two states (USNRC 2002).

The U.S. Department of Energy (DOE) is responsible for radioactive waste related to national defense, including nuclear weapons production and certain research activities. The NRC and some states regulate commercial radioactive waste produced by electricity generation and other nonmilitary uses of nuclear material. The Environmental Protection Agency, the Department of Transportation, and the Department of Health and Human Services also have smaller roles in regulation of radioactive material (Fentiman and Saling 2002). Commercial radioactive waste is of three basic types: mill tailings (discussed above), low-level waste, and high-level waste.

Low-Level Radioactive Waste

Commercial radioactive wastes that are not high-level wastes or uranium and thorium milling wastes are classified as low-level radioactive waste. Low-level waste includes items that have become contaminated with radioactive material or have become radioactive through exposure to neutron radiation. This waste typically consists of contaminated protective shoe covers and clothing, wiping rags, mops, filters, reactor water-treatment residues, equipment and tools, luminous dials, medical tubes, swabs, injection needles, syringes, and laboratory animal carcasses and tissues. Low-level waste is typically stored on-site by licensees, either until it has decayed away and can be disposed of as ordinary trash or until amounts are large enough for shipment to a low-level waste disposal site in containers approved by the U.S. Department of Transportation (USNRC 2011d). Three low-level waste facilities located in the United States are in Barnwell, South Carolina, Richland, Washington, and Clive, Utah. They accept waste only from certain states or only limited types of low-level wastes (USNRC 2002). Facilities licensed by NRC take steps to reduce the volume of radioactive waste after it has been produced. Common means are compaction and incineration. Approximately fifty-nine NRC licensees are authorized to incinerate certain low-level wastes, although most incineration is performed by a small number of commercial incinerators (USNRC 2002).

Radioactive waste with a short half-life is often stored temporarily before disposal in order to reduce potential radiation doses to workers who handle and transport the waste, as well as to reduce radiation levels at disposal sites. NRC authorizes some licensees to store short-half-lived material until the radioactivity is indistinguishable from ambient radiation levels and then dispose of the material as nonradioactive trash. This low-level waste is stored primarily at the sites where it was produced, such as hospitals, research facilities, clinics, and nuclear power plants (USNRC 2002).

High-Level Radioactive Waste

Today the conceptual system for high-level radioactive waste disposal includes: (1) short-term storage as liquid in tanks; (2) solidification; (3) short-term storage as a solid; (4) shipment to a repository; and (5) disposal. Provision for longer-term interim storage is an option (Bishop and Miraglia 1976, 2–3). These wastes require management that provides radiation shielding from the human environment, protections against releases, and a means of continuous heat dissipation.

Tank Storage

Temporary storage of liquid high-level radioactive wastes has been practiced in the United States for over sixty years. Tank designs generally use stainless steel tanks set in a stainless steel–lined concrete vault with air-driven circulators and cooling coils for heat transfer and removal, such as those at the Barnwell Nuclear Fuel Plant in Barnwell, South Carolina (Bishop and Miraglia 1976, 2–4).

Solidification

To prepare high-level radioactive waste for shipment and disposal, generally it is reduced to a glass form in a two-step process. First it is chemically converted to a calcine and then melted together with glass-forming materials. The end product is sealed in a canister for storage, shipment, or disposal (Bishop and Miraglia 1976, 2–4). This material is generally stored in secure warehouse facilities until a sufficient quantity is accumulated for shipment to a permanent repository, via means described above in the section on Transportation.

Currently, there are no permanent disposal facilities in the United States for high-level nuclear waste. Commercial high-level waste (spent fuel) is in temporary storage, mainly at nuclear power plant sites.

During the first forty years that nuclear waste was being created in the United States, no legislation was enacted to manage its disposal. Nuclear waste, some of which remains dangerously radioactive with a half-life of more than 1 million years, was kept in various types of temporary storage. The most troublesome transuranic elements in spent fuel are neptunium-237 (Np-237, half-life 2 million years) and plutonium-239 (Pu-239, half-life 24,000 years). Of particular concern during nuclear waste disposal are two long-lived fission products, technetium-99 (Tc-99, half-life 220,000 years) and iodine-129 (I-129, half-life 17 million years), which dominate spent fuel radioactivity after a few thousand years (Vandenbosch and Vandenbosch 2007, 21). The principal doses to humans from geological storage of nuclear wastes after long periods of time are likely to be from Tc-99 and I-129, because they are water-soluble and can move through groundwater (Sailor 1999, 109).

Most nuclear waste existing today came from production of nuclear weapons. About 77 million gallons of military nuclear waste in liquid form is stored in steel tanks, mostly in South Carolina, Washington, and Idaho. In the private sector, eighty-two nuclear plants used uranium fuel to produce electricity when the Nuclear Waste Policy Act of 1982 was enacted. Highly radioactive spent fuel rods were stored in pools of water at reactor sites, but many utilities were running out of storage space (*Congressional Quarterly* 1982, 304–310). The number of operating nuclear plants has increased significantly since then.

NUCLEAR WASTE POLICY ACT

The Nuclear Waste Policy Act of 1982 (96 Statutes at Large 2201; 42 U.S.C. §10101 et seq.) created a timetable and procedure for establishing a permanent underground repository for high-level radioactive waste by the mid-1990s and provided for some temporary federal storage of waste, including spent fuel from civilian nuclear reactors. State governments were authorized to veto a national government decision to place a waste repository within their borders; the veto would stand unless both houses of Congress voted to override it. The Act also called for developing plans by 1985 to build monitored retrievable storage (MRS) facilities, where wastes could be kept for fifty to a hundred years or more and then removed for permanent disposal or reprocessing.

Congress assigned responsibility to the U.S. Department of Energy to site, construct, operate, and close a repository for the disposal of spent nuclear fuel and high-level radioactive waste. An Office of Civilian Radioactive Waste Management was established in the Department of Energy to implement the act. The Environmental Protection Agency (EPA) was directed to set public health and safety standards for releases of radioactive materials from a repository, and the Nuclear Regulatory Commission was required to promulgate regulations governing construction, operation, and closure of a repository. Generators and owners of spent nuclear fuel and high-level radioactive waste were required to pay the costs of disposal of such radioactive materials. The waste program, which was expected to cost billions of dollars, would be funded through a fee paid by electric utilities on nuclear-generated electricity.

Permanent Repositories

The basic concept of the Nuclear Waste Policy Act was to locate a large, stable geologic formation and use mining technology to excavate a tunnel, or large-bore tunnel-boring machines (similar to those used to drill the Chunnel from England to France) to drill a shaft 500 to 1,000 meters below the surface where rooms or vaults could be excavated for disposal of high-level radioactive waste. The goal was to permanently isolate nuclear waste from the human environment (*Congressional Quarterly* 1982, 304–310). The act required the secretary of energy to issue guidelines for selection of sites for construction of two permanent underground nuclear waste repositories. DOE was to recommend three potential sites to the president by January 1985. Additional sites were to be recommended to the president by July 1, 1989, as possible locations for a second repository. A full environmental impact statement was required for any site recommended to the president.

Locations considered to be leading contenders for a permanent repository were basalt formations at the government's Hanford Nuclear Reservation in Washington, volcanic tuff formations at its Nevada nuclear test site, and several salt formations in Utah, Texas, Louisiana, and Mississippi. Salt and granite formations in other states from Maine to Georgia were also surveyed, but not evaluated in great detail (USDOE 1986; *Congressional Quarterly* 1982, 304–310). The president was required to review site recommendations and submit to Congress by March 31, 1987, his recommendation of one site for the first repository and by March 31, 1990, his recommendation for a second repository. The amount of high-level waste or spent fuel that could be placed in the first repository was limited to the equivalent of 70,000 metric tons until a second repository was built. The act required the national government to take ownership of all nuclear waste or spent fuel at all reactor sites, transport it to a repository, and thereafter be responsible for its containment. Ability to retrieve emplaced materials will be maintained for at least 100 years and possibly for as long as 300 years (Vandenbosch and Vandenbosch 2007, 109).

Temporary Spent Fuel Storage

The act authorized DOE to provide up to 1,900 metric tons of temporary storage capacity for spent fuel from civilian nuclear reactors. It required that spent fuel in temporary storage facilities be moved to permanent storage within three years after a permanent waste repository went into operation. Costs of temporary storage would be paid by fees collected from electric utilities using the storage.

Monitored Retrievable Storage

The secretary of energy was required to report to Congress by June 1, 1985, on the need for and feasibility of a monitored retrievable storage facility. The report was to include five different combinations of proposed sites and facility designs, involving at least three different locations. Environmental assessments were required for the sites. Construction of an MRS facility in a state under consideration for a permanent waste repository was prohibited.

State Veto of Selected Site

The act required DOE to consult closely throughout the site selection process with states or Indian tribes that might be affected by the location of a waste facility. The law allowed a state (governor or legislature) or Indian tribe to veto a federal decision to place within its borders a waste repository or temporary storage facility holding 300 tons or more of spent fuel, but provided that the veto could be overruled by a vote of both houses of Congress.

Payment of Construction and Operating Costs

A Nuclear Waste Fund was established by the act composed of fees levied against electric utilities to pay for the costs of constructing and operating a permanent repository. The fee was set by statute at one mill per kilowatt-hour of nuclear electricity generated. Utilities were charged a one-time fee for storage of spent fuel created before enactment of the law. Nuclear waste from defense activities was exempted from most provisions of the act, which required that if military waste were put into a civilian repository, the government would pay its pro rata share of the cost of development, construction, and operation of the repository. The act authorized impact assistance payments to states or Indian tribes to offset any costs resulting from location of a waste facility within their borders (*Congressional Quarterly* 1982, 304–310).

Yucca Mountain

In December 1987, Congress amended the Nuclear Waste Policy Act to designate Yucca Mountain, Nevada, a permanent repository for all of the nation's high-level radioactive waste (42 U.S.C. §10172). This amendment was added to the FY1988 budget reconciliation bill signed on December 22, 1987. It set aside a decision Congress made in 1982 declaring that selection of a site would be based purely on science and safety rather than politics. Working under the 1982 act, DOE had narrowed down the search for the first nuclear waste repository to three western states: Nevada, Washington, and Texas. The amendment repealed provisions of the 1982 law calling for a second repository in the eastern United States. No one from Nevada participated on the House-Senate conference committee on reconciliation (*Congressional Quarterly* 1987, 307–311). The amendment explicitly named Yucca Mountain as the only site where DOE was to construct a permanent repository for the nation's highly radioactive waste. Although years of study and procedural steps remained, investment of an estimated $1–$2 billion to test the geological suitability of the site was viewed as a virtual commitment to put the waste there. The amendment also authorized a monitored retrievable storage facility, but not until the permanent repository was licensed (*Congressional Quarterly* 1987, 307–311).

Early in 2002 the secretary of energy recommended Yucca Mountain for the only repository and President Bush approved the recommendation. Nevada exercised its state veto in April 2002, but the veto was overridden by both houses of Congress by July (Vandenbosch and Vandenbosch 2007, 21, 3–4). In 2004 the U.S. Court of Appeals for the District of Columbia Circuit upheld a challenge by Nevada, ruling that EPA's 10,000-year compliance period for isolation of radioactive waste was not consistent with National Academy of Sciences (NAS) recommendations and was too short (Vandenbosch and Vandenbosch 2007, 21, 111, 190–191; *Nuclear Energy Institute, Inc. v. EPA*, 373 F.3d 1251, D.C. Cir. 2004). The NAS report had recommended standards be set for the time of peak risk, which might approach a period of one million years (NRC 1995). By limiting the compliance time to 10,000 years, EPA did not respect a statutory requirement that it develop standards consistent with NAS recommendations (Vandenbosch and Vandenbosch 2007, 21, 111).

Subsequently it was revealed that volcanic tuff at Yucca Mountain is appreciably fractured and that movement of water through an aquifer below the waste repository is primarily through fractures (USDOE 2002). Future water transport from the surface to waste containers is likely to be facilitated by fractures. Moreover, there is evidence that surface water has been transported through the 700 vertical feet of overburden to the exploratory tunnel at Yucca Mountain in less than fifty years (Vandenbosch and Vandenbosch 2007, 21, 12, 106–107; Fabryka-Martin et al. 1998, 264–268; Levy et al. 1997, 901–908; Norris et al. 1990, 455–460).

President Obama rejected use of the Yucca Mountain site in the 2009 federal budget, which eliminated all funding except that needed to answer inquiries from the Nuclear Regulatory Commission "while the Administration devises a new strategy toward nuclear waste disposal" (Executive Office of the President 2009, 65). On March 5, 2009, the secretary of energy told a Senate hearing the Yucca Mountain site is no longer viewed as an option for storing reactor waste (Hebert 2009), leaving the United States without a permanent high-level radioactive waste repository.

PREREQUISITES FOR EFFECTIVE RADIOACTIVE WASTE MANAGEMENT

Many years ago, Hannes Alfvén, Nobel laureate in physics, described the as yet unresolved dilemma of permanent radioactive waste disposal:

> The problem is how to keep radioactive waste in storage until it decays after hundreds of thousands of years. The [geologic] deposit must be absolutely reliable as the quantities of poison are tremendous. It is very difficult to satisfy these requirements for the simple reason that we have had no practical experience with such a long term project. Moreover permanently guarded storage requires a society with unprecedented stability. (Abbotts 1979, 14)

Thus, Alfvén identified two fundamental prerequisites for effective management of high-level radioactive waste: (1) stable geological formations, and (2) stable human institutions over hundreds of thousands of years. However, no known human civilization has ever endured for so long. Moreover, no geologic formation of adequate size for a permanent radioactive waste repository has yet been discovered that has been stable for so long a period.

Because some radioactive species have half-lives longer than one million years, even very low container leakage and radionuclide migration rates must be taken into account (Vandenbosch and Vandenbosch 2007, 10). Moreover, it may require more than one half-life until some nuclear waste loses enough radioactivity so that it is no longer lethal to humans. Waste containers have an expected lifetime of 12,000 to over 100,000 years, depending on the design (USDOE 2002), and it is assumed they will fail in about two million years. A 1983 review of the Swedish radioactive waste disposal program by the National Academy of Sciences found that country's estimate of about 1 million years being necessary for waste isolation "fully justified" (Yates 1989, 33).

The Nuclear Waste Policy Act did not require anything approaching this standard for permanent deep geologic disposal of high-level radioactive waste in the United States. Department of Energy guidelines for selecting locations for permanent deep geologic high-level radioactive waste repositories required containment within waste packages for only 300 years (USDOE 1984, 47767; 10 Code of Federal Regulations 960.2). A site would be disqualified from further consideration only if groundwater travel time from the "disturbed zone" of the underground facility to the "accessible environment" (atmosphere, land surface, surface water, oceans, or lithosphere extending no more than ten kilometers from the underground facility) was expected to be less than 1,000 years along any pathway of radionuclide travel (USDOE 1984, 47760; 10 Code of Federal Regulations 960.4–2–1[d]). Sites with groundwater travel time greater than 1,000 years from the original location to the human environment were considered potentially acceptable, even if the waste would be highly radioactive for 200,000 years or more. Moreover, the term "disturbed zone" was defined in the regulations to exclude shafts drilled into geologic structures from the surface (USDOE 1984), so the standard applied to natural geologic pathways was more stringent than the standard applied to artificial pathways of radionuclide travel created during construction of the facility.

REPOSITORY CLOSURE

Nuclear waste repositories will be closed and sealed when their maximum capacity is reached. Current repository closure plans require backfilling of waste disposal rooms, tunnels, and shafts with rubble from initial excavation and sealing openings at the surface, but do not require complete or perpetual isolation of radioactive waste from the human environment. DOE guidelines contain no requirements for permanent off-site or on-site monitoring after closure. This may seem imprudent considering repositories will contain millions of dollars' worth of spent reactor fuel that might be recovered by legal or illicit means, reprocessed, and used again either in reactors generating electricity, in weapons applications, or possibly in terrorist activities.

Previous experiences sealing mine tunnels and shafts have not been particularly successful, especially where there is any hydraulic pressure from groundwater infiltration into disturbed underground geologic structures. Historical attempts to seal smaller boreholes created during exploration for oil, gas, and water are notorious for their high failure rates, often in less than fifty years (D'Appolonia Consulting Engineers 1979).

In many European countries (e.g., Britain, Finland, the Netherlands, Sweden, and Switzerland), the risk or dose limit for a member of the public exposed to radiation from a future high-level nuclear waste facility is considerably more stringent than that suggested by the International Commission on Radiation Protection or proposed in the United States. European limits are often more stringent than the standard suggested in 1990 by the International Commission on Radiation Protection by a factor of twenty, and more stringent by a factor of ten than the standard proposed by the U.S. Environmental Protection Agency for Yucca Mountain for the first 10,000 years after closure. Moreover, the EPA's proposed standard for greater than 10,000 years is 250 times more permissive than the European limit (Vandenbosch and Vandenbosch 2007, 248).

DISPOSAL VS. MANAGEMENT

In the struggle to determine where a high-level radioactive waste dump should be, a basic question has been lost: Is the disposal policy conceptually sound?

Disposal Is Legal Fiction

The Nuclear Waste Policy Act of 1982 endorsed the fictitious notion that disposal of high-level radioactive waste is possible. Disposal implies that if waste is thrown away it will stay away; if it is put deep in the ground it will stay there. But according to DOE guidelines, disposal means placement of highly radioactive materials in excavated holes 350 to 800 meters (1,000 to 2,620 feet) deep, where it will presumably remain isolated from the atmosphere, nearby land and surface waters, and surrounding rock "situated more than ten kilometers in a horizontal direction from the outer boundary of the original location of the waste" (10 Code of Federal Regulations, Part 960, 49 Federal Register 47757–47760). However, sites with groundwater travel time of more than 1,000 years from the original location of waste to the human environment are considered potentially acceptable (10 Code of Federal Regulations 960.4-2-1[d], 49 Federal Register 47767), even if the waste products have half-lives far longer than that.

In other words, disposal sounds like forever, but, according to DOE regulations, disposal is not really forever. DOE guidelines do not require complete or perpetual isolation of radioactive waste from the human environment. They only require the waste to be buried where we can predict that radionuclides with half-lives of 20,000 to 200,000 years will not show up for at least 300 years after permanent closure of the facility (49 Federal Register 47767), and then only in amounts considered acceptable under regulations of the Nuclear Regulatory Commission and the Environmental Protection Agency (10 Code of Federal Regulations, Part 60; 40 Code of Federal Regulations 191). Backfilling of waste disposal rooms and sealing of shafts is contemplated, but DOE guidelines contain no requirement for postclosure on-site or off-site monitoring of radiation or consideration of site suitability for placement of monitoring equipment during site selection.

Historical attempts to seal small-bore wells for oil, natural gas, and water are notorious for their failures. At the time the Nuclear Waste Policy Act of 1982 was enacted, the future status of borehole plugging and shaft sealing was uncertain, at best:

> There presently is not uniform agreement about the best material(s) to use in sealing penetrations associated with a nuclear waste repository. One important property of the seal is durability. The use of natural earth materials (clays) or melted salt circumvents the durability requirement. However, fractures in the surrounding host rock (which may have resulted during drilling operations) may not be filled by compacted clays. The thermal shock to the host rock resulting from introducing molten earth materials to the penetration may likewise cause microfractures, the healing time

and effects of which remain unknown. Low-temperature cement grouts can easily seal fractures and voids around a penetration but cannot be demonstrated as stable for the required 250,000 years. (D'Appolonia Consulting Engineers 1979, III-22–III-23)

Technology for permanently sealing large-borehole walls against water infiltration or fracture does not exist, and field research sponsored by DOE has revealed some spectacular failures of new technologies (Bush and Lingle 1986).

The apparent hope was that disposal will be permanent, but it is not required to be permanent. Little planning is required for periods after repository closure to deal with the possibility it will not be permanent. Nuclear physicist Arjun Makhijani characterized DOE site selection activities as "a record of astonishing scientific and technical incompetence" (Yates 1989, 33).

Management Is Forever

Disposal is conceptually and practically different from management. Disposal relies on luck in predicting the distant future; management depends upon continuous control. Deep geologic disposal of radioactive waste, as required by current policy, relinquishes control over radioactive materials to geohydrologic processes at repository closure. But existing models of these processes have not been empirically verified over periods of time equivalent to the lethal half-lives of high-level radioactive waste (Shrader-Frechette 1988, 1992, 1993). The models are likely to remain unverified for the foreseeable future. That is, there is no way of knowing how accurate they may be. Management of highly radioactive materials would seem to require continuous supervision and exercise of control, including periodic intervention if necessary to ensure the materials' isolation from the human environment until they are no longer lethal, a period approaching perpetuity.

A MODEST PROPOSAL

Given existing accumulations of radioactive materials, the wisest course may be to put them in secure, dry subsurface storage where they can be monitored. This appears preferable to the risks of putting them out of sight and out of mind, perhaps abandoning them in a deep geologic repository for future generations to discover in their drinking water. Subsurface geologic emplacement is required to mitigate the risk of sabotage in an unstable political world. Dry rock emplacement is required to minimize deterioration of containers and the frequency of handling radioactive waste in managed and monitored storage. Permanent management and continuous monitoring on-site and off-site are necessary to detect and mitigate any breach of isolation. Periodic on-site repackaging of entire containers in slightly larger containers should be contemplated, using the best available materials and handling technology at the time repackaging occurs. Over the next centuries, new materials are likely to be developed that will not break down as quickly when exposed to high neutron flux from decay of radionuclides, thus increasing the longevity of containers after they are permanently buried (Hamilton 1990, 6–7). Estimation of container deterioration rates and periodic examination of containers with stress and corrosion detection technology will determine necessity and timing of repackaging. This will allow use of improved container materials as they become available in future periods, presumably lengthening intervals between repackaging activities while providing greater assurance of continued waste isolation.

In its management of nuclear defense facilities, its previous radioactive waste disposal activities, and its attempts to construct a site selection process on the flawed concept of disposal, DOE has taken many actions that have undermined its scientific judgment and credibility in the eyes of citizens and state and local government officials. Future DOE efforts are unlikely to regain public acceptance (Hamilton 1986). Interviews with DOE scientists responsible for these efforts revealed no awareness on their part of the significance or causes of their failure to devise a credible site selection procedure for permanent waste disposal facilities (Hamilton 1986). Apparently so committed to a particular procedure they fail to see its shortcomings, their response to criticism has been denial, rather than adaptation. They appear to see all criticism as politics, and all politics as unscientific—unless it supports their version of science.

Therefore, a new, independent, radioactive waste management agency must be established separate from DOE to construct and manage radioactive waste facilities. Establishment of such an organization would require development of a new profession of radioactive waste managers, separate from organizations and professions that have primary roles in promotion or use of nuclear technology for weapons or civilian purposes. If the careers of these workers can be linked closely to, and only to, long-term management of radioactive wastes, it seems likely they will develop superior expertise in this crucial area and perform better than people whose careers depend directly upon continued use of nuclear technology. The agency should acquire employees with advanced training in health, physics, or other areas of expertise useful in handling radioactive materials, and establish physical standards for employee health and alertness as stringent as those required for air traffic controllers (Hamilton 1990, 6–7). The new agency should provide secure career paths and incentive bonuses for employees who detect and report safety violations or hazards in waste management facilities.

The DOE attempted to identify sites for construction of deep geologic, high-level radioactive waste disposal facilities that would gain public acceptance. It failed. One cannot build good government programs on bad ideas (Hamilton 1990, 6–7). The fiction of radioactive waste disposal is not an adequate basis on which to make policy capable of protecting humanity from the consequences of its prior errors in judgment (e.g., creating thousands of tons of high-level radioactive waste before figuring out how to deal with it responsibly). The Nuclear Waste Policy Act of 1982, as amended, is therefore fatally flawed and must be reformulated. Prohibiting selection of a second repository site in the eastern United States did not cure the basic infirmities of this policy. There is no moral or ethical justification for protecting residents of the eastern states, where most radioactive waste is created, while allowing residents of any western state to be victimized by a poorly conceived and poorly implemented national policy. The law should be thoroughly rewritten, even if existing waste must be kept in expanded temporary storage until a sound, credible policy is enacted and implemented.

NUCLEAR FUSION

Nuclear fusion is a process by which two or more atomic nuclei join together, releasing large amounts of energy. It is the process that powers the sun and other active stars, the hydrogen bomb, and experimental equipment exploring fusion power for electrical generation. Periodically hope is raised that nuclear fusion will solve all our energy problems and perhaps dispose of all our hazardous and radioactive waste as well. However, this would involve technology capable of creating and sustaining an environment equivalent to being in the center of the sun. This is a technically demanding task, much more difficult to accomplish than to imagine. To date, efforts to do so have been sustained only for the tiniest fraction of a second and used thousands of time more energy than was produced. Even if the technical challenges are someday overcome, the most optimistic predictions are that half the electricity produced by nuclear fusion will be consumed to sustain the fusion reaction (Nersesian 2010, 288). Consequently, even if it becomes technically feasible to generate electricity with nuclear fusion, its use on a commercial scale is unlikely to be economically feasible. In the absence of substantial direct subsidies, the capital costs of constructing such a large and technically complex facility would likely be beyond the capability of anyone other than government. Construction of a commercial nuclear fusion power plant is unlikely to commence before 2050 (Princeton Plasma Physics Laboratory 2005). In the United States it usually takes ten to fourteen years to bring a new fission plant online (Hamilton and Wengert 1980, 69), and it seems unlikely a fusion plant would take less time to build.

One nuclear fusion plant would not make a significant contribution to U.S. electricity demand in 2060. Under the most optimistic and favorable circumstances, it seems extremely unlikely nuclear fusion could provide a substantial contribution to meeting U.S. electricity demand before the year 2100. The American electric utility industry is not known for early adoption of new technologies, displaying instead a strong preference for tried-and-true generation and transmission technology. With few exceptions, electric utilities resisted interconnecting their networks with others (some still do), despite substantial financial and reliability benefits of doing so, and were notoriously slow to adopt simple, inexpensive load-shedding equipment to prevent blackouts in the 1960s and 1970s. Most electric utilities have been slow to adopt energy conservation, fluidized-bed coal combustion, solar photovoltaic, and wind technologies until strongly encouraged to do so by regulatory authorities. It took fifty years for the electric utility industry to build the nuclear fission power plants that now provide about 20 percent of total generating capacity in the United States. It seems unlikely it would take less time for the electric utility industry to construct enough nuclear fusion plants to make a significant contribution to meeting U.S. electrical demand.

COSTS OF URANIUM UTILIZATION

Dollar Costs of Utilizing Nuclear Power

The market cost to consumers for nuclear energy consumed in calendar year 2009 was estimated at a bit over $4.5 billion, and almost $4.0 billion in 2008 (USEIA 2011a, Table 3.5). Historically, the capital costs of constructing nuclear electric generating plants have been comparatively high, and operating costs, especially for fuel, have been relatively low when compared to other generating technologies. High capital costs are in part a reflection of the technological sophistication of nuclear generating plants and in part based on concerns for reactor safety: as concerns for safety have increased, capital and operating costs have increased. Still, most efforts to estimate the dollar costs of utilizing nuclear power have neglected to include the significant costs of repairing environmental damage done by the mining and milling of uranium, which have either been externalized or paid by the U.S. government, and the very long-term but as yet unknown costs of permanent high-level radioactive waste management, which under current policy will be paid by the U.S. government. Any discussion of the costs of utilizing nuclear electric power that failed to take such costs into account would be intellectually dishonest. Token contributions by industry for permanent high-level radioactive waste are limited by the Nuclear Waste Policy Act and will not be sufficient to pay for these additional unknown costs, which must be acknowledged as likely to be exceedingly large.

Capital Construction Costs

Electric utilities applying for U.S. government loan guarantees supporting construction of new nuclear generating units in October 2008 estimated their costs would average about $9 billion per 1,000 MWe generating unit, including financing costs and expected increases in construction costs. This would represent an average cost of more than $6,700 per kilowatt. Other independent analysts estimated construction costs as high as $10,000 per kilowatt, excluding fuel, financing, and cost escalations during construction, which historically have increased the total price of nuclear units by as much as 50 percent (UCS 2009b, 3). These estimates for new generating technology construction are somewhat higher than those provided by the U.S. Department of Energy of $3,820/kW (in 2008 dollars), but even the DOE estimate for nuclear plants is higher than for any other energy technology except fuel cells, central station photovoltaics, solar thermal, and offshore wind generation (USEIA 2010b, Table 8.2). Consequently, new nuclear generating units would be the most expensive nuclear units ever built. Without government subsidies and loan guarantees, it seems unlikely such costly investments would ever be made by profit-conscious electric utility managers.

Costs of Uranium Fuel

Compared to the capital costs of constructing new nuclear electric generating units, fuel costs are relatively low. U.S. consumption of uranium was about 54.8 million pounds of U_3O_8 equivalent in 2011. Calculating the weighted-average price for the total purchased at $55.64 per pound, the fuel cost of uranium utilization in the United States was about $3.05 billion in 2011 (USEIA 2012c, Table S1a, S1b).

Decommissioning Costs

The costs of decommissioning nuclear power plants are probably underestimated for most facilities that have not yet been decommissioned. Experience with a small number of sites that have been decommissioned indicates that such costs may be higher than the capital cost to build the same plants and may exceed funds set aside for decommissioning. For example, decommissioning costs for the 900 MWe Maine Yankee nuclear generating unit in Maine were about $377.6 million, or 163 percent of its $231 million construction cost, and decommissioning costs for the 50 MWe Big Rock Point nuclear unit in Michigan were about $290 million, or a little over ten times its $27.7 million construction cost. Moreover, decommissioning costs for such plants have not yet been completely paid, as spent fuel and high-level radioactive waste continues to be stored at these locations, increasing costs for monitoring and security while awaiting transfer of the waste to a permanent high-level radioactive waste repository that has not yet been built.

Experience has shown that the useful lifetime of many nuclear generating plants was often overestimated. Construction decisions for most plants were based on cost-benefit analysis anticipating a useful design life of thirty to forty years, but the average years of operation for twenty-two commercial reactors decommissioned as of January 2008 was only about 16.2 years (calculated from USNRC 2010). This means that nuclear generating units decommissioned to date were on average about twice as expensive over their useful lifetimes as was expected at the time investment decisions were made.

A frequent cause of decommissioning nuclear reactors, especially pressurized water reactors, before the end of their design lifetime has been embrittlement of welded steel in steam generator tubes and the vessel surrounding the reactor core. Embrittlement is the result of years of bombardment by neutrons, the subatomic particles that sustain a nuclear reaction, which may produce microscopic hairline cracks. It can often be cured by annealing (a process that tempers and strengthens the metal), but if embrittlement is widespread in older reactors, annealing is often uneconomic as compared to decommissioning the reactor. This was the case with several nuclear units decommissioned to date, including Maine Yankee, Big Rock Point, and Yankee Rowe in Massachusetts (Aker 2005, 2–1; Odette and Lucas 2001; Mager 1993; Jones 1989).

Decommissioning costs occur at a time when there is no cash flow from a plant to finance cost overruns. Required removal of all radioactive materials from nuclear generating plant sites will place a large volumetric burden on existing low-level radioactive waste dumps and high-level radioactive waste repositories that do not yet exist. Without permanent disposal facilities in the United States for high-level nuclear waste, total dollar costs to society for disposal (or management) are currently unknown, but expected to be high. Any costs not paid by consumers via utility payments to decommissioning funds may be expected to be paid by future taxpayers.

Subsidies

Nuclear electric generation technology has been the beneficiary of large government subsidies since its inception. Realizing that no electric utility was likely to build a nuclear generator for fear of opening itself up to enormous financial liability from a nuclear accident, Congress enacted the Price-Anderson Act of 1957 (Nuclear Industries Indemnity Act, 42 U.S.C. §2210 et seq.), limiting the direct financial liability of owners of reactors for a nuclear accident to $300 million, adjusted for inflation. A cost-sharing arrangement was provided whereby other nuclear generators would pay any costs above $300 million per accident through an insurance pool. Owners of the 104 operating reactors covered by the act must pay up to $95.8 million per reactor, adjusted for inflation, to cover costs in retrospective annual premiums capped at $10 million per year, establishing a potential total insurance pool of about $10.5 billion ($300 million plus $95.8 million from operating reactors). Any claims above $10.5 billion would be covered by the federal government. The average annual premium in 2008 for a single-unit reactor was $400,000, with premiums for additional reactors at a single site discounted somewhat (USNRC 2011a).

According to the public interest group Public Citizen, "the $10.5 billion provided by private insurance and nuclear reactor operators represents less than 2 percent of the $560 billion in potential costs of a major nuclear accident" in 2000 dollars (Public Citizen 2004, 2). Others have estimated the potential risk exposure to taxpayers at $360 billion to $1.6 trillion (Schlissel, Mullett, and Alvarez 2009). More than $200 million has been paid in claims and costs of litigation since the Price-Anderson Act came into effect, all of it funded by the insurance pools. Of this amount, some $71 million went toward litigation costs following the 1979 accident at Three Mile Island, Pennsylvania. Another $65 million was paid by the U.S. Department of Energy to cover claims for its own nuclear operations (Folkers 2010; UCS 2009a).

In the 1980s, due to overly optimistic projections of electricity demand and estimates of costs, electric utilities abandoned about 100 nuclear generator projects—about half of all those ordered— during construction. As a result, taxpayers and ratepayers paid an estimated $40 billion in costs for abandoned nuclear units; ratepayers paid over $200 billion (adjusted for inflation) to electric utilities in cost overruns for nuclear units that were completed, and an additional $40 billion in "stranded costs" of unfinished generators as a result of restructuring designed to introduce competition into the industry. This is not an impressive record of financial success. In fact, "the nuclear industry has an extremely poor record on cost overruns," with actual costs for seventy-five of the first generation of nuclear units exceeding initial cost estimates by more than 200 percent (Schlissel, Mullett, and

Alvarez 2009). Consequently, the U.S. Government Accountability Office estimates the average risk of default for DOE loan guarantees is about 50 percent (USGAO 2008). Government subsidies and limitations on liability insurance required for nuclear generating stations are evidence of the high risk of reactor safety and potentially high financial costs of a nuclear reactor accident.

Since enactment of the Atomic Energy Act of 1954, many of the costs of research, development, and uranium enrichment have been borne by the national government, not utilities or consumers. It has been estimated that these costs were worth $100 billion over the past half-century and that federal subsidies were worth up to $13 billion per plant in 2008 (Lovins and Sheikh 2008; Walsh 2008). In addition to insurance guarantees, federal subsidies and tax expenditures supporting nuclear electricity generation were estimated at almost $2.5 billion for FY2010 (USEIA 2011b, xi). No other energy fuel or technology has received comparable subsidies in the United States.

Historically, planning lead times for development and construction of nuclear generating plants have been much longer than for other energy technologies. The lack of construction starts on new nuclear generating units since the late 1970s provides little recent experience, but a 1980 study of new power-generating stations found planning lead times reported by electric utilities then typically ran ten to fourteen years for nuclear units, as compared to six to eleven years for coal-fired plants, three to six years for natural gas combustion turbines, and three to seven years for combined cycle units (Hamilton and Wengert 1980, 69). Long lead times to construct nuclear plants increase the financial costs of borrowing capital in the form of interest paid before revenues are generated, as compared to shorter lead times.

Evidence that the electric utility industry considers nuclear generating units too expensive to build without government subsidy is found in the fact that U.S. utilities have ordered no new nuclear units since 1978 and canceled all units they had ordered after 1973 (UCS 2009b, 1). In 2008 the Tennessee Valley Authority resumed work on a generating unit at Watts Bar 2, where construction had been stopped in 1988. The unit is now expected to be completed in 2013. The NRC reports that since 2007, seventeen companies have submitted applications to build thirty new units at twenty sites (USNRC 2011b). Two new pressurized water reactors totaling approximately 2,300 MWe generating capacity received combined construction and operating permits from the U.S. Nuclear Regulatory Commission in February 2012, for location at the existing Plant Vogtle south of Augusta, near Waynesboro, Georgia, on the border with South Carolina (Vartabedian and Duncan 2012). The Southern Company secured $8.3 billion in conditional loan guarantees from the U.S. Department of Energy toward the expected $14 billion price tag for the project (Piore 2011). Considering that Plant Vogtle's two existing nuclear reactors of 2,430 MWe generating capacity ran over budget by $8 billion and took sixteen years to build (Swartz 2012), it seems unlikely the new units will be completed on budget and on schedule to start producing electricity in 2016 and 2017. Serious questions have been raised about the durability of the containment structure steel liner of the new AP1000 Westinghouse design, which has not yet been built anywhere (Piore 2011; Gunderson 2010).

National Security Costs of Utilizing Nuclear Energy

The principal costs to national security from using nuclear electric power are nuclear proliferation, the risk of terrorist action, and overdependence on foreign sources of nuclear fuel.

Proliferation

Nonproliferation policies of the United States have long been based on control of access to fissile materials more than on control of knowledge about nuclear technologies. Education in nuclear physics and engineering has been relatively easy to obtain from American and European universities for capable students from foreign countries. But acquisition of nuclear materials was made more difficult as a matter of national policy in support of the Nuclear Nonproliferation Treaty of 1969.

It has long been feared that clandestine diversion of plutonium from reprocessing facilities could allow rogue states and terrorist groups access to nuclear materials and technologies. During the 1970s many people believed that U.S. government influence on the world nuclear power industry could curtail reprocessing and diminish the risk of proliferation of nuclear weapons. Yet President Ford expressed concern about nuclear proliferation from reprocessing facilities in October 1976 (Andrews 2008, 3). Fears about the consequences of creating an uncontrollable market for plutonium from reprocessed nuclear reactor fuel led the Nuclear Energy Policy Study Group formed by the Ford Foundation to recommend that the United States ban commercial reprocessing and defer indefinitely development of the liquid-metal fast breeder reactor, which would actually create more fuel than it would use: "The growth and diffusion of nuclear power thus inevitably enhance the potential for the proliferation of nuclear weapons. If widespread proliferation actually occurs, it will prove an extremely serious danger to U.S. security and to world peace and stability in general." The study group further argued that the "risks associated with reprocessing and recycle of plutonium weigh strongly against their introduction. The use of plutonium in the commercial fuel cycle would expose to diversion and theft material directly usable for weapons" (Nuclear Energy Policy Study Group 1977, 22, 30).

This was the principal reason President Jimmy Carter decided in 1977 to halt commercial reprocessing and restructure the breeder reactor program in the United States:

> The U.S. is deeply concerned about the consequences for all nations of a further spread of nuclear weapons or explosive capabilities. We believe that these risks would be vastly increased by the further spread of sensitive technologies which entail direct access to plutonium, highly enriched uranium, or other weapons usable material. (Sailor 1999, 111; Andrews 2008, 4)

President Carter waited to ban commercial reprocessing until he received assurances that the breeder reactor would be too expensive to compete with other nuclear technologies in the marketplace, that reprocessing would not resolve nuclear waste disposal problems, that a policy against reprocessing would not harm the nuclear power industry, and that reprocessing would not improve the economics of nuclear electric power generation (Sailor 1999, 108, 112).

However, there are additional difficulties concerning threats to national security from nuclear proliferation that were not addressed by banning commercial reprocessing of spent fuel. Many countries, including those who signed the Nuclear Nonproliferation Treaty of 1969 and thereby agreed not to acquire nuclear weapons, can come very close to manufacturing nuclear bombs without precisely violating the agreement. They can obtain fissile material, or the means to produce that material, from supplying countries that have promised not "in any way to assist" countries without weapons to obtain them (Wohlstetter et al. 1979, 1).

The critical time required to make a nuclear explosive from spent reactor fuel has been diminished from the two or three years originally anticipated, without any necessary violation of agreed rules, without any illicit diversion of nuclear materials, and therefore without any prospect of being curbed by nonproliferation treaty safeguards (Wohlstetter et al. 1979, 18, 25). Governments may be able to appropriate stocks of highly enriched uranium or plutonium acquired for other purposes in order to develop weapons. Those without the national means to produce such stocks may have acquired them legitimately for their research facilities or as fresh fuel for their commercial reactors. Governments may also accumulate plutonium for the initial loadings of future commercial breeder reactors. They do not have to steal these stocks or even divert them in order to be very close to being able to make nuclear explosives (Wohlstetter et al. 1979, 23).

With creation of new nuclear powers in Belarus, Kazakhstan, Russia, and Ukraine since the breakup of the former Soviet Union, concerns about proliferation of nuclear materials appear to have increased somewhat (Martinez 2002, 261; Sailor 1999, 112).

Vulnerability to Terrorist Action

Nuclear reactors, fuel enrichment and fabrication facilities, and temporary spent fuel storage facilities remain vulnerable to terrorist attack in the United States. A terrorists' goal could be either to impose massive radiation contamination on nearby populations or to obtain fissile materials for use in a subsequent attack on a different location. The most likely terrorist targets are considered to be nuclear reactors and pools storing spent fuel. Since 9/11, the International Atomic Energy Agency (IAEA), the NRC, and the United Kingdom Parliamentary Office for Science and Technology have all stated that no existing reactors were designed or built to withstand the impact of a large commercial aircraft loaded with jet fuel (Ruff 2006; Barnaby 2005; Farneth 2005).

To do unacceptable damage, it would not be necessary to breach a reactor core. Some structural damage plus a large hot fire sufficient to damage cooling water conduits or electrical wiring supplying reactor safety systems would be enough to cause loss of coolant to the reactor core, resulting in a meltdown. Although this would not produce a nuclear explosion, the resulting steam explosion might be sufficient to disperse highly radioactive particles over a wide geographic area, contaminating many square miles. Reactors located near large cities like New York or Chicago would be particularly attractive targets (Ruff 2006; Barnaby 2005; Farneth 2005), as their destruction would expose massive human populations to radioactivity, destroy property, and cause widespread fear. One study of a scenario in which a hijacked airliner crashes into a nuclear power plant outside Chicago estimated that more than 7.5 million people would be exposed to more than the maximum allowed annual population radiation dose, of whom more than 4.6 million would receive more than the maximum occupational radiation dose; more than 200,000 would develop radiation sickness and 20,000 might receive a lethal dose (Helfand et al. 2006; Ruff 2006). A meltdown at a nuclear power plant near New York City was estimated to result in 44,000 radiation deaths within one year and 518,000 excess cancer deaths over time. Huge areas would be uninhabitable for many years, and economic losses could run over US$2 trillion (Ruff 2006; Lyman 2004).

Spent fuel pools are attractive terrorist targets because buildings housing them are typically constructed like corrugated metal warehouses, which lack the hardening and multiple layers of containment a reactor has, and they often contain ten to twenty times the amount of radioactivity as a reactor core (Ruff 2006, 4). Consequently, an attack on a reprocessing plant or fuel storage pool could result in a greater and longer-duration radioactivity release than an attack on a nuclear reactor (Ruff 2006; Barnaby 2005). Terrorists seeking to impose such costs on a population might achieve their goal using any one of the following means:

- Exploding a truck or light aircraft carrying high explosives near a critical part of a nuclear facility
- Hijacking a commercial airliner and crashing it into a reactor building or spent fuel pond
- Attacking a facility with artillery, missiles, or small arms and detonating conventional high explosives in critical locations
- Using infiltration or insider sabotage by employees to damage critical systems

Figure 3.3 **The Costs of Utilizing Nuclear Technologies**

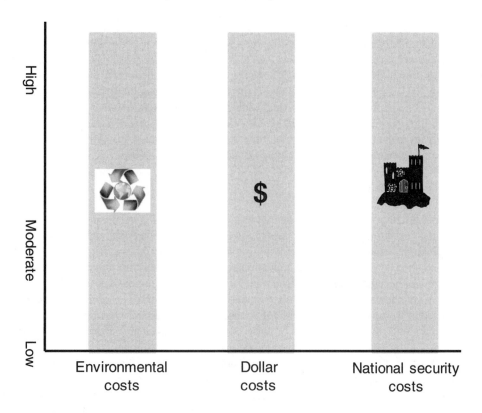

- Disrupting electrical power or cooling water supply to a reactor
- Draining cooling water from spent fuel ponds (Ruff 2006)

Any of these actions could lead to a massive release of radioactivity. Such operations would require sophisticated organization, advance planning, considerable skill, and coordination. None would require use of weapons, technical skills, or tactics that have not been used previously by terrorists in attacks such as the Pan Am jumbo jet bombing over Lockerbie, Scotland, in 1988; the Aum Shinrikyo nerve gas attacks on Tokyo subways in 1997; the simultaneous New York World Trade Center and Pentagon attacks in 2001; and the multiple bombings of commuter trains in Madrid in March 2004 (Ruff 2006).

Nuclear facilities are also vulnerable to attempts by terrorists to acquire fissile materials that may be used to construct a "dirty" bomb (Bunn and Wier 2006) that could be exploded at a target of choice. Fuel enrichment and fabrication facilities, as well as temporary spent fuel storage facilities containing quantities of radioactive materials with long half-lives, might be especially attractive to terrorists wishing to construct such explosives. The IAEA has documented more than 650 instances of intercepted smuggling of radioactive materials over the past decade, including eighteen cases of seizure of stolen plutonium or highly enriched uranium (Bunn and Wier 2006). A small group of people—or even a single person—could release enough radioactivity to make much of the United States uninhabitable (Lovins and Lovins 1982, 2).

Dependence on Foreign Fuel Supplies

Of the 49.8 million pounds of uranium reactor fuel consumed in the United States in 2009, 42.8 million pounds (85.9 percent) was imported from foreign sources (USEIA 2010a, Table S1a), a little over 20 percent of that from Russia (NERC 2009, 368). Other amounts came from Australia, Canada, Namibia, Kazakhstan, and Uzbekistan. Uranium fuel imports from Russia increased beginning in 2011, as the United States began to purchase weapons-grade uranium reprocessed into reactor fuel under the Megatons for Megawatts Agreement, and imports may reach 30 percent of fuel used in American reactors by 2013. This dependence on imported supplies of enriched uranium may leave the United States vulnerable to supply disruptions, especially if world demand for nuclear fuel increases as expected by 2018 (NERC 2009, 368–369).

SUMMARY OF COSTS

The costs of utilizing nuclear technologies are summarized in Figure 3.3 (see page 69). The environmental costs of nuclear electric generation to American society can only be described as "high" because the devastation of uranium mining and milling continues to be paid in the form of destroyed and unreclaimed mined lands, contaminated water supplies, Superfund cleanups, and the historic impact of nuclear technology on human lives. Some environmental costs of using nuclear power are not yet known, because the United States has not yet invented a viable, permanent high-level radioactive waste management technology and therefore certainly has not yet built such a facility to contain the thousands of tons of highly radioactive wastes and spent fuel that continue to accumulate at the nation's 104 operating nuclear electric generating units.

The dollar costs of nuclear electric generation are not as yet entirely known, due to the fact that some costs of cleanup activities have not yet been paid, others have been paid by the government, and still other costs for permanent high-level radioactive waste management will not be paid in the foreseeable future and, in the absence of a viable technology, cannot be estimated with assurance. Certainly the dollar costs will be "high" when they are paid in the distant future.

The national security costs of nuclear electric generation are certainly "high" due to the recent proliferation of nuclear technology and materials into the hands of nation-states who are not our friends, and the availability of such technology and materials to terrorist organizations via international black markets.

REFERENCES

Abbotts, John 1979. "Radioactive Waste: A Technical Solution?" *Bulletin of the Atomic Scientists* 35 (October): 12–18.
Aker, R. 2005. *Maine Yankee Decommissioning Experience Report: Detailed Experiences, 1997–2004.* Naperville, IL: New Horizon Scientific.
Andrews, Anthony. 2008. *Nuclear Fuel Reprocessing: U.S. Policy Development.* Washington, DC: Congressional Research Service.
Barnaby, Frank. 2005. *Security and Nuclear Power. Secure Energy: Options for a Safer World.* Oxford: Oxford Research Group. www.oxfordresearchgroup.org.uk/sites/default/files/factsheets1-2.pdf.
Bishop, William P., and Frank J. Miraglia. 1976. *Environmental Survey of the Reprocessing and Waste Management Portions of the LWR Fuel Cycle.* Washington, DC: U.S. Nuclear Regulatory Commission.
Bush, Daniel D., and Richard Lingle. 1986. *A Full-scale Borehole Sealing Test in Anhydrite under Simulated Downhole Conditions*, 2 vols. Columbus, OH: Battelle Memorial Institute, Office of Nuclear Waste Isolation.

Bunn, M., and A. Wier. 2006. "Terrorist Nuclear Weapon Construction: How Difficult?" *Annals of the American Academy of Political and Social Science* 607 (September): 133–149.

CNN Wire Staff. 2011. "3 Nuclear Reactors Melted Down After Quake, Japan Confirms." CNN Edition: International, June 7. http://edition.cnn.com/2011/WORLD/asiapcf/06/06/japan.nuclear.meltdown/index. html?iref=NS1.

Congressional Quarterly. 1982. "Comprehensive Nuclear Waste Plan Enacted." *Congressional Quarterly Almanac*, 304–310. Washington, DC: Congressional Quarterly.

———. 1987. "Nevada Chosen to Receive Nuclear Waste." *Congressional Quarterly Almanac*, 307–311. Washington, DC: Congressional Quarterly.

Cowell, Alan. 2011. "Germans' Deep Suspicions of Nuclear Power Reach a Political Tipping Point." *New York Times*, June 1. www.nytimes.com/2011/06/02/world/europe/02germany.html.

Dahlkamp, Franz J. 1993. *Uranium Ore Deposits*. Berlin: Springer-Verlag.

D'Appolonia Consulting Engineers. 1979. *The Status of Borehole Plugging and Shaft Sealing for Geologic Isolation of Radioactive Waste*. Columbus, OH: Battelle Memorial Institute, Office of Nuclear Waste Isolation.

Dempsey, Judy, and Jack Ewing. 2011. "Germany, in Reversal, Will Close Nuclear Plants by 2022." *New York Times*, May 30. www.nytimes.com/2011/05/31/world/europe/31germany.html.

Dingmann, Tracy. 2009. "New Attention to Church Rock Uranium Spill Comes 30 Years Later." *New Mexico Independent*, July 16. http://newmexicoindependent.com/31989/31989.

DiSavino, Scott. 2011. "Analysis: A Month On, Japan Nuclear Crisis Still Scarring." Reuters, April 8.

Dreesen, David R. 1978. *Uranium Mill Tailings: Environmental Implications*. Los Alamos, NM: Los Alamos Scientific Laboratory.

Energy Policy Act. 2005. 42 U.S.C. §13201 et seq.

Executive Office of the President. 1977. Nuclear Power Policy. Presidential Documents. Washington, DC: Office of the Federal Register. National Archives and Records Service, 1977–. Jimmy Carter, 506–507.

———. 2009. *A New Era of Responsibility: The 2010 Budget*. Washington, DC: U.S. Government Printing Office. www.whitehouse.gov/omb/assets/fy2010_new_era/A_New_Era_of_Responsibility2.pdf.

Fabryka-Martin, J.T., A.V. Wolfsberg, J.L. Roach, S.T. Winters, and L.E. Wolfsberg. 1998. "Using Chloride to Trace Water Movement in the Unsaturated Zone at Yucca Mountain." In *High Level Radioactive Waste Management: Proceedings of the Eighth International Conference*, 264–268. La Grange Park, IL: American Nuclear Society.

Farneth, M. 2005. *Nuclear Power and the Terrorist Threat*. Washington, DC: Physicians for Social Responsibility. www.psr.org/nuclear-weapons/nuclear-terrorism-threat-to.pdf.

Fentiman, Audeen W., and James H. Saling. 2002. *Radioactive Waste Management*, 2nd ed. New York: Taylor & Francis.

Folkers, Cindy. 2010. *Price-Anderson Act: Unnecessary & Irresponsible*. Washington, DC: Nuclear Information and Resource Service. www.nirs.org/factsheets/priceandersonactfactsheet1001.htm.

Gofman, John. 1981. *Radiation and Human Health*. San Francisco: Sierra Club Books.

Gottlieb, L.S., and L.A. Husen. 1982. "Lung Cancer Among Navajo Uranium Miners." *Chest* 81 (4): 449–452. www.chestjournal.org/cgi/content/abstract/81/4/449.

Gunderson, Arnold. 2010. *Nuclear Containment Failures: Ramifications for the AP1000 Containment Design*. Burlington, VT: Fairwinds Associates.

Hamilton, Michael S. 1986. *Selecting Potentially Acceptable Sites for a High-Level Radioactive Waste Repository in Maine: Comments on the Draft Area Recommendation Report of the U.S. Department of Energy*. Augusta: Maine Governor's High-Level Nuclear Waste Task Force.

———. 1990. "Radioactive Waste Disposal: Flawed Concept, Unworkable Policy." *Natural Resources and Environmental Administration* 14 (June): 6–7.

Hamilton, Michael S., and Norman I. Wengert. 1980. *Environmental, Legal and Political Constraints on Power Plant Siting in the Southwestern United States*. Fort Collins: Colorado State University Experiment Station.

Hebert, H. Josef. 2009. "Official: Nuclear Waste Won't Go to Nevada Site." *Huffington Post*, March 5. www. huffingtonpost.com/huff-wires/20090305/yucca-mountain/.

Helfand, Ira, Andrew Kantor, Michael McCally, Kimberly Roberts, and Jaya Tiwari. 2006. *The United States and Nuclear Terrorism: Still Dangerously Unprepared*. Washington, DC: Physicians for Social Responsibility.

Humble Oil and Refining Co. 1971. *Applicants Environmental Report, Highland Uranium Mill, Converse County, Wyoming*. Houston, TX: Humble Oil and Refining Co.

International Atomic Energy Agency (IAEA). 2006. *Environmental Consequences of the Chernobyl Accident and Their Remediation: Twenty Years of Experience*. Report of the Chernobyl Forum Expert Group "Environment." Vienna, Austria: International Atomic Energy Agency. www-pub.iaea.org/MTCD/publications/PDF/Pub1239_web.pdf.

———. 2011a. Frequently Asked Chernobyl Questions. www.iaea.org/newscenter/features/chernobyl-15/cherno-faq.shtml.

———. 2011b. Fukushima Nuclear Accident Update Log: Updates of 15 March 2011. www.iaea.org/newscenter/news/2011/fukushima150311.html.

Jacobs, D.G., and H.W. Dickson. 1979. *A Description of Radiological Problems at Inactive Uranium Mill Sites and Formerly Utilized MED/AEC Sites*. Oak Ridge, TN: Oak Ridge National Laboratory.

Jones, H.F. 1989. "Effectiveness of Flux Reduction Measures Instituted at the Maine Yankee Atomic Power Station." In *Radiation Embrittlement of Nuclear Reactor Vessel Steels: An International Review*, vol. 3, ed. L. E. Steele, 145–160. Philadelphia: American Society for Testing and Materials.

Kemeny, John G. 1979. *Report of the President's Commission on the Accident at Three Mile Island. The Need for Change: The Legacy of TMI*. October. Washington, DC: U.S. Government Printing Office. www.threemileisland.org/downloads/188.pdf.

Levy, S.S., J.T. Fabryka-Martin, P.R. Dixon, B. Liu, H.J. Turin, and A.V. Wolfsberg. 1997. "Chlorine-36 Investigations of Groundwater Infiltration in the Exploratory Studies Facility at Yucca Mountain, Nevada." In *Scientific Basis for Nuclear Waste Management XX, Proceedings*, ed. W.J. Gray and I.R. Triay, 901–908. Pittsburgh: Materials Research Society.

Lovins, Amory B., and L. Hunter Lovins. 1982. *Brittle Power: Energy Strategy for National Security*. Andover, MA: Brick House.

Lovins, Amory, and Imran Sheikh. 2008. *The Nuclear Illusion*. Snowmass, CO: Rocky Mountain Institute. www.rmi.org/rmi/Library/E08-01_NuclearIllusion.

Lyman, E. 2004. *Chernobyl on the Hudson? The Health and Economic Impacts of a Terrorist Attack on the Indian Point Nuclear Plant*. Washington, DC: Union of Concerned Scientists.

MacKenzie, Debora. 2011a. "Caesium Fallout from Fukushima Rivals Chernobyl." *New Scientist*, March 29. www.webcitation.org/5xZGE47q4.

———. 2011b. "Fukushima Radioactive Fallout Nears Chernobyl Levels." *New Scientist*, March 24. www.newscientist.com/article/dn20285-fukushima-radioactive-fallout-nears-chernobyl-levels.html.

Mager, T.R. 1993. "Utilization of Reactor Pressure Vessel Surveillance Data in Support of Aging Management." In *Radiation Embrittlement of Nuclear Reactor Vessel Steels: An International Review*, vol. 4, ed. L.E. Steele, 87–98. Philadelphia: American Society for Testing and Materials.

Makinen, Julie, and Ralph Vartabedian. 2011. "Containing a Calamity Creates Another Nuclear Nightmare." *Sydney Morning Herald*, April 9. www.smh.com.au/environment/containing-a-calamity-creates-another-nuclear-nightmare-20110408-1d7qn.html.

Martinez, J. Michael. 2002. "The Carter Administration and the Evolution of American Nuclear Nonproliferation Policy, 1977–1981." *Journal of Policy History* 14 (3): 261–292.

Mullin, John R., and Zenia Kotval. 1997. "The Closing of the Yankee Rowe Nuclear Power Plant: The Impact on a New England Community." *Journal of the American Planning Association* 63: 454–468. http://works.bepress.com/john_mullin/18.

National Research Council (NRC). 1995. *Technical Bases for Yucca Mountain Standards*. Washington, DC: National Academy Press.

Navajo Nation. 2005. "Navajo Nation President Joe Shirley, Jr. Signs Diné Natural Resources Protection Act of 2005." Press release, April 30. Window Rock, AZ: Navajo Nation.

Nersesian, Roy L. 2010. *Energy for the 21st Century*, 2nd ed. Armonk, NY: M.E. Sharpe.

Norris, A.E., H.W. Bentley, S. Cheng, P.W. Kubik, P. Sharma, and H.E. Gove. 1990. "36Cl Studies of Water Movements Deep within Unsaturated Tuffs." *Nuclear Instruments and Methods in Physics Research Section B: Beam Interactions with Materials and Atoms* 52 (2 December): 455–460.

North American Electric Reliability Corporation (NERC). 2009. *2009 Long-Term Reliability Assessment*. Princeton, NJ: North American Electric Reliability Corporation.

Nuclear Energy Institute, Inc. v. EPA, 373 F.3d 1251 (D.C. Cir. 2004). www.cadc.uscourts.gov/internet/opinions.nsf/8AC175A974D58E3A85256F82006D458C/$file/01-1258a.pdf.

Nuclear Energy Policy Study Group. 1977. *Nuclear Power Issues and Choices*. Cambridge, MA: Ballinger.

Nuclear Industries Indemnity Act. 1957. 42 U.S.C. §2210 et seq.

Nuclear Waste Policy Act. 1982. 96 Statutes At Large 2201, 42 U.S.C. 10101 et seq.

Nuclear Waste Policy Amendments. 1987. 101 Statutes at Large 1330–227, 42 U.S.C. 10101 et seq.

Odette, G.R., and G.E. Lucas. 2001. "Embrittlement of Nuclear Reactor Pressure Vessels." *Journal of Metals* 53 (7): 18–22. www.tms.org/pubs/journals/JOM/0107/Odette-0107.html.

Olesky, Karen R. 2008. *Nuclear Power's Emission Reduction Potential in Utah*. Master's project, May. Durham, NC: Duke University Press. http://dukespace.lib.duke.edu/dspace/bitstream/10161/500/1/MP_kr04_a_200805.pdf.

Organization for Economic Co-operation and Development and International Atomic Energy Agency (OECD and IAEA). 2008. Uranium 2007: Resources, Production and Demand. Paris: OECD.

———. 2009. "Uranium Resources Sufficient to Meet Projected Nuclear Energy Requirements Long into the Future." Press release, June 3. Paris: OECD.

Pasternak, Judy. 2006. "Navajos' Desert Cleanup No More Than a Mirage." *Los Angeles Times*, November 21. www.latimes.com/news/la-na-navajo21nov21,0,2271711.story.

Physicians for Social Responsibility. 2009. *Dirty, Dangerous and Expensive: The Truth About Nuclear Power*. Washington, DC: Physicians for Social Responsibility. www.psr.org/resources/nuclear-power-factsheet.html?print=t.

Piore, Adam. 2011. "Nuclear Energy: Planning for the Black Swan." *Scientific American*. 33 (June): 48–53.

Princeton Plasma Physics Laboratory. 2005. "Beyond ITER [International Thermonuclear Experimental Reactor]." The ITER Project. Princeton, NJ: Princeton Plasma Physics Laboratory. http://web.archive.org/web/20061107220145/www.iter.org/Future-beyond.htm.

Public Citizen. 2004. "Price-Anderson Act: The Billion Dollar Bailout for Nuclear Power Mishaps." September. www.citizen.org/documents/Price%20Anderson%20Factsheet.pdf.

Ruff, Tilman. 2006. *Nuclear Terrorism*. energyscience.org.au, Fact Sheet 10, November. University of Melbourne, Australian Centre for Science, Innovation and Society. www.energyscience.org.au/FS10%20Nuclear%20Terrorism.pdf.

Sailor, William C. 1999. "The Case Against Reprocessing." *Forum for Applied Research and Public Policy* 14 (Summer): 108–112.

Schlissel, D., M. Mullett, and R. Alvarez. 2009. *Nuclear Loan Guarantees: Another Taxpayer Bailout Ahead?* Cambridge, MA: Union of Concerned Scientists.

Sears, M.B., R.E. Blanco, R.C. Dahlman, G.S. Hill, A.D. Ryon, and J.P. Witherspoon. 1975. *Correlation of Radioactive Waste Treatment Costs and the Environmental Impact of Waste Effluents in the Nuclear Fuel Cycle for Use in Establishing 'as Low as Practicable' Guides: Milling of Uranium Ores*, 2 vols. Oak Ridge, TN: Oak Ridge National Laboratory.

Shears, Richard. 2011. "Fires STILL Raging at Stricken Fukushima Nuclear Reactor One Month After It Was Destroyed by Tsunami." *Daily Mail Online*, April 12. www.dailymail.co.uk/news/article-1375981/Japan-nuclear-crisis-Radiation-bad-Chernobyl-level-7-reached-2nd-time-history.html.

Shrader-Frechette, Kristin S. 1988. "Values and Hydrogeological Modeling: How Not to Site the World's Largest Nuclear Dump." In *Planning for Changing Energy Conditions*, ed. John Byrne and Daniel Rich, 101–137. New Brunswick, NJ: Transaction Books.

———. 1992. *Expert Judgment in Assessing Radwaste Risks: What Nevadans Should Know About Yucca Mountain*. Carson City: Nevada Agency for Nuclear Projects, Nuclear Waste Project.

———. 1993. *Burying Uncertainty: Risk and the Case Against Geological Disposal of Nuclear Waste*. Berkeley: University of California Press.

Swartz, Kristi E. 2012. Plant Vogtle Nuclear Expansion Approved 4-1. *Atlanta Journal-Constitution*. 9 February. www.ajc.com/business/plant-vogtle-nuclear-expansion-1340522.html.

Union of Concerned Scientists (UCS). 2009a. *Nuclear Loan Guarantees: Another Taxpayer Bailout?* Cambridge, MA: Union of Concerned Scientists. www.ucsusa.org/nuclear_power/nuclear_power_and_global_warming/nuclear-loan-guarantees.html.

———. 2009b. "Nuclear Power: A Resurgence We Can't Afford." Issue Briefing, August. Cambridge: Union of Concerned Scientists. www.ucsusa.org/nuclear_power/nuclear_power_and_global_warming/nuclear-power-resurgence.html.

U.S. Bureau of Land Management (USBLM). 1997. *Final Environmental Impact Statement for the Green Mountain Mining Venture, Jackpot Mine Project, Fremont and Sweetwater Counties, Wyoming*. Washington, DC: U.S. Government Printing Office.

U.S. Congress, House Committee on Interior and Insular Affairs. 1979. Mill Tailings Dam Break at Church Rock, New Mexico. Hearings before a subcommittee of the House Committee on Interior and Insular Affairs. 96th Cong. 1st sess. October 22, pp. 1–4.

U.S. Department of Energy (USDOE). 1984. "General Guidelines for Recommendation of Sites for Nuclear Waste Repositories." *Federal Register* 49 (6 December): 47753; 10 Code of Federal Regulations §960.2.

———. 1986. *Draft Area Recommendation Report for the Crystalline Repository Project*, vol. 1. Washington, DC: U.S. Government Printing Office.

———. 2002. *Yucca Mountain Science and Engineering Report: Technical Information Supporting Site Recommendation Consideration*. Washington, DC: U.S. Department of Energy, Office of Civilian Radioactive Waste Management.

U.S. Energy Information Administration (USEIA). 2010a. *2009 Domestic Uranium Production Report*. Washington, DC: U.S. Energy Information Administration. www.eia.gov/cneaf/nuclear/umar/summarytable1.html.

———. 2010b. *Assumptions to the Annual Energy Outlook 2010*. Washington, DC: U.S. Energy Information Administration. www.eia.gov/oiaf/aeo/assumption/pdf/electricity.pdf.

———. 2010c. "Summary Production Statistics of the U.S. Uranium Industry." Table, July 15. Washington, DC: U.S. Energy Information Administration. www.eia.doe.gov/cneaf/nuclear/dupr/usummary.html.

———. 2010d. *U.S. Uranium Reserves Estimates*. Washington, DC: U.S. Energy Information Administration. www.eia.gov/cneaf/nuclear/page/reserves/ures.html.

———. 2011a. *Annual Energy Review 2010*. Washington, DC: U.S. Government Printing Office.

———. 2011b. *Direct Federal Financial Interventions and Subsidies in Energy Markets 2010*. Washington, DC: U.S. Government Printing Office.

———. 2011c. *Electric Power Annual 2010*. Washington, DC: U.S. Government Printing Office. www.eia.gov/electricity/annual/.

———. 2011d. *Electric Power Annual 2011*. Washington, DC: U.S. Government Printing Office. www.eia.gov/electricity/annual/.

———. 2011e. "Nuclear Explained." Washington, DC: U.S. Energy Information Administration. www.eia.gov/energyexplained/index.cfm?page=nuclear_home.

———. 2012a. *2011 Domestic Uranium Production Report*. Washington, DC: U.S. Energy Information Administration. www.eia.gov/uranium/production/annual/pdf/dupr.pdf

———. 2012b. "Pressured-Water Reactor and Reactor Vessel." www.eia.gov/cneaf/nuclear/page/nuc_reactors/pwr.html.

———. 2012c. *Uranium Marketing Annual Report*. Tables S1a and S1b. Washington, DC: U.S. Energy Information Administration. www.eia.gov/uranium/marketing/html/summarytable1a.cfm and www.eia.gov/uranium/marketing/html/summarytable1b.cfm

U.S. Environmental Protection Agency (USEPA). 1973a. *Environmental Analysis of the Uranium Fuel Cycle: Part I—Fuel Supply*. Washington, DC: U.S. Government Printing Office.

———. 1973b. *Environmental Analysis of the Uranium Fuel Cycle: Part IV—Supplementary Analysis*. Washington, DC: U.S. Government Printing Office.

———. 1975a. *Evaluation of the Impact of the Mines Development, Inc., Mill on Water Quality Conditions in the Cheyenne River*. Denver, CO: U.S. Environmental Protection Agency, Region VIII.

———. 1975b. *Water Quality Impacts of Uranium Mining and Milling Activities in the Grants Mineral Belt, New Mexico*. Dallas, TX: U.S. Environmental Protection Agency, Region VI.

———. 2011a. "Addressing Uranium Contamination in the Navajo Reservation: Abandoned Uranium Mines." www.epa.gov/region9/superfund/navajo-nation/abandoned-uranium.html.

———. 2011b. "Addressing Uranium Contamination in the Navajo Reservation: Contaminated Water Sources." www.epa.gov/region9/superfund/navajo-nation/contaminated-water.html.

U.S. Government Accountability Office (USGAO). 1978. *The Uranium Mill Tailings Cleanup: Federal Leadership at Last?* Washington, DC: U.S. General Accounting Office.

———. 1979. *The U.S. Mining and Mineral-Processing Industry: An Analysis of Trends and Implications*. Report to the Congress of the United States, October 31. Washington, DC: U.S. General Accounting Office.

———. 2008. *New Loan Guarantee Program Should Complete Activities Necessary for Effective and Accountable Program Management*. Washington, DC: U.S. Government Printing Office.

U.S. Nuclear Regulatory Commission (USNRC). 1976. *Final Environmental Statement Related to the Operation of the Humeca Uranium Mill*. Washington, DC: U.S. Nuclear Regulatory Commission.

———. 1980. *Final General Environmental Impact Statement on Uranium Milling*, vol. 1. Washington, DC: U.S. Government Printing Office.

———. 1981. *Radon Releases from Uranium Mining and Milling and Their Calculated Health Effects*. Washington, DC: U.S. Government Printing Office.

———. 1997. *Final Environmental Impact Statement to Construct and Operate the Crownpoint Uranium Solution Mining Project, Crownpoint, New Mexico*. Washington, DC: U.S. Nuclear Regulatory Commission.

———. 2002. *Radioactive Waste: Production, Storage, Disposal*, 2nd rev. ed. Washington, DC: U.S. Government Printing Office.

———. 2010. "Fact Sheet on Decommissioning Nuclear Power Plants." Washington, DC: U.S. Nuclear Regulatory Commission. www.nrc.gov/reading-rm/doc-collections/fact-sheets/decommissioning.html.

———. 2011a. "Expected New Nuclear Power Plant Applications." Table, October 6. Washington, DC: U.S. Nuclear Regulatory Commission. www.nrc.gov/reactors/new-reactors/new-licensing-files/expected-new-rx-applications.pdf.

———. 2011b. "Fact Sheet on Nuclear Insurance and Disaster Relief Funds." Washington, DC: U.S. Nuclear Regulatory Commission. www.nrc.gov/reading-rm/doc-collections/fact-sheets/funds-fs.html.

———. 2011c. "Fact Sheet on Uranium Enrichment." Washington, DC: U.S. Nuclear Regulatory Commission. www.nrc.gov/reading-rm/doc-collections/fact-sheets/enrichment.html.

———. 2011d. "Low Level Waste." Washington, DC: U.S. Nuclear Regulatory Commission. www.nrc.gov/waste/low-level-waste.html.

———. 2012. "GE Laser Enrichment Facility Licensing." Washington, DC: U.S. Nuclear Regulatory Commission. http://www.nrc.gov/materials/fuel-cycle-fac/laser.html.

Vandenbosch, Robert, and Susanne E. Vandenbosch. 2007. *Nuclear Waste Stalemate*. Salt Lake City: University of Utah Press.

Vartabedian, Ralph, and Ian Duncan. 2012. "First New U.S. Nuclear Reactors in Decades Approved." *Los Angeles Times*, 9 February. www.latimes.com/news/nationworld/nation/la-na-nuclear-20120210,0,3657441.story.

Walsh, Bryan. 2008. "Is Nuclear Power Viable?" *Time*, June 6. www.time.com/time/health/article/0,8599,1812540,00.html.

Wasserman, Harvey, and Norman Solomon. 1982. *Killing Our Own: The Disaster of America's Experience with Atomic Radiation*. New York: Delacorte Press.

Winter, Michael. 2011. "Cooling System Fails at 3 Reactors at Another Japanese Nuclear Plant." *USA Today*, March 11.

Wohlstetter, Albert, Thomas A. Brown, Gregory S. Jones, David McGarvey, Henry Rowen, Vince Taylor, and Roberta Wohlstetter. 1979. *Swords from Plowshares: The Military Potential of Civilian Nuclear Energy*. Chicago: University of Chicago Press.

World Health Organization (WHO). 2005. "Chernobyl: The True Scale of the Accident." www.who.int/mediacentre/news/releases/2005/pr38/en/index.html.

Yates, Marshall. 1989. "DOE Waste Management Criticized: On-site Storage Urged." *Public Utilities Fortnightly* 124 (July 6): 33.

4

Oil and Natural Gas

~~~~~~~~~

Proven reserves in the United States at the end of 2008 were 19,121 million barrels of crude oil and 244,656 billion cubic feet of dry (consumer-grade) natural gas (USEIA 2011a, 2010b). U.S. crude oil reserves have continued to decline since the 1970s, while reserves of natural gas have increased steadily since price deregulation in 1998.

The United States consumed 19.1 million barrels per day of petroleum products in 2010 (USEIA 2011e), comprising about 37 percent of all energy used, more than from any other energy source (USEIA 2011a, Figure 2.0). That represented about 22.4 percent of the 85.3 million barrels per day consumed worldwide (USEIA 2011e). The United States also consumed 23,775 billion cubic feet of natural gas (methane) in 2010, comprising about 24.6 percent of energy used nationally (USEIA 2011a, Figure 2.0). That represented about 21 percent of the estimated 112.9 trillion cubic feet of natural gas consumed worldwide in 2010 (USEIA 2011d).

Combustion of petroleum products is used for transportation of people, goods and services, to heat buildings, and to produce electric power. About 71 percent of total U.S. petroleum consumption is for transportation (USEIA 2011a, Figure 2.0). Gasoline is used in automobiles and light trucks; diesel fuel is used in heavy construction equipment, trucks, buses, tractors, boats, trains, and some automobiles; and jet fuel is used in airplanes.

Heating or fuel oil is used to heat homes and buildings, for industrial heating, and for producing electricity. Liquefied petroleum gases are mixtures of propane, ethane, butane, and other gases produced at oil refineries and natural gas processing plants. Propane is used in homes for space and water heating, clothes drying, and cooking and by farmers for heating greenhouses, livestock housing, and drying crops. The chemical industry uses about half of all propane consumed in the United States as a raw material feedstock for making plastics, nylon, and other materials. In addition, liquid petroleum is used as feedstock for production of plastics, polyurethane, solvents, asphalt, and hundreds of other products. Most of the natural gas consumed in the United States is produced in the United States, but about 16 percent is imported, mostly from Canada via pipelines (USEIA 2011a, Table 6.3). About 11.5 percent of imported natural gas was shipped to the United States as liquefied natural gas in 2010 (USEIA 2011d).

OIL AND NATURAL GAS EXPLORATION

The oil and natural gas fuel cycle, shown in Figure 4.1, includes exploration, drilling, well development and completion, transportation, refining and processing, reclamation of wellhead disturbances, utilization, and disposal of waste by-products. Human exposure to toxic, hazardous, and flammable materials is associated with each of these activities. Although there are some variations in the initial parts of the fuel cycle based on whether the fuels are found under land or water, oil and natural gas are often found together and pumped from the same wells, so their costs are sufficiently similar as to warrant treatment in a single chapter.

Oil and natural gas are often associated with coal deposits, in or below the coal. All coal deposits

Figure 4.1 **The Oil and Gas Fuel Cycle**

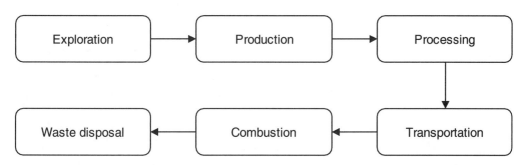

contain several volatile organic compounds, including methane. Natural gas is mostly methane, and coal bed methane is an economically recoverable resource in some areas of the United States. If these resources are to be developed in an economically efficient manner, the oil and gas must be developed before the coal is mined or significant portions of economically recoverable gas reserves may be lost.

Exploration for oil and natural gas is similar to that for coal in the United States (see Chapter 2 in this volume), but often includes remote sensing from aircraft to identify geologic structures, and geophysical seismic surveying to detect the differential in return of high-intensity acoustic signals through solid material from masses of liquid and gas. Because oil and gas are considerably less dense than surrounding rock, sound waves reflect back in distinctive patterns that reveal the presence of such resources. Although the equipment varies, with heavy truck equipment on land and ships on water, similar technologies are used to explore onshore and offshore resources.

Earlier use of explosives to generate high-intensity acoustic signals produced some destruction of marine life, but current electronic technologies are thought to be safe for fish and invertebrates, although there continue to be some concerns about the effects of seismic surveying on marine mammals, especially whales and others that communicate with acoustic signals (Neff, Rabalais, and Boesch 1987, 150).

Following a search of available records and geophysical surveying, core drilling and logging of boreholes determine the amounts of oil and gas that are extractable at specified depths and costs. On land this may involve building roads in roadless areas for transportation of drilling rigs similar to those used for coal and uranium prospecting, but offshore it involves mobile drilling rigs on barges, drill ships, and semisubmersibles fabricated at coastal or inland shipyards.

OFFSHORE RESOURCES

Crude oil seeps naturally into the marine environment, establishing a contaminant "background" that must be estimated in order to determine the extent of pollution from human activities. This background rate of natural seepage of crude oil has been estimated at 58.8 to 588 million gallons per year globally (NRC 2003, 67–69). Activities associated with oil and gas exploration or production introduce an estimated 11 million gallons of oil to the seas worldwide each year, including about 880,000 gallons to North American waters (2). Releases from oil and gas extraction include accidental spills of crude oil from blowouts of drilling rigs, surface spills of crude from platforms, and slower chronic releases associated with disposal of produced water and oil-bearing cuttings created during the drilling process. Volatile organic compounds are commonly associated with or

Figure 4.2 **Oil Spill Influences on Seabirds**

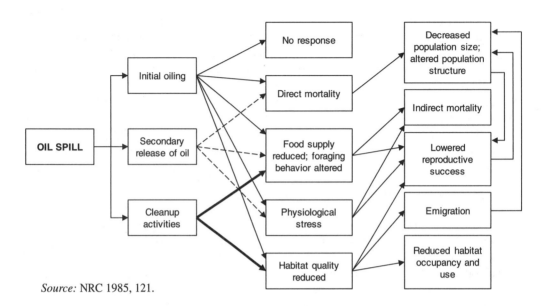

Source: NRC 1985, 121.

dissolved in petroleum and are released during extraction, contributing to the total load of hydrocarbon input to the seas (3). Some, such as polycyclic aromatic hydrocarbons (PAH) are known human carcinogens, and others are highly toxic to marine organisms. According to the National Research Council, "the more turbulent the release (i.e., if it is during a storm or from a blowout or pipeline under pressure), the higher the relative concentrations of the more toxic PAH, and the higher the impacts to water column organisms" (NRC 2003, 140).

No spill of petroleum is benign (NRC 2003, 4). Oil can kill marine organisms, reduce their fitness through sublethal effects, and disrupt the structure and function of marine communities and ecosystems (120). The effect of petroleum releases into the natural environment is a complex function of the rate of release, the nature of the released petroleum, the proportions of toxic compounds it may contain, and characteristics of the local ecosystem exposed to it (4). For example, the complex effects of oil spills on seabirds are illustrated in Figure 4.2. Similar pathways for the impact of oil spills would be evident for marine mammals, fishes, mollusks, and other benthic organisms. After an oil spill, birds, mammals, and reptiles are primarily impacted by direct exposure to floating oil, ingestion of contaminated prey, or depletion of food resources (139).

Much of what is known about the fate and effect of spilled oil has been derived from a very few well-studied spills. Although there is now good evidence for the toxic effects of oil pollution on individual organisms and species composition of affected communities, little is known about the effects of either acute or chronic oil pollution on entire populations or on the functions of communities or ecosystems (NRC 2003, 4). For example, we do not know the upper boundary for the potential length of a long-term effect of oil pollution, which is likely to be at least the length of a generation of affected organisms and may be much longer (119). Spill clean-up activities are also harmful to some organisms and ecosystems.

Sublethal effects from hydrocarbon exposure occur at concentrations several orders of magnitude lower than those that induce acute toxic effects (Vandermeulen and Capuzzo 1983). Impairment of feeding mechanisms, growth rates, development rates, energetics, reproductive output, recruitment rates, and increased susceptibility to disease and other histopathological disorders are examples of the types of sublethal effects that may occur with exposure to petroleum hydrocarbons (Capuzzo 1987). Early developmental stages of species can be especially vulnerable, and several studies have demonstrated that oil residuals in beach sediments may have significant toxic effects on fish eggs and embryos (NRC 2003, 127–129). In addition to the incidence of tumors and other histopathological disorders, sublethal toxic effects of contaminants in marine organisms include impairment of physiological processes that may alter the energy available for growth and reproduction and may include direct genetic damage (Capuzzo 1987; Capuzzo, Moore, and Widdows 1988).

Marine birds and mammals can be affected by oil in the sea through several pathways:

> As air-breathing organisms that obtain much or all of their food from beneath the surface of the sea, marine birds and mammals must frequently pass through the water's surface. When floating oil is present, they become fouled. Additionally, many species of birds frequent the intertidal zone while foraging and resting, as do seals, sea lions, sea ducks, shorebirds, and sea otters. While there, these warm-blooded vertebrates or their food may become coated with oil that has come ashore. The presence of oil on the feathers of a seabird or the pelage of a marine mammal can destroy the waterproofing and insulating characteristics of the feathers or fur and lead to death from hypothermia. Seabirds and marine mammals may be poisoned when they ingest oil while trying to remove it from their feathers or pelage, or when it adheres to food items. (NRC 2003, 132–133)

Marine mammals such as sea otters that depend on clean fur for insulation are vulnerable to surface oiling (Geraci and St. Aubin 1990). If seabirds transfer oil from their feathers to the surface of eggs during incubation, embryos may fail to develop. Oil may also reduce the distribution, abundance, and availability of prey, indirectly reducing the survival or reproductive success of marine birds and mammals (NRC 2003, 132–133). Ingestion of oil or oil-contaminated prey by seabirds may compromise the ability of blood to carry oxygen, an effect that persists long after the birds appear to have recovered from exposure (Fry and Addiego 1987). These effects on wildlife may be exacerbated by stress from handling during oil cleaning (Briggs, Yoshida, and Gershwin 1996). A general rule of thumb among researchers is that the body count of birds recovered after a spill represents about 10 percent of those actually killed by the spill (NRC 2003, 135), but there is no way to verify this estimate. A variety of significant indirect, chronic, and delayed adverse responses of various bird populations were chronicled after the *Exxon Valdez* oil spill of 1979 (136). Affected sea otter populations in Prince William Sound had not recovered from that spill as recently as 1998 (Dean et al. 2000). Sublethal effects can be identified in marine birds and mammals for many years after the acute effects of an oil spill have passed (NRC 2003, 138).

Effects of oiling on biogenically structured habitats may result from acute damage to coral reefs, live-bottom habitats, mangrove swamps, salt marshes, oyster reefs, and seagrass and kelp beds. Even though oil may not persist following a spill, the time required for recovery of damaged populations of organisms that provide the physical structure of the habitat may be many years (NRC 2003, 141). Mixtures of dispersants and oil are more toxic to coral than oil by itself (Peters et al. 1997). Oil spills are known to cause severe and long-term damage to mangrove and salt marsh ecosystems (Mille et al. 1998; Duke, Pinzon, and Prada 1997). Oil may persist in marsh sediments for many years (Teal and Howarth 1984), and vegetation recovery times range from a few weeks to decades (Hoff 1996). Oiling of mangroves can kill the plants and lead to unstable habitats and sediment erosion (Garrity, Levings, and Burns 1994), producing long-term ecosystem change and destroying the value of that habitat for nursery fish. These facts led the National Research Council to the following conclusion: "Biogenically structured habitats, such as salt marshes and mangrove forests, are subject to destruction or alteration by acute oiling events. Because the structure of these habitats depends upon living organisms, when these are killed, the structure of the habitat, and sometimes the substrate on which is grows, is lost" (NRC 2003, 157). The NRC recommends that government oil spill contingency plans contain mechanisms for higher levels of prevention to protect these areas from oil spills than are generally included in them.

Surface oil weathers, loses buoyancy, and sinks down in the water, where it can associate with particulate matter suspended in the water and eventually sink to the seabed, where it affects the benthic community (Elmgren et al. 1983). The most sensitive organisms there appear to be crustaceans, some of which, like American lobsters, have commercial value. Sedimented oil provides a long-term pathway for exposure to benthic fisheries (Kingston 1999).

Exploration

Mobile drilling rigs are towed or move under their own power to sites for exploratory drilling and are anchored at multiple mooring points, or they may be dynamically positioned in deeper waters. Initial drilling into the seabed to place risers to the surface results in direct discharge of sediment, drill cuttings, and drilling fluids at the seafloor. After the drilling rig is secured in place, drilling fluids necessary to cool, lubricate, and transport solids from the drill bit to the surface are separated from cuttings (pulverized rock from the formation) on the rig. Cuttings are usually discharged overboard continuously, while drilling fluids are reused and disposed of later, generally overboard at the drill site. Water drainage from the drill platform may contain drilling fluids, oil, and small quantities of industrial chemicals. Exploration wells are sparsely distributed and generally produce brief operational discharges compared to production facilities, in the absence of a blowout (Neff, Rabalais, and Boesch 1987, 150).

During exploratory drilling, several drilling fluid and cuttings-related effluents are discharged to the ocean. Used drilling fluids may be discharged in bulk quantities of 1,000 to 2,500 barrels several times during a drilling operation. Over the life of an exploratory well, 5,000 to 30,000 barrels of drilling fluids may be used, and 50 to 80 percent of this material may be discharged to the ocean (Neff, Rabalais, and Boesch 1987, 157, 158).

Production

After discovery of a promising reserve of oil or gas, a fixed platform may be placed from which several development wells may be drilled in different directions, producing more heavily concentrated discharges of drilling fluids and cuttings, and greater risks of oil spills. In some near-shore locations, an artificial island may be built of sand or gravel to support drilling and production, with resulting destruction of marine habitats (Neff, Rabalais, and Boesch 1987, 151). During drilling of a 10,000-foot production well, approximately 900 metric tons of drill cuttings are generated and about 1,000 tons of drilling fluid solids are discharged. As many as fifty to a hundred wells may be drilled from a single offshore development platform over four to twenty years, resulting in discharge of about 95,000 metric tons of drilling fluid and cuttings solids to the ocean (Neff, Rabalais, and Boesch 1987, 159).

Pipeline Construction

Transport of oil and gas across coastal wetlands often entails dredging channels for laying pipelines and burying them in the seafloor, except where economically impractical. If use of pipelines is uneconomic, the product may be stored offshore and loaded onto tankers or barges. All transport methods involve some risk of accidental spills (Neff, Rabalais, and Boesch 1987, 151).

Field Operations

During well drilling and production of oil and gas offshore, a variety of liquid, solid, and gaseous wastes are produced on the platform, some of which are discharged into the ocean. They include crude oil, natural gas, petroleum condensates, nonhydrocarbon waste gases, and water produced from sedimentary rock formations. Submerged parts of the platform must be protected against corrosion and growth of biological organisms with antifouling paints and use of electrodes that may release small amounts of toxic metals, such as aluminum, copper, mercury, indium, tin, and zinc (Dicks 1982).

The most significant discharges associated with exploratory drilling are drill cuttings and drilling fluids. Cuttings are particles of crushed sedimentary rock, ranging in size from clay to coarse gravel, produced by the drill bit as it penetrates into the rock strata. They have an angular configuration, as distinguished from the rounded shape of most weathered natural sediments, and represent a potential input of trace metals, hydrocarbons, drilling fluids, and suspended sediments to receiving waters (Neff, Rabalais, and Boesch 1987, 153).

Drilling fluids are mixtures of natural clays and polymers, weighting agents, and other materials suspended in water or a petroleum material. Discharge of oil-based drilling fluids to the waters of the United States is prohibited, but they are used widely in other parts of the world. During drilling, a mud engineer continually tests the drilling fluid and adjusts its composition to accommodate downhole conditions so as to provide adequate cooling and lubrication of the drill bit and to float cuttings up the borehole for removal at the platform. Consequently, no two drilling fluids are identical in composition (Neff, Rabalais, and Boesch 1987, 155).

> Drilling fluid is pumped under high pressure from the drilling fluid holding tanks on the platform down through the drill pipe and exits through nozzles in the drill bit. There it hydraulically removes cuttings generated by the grinding action of the drill bit. The drilling fluid, carrying cuttings with it, then passes up through the annulus (area between the drill pipe and the borehole wall or casing) to the drilling fluid return line. The drilling fluid passes through several screens and other devices which remove the cuttings from the fluid. The drilling fluid is returned to the holding tanks for recirculation down-hole, and the cuttings are discharged to the ocean. (157)

In addition to fresh or salt water, the five major ingredients of water-based drilling fluids are barite (barium sulfate), bentonite clay, lignosulfonate (derived from the lignin of wood), lignite (soft coal), and caustic sodium hydroxide (Neff, Rabalais, and Boesch 1987, 155). Specialty materials that may be added to water-based drilling fluids include sodium bicarbonate; cellulose polymers or starch; paraformaldehyde bactericide; zinc compounds; diesel or vegetable oil lubricant; aluminum stearate or alcohols; sodium chloride; sodium chromate; ground nut shells, mica, or cellophane; KCL-polymer drilling fluids; and asbestos (Neff, Rabalais, and Boesch 1987, 153–154). Several metals of major concern for their toxic and environmental effects are found in drilling fluids, including arsenic, barium, chromium, cadmium, copper, iron, lead, mercury, nickel, and zinc. Those most frequently present in drilling mud at concentrations significantly higher than in natural marine sediments are barium, chromium, lead, and zinc (Neff, Rabalais, and Boesch 1987, 155), all of which can be toxic to marine life forms. Discharged cuttings may contain 5 to 10 percent drilling fluid solids (Neff, Rabalais, and Boesch 1987, 157).

Fossil water that has been out of contact with the atmosphere for a large part of a geologic period may accumulate in reservoirs of oil and gas, and some of it may be pumped up during production as oilfield brine or produced water (White 1957). In older fields, production may be 95 percent water and 5 percent oil and gas (Neff, Rabalais, and Boesch 1987, 159). In 1970 daily production of produced water in the United States was 3.78 trillion liters. In the northwestern Gulf of Mexico, an estimated 47.7 million liters per day of produced water were discharged to outer continental shelf waters, and 47 million liters per day were treated onshore and discharged to coastal waters (Brooks, Bernard, and Phillips 1977). Produced water discharges from a single platform are usually less than 1.5 million liters per day, but discharges from large facilities handling several platforms may be as high as 25 million liters per day (Menzie 1982).

Produced water and oily wastes from platform deck drainage are processed with an oil-water separator, and domestic sewage is treated in an activated sludge system before discharge. Produced water treatment systems are designed to remove particulate or dispersed oil and have little effect on the concentration of dissolved petroleum hydrocarbons, other organics, and metal ions in produced water (Lysyj 1982; Jackson et al. 1981). Treated water containing up to 48ppm oil and grease is permitted for discharge to the oceans; consequently, discharges of produced waters often contain significant concentrations of various aromatic hydrocarbons such as benzene, toluene, ethylbenzene, xylene, naphthalene, and some alkanes (Neff, Rabalais, and Boesch 1987, 153, 165–166), many of which are known carcinogens. Other organics found in produced waters include ketones from solvents used to clean rig structures, phenols, and biocides used to inhibit organic growths in the production system (Middleditch 1981; Collins 1975). A wide variety of chemicals may be added to the process stream and appear in effluent water, including coagulents, corrosion inhibitors, cleaners, dispersants, emulsion breakers, paraffin control agents, reverse emulsion breakers, and scale inhibitors (Middleditch 1984).

Several toxic metals may be present at elevated levels in some produced waters; those present at substantially higher concentrations than in seawater include barium, beryllium, cadmium, chromium, copper, iron, lead, nickel, silver, and zinc, along with small amounts of radionuclides, principally radium (Neff, Rabalais, and Boesch 1987, 162).

Platform Removal

After development wells have been drilled and transportation or pipeline infrastructure is in place, drilling platforms are removed, often used in nearby areas for additional drilling, scuttled, or dismantled for scrap (Neff, Rabalais, and Boesch 1987, 162). Little or no reclamation of the seabed around offshore well heads is attempted, so these locations remain contaminated by drilling muds and materials discharged from drilling platforms for the indefinite future. Little research has been completed concerning the distribution or dissolution of such materials after removal of drilling platforms.

ONSHORE RESOURCES

Preliminary geological exploration on land involves ground and aerial survey of an area, along with aerial photo and geologic map interpretation. On-the-ground geologic mapping and rock sampling necessitates use of vehicles and sometimes helicopters to transport geologists into inaccessible areas. Geophysical exploration obtains data about subsurface geology. Gravitational and magnetic surveys are conducted by means of aerial and ground surveys (MDFWP 1983). Small trucks and jeeps with crews of several people are used at this stage of subsurface data gathering, and off-road travel is frequent (USDOI 1981a).

Seismic surveys are the most common geophysical methods and seem to give the most reliable results (USFS 1979). Methods used in seismic exploration vary, but the premise basic to all involves imparting an artificially generated shock wave into the ground so that the reflected waves from layers of different density rock can be recorded. Methods of producing the shock wave vary from using explosives to dropping a heavy object on the ground. Each formation reflects the shock wave back to the surface, where sensitive instruments record and measure the intensity of reflections. The resulting data are analyzed to predict where fossil fuels may have collected (API 1978).

One method uses a thumper unit consisting of one or more large trucks from which a suspended 3-ton slab is repeatedly dropped to the ground from a height of several feet. Additional support vehicles for equipment and crew are required. The vibroseis method involves use of three or four large trucks, under each of which is mounted a platform. The platform can be lowered and the truck hydraulically raised above it to provide the necessary weight. When a motor is turned on, vibrating the entire unit, a shock wave is generated. In the dinoseis method, a large bell-shaped metal chamber is mounted beneath a truck and lowered to the ground at test sites. Propane and oxygen are ignited inside the chamber with a spark to create an explosion, which, in turn, drives the required shock wave into the ground. A subsurface explosion method may utilize a large truck mounted with equipment used to drill a two- to six-inch diameter hole from twenty-five to 200 feet deep, into which five to fifty pounds of explosives are placed. When detonated, the explosion generates a shock wave (API 1978).

Liquid releases from oil and gas extraction include accidental spills of crude oil from blowouts of drilling rigs, surface spills of crude from drilling pads, and slower chronic releases associated with disposal of water produced from oil- or gas-bearing formations ("produced water") and oil-bearing cuttings created during the drilling process.

Access Road Construction

Exploration for oil and gas produces environmental effects on roadless areas not regularly visited by humans similar to those discussed for exploration of coal resources in Chapter 2. In some terrain, road construction is necessary to provide access to drill sites for large equipment, with attendant disruption of the natural environment. Each of the four seismic survey techniques described above requires various vehicles such as jug trucks, equipment trucks, recording trucks, and personnel carriers. Shot hole drilling also may require water trucks. A typical seismic operation may use ten to fifteen men and five to seven trucks (USDOI 1981b). The seismic sensors and energy source are located along lines on a one- to two-mile grid. Existing roads are used if possible. Lines may require clearing of vegetation and loose rock to improve access for trucks. Each mile of line cleared to a width of eight to fourteen feet represents disturbance of about one acre of land. After initial testing, road spacing may be reduced if results are favorable, and the process is repeated. There can be little modification of the road system to accommodate topography, since a line should not deviate more than eleven degrees from straight (USDOI 1981b) to get accurate data.

When rugged terrain prevents use of ground vehicles, portable drills may be backpacked or flown by helicopter onto location. A series of twenty-five-foot-deep holes is drilled and loaded with explosives; then all are detonated simultaneously. Another technique involves a surface explosion that consists of draping explosive packs over stakes driven into the ground. Five to fifty pounds of explosives in each pack are detonated simultaneously (MDFWP 1983).

An area may be explored with seismic methods several times by the same or different companies over a period of time. Frequently companies do not share their information and seismic methodology is constantly being upgraded to find deeper, smaller, and more subtle targets. There appears to be no consensus about which methods are the best (MDFWP 1983).

Drilling

If preliminary exploration reveals favorable results, exploratory drilling may take place. When an area's fossil fuel potential is unknown, the drilling operation is called a "wildcat." Prior to drilling, a drill pad (well site) is cleared and leveled for the drill rig and associated equipment and structures. Only by drilling a "wildcat well" (i.e., a well drilled in unproven territory) will a company know if subsurface strata contain oil or gas and if its quality and quantity are adequate for profitable sale.

The depth of wildcat wells and their rig size depend on the geology of an area. Wells drilled to a depth of 10,000 to 15,000 feet are not uncommon. For deep wells, as much as five acres may be needed to establish a drill pad, the drill rig, mud pit, tool shack, pipe rack, and generators. Drilling equipment may remain on-site for six months. In other areas, shallower wells up to a few thousand feet are common and may be completed in a few weeks (USDOI 1981a). Stratigraphic tests involve drilling relatively shallow holes (100 to several thousand feet deep) to supplement seismic data. These holes are usually drilled by truck-mounted rotary rigs that are fairly mobile; consequently, roads and trails to test sites on level, solid ground are temporary and may involve minimal construction. From 50,000 to 100,000 gallons of water a day may be needed for mixing drilling mud, cleaning equipment, and cooling engines (USDOI 1981b). A surface pipeline may be laid to a stream or a water well, or water may be trucked to the site. Once drilling is started, it continues twenty-four hours a day until completion.

Drilling activities can have detrimental impacts on surface and ground waters, resulting in harm to aquatic organisms, vegetation, and humans. Exploration drill holes may penetrate several aquifers and result in leakage between aquifers and to the surface with possible degradation of water quality (USDOI 1981b). Lowering the groundwater level in an aquifer can result in increased pumping costs at nearby wells or can cause wells to go dry. Open holes present a danger to domestic and wild animals, as well as humans. Improperly plugged drill holes allow surface water to enter an aquifer. This may be detrimental to groundwater, depending on the quality and degree of contamination of surface water. Other impacts from exploration drilling include noise, damage to archeological and historical sites, and possible contamination by drilling muds and fluids (USDOI 1981b).

Production Facilities

If wildcatting produces commercial quantities of hydrocarbons, a development phase is initiated. Additional wells are drilled to establish the extent of a field. Field size may vary from less than 1,000 acres to several thousand acres, and some cover several townships. Generally a state agency governs the spacing of oil and gas wells. Often oil wells less than about 6,000 feet deep are placed one per 40 acres; wells 6,000 to 11,000 feet, one per 160 acres; wells greater than 11,000 feet deep are one per 320 acres. Gas wells are often located one well per 640 acres. If an oil field is developed on the minimum spacing pattern of forty acres per well and if the field is a section (640 acres) in size, at least four miles of roads will be needed (USFS 1979). In addition to roads, other surface uses needed for development are more well drill sites, on-site processing facilities, and storage tanks.

Pipeline Construction

Construction of gathering and transmission pipelines is necessary before production can commence. Oil from a small field can be trucked to storage facilities, but larger amounts of oil and natural gas require pipelines. It is not practical to truck natural gas, so pipelines are necessary. Gathering lines transport the oil and gas from the well site to collection facilities, while transmission lines move it from storage to refineries. In the United States there are over 174,000 miles of oil pipelines and over 1.5 million miles of natural gas pipelines (USDOT 2011, Table 1.1).

Field Operations

Production begins when the field and its transportation networks are developed for the initial discovery wells. Many oil wells require an artificial lift to bring the oil to the surface. This primary production accounts for about 25 percent of the oil in a reservoir. In fields where it is economically feasible, "secondary" recovery methods are used. This involves pumping water or gas into the reservoir to increase oil production by increasing the pressure in the reservoir. "Tertiary" recovery methods can sometimes increase recovery rates if the viscosity of the oil is lowered so that it flows more easily—either by heating the oil or by injecting chemicals into the reservoir (USDOI 1981b). Most gas wells produce by normal flow and do not require pumping.

Hydraulic fracturing (fracking), an increasingly used, controversial method of oil and gas extraction, involves injecting pressurized water or other drilling fluids with sand and chemicals into wells to fracture rock layers and release oil and gas so they may be extracted more easily (Urbina 2011). The sand is to keep fractures open after they have been made. Elevated levels of total dissolved solids and radioactivity have been found in shale drilling wastewater from fracking. Total dissolved solids are a mixture of salt and other minerals from deep underground during gas production. Drilling wastewater can be more than five times as salty as sea water, and large amounts of these minerals can damage machinery at downstream power plants (*New York Times* 2011).

Hydraulic fracturing has resulted in significant increases of radioactive material, including radium, and carcinogens, including benzene, in major rivers and watersheds (*New York Times* 2011; Urbina 2011). Dilution of drilling wastes containing radium by discharge to rivers does not eliminate the health risks posed by that waste. Such discharges constitute a potential increased risk of cancer among people who often eat fish from waters where drilling waste is discharged (*New York Times* 2011). Fracking entails the risk of spills of hazardous hydraulic fracturing fluids (Litvak 2010; Mayer 2010). Fracking has seriously contaminated shallow groundwater supplies in northeast Pennsylvania with flammable levels of methane (Lustgarten 2009). Methane concentrations seventeen times above normal have been detected in samples taken from water wells near shale gas drilling sites employing hydraulic fracturing (Lustgarten 2011; Osborn et al. 2011). It is possible that natural gas drilling with hydraulic fracturing may have caused earthquakes in North Texas (Keenan 2011; Casselman 2009). There is evidence that the frequency of local earthquakes can be increased by injection of fluids in deep wells (Keenan 2011; Hsieh and Bredehoeft 1981) even without fracking.

Various treating and separating facilities are located near wells to treat the oil before storage and transportation. Similar units are used to separate condensate, moisture, and other undesirable products from natural gas. Depending on numerous factors, the life span of a field can vary considerably; however, the estimated average life of a typical field is fifteen to twenty-five years. Many fields go through several development phases. A field may be considered fully developed and produce for several years; then wells may be drilled to a deeper pay zone, thus creating a new field beneath the old field.

Reclamation

When a well field is abandoned, drilled holes are sealed and surface markers are established to record the well name and location. Disturbed land surfaces are restored to their previous grade and productive capability, and necessary measures are taken to prevent adverse hydrological effects from the wells.

Transportation

It has been estimated that activities associated with oil and gas transportation (including refining and distribution) of crude oil or refined products results in the release of about 44 million gallons of oil to the seas worldwide each year, about 2.7 million gallons to North American waters (NRC 2003, 3). This includes spills from onshore production and transportation facilities that run off into rivers and streams. Oil and gas transportation activities account for about 45.2 percent of all input of petroleum to the environment worldwide from all sources, including natural seeps (Neff, Rabalais, and Boesch 1987, 170).

> Offshore oil and gas development carries with it the risk of oil spills at the platform and in transporting the oil from the platform to shore. Spills at the platform result from leaks or blowouts during both exploratory and production drilling. Most oil and gas produced offshore is transported ashore through pipelines. Oil spills result from pipeline ruptures or chronic leaks. Where technologically difficult or economically infeasible, transport of oil by pipelines is replaced by storage of the product offshore, then transfer to tankers or barges. This method is commonly viewed as less safe than pipelines. (Neff, Rabalais, and Boesch 1987, 167)

Most oil and gas produced onshore is transported through pipelines or by tank trucks on roads and highways used by other vehicles. Large spills from outer continental shelf production and onshore production are rare. Although the number of small spills from transportation activities is larger, the total amount of oil from these is relatively small compared to the total amount attributable to large offshore spills (Neff, Rabalais, and Boesch 1987, 169).

For example, the largest oil spill in the Gulf of Mexico prior to 2010 was from a blowout of an exploratory well, IXTOC-I in the Bay of Campeche, Mexico, in June 1979, which released about 140 million gallons of crude to the marine environment, fouling largely uninhabited shorelines in Mexico and beaches in Texas. Less than 10 percent of the oil from this spill was recovered (Neff, Rabalais, and Boesch 1987, 170).

IXTOC-I was dwarfed in comparison by the BP Macondo well blowout after the Deepwater Horizon rig exploded and sank on April 20, 2010, releasing over 205 million gallons of crude oil by July 15 at a rate estimated at that time of about 2.52 million gallons per day (Henry 2010). This was easily the largest oil spill ever directly affecting the United States and ranks as the second-largest known release of oil in world history. Although the final tally of oil released during this incident is as yet unknown, its effects on the Gulf of Mexico will be profound for many years to come.

Early surveys in May 2010 discovered large subsurface plumes of oil droplets had formed in deep waters of the Gulf of Mexico, some ten miles long, three miles wide, and 300 feet thick in spots. Some plumes contained a great deal of oil in multiple layers in the water column. Scientists suspected the heavy use of chemical dispersants at the wellhead on the sea floor may have broken the oil into droplets too small to rise rapidly, producing plumes at 2,300 to 4,200 feet deep in the sea. The impacts of possible oxygen depletion caused by such plumes on marine flora and fauna were of considerable concern, and some feared they might create large "dead zones" on the seabed (Gillis 2010).

In August 2010, University of Georgia oceanographer Samantha Joye suggested that three-quarters of the oil spilled into the gulf—about 3 million barrels—remained in marine ecosystems there (Sutter 2010). Her empirical field research contradicted an earlier report from the National Oceanic and Atmospheric Administration that three-quarters of the oil had disappeared from the ecosystem. Joye's research at various locations near the BP Deepwater Horizon site collected numerous seabed core samples containing several centimeters of flocculated oil deposited from above, which distinguished them from natural seabed oil seeps (Joye 2010). More recent surveys in November 2010 discovered extensive damage to deep sea corals near the BP Deepwater Horizon site, appearing to support Joye's hypothesis (Burdeau 2010). Research into the impacts of this enormous oil spill had only just begun at this writing, and it appears we may learn a great deal more about the environmental damage done by the BP Deepwater Horizon spill in the coming years.

Refining and Processing

Activities associated with oil and gas development often cover large areas, especially in shore land areas. Each of these activities entails disturbance of land and its dedication to a single use for as long as development and production continue. Such facilities and structures include oil and gas treatment facilities and refineries; crude oil storage tanks; supply and crew boat bases; oil and gas pipeline terminals; temporary support bases for onshore and offshore pipeline installation activities; and use of existing or expanded airports for helicopter support activities (USDOI 1986, IV.A.65).

TAR SANDS

Bituminous oil sands, or tar sands, present a special type of unconventional heavy crude oil so thick it cannot be pumped from wells and requires special upgrading before it can be refined or transported by pipeline. Tar sands are naturally occurring mixtures of sand, clay, water, and a dense, extremely viscous form of petroleum known as bitumen, which has a tar-like appearance, odor, and color. This thick, sticky form of crude oil is so heavy and viscous it will not flow unless heated or diluted with lighter hydrocarbons or chemical solvents, appearing much like cold molasses at room temperature (Government of Alberta 2008b). Although there are large reserves in Utah and small deposits in Alabama, Texas, California, Kentucky, Alaska, and some other states, in 2011 there was no commercial production from tar sands in the United States. In 2008 Canada supplied about 20 percent of U.S. oil consumption, almost half from tar sands (USBLM 2008).

Making liquid fuels from oil sands requires considerable energy for steam injection and upgrading, before refining. This generates two to four times the amount of greenhouse gases per barrel of final product as production of conventional petroleum (Romm 2008, 181–182). Including combustion of the final products, oil sands extraction, upgrade, and use of tar sands emits 10 to 45 percent more greenhouse gases than conventional crude oil (Weber 2009).

Because bitumen flows very slowly, if at all, toward producing wells under normal reservoir conditions, tar sands must be extracted by strip mining or the oil made to flow into wells by in situ techniques, which reduce the viscosity by injecting steam, chemical solvents, or hot air into deposits underground. These processes can use more water and require larger amounts of energy than conventional oil extraction. In the Athabasca tar sands of Alberta, there are very large amounts of bitumen covered by little overburden, making surface mining the most efficient method of extracting it. Overburden consists of water-laden muskeg (peat bog) over clay and sand. Athabasca oil sands are typically forty to sixty meters deep, sitting on top of flat limestone rock, mined with truck and shovel operations using some of the largest power shovels (100 or more tons) and dump trucks (400 tons) in the world. Surface mining with such large equipment has held production costs to around $27 per barrel of synthetic crude oil despite rising energy and labor costs (Canadian Oil Sands Trust 2007). Consequently, surface mining tar sands entails environmental degradation of land similar to that described for coal strip mining in Chapter 2.

After excavation, hot water and caustic soda (NaOH) are added to the sand, and the resulting slurry is piped to an extraction plant where it is agitated and oil skimmed from the top. Bitumen separates from sand and clay, and small air bubbles attach to bitumen droplets. Bitumen froth floats to the top in separation vessels and is further treated to remove residual water and fine solids. Bitumen is much thicker than conventional crude oil, so it must be mixed with lighter petroleum (either liquid or gas) or chemically split before it can be transported by pipeline for upgrading into synthetic crude oil. Extraction plants can recover over 90 percent of the bitumen from the sand. About two tons of oil sands are required to produce one barrel (roughly one-eighth of a ton) of oil. After oil extraction, the spent sand and other materials are usually returned to a mine, which is eventually reclaimed.

Heavy metals such as vanadium, nickel, lead, cobalt, mercury, chromium, cadmium, arsenic, selenium, copper, manganese, iron, and zinc are present in Athabasca oil sands (Kelly et al. 2009). Some but not all are removed during the extraction process, and the remainder must be removed before or during refining. Air monitoring has shown significant increases in violations of hydrogen sulfide (H_2S) standards both in the Fort McMurray area and near oil sands upgraders. Hydrogen sulfide, a significant safety hazard, is a colorless, toxic, flammable gas responsible for the foul odor of rotten eggs. A major hindrance to monitoring produced waters from oil sands has been the lack of identification of individual compounds present in the effluent. Better understanding of the complex mixture of compounds, including naphthenic acids, would make it possible to monitor rivers for leachate and to remove toxic components (Rowland et al. 2011). In 2007 a study of Lake Athabasca, downstream of the oil sands, was initiated due to occurrence of deformities and tumors found in fish caught there (Weber 2010). High deformity rates in fish embryos in the Athabasca River and its tributaries were attributed to aromatic polycyclic compounds, some of which are known carcinogens (Kelly et al. 2009).

In spring 2008, a reported 1,600 waterfowl died in the oily tailings waste of a tar sands mine in Alberta (Dyer and Simieritsch 2010). Tailings ponds now cover fifty square miles and contain 190 billion gallons of toxic liquid by-products from oil sands mining, including acids, ammonia, mercury, and other compounds and trace metals (Nix and Martin 1992) toxic to aquatic organisms and mammals (MacKinnon and Boerger 1986). Woodland caribou herds in Alberta have declined and are now considered non-self-sustaining, partly due to habitat loss from oil sands development (Environment Canada 2008). Researchers project that over the next thirty to fifty years, over 160 million boreal songbirds with be lost due to habitat loss and fragmentation, tailings pond deaths, loss of wetlands, toxin accumulations, and impacts from climate change (Dyer and Simieritsch 2010; Wells et al. 2008).

The Keystone Pipeline System transports synthetic crude oil and diluted bitumen from northeastern Alberta through Montana, South Dakota, Nebraska, Kansas, and Oklahoma to refineries in Illinois, Oklahoma, and the Gulf Coast of Texas. It consists of the Keystone Pipeline, completed in

2011, and the proposed Keystone XL expansion pipeline to be completed in 2013. The Keystone Pipeline is 2,447 miles long, and the Keystone XL expansion pipeline will be 757 miles long (TransCanada Corporation 2008). The diameter of the pipeline is thirty-six inches (TransCanada Corporation 2008), and it will have a minimum ground cover of four feet of earth on top of it (Hovey 2008).

Initial capacity of the Keystone Pipeline was 435,000 barrels per day, which will be increased to 590,000 barrels per day (O'Meara 2010). Keystone XL will add 510,000 barrels per day, increasing the total capacity to 1.1 million barrels per day. Domestic oil will be added to the pipeline at Baker, Montana and Cushing, Oklahoma to help move the bitumen to Port Arthur, Texas (TransCanada Corporation 2008). The original Keystone Pipeline cost US$5.2 billion, with the Keystone XL expansion slated to cost approximately US$7 billion. Upon completion, the Keystone Pipeline System will provide about 5 percent of 2013 U.S. petroleum consumption needs and represent 9 percent of U.S. petroleum imports (McDermott 2010).

The U.S. Fish and Wildlife Service issued a biological opinion saying that the only threatened or endangered species likely to be affected by Keystone XL is the American burying beetle (*Nicrophorus americanus*), known as the ABB. According to the agency, "After reviewing the current status of the ABB, the environmental baseline for the action area, the effects of the proposed action, and the cumulative effects, it is the Service's biological opinion that the proposed project is not likely to jeopardize the continued existence of the ABB. No critical habitat has been designated for this species; therefore, none would be affected." Moreover, "the proposed action would not appreciably reduce the survival and recovery of the ABB because conservation measures included as part of the Keystone XL Project would likely result in a net increase in protected ABB habitat" (USFWS 2011, 64, 67). The logic of these two statements is unclear. If there is no critical habitat designated and it will not be affected, how can that same critical habitat be increased by conservation measures of the project? If one does not know what the baseline is, how can one project an increase?

It is unclear what the composition of the material received from the Keystone XL pipeline will be in Texas. The pipeline environmental impact statement focused on effects of construction of the pipeline, while largely ignoring its contents (USDOS 2011). Refining heavy oils produces particulate matter (soot or fly slag) containing unconverted carbon, fused ash, and fused trace metals, primarily vanadium and nickel. Hydrogen sulfide, ammonia, carbonyl sulfide, hydrogen cyanide, and sulfur may also be produced while refining heavy oil. If this bitumen was refined in Alberta, the toxic waste by-products could be returned to the mine site and buried, but there are no tar sands mine sites for it in East Texas. It is unclear what the benefit is to the United States of refining Canadian bitumen in Texas.

Bitumen cannot be refined in an ordinary refinery, but requires specialized equipment to deal with its special characteristics. Merely refining the bitumen in Texas will substantially increase greenhouse gas emissions and hazardous waste disposal in the United States. Alberta's greenhouse gas emissions are projected to be nearly six times as large in 2050 as they were in 2006, largely due to expected development of oil sands (Government of Alberta 2008a), if Keystone XL is built. One may reasonably wonder why refineries were not proposed to be built in Alberta, alongside required upgrading facilities, so greenhouse gases and hazardous waste from their bitumen are emitted there. Moving refined products by pipeline would be much easier, less expensive, and contribute less degradation of the environment in the United States.

Economist Philip Verleger maintains that construction of the Keystone XL pipeline will increase the dollar costs to American consumers for gasoline and diesel fuel by ten to twenty cents per gallon, totaling almost $5 billion per year beginning in 2012 or 2013. Most of the increase would come in the fourteen-state refining and marketing region of the north central midwestern United States. Food prices will also rise because they reflect farm operating costs for fuel (Verleger 2011). Moreover, a report by the Cornell University Global Labor Institute maintains that TransCanada's claim that the Keystone XL pipeline will create a total of 119,000 jobs (direct, indirect, and induced) is based on a flawed and poorly documented study by the Perryman Group, which wrongly included over $1 billion in spending and over 10,000 person-years of employment for a section of the project in Kansas and Oklahoma that is not part of Keystone XL and has already been built (Cornell University Global Labor Institute 2011, 2). Thus, it appears the environmental and dollar costs of Keystone XL may be much higher, and the employment benefits much lower, than claimed by proponents of the project.

OIL AND NATURAL GAS CONSUMPTION

Seventy-one percent of oil consumption in the United States occurs in transportation, mostly as fuel for cars and trucks where impacts are mostly on local air quality; only about 1 percent is used to generate electricity, usually in emergency diesel generators (USEIA 2011a, Figure 2.0). Thirty percent of natural gas is consumed generating electricity, and only 2 percent is used in transportation, mostly in urban mass transit buses (USEIA 2011a, Figure 2.0). Electricity can be generated using either fuel in combustion turbines, which are designed to start quickly to meet peak demand for electricity. They normally run with natural gas as a fuel, although low-sulfur fuel oil can also be used as needed. Combustion turbines operate like a jet engine: They draw in air at the front of the unit, compress it, mix it with fuel, and ignite it. The hot combustion gases then expand through turbine blades connected to a generator to produce electricity, as illustrated in Figure 4.3.

COSTS OF UTILIZING OIL AND NATURAL GAS

Environmental Costs

Because there are so many different impacts with varying degrees of intensity possible in a given area, this chapter presents only a general discussion of the impacts of oil and gas exploration and development upon the environment. Potential impacts are site-specific and can be determined only by intensive and extensive studies of each site (USFS 1979).

Air quality is affected by all active phases of oil and gas exploration and development. The primary air pollutants come from dust generated from vehicles on roads and around drilling sites and emissions from vehicle and stationary engines used in drilling operations. In the production phase, air pollutants can be produced by separation facilities, burning of unwanted gas, and venting of noxious vapors from storage tanks. Accidental explosions, fires, blowouts, oil spills, and leaks can occur, causing potentially serious air pollution problems.

A serious problem can develop when working with "sour" natural gas. This gas contains hydrogen sulfide, which is highly toxic and flammable. It can represent a deadly hazard to personnel and can form an explosive mixture. In Wyoming, it has resulted in wildlife mortalities (USFS 1979). Sour gas must be "sweetened" (sulfur removed) near producing wells, since long-distance piping is not possible. The process of removing sulfur from gas is complex; plants needed to accomplish this can use up to 1,000 acres of land and cost several hundred million dollars. Plants can require extensive pipeline systems and/or railroads to ship the sulfur. From 500 to 1000 construction workers may be needed initially, and some 50 to 120 employees may be needed for operation and

Figure 4.3   **Combustion Turbine Power Plant**

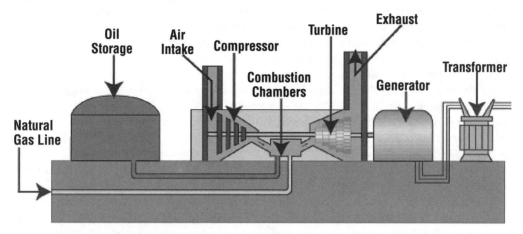

Source: Tennessee Valley Authority 2011.

maintenance of a plant (USDOI 1980). When smaller amounts of sulfur are produced, it may be trucked away or incinerated.

Soil productivity and capability can be adversely impacted. Wherever the earth's surface is disturbed, soil compaction and surface erosion can take place. Mechanized equipment has the greatest effects on compaction and erosion. Thus, any activities requiring equipment are prone to these impacts. Mass movement stability hazards such as potential landslides, avalanches, rockfalls, earthflows, and expansive soil and rock can occur if they are not identified and corrective measures taken. When soil is destroyed, the vegetation dependent upon it is also lost (MDFWP 1983, 14). Vegetation is primarily impacted by construction of roads and facilities. Wildfires, which may occur accidentally during any of the phases of oil and gas exploration and development, may cause destruction of considerable vegetation. After vegetation destruction, erosion may follow and destroy soils and water quality (MDFWP 1983, 14).

Water quality can be adversely affected by sedimentation resulting from erosion where roads and trails cross streams. This is particularly common in the exploration (seismic) phase and when high-grade roads, drill pads, processing facilities, and pipelines are constructed. Stream channels may be scoured if sumps or retention pond walls rupture. Surface water contamination may occur from leaks in mud and evaporation pits, oil spills (both crude and refined), produced water ponds, and well blowouts (MDFWP 1983, 14). Produced water, which ranges from brackish to highly saline, must be treated to meet water quality standards before being discharged into surface waters. Produced waters are often injected into dry holes, depleted wells, or back into the producing formations during secondary recovery. Groundwater contamination may occur from surface leaching, introduction of well fluids into deep groundwater aquifers, or spills from pipelines (USFS 1979). Geological hazards other than those associated with surface soil movement (landslides, mudflows, and avalanches) include subsidence and earthquakes. There is little evidence that oil and gas production can trigger earthquakes (MDFWP 1983, 15). Cultural values, including archeological and historical sites, may be adversely impacted by any surface-disturbing activity. A cultural resource inventory of the entire area that will be disturbed is required by the National Historic Preservation Act of 1966 prior to any ground disturbance that might adversely affect archeological sites on federal lands (MDFWP 1983, 15). Private lands are governed by state historic preservation laws.

When a government agency prepares an environmental impact statement (EIS) pursuant to national or state environmental legislation, it must consult with the appropriate historic preservation officer concerning identification and location of any properties or remains that may be in the area. When any of these properties or remains are located, the EIS must describe a plan for avoidance or mitigation of damage to these properties or remains.

Any of the phases of oil and gas activity can impair various recreational pursuits that are enjoyed on public lands, such as hiking, camping, ski touring, snowmobiling, hunting, fishing, picnicking, pleasure driving, and boating. The development of additional access (roads) into an area can affect recreational pursuits in different ways. More access can change the types of recreational uses available, but additional roads necessitated by oil and gas development are usually closed and reclaimed as soon as possible (MDFWP 1983, 16). The visual quality (aesthetics) of an area is impacted during all phases of activity from the perspective of those who value undisturbed landscapes.

The scope and severity of social and economic impacts as a result of oil and gas development are determined largely by the size of the discovery and the specific location (USFS 1979). The larger the field and the more isolated it is from an existing area of high population density, the more prominent impacts can become. The discovery of a large oil field far from any large towns is likely to place significant burdens on community and county infrastructure, including housing, water supply, sewage treatment, schools, recreational opportunities, roads, and police and fire protection. Social impacts are more difficult to analyze, but there will be a radical change of lifestyles in the impacted area that can be difficult for local people to handle. Adverse impacts such as an increase in violent crime, drug abuse, divorce, and other forms of family and social disruption must be anticipated (MDFWP 1983, 16–17).

Fish and wildlife are impacted by onshore oil and gas exploration and development in ways similar to those described for coal in Chapter 2. Because of the diversity of fish and wildlife species and their unique habitat needs, impacts on these species can be significant and vary immensely, falling within several major categories (USDOI 1981a):

1. Surface disturbance generally reduces the quantity and quality of forage and cover available for fish and wildlife.
2. Short- or long-term displacement of wildlife can occur as a result of disturbance, depending upon the species involved and the magnitude of the impact.
3. Stress to wildlife varies with the season during which an activity occurs and the species involved. In winter and spring, stress on wildlife is most significant.
4. Increased road access can cause increased hunting and fishing pressure. Nonconsumptive recreational use of an area may increase, adding to stress and displacement impacts caused by oil and gas activities.
5. Special management provisions may be necessary to close roads, increasing management costs and enforcement requirements.
6. Noise from many oil and gas activities may displace wildlife species.
7. Direct mortality to wildlife can result from operation of equipment and machinery, but primarily from collisions between vehicles and wildlife.
8. Vegetation removal and soil disturbances along streams for access roads may alter stream flow patterns, raise water temperature, decrease insect production, and increase siltation levels, adversely affecting fish and wildlife in the vicinity.
9. Retention ponds of produced water, drilling muds, and oil products may attract wildlife to their detriment, unless measures are taken to cover them with screens or nets.

In summary, clearing and earth-moving activities associated with construction of well pads and roads, and human activity involved with oil and gas production create the most significant impacts to animals. Many effects upon wildlife are indirect; for example, a loss of vegetation may result in a loss of forage for animals, or a change in water quality may result in a change in fish populations. Other impacts would be direct; continued disturbance could result in complete abandonment of disturbed areas by some wildlife species (MDFWP 1983; USDOI 1981a). Special care must be taken to survey each location to identify any endangered species present, because they may require special treatment to ensure they are not harmed by oil and gas development activities and that any unavoidable impacts are successfully mitigated.

Liquefied Natural Gas

Cooling natural gas to about –260°F at normal pressure results in condensation of the gas into liquid form, known as liquefied natural gas (LNG). LNG is useful for transportation of natural gas, since LNG takes up about one six-hundredth the volume of gaseous natural gas (Natural Gas Supply Association 2010). Oceangoing tankers transport large amounts of LNG from distant natural gas fields. They are equipped with up to five LNG cargo tanks housed inside a double-walled hull. Each cargo tank can store several thousand cubic feet of LNG. These ships are up to 1,000 feet long and, when fully loaded, require a minimum water depth of forty feet, deeper than many U.S. harbors. Docking facilities, which are normally designed to accommodate the sizes of anticipated LNG tankers, may consist of a pier about 1,800 feet long and 30 feet wide with moorings and off-loading facilities (California Energy Commission 2003). Construction of such facilities involves substantial modification of onshore and marine environments.

In most respects, an LNG docking facility would be similar in size to those that currently handle supertankers delivering crude oil to deepwater ports. One difference is that an LNG tanker has a much higher profile (125 feet). Therefore, when considering the placement of docking facilities, facility designers must account for the effect of prevailing winds on the maneuverability of such ships. Despite peak flow rates of about 12,000 cubic meters per hour, unloading times for a full-sized LNG tanker average twelve to fifteen hours. While unloading their cargoes, LNG tankers could be subject to substantial tidal and wave forces that might jeopardize the integrity of the ship-to-shore interface. Consequently, LNG ports and jetties must have built-in safety features to prevent releases of LNG during ship-to-shore transfers (California Energy Commission 2003, 2–3).

A shore-based LNG terminal—consisting of a docking facility, LNG storage tanks, LNG vaporization equipment, and vapor-handling systems—occupies twenty-five to forty acres of land, with associated facilities, such as roads, electric transmission lines, and gas and water lines that would also be needed. These acreages represent considerable loss of habitat for shorebirds and marine mammals. Currently, the United States has LNG receiving and regasification terminals in Massachusetts, Maryland, Georgia, Louisiana, Texas, and Puerto Rico (California Energy Commission 2003).

Such facilities may be operated without incident, but the consequences of a major LNG spill could be catastrophic. When cold LNG comes in contact with warmer air, it becomes a visible vapor cloud. As it warms, the vapor cloud becomes lighter than air and rises. When LNG vapor mixes with air, it is flammable if the mixture contains between 5 and 15 percent natural gas. If there is less than 5 percent natural gas in the air, there is not enough natural gas to burn. If there is more than 15 percent natural gas, there is too much gas in the air and not enough oxygen for it to burn (Natural Gas Supply Association 2010).

When enough LNG is spilled on water at a fast rate, heat is transferred from the water, causing the LNG to instantly convert from its liquid phase to its gaseous phase in a boiling "rapid phase transition." The volume of the LNG instantly expands 600 times, releasing a large amount of energy and resulting in a physical expansion or explosion that can be devastating to any living organisms or buildings nearby (Natural Gas Supply Association 2010), although there is no immediate combustion.

LNG weighs slightly less than half as much as water, so it floats on fresh water or seawater. In shallow-water marine ecosystems such as coastal wetlands and marshes, it would instantly freeze any living organisms present. As the LNG vaporizes, a vapor cloud resembling ground fog will form under relatively calm atmospheric conditions. The vapor cloud is initially heavier than air because it is so cold, but as it absorbs more heat, it becomes lighter than air, rises, and may be dissipated by a breeze. Although an LNG vapor cloud cannot explode in the open atmosphere, exterior portions may ignite if the vapor comes in contact with an ignition source. Otherwise, an LNG vapor cloud may simply dissipate into the atmosphere (California Energy Commission 2003, 2–3).

The extreme cold of LNG can directly cause injury to living organisms or damage to physical structures. Although not poisonous, exposure to the interior of a vapor cloud would cause asphyxiation due to the absence of oxygen. Although momentary skin contact can be harmless, extended contact will cause severe frostbite or freeze burns. On contact with certain metals, such as ship decks, LNG can cause immediate cracking (California Energy Commission 2003, 2–3).

An ignited LNG vapor cloud is very dangerous because of its tremendous radiant heat output. Furthermore, as a vapor cloud continues to burn, the flame may burn back toward an evaporating pool of spilled liquid, ultimately burning quickly evaporating natural gas immediately above the pool, giving the appearance of a "burning pool" or "pool fire." An ignited vapor cloud or a large LNG pool fire can cause extensive damage to life and property (California Energy Commission 2003, 2–3).

Spilled LNG would disperse faster on the ocean than on land, because water spills provide very limited opportunity for containment. Furthermore, LNG vaporizes more quickly on water, because the ocean provides an enormous heat source. For these reasons, most analysts conclude that the risks associated with shipping, loading, and off-loading LNG are much greater than those associated with land-based storage facilities (California Energy Commission 2003, 2–3).

Dollar Costs of Utilizing Oil and Natural Gas

U.S. consumption of oil was about 19.1 million barrels per day and consumption of natural gas was about 23.8 quadrillion cubic feet in 2010 (USEIA 2011c, 2011d). The market cost to consumers for petroleum products in calendar year 2009 was estimated at a bit over $578.5 billion, and a little less than $871 billion in 2008 (USEIA 2011a, Table 3.5). The market cost to consumers for natural gas consumed in calendar year 2009 was estimated at a bit over $159 billion, and a little more than $230 billion in 2008 (USEIA 2011a, Table 3.5). Federal subsidies and tax expenditures for natural gas and petroleum liquids were estimated at a bit over $2.8 billion for FY2010 (USEIA 2011b, xiii), including $654 million for production of electricity (USEIA 2011b, xviii).

The United States relied on imported oil for about 49 percent of its consumption at an estimated cost of about $530.3 billion to the economy in 2010 (calculated from USEIA 2011e), about $9.8 billion of which went to OPEC countries. Imports of crude oil and petroleum products from OPEC countries accounted for about 55.5 percent of all imports in 2010 (calculated from USEIA 2011e). Domestic production of natural gas accounted for 83.7 percent of consumption and the United

States spent about $137.1 billion for natural gas in 2010 (calculated from USEIA 2011d). Oil and natural gas imports came principally from Canada via pipeline in 2010.

National Security Costs of Utilizing Oil and Natural Gas

It has been said that the flow of dollars from the United States to countries such as Saudi Arabia to purchase oil constitutes the largest transfer of wealth from one country to another in the history of the world (Pickens 2008). "Of America's $0.9 trillion oil bill in 2008, $388 billion went abroad. Some of this money paid for state-sponsored violence, weapons of mass destruction, and terrorism. This wealth transfer also worsens U.S. trade deficits, weakens the dollar, and boosts oil prices even higher as sellers try to protect their purchasing power" (Lovins and Rocky Mountain Institute 2011, 3). "It is equivalent to a roughly 2 percent tax on the whole economy, without the revenues" (Goldstein 2010, 73). From 1975 to 2009, oil imports to the United States removed well over $3 trillion of cash out of other expenditures and investments (Greene 2010; Greene and Hopson 2010).

To the extent that such transfers of wealth make investment capital scarcer in the United States and cause interest rates to rise, they slow growth in the U.S. economy and contribute to higher prices, higher unemployment, and increased government expenditures for social services. When petrodollars leave the United States and do not return to purchase goods made in the United States, unemployment stays high and gets higher. Dollars paid by consumers of imported energy resources also may add up to a substantial drain on capital available for investment in the United States. Energy policies that allow such enormous transfers of wealth from the United States to other countries, and their associated domestic impacts, do not advance the national interests of the United States.

Dependence on Foreign Fuel Supplies

Of the nearly 7 billion barrels of oil consumed in the United States in 2009, about 4.3 billion barrels (49 percent) were imported, of which about 1.78 billion barrels came from OPEC countries that do not support U.S. foreign policies concerning Israel and the Middle East (e.g., Saudi Arabia, Iraq, Libya, Nigeria). Some of them are hostile toward the entire U.S. economic system on ideological grounds (e.g., Venezuela) (USEIA 2011a, Table 5.4). These imports cannot be replaced by domestic production or imports from more friendly countries (e.g., Canada) in the near future.

Dependence of the United States on oil imports from hostile nation-states threatened U.S. freedom of action in its foreign affairs during the Arab oil embargo of 1973, when OAPEC countries reduced sales of oil to the United States in retaliation for U.S. support of Israel during and after the war of 1967 (Nersesian 2010, 150–151; Halabi 2009; Geller 1993). This embargo produced a great deal of discussion about the possibility of U.S. military intervention to secure adequate oil supplies, including a conspicuous bit of sword rattling in the form of congressional publication of "plans" for the U.S. invasion of some Middle Eastern countries to seize control of their oil fields (U.S. Congress 1974). Maps and tactics discussed in this publication were crude and insufficient for use in any actual military exercise, but sufficient numbers of the document were produced to make one available to every member of Congress and every foreign embassy in Washington, DC, and the point was well taken by all.

Although the effects of the embargo were relatively short-lived, they did produce significant inconvenience to consumers and disruption of the U.S. economy for several months, rendering U.S. foreign policy makers more sensitive to the views of OAPEC countries than they had been previously and stimulating expansion of strategic oil reserves in the United States (Barton et al. 2004, 153; Davis 1993; Kalt 1981). The exact degree to which U.S. support of Israel has been reduced or has shifted in subsequent years is undetermined, but there has certainly been an increase in concern for the views of OAPEC countries toward U.S. foreign policy in the Middle East.

Concern for Global Climate Change

Combustion of fossil fuels is the greatest source of carbon emissions in the United States, contributing to global climate change; oil combustion contributed the largest share of all sources at 2,551 million metric tons, or 41.7 percent of total emissions of carbon dioxide in 2010. Natural gas utilization was the third greatest source of carbon emissions in the United States, contributing 1,285 million metric tons, or 22.8 percent of the total in 2010. When combined with emissions from coal combustion, the third-greatest source, energy-related carbon emissions from utilization of oil, coal, and natural gas accounted for 99.9 percent of all greenhouse gas emissions in the United States in 2010. Total U.S. carbon emissions from all sources were 5,633 million metric tons in 2010 (USEIA 2011a, Table 11.2).

As discussed in Chapter 1, continued large-scale use of carbon fuels such as oil, natural gas, and coal promises to directly and adversely affect many nation-states, including the Philippines, Indonesia, Bangladesh, Vietnam, China, and Egypt (Henley 2008; O'Carroll 2008; Nicholls et al 2007, 315–356). As many as 200 million climate change refugees could be displaced by 2050 in the South Pacific and Indian Ocean regions (MacFarquhar 2009). The impact on nearby nation-states of an influx of so many refugees seems likely to destabilize some governments in these regions, especially Bangladesh and perhaps Australia (Cart 2009). Actions that affect key allies like Indonesia, Australia, or Egypt, or key rivals such as China, may reasonably be expected to have some impact on U.S. foreign policy. Large-scale reliance on fossil fuels may threaten our freedom of action in foreign affairs and constrain choices in use of energy technologies for domestic purposes.

To the extent that other nations are concerned about or harmed by climate change and perceive such effects to be caused in part by United States consumption of fossil fuels, our relationships with some countries are likely to be damaged by continued utilization of large quantities of oil and natural gas. At the current time, the national security costs of utilizing oil and natural gas resources are considered by the general public and many government decision makers to be low, but they may be expected to increase in the future, as different countries are affected and make their concerns known to the United States through diplomatic channels or in the international arena.

Infrastructure Centralization and Vulnerability to Terrorism

The oil and gas industry infrastructure in the United States is highly centralized in very large facilities in only a few states. Three-fourths of domestic oil production occurs in only four states: Texas, Louisiana, Alaska, and California; over half the refinery capacity is concentrated in three states: Texas, Louisiana, and California (Lovins and Lovins 1982, 109). "A handful of people could shut off three-fourths of the oil and gas supply to the eastern United States in one evening without even leaving Louisiana" (Lovins et al. 2002, 47). Terrorist attacks against such facilities have actually occurred, both in the United States and other countries, causing many millions of dollars in damage, and recent structural changes in the industry have tended to accentuate the vulnerabilities of centralization (Lovins and Lovins 1982, 111).

Figure 4.4 **The Costs of Utilizing Petroleum**

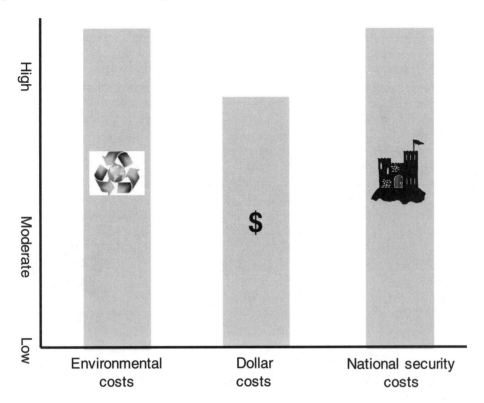

SUMMARY OF COSTS

The costs of utilizing petroleum products are summarized in Figure 4.4. If Americans really understood the extent and severity of the environmental costs associated with development and use of oil and natural gas, it seems unlikely they would willingly continue to rely on these resources so heavily when there are other technologies and fuels available to meet our transportation and heating needs. The environmental costs of petroleum utilization can only be described as "high" because the devastation of petroleum development and utilization continues to be paid in the form of destroyed marine ecosystems and global climate change. Many environmental costs of using petroleum occur in remote areas or in submarine environments, out of sight of the consumer and out of mind, or else in the form of invisible air contaminants that have few obvious impacts, but severe long-term effects on the atmosphere.

Although consumer prices have been artificially suppressed by government subsidies and favorable tax treatment of oil companies, the dollar costs of petroleum use are substantial in terms of transfers of wealth from the U.S. economy to other nation-states. The significance of such transfers for national economies in draining scarce investment capital, increasing interest rates, contributing to higher prices for consumer goods, slowing economic growth, and increasing government expenditures for social services has seldom been examined and is poorly understood. Certainly the dollar costs of petroleum utilization are increasing and will be "moderately high" before adequate substitutes are widely utilized in the transportation sector.

Figure 4.5 **The Costs of Utilizing Natural Gas Technologies**

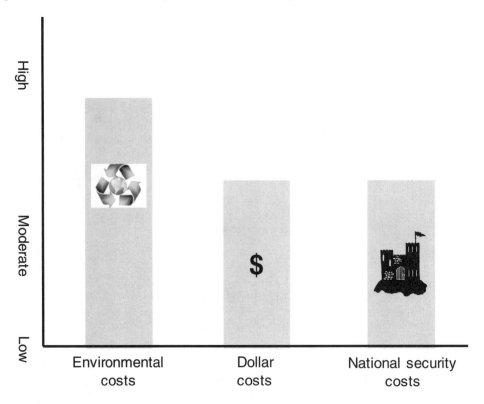

The national security costs of petroleum use are certainly "high" due to dependence of the United States on foreign sources of oil in the hands of nation-states who are not our friends, their supplies' vulnerability to interruption via cartel activity or terrorist action against supply lines, and the effect of global climate change on several friendly and not so friendly nation-states.

The costs of utilizing natural gas are summarized in Figure 4.5. The environmental costs of utilizing natural gas are difficult to separate from the costs of using petroleum because the two resources are so often produced from the same wells; therefore environmental costs of natural gas must also be considered at least "moderately high." Natural gas is a cleaner burning fuel than petroleum due to its generally lower content of contaminants such as sulfur and higher efficiency of combustion, but it does make substantial contributions to global climate change in the form of carbon dioxide emissions. Although not yet widely transported in bulk or used in the United States, the environmental costs of LNG are generally comparable to those for utilizing natural gas, except in the event of a major spill from a transportation or storage facility, where they would be potentially catastrophic. Very low temperatures, very high volumes, and the high combustibility of LNG when accidentally discharged into human or marine environments make it exceedingly dangerous and potentially disastrous in its effects on human population concentrations and marine environments.

The dollar costs of utilizing natural gas are "moderate" due to low transportation costs and plentiful reserves in the United States. Estimates of economically recoverable reserves increased steeply after deregulation of the wellhead price and are expected to continue to rise. Natural gas has been the preferred fuel for new electric power generating plants constructed in the United States for many years and is expected to continue to be so. It is used increasingly in municipal bus and other vehicle fleets nationwide as a cleaner alternative to diesel fuel or gasoline, and its potential for greater use in transportation is great.

The national security costs of utilizing natural gas are "moderate" due to its availability as a domestic resource or one available from neighboring Canada via pipeline. Although supply interruptions by terrorist action are conceivable, none have yet occurred in the United States and would require sophisticated planning and operations to implement. Moreover, it would require considerable coordination of effort to effect a supply interruption of more than local significance, in the absence of LNG supertanker ports.

REFERENCES

American Petroleum Institute (API). 1978. *Primer of Oil and Gas Production*. Dallas: American Petroleum Institute.

Barton, Barry, Catherine Redgwell, Anita Ronne, and Donald N. Zillman. 2004. *Energy Security: Managing Risk in a Dynamic Legal and Regulatory Environment*. Oxford: Oxford University Press.

Briggs, K.T., S.H. Yoshida, and M.E. Gershwin. 1996. "The Influence of Petrochemicals and Stress on the Immune System of Seabirds." *Regulatory Toxicology and Pharmacology* 20: 145–155.

Brooks, J.M, B.B. Bernard, and A.J. Phillips. 1977. "Input of Low-Molecular-Weight Hydrocarbons from Petroleum Operations into the Gulf of Mexico." In *Fate and Effects of Petroleum Hydrocarbons in Marine Ecosystems and Organisms*, ed. D.A. Wolfe, 373–384. New York: Pergamon Press.

Burdeau, Cain. 2010. "Scientists Find Damage to Coral Near BP Well." Associated Press. 6 November. http://phys.org/news/2010-11-scientists-coral-bp.html.

California Energy Commission. 2003. *Liquified Natural Gas in California: History, Risks, and Siting*. Staff White Paper, July. www.energy.ca.gov/reports/2003-07-17_700-03-005.PDF.

Canadian Oil Sands Trust. 2007. "Canadian Oil Sands Provides 2008 Budget." News release, December 14. http://web.archive.org/web/20080216235949/http:/www.cos-trust.com/news/news12140701.aspx.

Capuzzo, J.M. 1987. "Biological Effects of Petroleum Hydrocarbons: Assessments from Experimental Results." In *Long-Term Environmental Effects of Offshore Oil and Gas Development*, ed. Donald F. Boesch and Nancy N. Rabalais, 343–410. London: Elsevier Applied Science.

Capuzzo, J.M., M.N. Moore, and J. Widdows. 1988. "Effects of Toxic Chemicals in the Marine Environment: Predictions of Impacts from Laboratory Studies." *Aquatic Toxicology* 11: 303–311.

Cart, Julie. 2009. "The Writing on the Wall; Drought, Fire, Killer Heat and Suicides—Scientists Say Climate Change Fears Have Become Reality in Australia." *Los Angeles Times*, April 9.

Casselman, Ben. 2009. "Wastewater Disposal Well May Have Caused Texas Earthquakes." *Wall Street Journal*, August 13. http://online.wsj.com/article/SB125020088034530363.html.

Collins, A.G. 1975. *Geochemistry of Oilfield Waters*. New York: Elsevier Scientific.

Cornell University Global Labor Institute. 2011. *Pipe Dreams? Jobs Gained, Jobs Lost by the Construction of Keystone XL*. Ithaca, NY: Cornell University School of Industrial and Labor Relations.

Davis, David H. 1993. *Energy Politics*, 4th ed. New York: St. Martin's Press.

Dean, T.A., J.L. Bodkin, S.C. Jewett, D.H. Monson, and D. Jung. 2000. "Changes in Sea Urchins and Kelp Following a Reduction in Sea Otter Density as a Result of the *Exxon Valdez* Oil Spill." *Marine Ecology Progress Series* 199: 281–291.

Dicks, B.M. 1982. "Monitoring the Biological Effects of North Sea Platforms." *Marine Pollution Bulletin* 13: 221–227.

Duke, N.C., Z.S. Pinzon, and M.C. Prada. 1997. "Large-Scale Damage to Mangrove Forests Following Two Large Oil Spills in Panama." *Biotropica* 29: 2–14.

Dyer, Simon, and Terra Simieritsch. 2010. "Will Oil Trump Nature in Canada?" *Wildlife Professional* 4 (Spring): 58–61.

Elmgren, R., S. Hanson, U. Larson, B. Sundelin, and P.D. Boehm. 1983. "The Tsesis: Acute and Long-term Impact on the Benthos." *Marine Biology* 73: 51–65.

Environment Canada. 2008. *Scientific Review for the Identification of Critical Habitat for Woodland Caribou* (Rangifer tarandus caribou), *Boreal Population, in Canada*. Ottawa: Environment Canada.

Fry, D.M., and L.A. Addiego. 1987. "Homeolytic Anemia Complicates the Cleaning of Oiled Seabirds." *Wildlife Journal* 10: 3–8.

Garrity, S., S. Levings, and K.A. Burns. 1994. "The Galeta Oil Spill I: Long-Term Effect on the Structure of the Mangrove Fringe." *Estuarine Coastal and Shelf Science* 38: 327–348.

Geller, Howard S. 1993. *Twenty Years After the Embargo: U.S. Oil Import Dependence and How It Can Be Reduced*. Washington, DC: American Council for an Energy-Efficient Economy.

Geraci, J.R., and D.J. St. Aubin, eds. 1990. *Sea Mammals and Oil: Confronting the Risks*. San Diego: Academic Press.

Gillis, Justin. 2010. "Giant Plume of Oil Forming under the Gulf." *New York Times*, May 16. www.nytimes. com/2010/05/16/us/16oil.html.

Goldstein, D.B. 2010. *Invisible Energy: Strategies to Rescue the Economy and Save the Planet*. Point Richmond, CA: Bay Tree.

Government of Alberta. 2008a. *Alberta's 2008 Climate Change Strategy*. Alberta: Government of Alberta. www.environment.alberta.ca/1319.html.

———. 2008b. *Alberta's Oil Sands: Opportunity, Balance*. Alberta: Government of Alberta. www. environment.alberta.ca/documents/Oil_Sands_Opportunity_Balance.pdf.

Greene, David L. 2010. "Measuring Energy Security: Can the United States Achieve Oil Independence?" *Energy Policy* 38: 1614–21.

Greene, David L., and Janet Hopson. 2010. *The Costs of Oil Dependence*. Oak Ridge, TN: Oak Ridge National Laboratory.

Halabi, Yakub. 2009. *U.S. Foreign Policy in the Middle East: From Crises to Change*. Farnham, UK: Ashgate.

Henley, Jon. 2008. "The Last Days of Paradise." *Guardian*, November 11. www.guardian.co.uk/ environment/2008/nov/11/climatechange-endangered-habitats-maldives.

Henry, Ray. 2010. "Scientists Up Estimate of Leaking Gulf Oil." Associated Press, July 15. www.msnbc. msn.com/id/37717335/#slice-2.

Hoff, R.Z. 1996. "Responding to Oil Spills in Marshes: The Fine Line Between Help and Hindrance." In *Symposium Proceedings: Gulf of Mexico and Caribbean Oil Spills in Coastal Ecosystems: Assessing Effects, Natural Recovery, and Progress in Remediation Research*, ed. C.E. Proffitt and P.F. Roscigno, 146–161. New Orleans: U.S. Department of the Interior, Minerals Management Service.

Hovey, Art. 2008. "TransCanada Proposes Second Oil Pipeline." *Lincoln Journal-Star*, June 12.

Hsieh, Paul A., and John D. Bredehoeft. 1981. "A Reservoir Analysis of the Denver Earthquakes: A Case of Induced Seismicity." *Journal of Geophysical Research* 86: 903–920.

Jackson, G.F., E. Hume, M.J. Wade, and M. Kirsch. 1981. *Oil Content in Produced Brine on Ten Louisiana Production Platforms*. Cincinnati: Municipal Environmental Research Laboratory.

Joye, Samantha. 2010. "Focusing in on Oil." Gulf Oil Blog, September 6. http://gulfblog.uga.edu/2010/09/ focusing-in-on-oil/.

Kalt, Joseph P. 1981. *The Economics and Politics of Oil Price Regulation: Federal Policy in the Post-Embargo Era*. Cambridge, MA: MIT Press.

Keenan, Chris. 2011. "Fracking Disposal Wells Linked to Earthquakes, Banned in Arkansas." Planetsave, September 16. http://planetsave.com/2011/09/16/fracking-disposal-wells-linked-to-earthquakes-banned-in-arkansas/.

Kelly, E.N., J.W. Short, D.W. Schindler, P.V. Hodson, M. Ma, A.K. Kwan, and B.L. Fortin. 2009. "Oil Sands Development Contributes Polycyclic Aromatic Compounds to the Athabasca River and Its Tributary." *Proceedings of the National Academy of Sciences of the United States of America* 106: 22346–22351.

Kingston, P. 1999. "Recovery of the Marine Environment Following the *Braer* Spill, Shetland." In *Proceedings of the 1999 Oil Spill Conference*, 103–109. Seattle, Washington, March 8–11. Washington, DC: American Petroleum Institute.

Litvak, Anya. 2010. "Marcellus Shale Well Blowout Prompts Second DEP Suspension." *Pittsburgh Business Times*, June 9. www.bizjournals.com/pittsburgh/stories/2010/06/07/daily32.html.

Lovins, Amory B., and L. Hunter Lovins. 1982. *Brittle Power: Energy Strategy for National Security*. Andover, MA: Brick House.

Lovins, Amory B., E. Kyle Datta, Thomas Feiler, Karl R. Rábago, Joel N. Swisher, André Lehmann, and Ken Wicker. 2002. *Small Is Profitable*. Snowmass, CO: Rocky Mountain Institute.

Lovins, Amory L., and Rocky Mountain Institute. 2011. *Reinventing Fire: Bold Business Solutions for the New Energy Era*. White River Junction, VT: Chelsea Green.

Lustgarten, Abraham. 2009. "Water Problems From Drilling Are More Frequent Than PA Officials Said." *ProPublica*, July 31. www.propublica.org/article/water-problems-from-drilling-are-more-frequent-than-officials-said-731.

———. 2011. "Scientific Study Links Flammable Drinking Water to Fracking." *ProPublica*, May 9. www.propublica.org/article/scientific-study-links-flammable-drinking-water-to-fracking.

Lysyj, I. 1982. *Chemical Composition of Produced Water at Some Offshore Oil Platforms*. Cincinnati, OH: Municipal Environmental Research Laboratory.

MacFarquhar, Neil. 2009. "Refugees Join List of Climate-Change Issues." *New York Times*, May 29.

MacKinnon, M.O., and Hans Boerger. 1986. "Description of Two Treatment Methods for Detoxifying Oil Sands Tailings Pond Water." *Water Pollution Research Journal of Canada* 21: 496–512.

Mayer, Fritz. 2010. "Gas Eruption Fallout: Blowout Preventer Fails after Fracking." *River Reporter* (Narrowsburg, NY), June 10–16.

McDermott, Michael. 2010. "Oil Pipeline Work Near Finish." *Augusta Gazette*, September 24.

Menzie, C.A. 1982. "The Environmental Implications of Offshore Oil and Gas Activities." *Environmental Science & Technology* 16: 454A–472A.

Middleditch, B.S. 1981. "Hydrocarbons and Sulfur." In *Environmental Effects of Offshore Oil Production: The Buccaneer Gas and Oil Field Study*, ed. B.S. Middleditch, 15–54. New York: Plenum Press.

———. 1984. *Ecological Effects of Produced Water Discharges from Offshore Oil and Gas Production Platforms*. Final report on API Project No. 248. Washington, DC: American Petroleum Institute.

Mille, G., D. Munoz, F. Jacquot, L. Rivet, and J.-C. Bertrand. 1998. "The Amoco Cadiz Oil Spill: Evolution of Petroleum Hydrocarbons in the Ile Grande Salt Marshes (Brittany) After a 13-Year Period." *Estuarine, Coastal and Shelf Science* 47: 547–559.

Montana Department of Fish, Wildlife and Parks (MDFWP). 1983. *Programmatic Environmental Impact Statement: The Effects of Leasing Department Lands for Oil and Gas Exploration and Development*. Butte: Montana Department of Fish, Wildlife and Parks.

National Research Council (NRC). 1985. *Oil in the Sea: Inputs, Fates, and Effects*. Washington, DC: National Academy Press.

———. 2003. *Oil in the Sea III: Inputs, Fates, and Effects*. Washington, DC: National Academy Press.

Natural Gas Supply Association. 2010. "Liquefied Natural Gas (LNG)." NaturalGas.org. www.naturalgas.org/lng/lng.asp.

Neff, Jerry M., Nancy N. Rabalais, and Donald F. Boesch. 1987. "Offshore Oil and Gas Development Activities Potentially Causing Long-Term Environmental Effects." In *Long-Term Environmental Effects of Offshore Oil and Gas Development*, ed. Donald F. Boesch and Nancy N. Rabalais. New York: Elsevier Applied Science.

Nersesian, Roy L. 2010. *Energy for the 21st Century,* 2d ed. Armonk, NY: M.E. Sharpe.

New York Times. 2011. "Documents: Natural Gas's Toxic Waste." February 26. www.nytimes.com/interactive/2011/02/27/us/natural-gas-documents-1.html#document/p416/a9943.

Nicholls, R.J., P.P. Wong, V.R. Burkett, J.O. Codignotto, J.E. Hay, R.F. McLean, S. Ragoonaden, and C.D. Woodroffe. 2007. "Coastal Systems and Low-Lying Areas. Climate Change 2007: Impacts, Adaptation and Vulnerability." In *Climate Change 2007: Impacts, Adaptation and Vulnerability. Contribution of Working Group II to the Fourth Assessment Report of the Intergovernmental Panel on Climate Change*, ed. M.L. Parry, O.F. Canziani, J.P. Palutikof, P.J. van der Linden, and C.E. Hanson. Cambridge, UK: Cambridge University Press. www.ipcc-wg2.gov/AR4/website/spm.pdf.

Nix, P.G., and R.W. Martin. 1992. "Detoxification and Reclamation of Suncor's Oil Sand Tailings Ponds." *Environmental Toxicology and Water Quality* 7: 171–188. doi: 10.1002/tox.2530070208.

O'Carroll, Eoin. 2008. "Faced with Rising Sea Levels, the Maldives Seek New Homeland." *Christian Science Monitor*, November 11. www.csmonitor.com/Environment/Bright-Green/2008/1111/faced-with-rising-sea-levels-the-maldives-seek-new-homeland.

O'Meara, Dina. 2010. "U.S. Delays Decision on Keystone XL." *Calgary Herald*, July 27. www2.canada.com/calgaryherald/news/calgarybusiness/story.html?id=851d435b-2298-4d14-8814-2b93e17bea14.

Osborn, Stephen G., Avener Vengosh, Nathaniel R. Warner, and Robert B. Jackson. 2011. "Methane Contamination of Drinking Water Accompanying Gas-Well Drilling and Hydraulic Fracturing." *Proceedings of the National Academy of Sciences of the United States of America* 108: 8172–8176.

Peters, E.C., N.J. Gassman, J.C. Firman, R.H. Richmond, and E.A. Power. 1997. "Ecotoxicology of Tropical Marine Ecosystems." *Environmental Toxicology and Chemistry* 16: 12–40.

Pickens, T. Boone. 2008. "America Is Addicted to OPEC Oil." www.pickensplan.com/theplan.

Romm, Joseph J. 2008. *Hell and High Water: The Global Warming Solution*. New York: HarperPerennial.

Rowland, S.J., A.G. Scarlett, D. Jones, C.E. West, and R.A. Frank. 2011. "Diamonds in the Rough: Identification of Individual Naphthenic Acids in Oil Sands Process Water." *Environmental Science & Technology* 45: 3154–3159.

Scanlon, Bill. 1992. "Twenty-Five Years Ago, the Ground Shook Around Denver." *Rocky Mountain News*, November 27.

Sutter, John D. 2010. "Defender of the Deep: The Oil's Not Gone." CNN, August 24. http://articles.cnn.com/2010-08-24/us/samantha.joye.gulf.oil_1_oil-spill-samantha-joye-ecological-disaster?_s=PM:US.

Teal, J.M., and R.W. Howarth. 1984. "Oil Spill Studies: A Review of Ecological Effects." *Environmental Management* 8: 27–44.

Tennessee Valley Authority. 2011. "Combustion Turbine Power Plant." www.tva.gov/power/cumb_turbineart.htm.

TransCanada Corporation. 2008. "TransCanada, ConocoPhillips to Expand Keystone to Gulf Coast." *Downstream Today*, July 16. www.downstreamtoday.com/news/article.aspx?a_id=11890.

Urbina, Ian. 2011. "Chemicals Were Injected into Wells, Report Says." *New York Times*, April 16.

U.S. Bureau of Land Management (USBLM). 2008. "About Tar Sands." Argonne, IL: Argonne National Laboratory. http://ostseis.anl.gov/guide/tarsands/index.cfm.

U.S. Congress, Committee on International Relations, Special Subcommittee on Investigations. 1974. *Oil Fields as Military Objectives*. Report Prepared by the Congressional Research Service, 94th Cong., 1st sess., August 21. Washington, DC: U.S. Government Printing Office.

U.S. Department of the Interior (USDOI). 1980. *Environmental Assessment of the Whitney Canyon and Carter Creek Natural Gas Processing Plants*. Rock Springs, WY: U.S. Department of the Interior, Bureau of Land Management.

———. 1981a. *Oil and Gas Environmental Assessment of BLM Leasing Program, Butte District*. Butte, MT: U.S. Department of the Interior, Bureau of Land Management.

———. 1981b. *Oil and Gas Environmental Assessment of BLM Leasing Program, Lewistown District*. Lewistown, MT: U.S. Department of the Interior, Bureau of Land Management.

———. 1986. *Proposed 5-Year Outer Continental Shelf Oil and Gas Leasing Program, January 1987–December 1991: Draft Environmental Impact Statement*. Washington, DC: U.S. Department of the Interior.

U.S. Department of State (USDOS). 2011. *Final Environmental Impact Statement for the Proposed Keystone XL Project*. Washington, DC: U.S. Government Printing Office.

U.S. Department of Transportation (USDOT). 2011. *National Transportation Statistics*. Washington, DC: U.S. Government Printing Office.

U.S. Energy Information Administration (USEIA). 2007. *Federal Financial Interventions and Subsidies in Energy Markets 2007*. Report No. SR/CNEAF/2008-01, April. Washington, DC: U.S. Government Printing Office.

———. 2010a. "Crude Oil Proved Reserves, Reserves Changes, and Production." Table, December 30. www.eia.gov/dnav/pet/pet_crd_pres_dcu_NUS_a.htm.

———. 2010b. "Natural Gas Reserves Summary as of December 31." Table, December 30. www.eia.gov/dnav/ng/ng_enr_sum_dcu_NUS_a.htm.

———. 2011a. *Annual Energy Review 2010*. Washington, DC: U.S. Government Printing Office.

———. 2011b. *Direct Federal Financial Interventions and Subsidies in Energy Markets 2010*. Washington, DC: U.S. Government Printing Office.

———. 2011c. *International Energy Outlook 2011*. Washington, DC: U.S. Government Printing Office. www.eia.gov/forecasts/ieo/index.cfm.

———. 2011d. "Natural Gas Summary." www.eia.gov/dnav/ng/ng_sum_lsum_dcu_nus_a.htm.

———. 2011e. "Oil: Crude and Petroleum Products Explained. Data and Statistics." July 5. www.eia.gov/energyexplained/index.cfm?page=oil_home#tab2.

U.S. Fish and Wildlife Service (USFWS). 2011. *Biological Opinion on the Effects to Threatened and Endangered Species from the Issuance of a Presidential Permit to TransCanada Keystone Pipeline, LP (Keystone)*. FWS-NE: 2010-377, September 23. Grand Island, NE: U.S. Fish and Wildlife Service.

U.S. Forest Service (USFS). 1979. *Oil and Gas Guide*. Missoula, MT: U.S. Department of Agriculture, Forest Service.

Vandermeulen, J.H., and J.M. Capuzzo. 1983. "Understanding Sublethal Pollutant Effects in the Marine Environment." In *Ocean Waste Management: Policy and Strategies*. Kingston: University of Rhode Island.

Verleger, Philip. 2011. "If Gas Prices Go Up Further, Blame Canada: Pipeline Plan Would Manipulate What Midwest Farmers and Consumers Pay." *Star Tribune* (Minneapolis, MN), March 13.

Weber, Bob. 2009. "Alberta's Oilsands: Well-Managed Necessity or Ecological Disaster?" *Moose Jaw Herald Times*, December 10. www.mjtimes.sk.ca/Canada--World/Business/2009-12-10/article-243834/Albertas-oilsands:-well-managed-necessity-or-ecological-disaster%3F/1.

———. 2010. "Deformed Fish Found in Lake Downstream from Oilsands." *Toronto Star*, September 17. www.thestar.com/news/canada/article/862603--deformed-fish-found-in-lake-downstream-from-oilsands.

Wells, Jeff, Susan Casey-Lefkowitz, Gabriela Chavarria, and Simon Dyer. 2008. *Danger in the Nursery: Impact of Tar Sands Oil Development in Canada's Boreal on Birds*. NRDC Report, December. New York: Natural Resources Defense Council.

White, D.E. 1957. "Magmatic, Connate and Metamorphic Waters." *Bulletin of the Geological Society of America* 68: 1669.

5

Solar

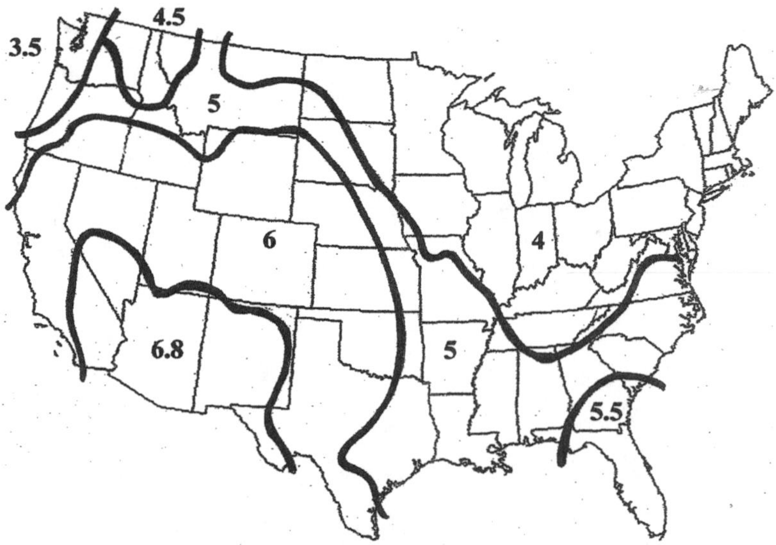

~~~~~~~~~~~~~

Every hour, the sun radiates more energy onto the earth than the entire human population uses in an entire year. The sun shines nearly everywhere in the United States nearly every day, with the exception of Alaska during winter. Solar energy is available everywhere the sun shines, and it can be used to generate both heat and electricity. Every square meter of the earth's surface, when exposed to direct sunlight, receives about 1,000 watts (one kilowatt) of energy from the sun's light. Depending on the angle of sunlight, which changes with the time of day and geographical location, the power of the sun's light will be somewhat more or less than one kilowatt-hour.

On average every square meter exposed to direct sunlight receives about one kilowatt per hour of solar energy. But because during the early and late hours of the day the angle of the sun's light is low, sunlight will provide useful solar energy for only about six or seven hours per day. Thus, a square meter of land in direct sunlight receives about six kilowatt-hours of solar energy per day. Of course, the amount of sunlight that arrives at the earth's surface is variable, depending on location, time of day, time of year, and weather conditions. Consequently, a square meter of land in direct sunlight in the continental United States receives from 3.5 to 6.8 kilowatt-hours of solar energy per day, depending on location. Areas in the southwestern United States receive the most solar radiation, and areas in the northwest and northeast receive the least insolation, as illustrated in Figure 5.1, which shows the approximate daily insolation in kilowatt-hours per square meter falling on a south-facing surface tilted at an angle equal to local latitude, for an average day in the year.

Figure 5.1 **Photovoltaic Solar Resource of the United States**

Source: Zones interpolated from USEIA 2008.
Notes: Numbers apply to areas between the isobars. Average annual kWh/m^3/day.

More than half of the United States receives five kilowatt-hours or more of solar radiation per square meter per day. Alaska receives less solar radiation during a year than Arizona, yet solar hot water heating units are common in northern climes such as Maine and Montana. Although it is intermittent, solar energy can be easily supplemented by thermal energy storage or another energy source, such as natural gas, geothermal heat pumps, wind power, or hydropower, to provide a reliable mix of energy supplies.

Solar energy is utilized in three ways: thermal collectors, solar power plants, and photovoltaic collectors. The first type of technology makes direct use of heat from the sun and the other two involve converting solar energy to electricity.

SOLAR THERMAL TECHNOLOGIES

Thermal energy (heat) from the sun can be collected to heat air or water for use in homes, buildings, industrial processes, and swimming pools, or to directly heat spaces inside homes, greenhouses, and other buildings. Primitive collectors may involve locating loops of a dark-colored garden hose on a roof and allowing gravity to draw heated water down for use in washing dishes, laundry, or people. More sophisticated collectors involve the use of metal cabinets containing surfaces that absorb heat and plumbing that circulates it into a building, often using water or antifreeze as a heat-transfer medium, the flow of which is controlled by computer-assisted valves and storage devices.

Solar space heating systems are often classified as passive or active. In a passive solar building, windows, walls, and floors are designed to collect, store, and distribute solar energy in the form of heat in the winter and reject solar heat in the summer. This is called passive solar design because, unlike active solar heating systems, it does not involve the use of mechanical and electrical devices. Passive solar design can convert into useful heat 65 to 70 percent of the solar energy that strikes a surface. The key to designing a passive solar building is to best take advantage of local climate. Elements to be considered include window placement and glazing type, thermal insulation, thermal mass, and shading. This can be done most easily when designing a new home. However, existing buildings can be adapted or retrofitted to passively collect and store solar heat (Mazria 1979).

Active heating systems require a collector to absorb solar radiation. Fans or pumps are used to circulate heated air or heat-absorbing fluid. Active systems often include some type of energy storage system such as a tank of water or rocks. Active solar thermal collectors use nonconcentrating or concentrating equipment. Flat-plate collectors, the most common type of nonconcentrating collector, are used when temperatures below about 200°F are required. In nonconcentrating collectors, a surface absorbs solar radiation, which is then moved to an area requiring heat. Such collectors are often used for heating buildings and water for washing.

There are many flat-plate collector designs but generally all consist of the following components:

- A flat-plate absorber that intercepts and absorbs solar energy
- A transparent cover(s) that allows solar energy to pass through but reduces heat loss from energy-absorbing surfaces
- A heat-transport medium (air or water) flowing through tubes to remove heat from the absorber
- A heat-insulating backing. (USEIA 2011f)

Often flat-plate collectors are located on roofs of buildings or on the ground, tilted toward the prevailing direction of the sun and fixed in place. Some may be mechanized to follow the path of the sun through the sky.

SOLAR POWER PLANTS

In concentrating collectors, the area intercepting solar radiation is sometimes hundreds of times greater than the absorber area (USEIA 2011f). Solar thermal power plants use the sun's rays to heat a fluid to very high temperatures. The fluid is then circulated through pipes so it can transfer heat to water and produce steam. The steam, in turn, is converted into mechanical energy in a turbine and into electricity by a conventional generator coupled to the turbine.

Solar thermal power generation works essentially the same way as generation from fossil fuels except that instead of steam being produced from combustion of fossil fuels, steam is produced by the heat collected from sunlight. Solar thermal technologies use concentrator systems to achieve high temperatures needed to heat the fluid. The three main types of solar thermal concentrating power systems are parabolic trough, solar dish, and solar power tower.

Parabolic Trough

In the most common type of solar power plant, a parabolic trough collector has a long parabolic-shaped reflector that focuses the sun's rays on a receiver pipe located at the focus of the parabola. The collector tilts with the sun as it moves from east to west during the day to ensure it is continuously focused on the receiver. Because of its parabolic shape, a trough can focus the sun at thirty to 100 times its normal intensity (concentration ratio) on the receiver pipe located along the focal line of the trough, achieving operating temperatures over 750°F (USEIA 2011d).

Many parallel rows of solar parabolic trough collectors are aligned on a north-south horizontal axis in a solar field. A heat transfer fluid is heated as it circulates through the receiver pipes and returns to a series of heat exchangers at a central location. Here, the fluid circulates through pipes so it can transfer heat to water and generate high-pressure, superheated steam. The steam is then fed to a conventional steam turbine and generator to produce electricity. When the hot fluid passes through heat exchangers, it cools down and is then recirculated through the solar field to heat it up again. Parabolic troughs are used in the largest solar power facility in the world, located in the Mojave Desert at Kramer Junction, California. This facility has operated since the 1980s and accounts for most solar electricity produced by the electric utility industry in the United States today (USEIA 2011d).

Solar Dish

A solar dish/engine system uses concentrating solar collectors that track the sun and concentrate solar energy at the focal point of a dish. A solar dish's concentration ratio is much higher than a solar trough's, typically over 2,000, with a working fluid temperature over 1,380°F (USEIA 2011f). Power-generating equipment used with a solar dish can be mounted at the focal point of the dish or, as with the solar trough, energy may be collected from a number of installations and converted to electricity at a central point.

The engine in a solar dish/engine system converts heat to mechanical power by compressing the working fluid when it is cold, heating the compressed working fluid, and then expanding the fluid through a turbine or with a piston to produce work. The engine is coupled to an electric generator to convert mechanical power to electric power (USEIA 2011f).

Solar Power Tower

Concentrating solar power plants generate electricity by using the heat from solar thermal collectors to heat a fluid which produces steam used to power a generator. A solar power tower or central receiver generates electricity from sunlight by focusing concentrated solar energy on a tower-mounted heat exchanger (receiver). This system uses hundreds or thousands of flat sun-tracking mirrors called heliostats to reflect and concentrate the sun's energy onto a central receiver tower. The energy can be concentrated as much as 1,500 times that of the energy coming in from the sun (USEIA 2011f). Power towers must be large to be economical. Though power towers are in the early stages of development compared with parabolic trough technology, a number of test facilities have been constructed around the world. Of thirteen large concentrating solar power generating units operating in the United States at the end of 2008, eleven were in California, one in Arizona, and one in Nevada (USEIA 2011c).

SOLAR PHOTOVOLTAIC TECHNOLOGIES

Photovoltaic (PV) solar cells change sunlight directly into electricity. Individual PV cells are grouped into interconnected panels and arrays of panels that can be used in a wide range of applications, ranging from single small cells that charge calculator and watch batteries, to systems that power single homes, to large power plants covering many acres.

French physicist Edmond Becquerel discovered the process of using sunlight to produce an electric current in a solid material as early as 1839. More than a century later, scientists eventually learned that the photoelectric or photovoltaic effect caused certain materials to convert light energy into electrical energy at the atomic level (USDOE 2011b). The first practical photovoltaic cell was developed in 1954 by Bell Telephone researchers examining the sensitivity of a silicon wafer to sunlight. Beginning in the late 1950s, PV cells were used to power U.S. space satellites. PV cells were next widely used for small consumer electronics like calculators and watches and to provide electricity in remote or "off-grid" locations where there were no electric power lines. More complicated systems provide electricity to pump water, power communications equipment, and provide electricity to homes. Technology advances, government financial incentives, and innovations in financing them have helped to greatly expand PV use since the mid-1990s. Shipments of PV cells and panels by U.S. manufacturers in 2006 were the equivalent of about 337 megawatts, about twenty-five times greater than shipments of about thirteen megawatts in 1989. Since about 2004, most of the PV panels installed in the United States have been in grid-connected systems on homes, buildings, and central-station power facilities. There are now PV products available that can replace conventional roofing materials while generating electricity (USEIA 2011d).

Sunlight is composed of photons, or particles of solar energy. When photons strike a photovoltaic cell, some are absorbed by a semiconductor material, and electrons are dislodged from the material's atoms. Special treatment of the material surface during manufacturing makes the front surface of the cell more receptive to free electrons, so the electrons naturally migrate to the front surface. When the dislodged electrons, each carrying a negative charge, travel toward the front surface of the cell, the resulting imbalance of charge between the cell's front and back surfaces creates a voltage potential like the negative and positive terminals of a battery. When the two surfaces are connected through an external load, such as an appliance, electricity flows (USEIA 2011d).

The photovoltaic cell is the basic building block of a photovoltaic system. Individual cells can vary in size from about 0.5 inches to about 4 inches across. One cell produces one or two watts, not enough power for most applications. To increase power output, cells are electrically connected into a packaged weather-tight module. Multiple modules can be further connected to form an array of one or several thousand modules. The number of modules connected together in an array depends on the amount of power output needed (USEIA 2011d).

Climate conditions (such as clouds or fog) have a significant effect on the amount of solar energy received by a photovoltaic array and, in turn, on its performance. Most modern modules are about 10 percent efficient in converting sunlight to electricity (USEIA 2011d). Recent research by the SunPower Corporation raised this efficiency to above 22 percent in commercial applications (USDOE 2011a).

With photovoltaic cells, conversion from sunlight to electricity is direct, so bulky mechanical generator systems are unnecessary. PV arrays of any size can be installed quickly on any flat or tilted surface. Using the existing interconnected electric transmission and distribution grid system eliminates the need for power storage devices (Oregon Department of Transportation 2008). Photovoltaic cells, like batteries, generate direct current (DC), which is generally used for small loads (electronic equipment). When DC from photovoltaic cells is used for commercial applications or sold to electric utilities for use in the electric grid, it must be converted to alternating current (AC) using inverters, solid-state devices that convert DC power to AC.

COSTS OF USING SOLAR ENERGY

Environmental Costs of Using Solar Energy

The solar technology "fuel cycle" is quite simple, involving acquisition of materials, manufacture and installation of solar collectors and control equipment, operation of this equipment, and disposal or recycling of waste materials from manufacturing processes and decommissioning, as illustrated in Figure 5.2. Manufacturing involves producing industrial-scale semiconductors, and aluminum and sheet metal fabrication of collectors, with installation of plumbing and electrical components, appropriate to the specific technology utilized. Utility-scale solar energy environmental costs include land disturbance and land use impacts, visual impacts, potential impacts on water resources, hazardous materials disposal, and adverse effects on other resources, depending on the solar technology employed.

Land Use Impacts

All commercial-scale solar energy facilities require relatively large areas for solar radiation collection when used to generate electricity. These large arrays of solar collectors may interfere with natural sunlight, rainfall, and drainage, causing a variety of effects on plants and animals. Solar arrays may create avian perching opportunities that could affect both bird and prey populations. Large solar thermal power plants may harm desert ecosystems if not properly managed. Birds and insects can be killed if they fly into a concentrated beam of sunlight, such as that created by a solar power tower (USDOE, USDOI, and ANL 2011).

Land disturbance may also adversely affect archeological resources, and solar facilities may interfere with existing land uses, such as livestock grazing. There are concerns that the large spaces required for solar energy production will result in loss of critical wildlife habitat (Leitner 2009; Tsoutsos, Frantzeskaki, and Gekas 2005). There have been several estimates of the total land area required to meet electricity demand from photovoltaic cells (Love et al. 2003; Turner, 1999). One study asserts that "huge tracts of land would have to be covered with photovoltaic panels and solar heating troughs" and "a direct-current (DC) transmission backbone would also have to be

Figure 5.2 **The Solar Fuel Cycle**

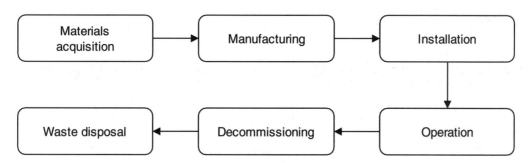

erected to send that energy efficiently across the nation" (Zweibel, Mason, and Fthenakis 2008). Another study suggests it would take about 10 million acres, or only about 0.4 percent of the area of the United States, to supply all of the nation's electricity using photovoltaic collectors (USDOE 2004). However, perhaps due to a bias in favor of utility-scale energy solutions, these studies have not given adequate consideration to the substantial areas of existing underutilized flat or slightly tilted surfaces—building roofs, uncovered parking lots, highway walls, the sides of buildings—on which photovoltaic collectors might be mounted.

Impervious surfaces such as roads, parking lots, and rooftops cover 43,000 square miles of the contiguous United States, according to research published in 2004 in *Eos*, the newsletter of the American Geophysical Union (Frazer 2005). That is an area about the size of Ohio. About one-third of it, 14,333 square miles, is building roofs. Continuing development adds another quarter of a million acres per year (Schueler 2000). Thus, there were nearly 400 billion square feet of underutilized rooftop space already in existence in the United States in 2004 that might be usable for placement of solar photovoltaic or flat-plate thermal collectors. In the United States, one square yard receives on average about five kilowatt-hours of solar energy per day. The average efficiency of commercially available solar photovoltaic panels is about 15 percent (some claim 20 percent), so a square yard of solar photovoltaic cells will produce about 0.75 kilowatt-hours of electric energy per day (AmericanEnergyIndependence.com 2011). Using commercially available solar photovoltaic panels, it is estimated that the underutilized rooftop space already in existence in the United States in 2004 would be capable of generating almost 33.3 billion kilowatt-hours of electric energy per day. That is a little over three times the average amount of electricity consumption per day in the United States in 2010 (calculated from USEIA 2011a, Table 8.9). Thus, if only one-third of the existing underutilized rooftop space was used for photovoltaic collectors, it would be enough to generate all of the electricity consumed in the United States today. These calculations do not take into consideration additional capacity needed to meet demand during peak consumption periods, but they do call into serious question the need to build new electric generating stations of any kind, solar or otherwise, on undeveloped land such as public lands in the desert southwest. Better utilization of existing developed building sites would make such environmentally disruptive construction unnecessary.

Utilizing existing roof space for location of solar facilities would greatly mitigate the potential impacts on existing land uses, archeological resources, wildlife habitat and ecosystems, perhaps reducing the need for changing land uses to zero for photovoltaic collectors and nonconcentrating thermal collectors (U.S. Department of Energy 2004). Solar power towers remain the single solar technology having potential for large-scale land use impacts. Proper site selection can minimize land disturbance and land use impacts (USDOE, USDOI, and ANL 2011). Use of decentralized photovoltaic systems instead of central-station solar power towers would reduce the need for such land disturbance to nothing.

Visual Impacts

Because they are generally large facilities with numerous highly geometric and sometimes highly reflective surfaces, solar energy facilities, which are often located in rural areas, may create visual impacts; however, being visible is not necessarily the same as being intrusive. Aesthetic issues are by their nature highly subjective. Many Americans are increasingly viewing solar photovoltaic panels as attractive symbols of progress and possible independence from foreign sources of energy supplies. Again, proper siting decisions can help avoid negative aesthetic impacts on the landscape (USDOE, USDOI, and ANL 2011).

Water Resources

Parabolic trough and central tower systems typically use conventional steam plants to generate electricity, which commonly consume water for cooling. In arid settings, increased water demand could strain available water resources. If cooling water was contaminated through an accident, pollution of water resources could occur, although the risk may be minimized by sound operating practices (USDOE, USDOI, and ANL 2011). Concentrating solar systems require water for regular cleaning of concentrators and receivers and for cooling the turbine-generator. Using water from underground wells may affect the ecosystem in some arid locations (USEIA 2011e).

Hazardous Waste Disposal

Some solar thermal systems transfer heat by using potentially hazardous fluids that require proper handling and disposal. Some toxic materials and chemicals, such as silicon tetrachloride, and various solvents and alcohols are used in the manufacturing process for photovoltaic cells, but no more (and often less) than are used when manufacturing other energy technologies.

Photovoltaic panels may contain hazardous materials, and although they are sealed under normal operating conditions, there is a potential for environmental contamination if they were damaged or improperly discarded upon decommissioning. An Oregon study on the life cycle of solar panels notes that arsenic, cadmium, and other chemicals are used during construction of photovoltaic panels, requiring environmentally sensitive disposal. However, pollutant and heavy metal emissions associated with solar photovoltaic panels are due primarily to raw material extraction and energy consumption during the manufacturing process (Fthenakis, Kim, and Alsema 2008; Oregon Department of Transportation 2008). Cadmium, which is extremely toxic, is used in very small amounts in cadmium telluride solar cells as a semiconductor to convert solar energy into electricity. Firms that make these solar cells often have recycling programs so unusable cells do not inadvertently damage the surrounding environment (USDOE, USDOI, and ANL 2011).

Concentrating solar power systems may employ liquids such as oils or molten salts that may be hazardous and present spill risks. In addition, various fluids, such as hydraulic fluids, coolants, and lubricants, are commonly used in most industrial facilities. These fluids may in some cases be hazardous and present a spill-related risk. Proper planning and sound maintenance practices can minimize impacts from hazardous materials. As with other industrial applications, waste materials must be disposed of in licensed waste disposal facilities (USDOE, USDOI, and ANL 2011).

Overall, active solar space heating technologies require more use of hazardous materials during manufacture and operation than passive solar technologies; concentrating solar technologies require more use of hazardous materials than nonconcentrating solar technologies; and solar power plants entail more use of hazardous materials than solar photovoltaic technologies. Photovoltaic technologies entail use of hazardous materials only during production of solar cells and arrays, but not during their operation, greatly limiting areas of potential contamination. Thus, the only pollutants associated with the use of solar power are those involved in the construction and transportation of its parts (USDOE, USDOI, and ANL 2011; Tsoutsos, Frantzeskaki, and Gekas 2005).

Other Concerns

Concentrating solar power systems might potentially cause interference with aircraft operations if reflected light beams become misdirected into aircraft pathways. However, this would not occur under normal operating circumstances, would likely be limited to areas near airports, and would be unlikely to interfere with aircraft instrumentation in use today. Operation of solar energy facilities, and especially concentrating solar power facilities, involves high temperatures that may pose an occupational safety risk to employees. Construction and decommissioning of utility-scale solar energy facilities would involve a variety of familiar possible impacts normally encountered during construction and decommissioning of large-scale industrial facilities and are therefore manageable.

Most photovoltaic cells are currently made of silicon, one of the most common minerals found on this planet. Producing the components is extremely easy and does not require mining or drilling in dangerous locales. However, silicon dust is a harmful substance when inhaled, especially over long periods of time. Exposure to this dust in a manufacturing environment can result in a lung disease called silicosis, which causes scar tissue to form in the lungs, reducing the lungs' capacity to process oxygen (USDOE, USDOI, and ANL 2011). Such exposure, therefore, must be controlled during the manufacturing process.

Like all bulk electric power generating facilities, solar power plants produce electric and magnetic fields. Modern solar energy systems use components that radiate high levels of radio-frequency electromagnetic radiation, which may pose health risks to persons with electromagnetic hypersensitivity (EHS). The primary health hazard involved with solar energy generation is that people with EHS may get ill from electromagnetic radiation in very small amounts. Such a health problem may be triggered by small frequencies from cell phones, computers, and other electronic appliances. The production of solar energy may further aggravate this situation for a relatively small portion of the population.

Operation of solar energy technologies produces no air or water pollution and no greenhouse gases. Manufacture of solar energy facilities entails no more, and often less, disposal of solid and hazardous waste materials than construction of any other energy supply technology. The environmental impact from use of photovoltaic electricity is minimal, requiring no water for system cooling and generating no by-products (USEIA 2011e).

Dollar Costs of Utilizing Solar Power

The market cost to consumers for purchase of solar photovoltaic modules in calendar year 2009 was estimated at a bit less than $3.58 billion for almost 1.3 million peak kilowatts (USEIA 2011a, Table 10.8). The value of electricity generated from photovoltaic modules was a little over $80 million in 2009 and about $116 million in 2010 (calculated from USEIA 2011a, Table 8.2c, Table

8.10). Federal subsidies and tax expenditures for solar energy technologies were estimated at $1.1 billion for FY2010, including $968 million for solar electricity production (USEIA 2011b, xviii, xvi).

During the past ten years, the U.S. Department of Energy invested more than $1 billion in pursuit of research and development to advance solar energy technologies and bring down the costs of solar energy systems. Technological innovations have helped to reduce solar energy costs by more than 60 percent since 1995 and are expected to enable large-scale solar energy to achieve cost-competitiveness with fossil-fueled electricity generation by the end of the decade, without any further subsidies. This means DOE expects the installed price of utility-scale solar energy to be reduced to about $1 per watt, or roughly 6 cents per kilowatt-hour, making it cost-competitive with conventional fossil fuel–based electricity sources (USDOE 2011a).

This unfortunate focus on large utility-scale solar energy obscures the fact that solar photovoltaic arrays are cost-competitive for many applications in the marketplace today and have been for some time. With less restrictive assumptions, photovoltaic arrays were cost-competitive for some homeowners in 1981—if the homeowner was in the 50 percent tax bracket, paid $0.12 per kilowatt-hour, received 2,500 kilowatt-hours of insolation annually, obtained a 50 percent tax rebate, and could depend on the utility grid to back up the system (Maycock and Stirewalt 1981, 103).

There is no single figure at which photovoltaics become cost-competitive. Within each class of applications, the tax structure, utility costs, and income of the property owner all collaborate to determine a break-even point for investments (Maycock and Stirewalt 1981, 103). Specific financial returns on photovoltaic systems vary by geographic location and are affected by federal tax credits, state and utility rebates, current and future electric rates, and average solar insolation of a location.

State net-metering laws that require electric utilities to credit homeowners for any excess power they generate from solar technologies on their homes have proven particularly useful in encouraging homeowners to purchase photovoltaic equipment. With net metering, if a solar installation produces more power than necessary for immediate use, the residential electric meter "spins backwards" and excess power is sent into the grid for credit on the next electric bill (SunEdison 2011d). Net metering has made it possible for electric utilities to offer rebate programs encouraging on-site consumers of electricity to install significant renewable energy resources such as solar photovoltaics and wind generators, which have enabled the utility to meet electricity demand without construction of new, environmentally disruptive central-station generating facilities. For example, during 2010, Black Hills Energy, an investor-owned utility, was able to meet its obligations under Colorado law to provide a portion of its energy through on-site solar installations through a standard rebate offer program using net metering (Black Hills Energy 2011, 9). As a result of this longstanding program, Black Hills Energy has been able to meet expanding demand for electricity without construction of new power plants for many years.

Provided a photovoltaic system is installed in an aesthetically pleasing manner, it immediately adds resale value to a home. Panels are typically warranted to produce power for twenty-five years. Some last longer. After installation, the remaining production under warranty may be calculated and multiplied by the current electric rate to determine an accurate dollar value that the system adds to a home. Homes equipped with solar photovoltaics have lower operating costs in the form of monthly electric bills than do comparable nonsolar homes. And with twenty-five years of guaranteed production, a photovoltaic system allows a homeowner to fix the costs for electricity at the cost of installation of the system, providing protection against future electric rate increases. Moreover, a solar photovoltaics system typically provides electric bill savings equal to two to three times the initial price of the system (SunEdison 2011b).

Investments in the stock market or savings accounts are taxable income, but investments in photovoltaics provide savings on electric bills, which are not taxable. Depending on state rebates and local electric rates, the twenty-five-year electric bill savings from an investment in solar photovoltaics typically provides a 10 to 20 percent average annual return on the initial investment. By financing a photovoltaics system in a thirty-year home mortgage or other secured loan, the net loan cost after tax benefits is often equal to or less than the first year's monthly electric bill savings—and the loan is a fixed payment, while electric rates are always increasing (SunEdison 2011b) at the rate of inflation or more.

Solar photovoltaics are cost-competitive with central-station generation of electricity today and are being installed at an increasing rate in the commercial, industrial, and residential sectors. Innovations in the private sector and incentives in government policies are accelerating the adoption of solar technologies. In May 2010, solar project developer SunEdison secured a financing package projected to reach $1.5 billion to install solar power at businesses and utilities. SunEdison and First Reserve, a private equity firm that invests in energy, announced a joint venture to finance, build, and operate solar photovoltaic projects. The deal paves the way for installation of hundreds of megawatts worth of large solar photovoltaic projects in the United States, Italy, Spain, and Canada (LaMonica 2010).

Rather than pay the cost of installation up front, many commercial customers of the joint venture are expected to sign an innovative long-term power purchase agreement (PPA). The solar PPA structure allows SunEdison to maximize use of the federal investment tax credit and other local incentives and participate in the solar renewable energy credit market. Using the PPA as collateral to secure capital on the open market, SunEdison builds, operates, and repairs the systems, and customers just contract to pay their utility bills. Under this arrangement, the customers buy electricity that the solar array produces, but the actual equipment is owned by SunEdison (LaMonica 2010). The customers run no risk for generation or transmission price increases during the entire period of operation, at the end of which electricity prices will certainly be more expensive than they were at the beginning. The customers incur no up-front capital costs and are not responsible for maintenance or operation of the equipment, but reap the benefit of fixed energy costs for a long period, ten to twenty-five years, allowing them to garner favorable media attention for minimizing their carbon footprint.

SunEdison has considerable experience financing and installing solar photovoltaic systems in this manner. North America's largest solar energy services provider, SunEdison provides solar-generated energy at or below current retail utility rates to a diverse client base of commercial, municipal, and utility customers. Founded in 2003 and headquartered in Beltsville, MD, SunEdison has completed solar photovoltaic projects in the United States, Spain, and Italy and has projects under development in Canada, France, and Germany (SunEdison 2008). In North America, SunEdison has installed more than 260 MWe of solar photovoltaic capacity at 450 operational sites since 2003. Familiar organizations that have contracted with SunEdison for services and solar power systems, include Anheuser-Busch, Staples, Kohl's, the City of San Diego, Duke Energy, Progress Energy, Xcel Energy, the U.S. Department of Energy National Renewable Energy Laboratory in Golden, Colorado, the U.S. General Services Administration, the State of California Department of General Services, and Montgomery County Public Schools. SunEdison recently completed a 70 MWe photovoltaic power plant in Rovigo, Italy (SunEdison 2011a, 2011c).

The attractiveness of this business model was evident in November 2009 when SunEdison was acquired by the Monsanto Energy Materials Company (MEMC) for $200 million (MEMC 2011). MEMC has been a pioneer in the design and development of silicon wafer technologies for over fifty years and is a global leader in semiconductor and solar technology, with research, development, and manufacturing facilities in the United States, Europe, and Asia. With acquisition of its SunEdison subsidiary, MEMC is also now a developer of solar power projects and a worldwide leader in solar energy services (MEMC 2011).

Major changes to MEMC's business model were announced with acquisition of SunEdison. MEMC made further inroads into the project arena and leveraged its US$1 billion in cash and short-term investments to fuel demand for its solar wafers. MEMC now participates in the actual development of solar power plants and commercialization of photovoltaic technology, in addition to supplying the solar and semiconductor industries with their traditional silicon wafer products. MEMC expected a significant percentage of projects undertaken by SunEdison in the future to use its wafers (MEMC 2011).

SunEdison's PV project pipeline rose sharply in early 2011, increasing by 32 percent, or 454 MWe, to 1,870 MWe, making it a major player in the PV project development market. MEMC expected SunEdison's PV installations to more than double in 2011, with the United States remaining the largest market (Osborne 2010). Similar expansions were projected by other photovoltaic developers—Sungevity (www.sungevity.com) and SunRun (www.sunrunhome.com).

Mainstream adoption of residential solar photovoltaic technology took another step forward with the announcement that cost estimates for Sungevity photovoltaic installations utilizing the company's Solar Lease arrangement will be available at Lowe's home improvement stores and that Lowe's has taken an equity position in Sungevity. The partnership began in summer 2011 at all Lowe's stores in states where Sungevity provides services, including Arizona, California, Colorado, Delaware, Maryland, Massachusetts, New Jersey, and New York (Kennedy 2011). Another approach to the retail market is being taken by SunPower Corporation, which will offer California purchasers of new Ford Focus electric and electric-hybrid vehicles in 2012 the option of installing a PV solar array at their homes to offset the electricity they use to charge their vehicles (Hull 2011, J10). In this way, SunPower hopes to expand its market share by encouraging purchasers of electric vehicles to add additional solar panels to cover their household energy use.

Meanwhile, Google Inc. has created a $280 million fund to help finance rooftop installations by SolarCity, a solar panel installation company based in San Mateo, California. SolarCity now has fifteen such funds in place, with partners such as Citigroup Inc. and U.S. Bancorp. According to the Solar Energy Industries Association, residential installations nationwide have grown steadily and are expected to keep expanding; by the end of 2010, home solar panels were capable of producing seventy-four megawatts of electricity, or enough to power about 74,000 average California homes. That was up 33 percent from the beginning of the year (Hsu 2011).

In January 2009, Interlock Roofing Ltd., one of North America's leading manufacturers of Energy Star aluminum lifetime metal roofing products, announced the availability of an aluminum roofing product comprised of a thin-film solar laminate integrated onto the surface of their standing seam aluminum roofing panels. No roof penetrations and no additional structural support are required for this roofing system. A person can walk on the laminated panels, and the panel/laminate bond has been proven to withstand wind forces of 160 mph. Moreover, Interlock aluminum roofing is made from recycled and recyclable materials and is therefore an environmentally sustainable roofing choice. These roofing panels, with complete electrical control systems, are available through building contractors throughout North America, with financing provided by Interlock Roofing (Interlock Roofing Ltd. 2009).

Another company finding new financial benefits in utilizing underutilized roof space for photovoltaic systems is Prologis, which provides industrial warehouse and distribution space worldwide. Headquartered in Denver, Prologis owns 475 million square feet of this type of space, making it one of the largest owners of roof space in the world (NREL 2009). The large, flat roofs make them ideal for rooftop photovoltaic (PV) systems, and their locations near major population centers make good host sites from which to generate and sell energy back into the electric grid. The main use for Prologis's industrial space is storage and distribution, so although the buildings are large, their energy consumption is small, since the buildings typically contain merchandise and are not air-conditioned. While it would be possible for Prologis's customers in these distribution centers to use the energy produced, they would not come close to using all of it (NREL 2009).

Prologis partnered with Portland General Electric to install 1.1 megawatts of thin film solar panels on three warehouses in Portland, Oregon. Prologis also worked with Southern California Edison to complete a 2.4-megawatt installation in California. In total, the company currently has ten PV projects completed on three continents, resulting in just over six megawatts of solar power. These ten Prologis PV projects occupy roughly 3 million square feet of roof space (NREL 2005).

Solar photovoltaic systems are increasingly available and are being installed at an increasing rate in the commercial, industrial, and residential sectors today. Solar energy installations grew at a compound annual growth rate in excess of 40 percent during the past decade (MEMC 2011), a rate that is accelerating. This would not be happening if photovoltaics were not cost-competitive with central-station generation of electricity. Previous projections of market penetration (Paidipati et al. 2008) seem pessimistic in light of recent evidence of expanded market penetration and moves by financial institutions to position themselves for market takeoff. The "silent revolution" of rapid photovoltaic market expansion predicted by Paul Maycock and Edward Stirewalt twenty-five years ago (Maycock and Stirewalt 1985) appears to be well under way, although it remains seldom noticed.

National Security Costs of Utilizing Solar Power

Sunlight is ubiquitous in the world. Silicon is commonplace worldwide and can be acquired without dependence on politically unstable areas such as the Middle East. No country or group of countries holds a large enough share of the silicon resource to enable it to control supplies or determine price. Solar energy produces almost no carbon emissions or greenhouse gases, and what little it does produce is generated during the manufacture of solar equipment, not during ongoing operations. Consequently, utilizing solar technologies will not produce climate change or a rise in sea level. Solar technologies do not produce substantial amounts of toxic waste that must be isolated from the human environment for millennia. Solar energy utilization does not produce materials useful to terrorists. Consequently, the national security costs of utilizing solar technologies are nil. As compared to other energy technologies, utilization of solar technologies can be conceptualized as having net national security benefits.

SUMMARY OF COSTS

The costs of utilizing solar technologies are summarized in Figure 5.3. Overall, the environmental costs of producing and using solar technologies are incurred mostly during production of equipment and are "low" compared to the costs of most conventional fuel technologies in use today. The environmental costs of producing electricity from solar thermal concentrating power systems in power plants comprised of parabolic trough, solar dish, and power tower technology are moderately competitive to most conventional fuels in use today, due to the high costs of disruption of relatively large acreages of land that must be dedicated to such facilities.

Figure 5.3 **The Costs of Utilizing Solar Technologies**

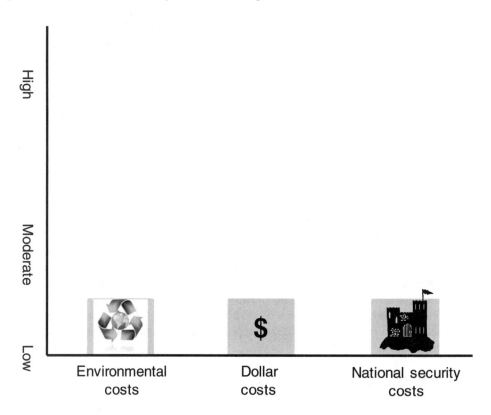

Dollar costs for decentralized application of solar thermal collectors for heating residential, commercial, and industrial hot water and some space heating applications, and for solar photovoltaic collectors generating electricity, are "low" and competitive today with conventional fuels in all but the most northern climates and in instances where collectors might be shaded from the sun. Dollar costs for central-station generation of electricity by solar power plants are generally higher than for decentralized nonconcentrating solar thermal technologies and photovoltaic systems, due to more complex operating systems, although they may be approaching competitiveness with conventional fuels for central-station generation of electricity. National security costs for all solar technologies are very "low" or negligible because the materials for producing them are all available in the United States or from friendly nations. This is a very distinct and significant advantage that solar technologies hold over other energy technologies that may have to be acquired from foreign sources, may contribute to global climate change, or may leave a legacy of long-term waste products attractive to terrorists.

Solar energy technologies do not produce much hazardous waste, and their general lack of moving parts reduces the probability of an environmentally devastating accident to nil. Solar power is also environmentally advantageous because its energy supply will never run out and cannot be controlled by any combination of foreign governments. For the foreseeable future, sunlight will always shine upon this planet, providing energy that solar technologies can exploit. This means that creating the components of solar technology is extremely easy, does not require mining or drilling in a dangerous locale, and can be achieved without involvement of unreliable political allies. The environmental effects of utilizing solar technologies are sometimes subtle but, because fewer resources are expended in the acquisition and utilization of silicon, the overall effect on ecosystems of utilizing solar technologies is less than for other fuel sources.

To capture appreciable amounts of energy, solar photovoltaics require a large number of cells, which can take up a considerable amount of space. A practical solution to this issue is to decentralize their utilization by mounting the cells on existing rooftops, near electricity consumers, thereby reducing the impact of space utilized while still allowing maximum exposure to the sun and minimum electrical transmission distances. Of course, trees and bushes must be set back lest they block sunlight from collectors, but this issue may be dealt with successfully through local zoning ordinances. Of the various solar technologies, solar photovoltaic systems hold the greatest promise for rapid market penetration utilizing recent innovations in financing, installation, and ownership arrangements.

It takes about fourteen years to build a new 1,000 MWe nuclear plant in the United States (Hamilton and Wengert 1980), but SunEdison built 260 MWe of solar photovoltaic generating capacity in eight years (SunEdison 2011c), and Black Hills Energy acquired about 330 MWe of customer-sited solar photovoltaic generating capacity in four years (Black Hills Energy 2010, Exhibits 6 and 7). More than two-thirds of the installed capacity of customer-sited solar photovoltaic capacity acquired by Black Hills Energy was in projects of less than ten kilowatts per project (Black Hills Energy 2010, Exhibits 6 and 7). At these rates, it appears that decentralized solar photovoltaic generating capacity can be installed in a fraction of the time it takes to construct new central-station nuclear capacity. This means that at least 1,140 MWe of decentralized photovoltaic generating capacity (and probably much more) can be installed in the time it takes to construct 1,000 MWe of nuclear generating capacity.

Pursuant to the Energy Policy Act of 2005, each state regulatory authority (e.g., public service commission) and each unregulated electric utility (e.g., municipals and cooperatives) must consider rulemaking for investor-owned utilities providing

> net metering service to any electric consumer that the electric utility serves. For purposes of this paragraph, the term "net metering service" means service to an electric consumer under which electric energy generated by that electric consumer from an eligible on-site generating facility and delivered to the local distribution facilities may be used to offset electric energy provided by the electric utility to the electric consumer during the applicable billing period. (16 U.S.C. 2621[d][11] 2005)

Net metering is offered in forty-three states, Washington, DC, and Puerto Rico (NCSC and IREC 2011). Some state legislatures have been slow to authorize, and some state regulatory authorities slow to implement this mandate, or included regulatory provisions that resulted in higher installation costs and increased the amount of time it took to receive interconnection approval for solar photovoltaic installations (NREL 2009). Investor-owned electric utilities are significantly more inclined to adopt decentralized generation technologies than cooperatives and other types of public utilities (Carley 2009).

State or national legislation requiring effective implementation of net metering would probably do more for American energy independence than policy favoring any particular energy fuel or technology, and at considerably less expense to the taxpayer. Legislation mandating that usable rooftop space of greater than 1,000 square meters atop new buildings must be available for installation of photovoltaic collectors would also be useful in stimulating greater use of this environmentally benign energy technology with its low national security cost.

REFERENCES

AmericanEnergyIndependence.com. 2011. "America's Solar Energy Potential." www.americanenergyindependence.com/solarenergy.aspx.

Black Hills Energy. 2010. *Black Hills Energy 2011 Renewable Energy Compliance Report*. Hearing before the Public Utilities Commission of the State of Colorado, Docket No. 10A-805E. In the Matter of the Application of Black Hills/Colorado Electric Utility Company LP, for an Order Approving Its 2011 Qualifying Retail Utility Compliance Plan. November 5, Denver, CO. Available from Colorado Public Utilities Commission, 1560 Broadway, Suite 250, Denver, CO 80202.

———. 2011. *Black Hills Energy 2010 Renewable Energy Compliance Report*. Before the Public Utilities Commission of the State of Colorado, Docket No. 09A-494E. In the Matter of the Application of Black Hills/Colorado Electric Utility Company LP, for an Order Approving Its 2010 Qualifying Retail Utility Compliance Plan. Attachment A. June 1, Denver, CO. Available from Colorado Public Utilities Commission, 1560 Broadway, Suite 250, Denver, CO 80202.

Carley, S. 2009. "Distributed Generation: An Empirical Analysis of Primary Motivators." *Energy Policy* 37 (May): 1648–1659.

Frazer, Lance. 2005. "Paving Paradise: The Peril of Impervious Surfaces." *Environmental Health Perspectives* 113: A457–A462. www.ncbi.nlm.nih.gov/pmc/articles/PMC1257665/.

Fthenakis, V.M., H.C. Kim, and E.A. Alsema. 2008. "Emissions from Photovoltaic Life Cycles." *Environmental Science & Technology* 42: 2168–2174. http://pbadupws.nrc.gov/docs/ML1036/ML103620062.pdf.

Hamilton, Michael S., and Norman Wengert. 1980. *Environmental, Legal and Political Constraints on Power Plant Siting in the Southwestern United States*. A report to the Los Alamos Scientific Laboratory. Fort Collins, CO: Colorado State University Experiment Station, 1980.

Hsu, Tiffany. 2011. "Google Creates $280-Million Solar Power Fund." *Los Angeles Times*, J11. June 14. www.latimes.com/business/la-fi-google-solar-20110614,0,4289667.story.

Hull, Dana. 2011. "Solar-Panel to Be Offered with Ford Focus Electric." *Maine Sunday Telegram*, August 21.

Interlock Roofing Ltd. 2009. "Interlock Roofing Becomes a Provider of Building Integrated Photovoltaic System." Press release, January 29. http://solar.interlockroofing.com/interlock-roofing-becomes-provider-of-building-integrated-photovoltaic-bipv-system.

Kennedy, Danny. 2011. "Coming Soon to a Lowe's Store Near You: Solar Home Improvement Made Easy, Efficient and Affordable." http://blog.sungevity.com/2011/05/coming-soon-to-a-lowe%E2%80%99s-store-near-you-solar-home-improvement-made-easy-efficient-and-affordable/.

LaMonica, Martin. 2010. "SunEdison Banks Money to Finance Solar Projects." CNET, May 25. http://news.cnet.com/8301-11128_3-20005855-54.html.

Leitner, Philip. 2009. "The Promise and Peril of Solar Power." *Wildlife Professional* 3 (Spring): 48–53.

Love, M., L. Pitt, T. Niet, and G. McLean. 2003. "Utility-Scale Renewable Energy Systems: Spatial and Storage Requirements." Proceedings of the Hydrogen and Fuel Cells 2003 Conference and Trade Show. Vancouver, BC, June 8–11.

Maycock, Paul D., and Edward N. Stirewalt. 1981. *Photovoltaics: Sunlight to Electricity in One Step*. Andover, MA: Brick House.

———. 1985. *A Guide to the Photovoltaic Revolution: Sunlight to Electricity in One Step*. Emmaus, PA: Rodale Press.

Mazria, Edward. 1979. *The Passive Solar Energy Book*. Emmaus, PA: Rodale Press.

Monsanto Electronic Materials Company (MEMC). 2011. "About MEMC." www.memc.com/index.php?view=About-MEMC.

National Renewable Energy Laboratory (NREL). 2005. *Overcoming Net Metering and Interconnection Objections: New Jersey Million Solar Roofs Partnership*. www.nrel.gov/docs/fy05osti/38666.pdf.

———. 2009. "NREL Energy Execs Make an Impact Nationally." Press release, September 4. www.nrel.gov/news/features/feature_detail.cfm/feature_id=1682.

North Carolina Solar Center and the Interstate Renewable Energy Council (NCSC and IREC). 2011. "Rules, Regulations & Policies for Renewable Energy." Table. www.dsireusa.org/summarytables/rrpre.cfm.

Oregon Department of Transportation. 2008. "Life-Cycle Environmental Performance of Silicon Solar Panels." Good Company.com, August. www.oregon.gov/ODOT/HWY/OIPP/docs/solar_panel_lifecycle.pdf?ga=t.

Osborne, Mark. 2009. "MEMC Acquires SunEdison in Bid to Further Build Downstream Solar Business." PV-Tech, October 23. www.pv-tech.org/news/memc_acquires_sunedison_in_bid_to_further_build_ downstream_solar_business.

———. 2010. "MEMC's SunEdison Project Pipeline Stands at 1870MW." PV-Tech, May 5. www.pv-tech. org/news/memcs_sunedison_project_pipeline_stands_at_1870mw.

Paidipati, J., L. Frantzis, H. Sawyer, and A. Kurrasch. 2008. *Rooftop Photovoltaics Market Penetration Scenarios*. Golden, CO: National Renewable Energy Laboratory.

Schueler, Thomas R. 2000. "The Importance of Imperviousness." *Practice of Watershed Protection* 1 (3): 100–111.

SunEdison. 2008. "SunEdison Starts Construction on Photovoltaic Power Plants in Spain." Press release, January 30. www.reuters.com/article/2008/01/30/idUS136656+30-Jan-2008+BW20080130.

———. 2011a. "Case Studies & Customer Testimonials." www.sunedison.com/wps/portal/memc/publicsector/ federalgovt/casestudies/.

———. 2011b. "Economics of Solar Energy Systems." www.sunedison.com/pdf/Solar_Economics.pdf.

———. 2011c. "Our Experience." www.sunedison.com/wps/portal/memc/aboutus/whoweare/ ourexperience.

———. 2011d. "Save Money: SunEdison Brings Solar Benefits to Light." www.sunedison.com/wps/portal/ memc/homeowners/whysolar/benefitsofsolar/!ut/p/b0/04_Sj9CPykssy0xPLMnMz0vMAfGjzOKNDV0N-jIxNDD3cLcIMDDwtPUIMQt2cDYLdjfULsh0VAcYmGbA!/.

Tsoutsos, Theocharis, Niki Frantzeskaki, and Vassilis Gekas. 2005. "Environmental Impacts from the Solar Energy Technologies." *Energy Policy* 33: 289–296.

Turner, J.A. 1999. "A Realizable Renewable Energy Future." *Science* 285: 687.

U.S. Department of Energy (USDOE). 2004. "How Much Land Will PV Need to Supply Our Electricity?" *PV FAQs*, February (revised). www.nrel.gov/docs/fy04osti/35097.pdf.

———. 2011a. "Fact Sheet: Department of Energy Investments in Solar Energy." www.eere.energy.gov/ pdfs/fact_sheet_doe_investments_in_solar.pdf.

———. 2011b. "Photovoltaics." www.eere.energy.gov/basics/renewable_energy/photovoltaics.html.

U.S. Department of Energy, U.S. Department of the Interior, and Argonne National Laboratory (USDOE, USDOI, and ANL). 2011. Solar Energy Development Programmatic EIS. http://solareis.anl.gov/about/ index.cfm.

U.S. Energy Information Administration (USEIA). 2008. "Photovoltaic Solar Resource of the United States." Washington, DC: U.S. Energy Information Administration.www.eia.gov/energyexplained/index. cfm?page=solar_where.

———. 2011a. *Annual Energy Review 2010*. Washington, DC: U.S. Government Printing Office.

———. 2011b. *Direct Federal Financial Interventions and Subsidies in Energy Markets 2010*. Washington, DC: U.S. Government Printing Office.

———. 2011c. "Solar Explained." Washington, DC: U.S. Energy Information Administration. www.eia. gov/energyexplained/index.cfm?page=solar_home.

———. 2011d. "Solar Explained: Photovoltaics and Electricity." Washington, DC: U.S. Energy Information Administration. www.eia.gov/energyexplained/index.cfm?page=solar_photovoltaics.

———. 2011e. "Solar Explained: Solar Energy and the Environment." Washington, DC: U.S. Energy Information Administration. www.eia.gov/energyexplained/index.cfm?page=solar_environment.

———. 2011f. "Solar Explained: Solar Thermal Collectors." Washington, DC: U.S. Energy Information Administration. www.eia.gov/energyexplained/index.cfm?page=solar_thermal_collectors.

Zweibel, Ken, James Mason, and Vasilis Fthenakis. 2008. "A Solar Grand Plan." *Scientific American*, January. www.geni.org/globalenergy/library/technical-articles/generation/solar/scientific-american/a-solar-grand-plan/index.shtml.

6

Wind

~~~~~~~~~~~~~~~

If sunlight falls on nearly every square foot of the earth's surface nearly every day, the same cannot be said of wind blowing everywhere, except perhaps on top of Mount Washington, New Hampshire, home of the horizontal icicle. Wind is common, but more variable than sunlight. Technically, wind is a form of solar energy because it is caused by uneven heating of the atmosphere by the sun, moderated by irregularities of the earth's surface and by rotation of the earth. But the technologies for utilizing wind energy are so different from utilizing other forms of solar energy that wind deserves separate treatment here.

Wind resources in total are adequate to generate electricity for every home and business in the United States, but not all locations are suitable for wind energy development. Areas with annual average wind speeds around 6.5 meters per second and greater at eighty meters in elevation are generally considered to have suitable wind resources for development (AWS Truepower 2011). These areas are mostly in the northern Great Plains, as illustrated in Figure 6.1. Areas unlikely to be developed, such as wilderness areas, parks, urban areas, and water features, were excluded from this assessment.

Figure 6.1 **Wind Resources of the United States**

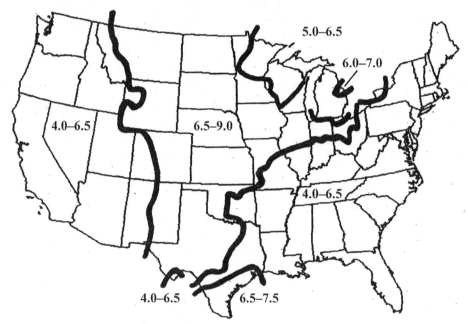

Source: Zones interpolated from USDOE 2011d.
Notes: Numbers apply to areas between the isobars. Average annual m/s at 80 meters elevation.

Figure 6.2   **Offshore and Onshore Wind Energy Potential, by Wind Power Classification**

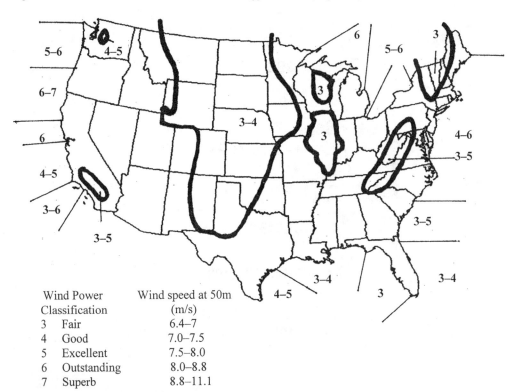

Wind Power Classification	Wind speed at 50m (m/s)
3 Fair	6.4–7
4 Good	7.0–7.5
5 Excellent	7.5–8.0
6 Outstanding	8.0–8.8
7 Superb	8.8–11.1

Source: Zones interpolated from USDOE 2011c.
Notes: Numbers apply to areas between the isobars.

Reducing the elevation to fifty meters, adding offshore areas to the assessment, and applying a technology-based rating system to the data reveals a very different picture of areas economically desirable for wind energy development, as illustrated in Figure 6.2. Using a rating scheme developed by the National Renewable Energy Laboratory, coastal areas near the Great Lakes and offshore of the northern East and West Coasts appear more desirable for wind energy development than most onshore areas in the contiguous United States. One notable exception appears to be a narrow north-south line of small areas rated as "superb" running roughly parallel to the Rocky Mountains from southeastern Wyoming through southern New Mexico. The Aleutian Islands of Alaska, although having "superb" wind resource potential, are located at such great distances from population centers with high electricity demand as to render them undesirable for large-scale energy development. Offshore areas in the Gulf of Mexico appear less desirable for development, about on a par with most onshore areas. Although it is true that winds are generally stronger at higher elevations, due to differences in wind resource potential onshore and offshore taller wind turbines may be more suitable for onshore wind energy development, and shorter turbine towers more suitable for offshore development in the United States.

WIND TECHNOLOGIES

Windmills convert the motion or kinetic energy in wind into mechanical power, which can be used for grinding grain or pumping water, or a generator turbine can convert it into electricity.

Figure 6.3 **Wind Turbine**

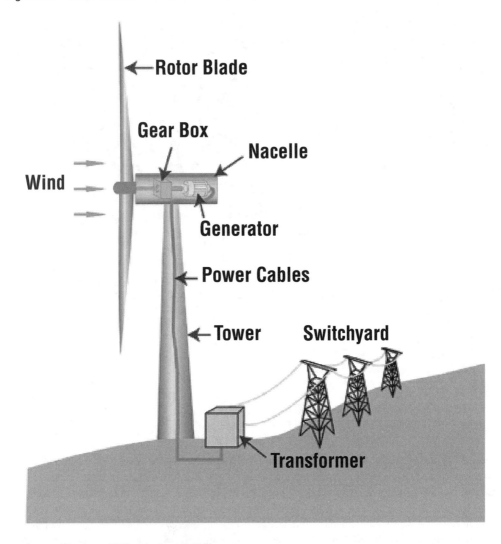

Source: Tennessee Valley Authority 2011.

In turbines, wind is used to turn blades, which rotate a shaft, which connects to a generator and makes electricity, as illustrated in Figure 6.3. Modern wind turbines are based on two basic technologies: the familiar horizontal-axis variety and the less familiar vertical-axis design, like the eggbeater-style Darrieus model, named after its French inventor (USDOE 2011b). Horizontal-axis wind turbines typically have either two or three blades.

Utility-scale turbines range in size from 100 kilowatts to as large as several megawatts. A typical commercial wind turbine may stand 390 feet above ground with blades 130 feet in diameter (Nersesian 2010, 312). Large turbines are often grouped together into "wind farms," which provide bulk power to an interconnected electrical grid. After they are constructed, turbine towers have relatively small footprints, and agricultural activities such as cultivating crops and grazing

Figure 6.4 **The Wind Fuel Cycle**

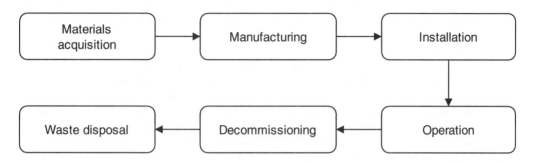

livestock can continue around them, making them attractive as a supplemental land rental income source for some farmers. Single small turbines, less than 100 kilowatts and some with towers of 40 feet or less, are used for individual homes, telecommunications dishes, or pumping water for livestock. Small turbines are sometimes used in connection with diesel generators, batteries, and photovoltaic systems. These hybrid systems are typically used in remote, off-grid locations, where a connection to the utility grid is not available.

COSTS OF UTILIZING WIND POWER

Environmental Costs of Utilizing Wind Power

The wind technology "fuel cycle" is quite simple, involving acquisition of materials, manufacture, installation and operation of wind turbines and control equipment, disposal or recycling of waste materials from manufacturing processes, and decommissioning, as illustrated in Figure 6.4. Manufacturing involves industrial-scale fabrication of turbines, with installation of electrical components depending on the specific technology utilized. Utility-scale wind energy environmental costs include land disturbance and land use impacts, wildlife impacts, offshore impacts, visual impacts, and waste disposal, depending on the wind technology and location employed.

Land Use Impacts

Commercial wind turbines in use today generally have a high profile and are highly visible (Nersesian 2010, 312), as they are elevated hundreds of feet above features of the surrounding terrain. Land disturbance for wind energy development may adversely affect archeological resources, and wind facilities may make existing land uses, such as livestock grazing, more difficult.

Wildlife Impacts

There are concerns that the large spaces required for wind energy production will lead to loss of wildlife habitat. Wind installations may create obstacles to avian movement, as the tips of rotor blades often move at speeds in excess of 200 miles per hour, and birds are not adapted to solid objects moving at such speeds in their environments. A review of existing studies on avian collisions with wind turbines found there is an average of 2.19 bird deaths per turbine per year in the United States for all species, with an annual range of about 10,000 to 40,000 bird deaths per year (Erickson et al. 2001). Areas cleared of trees and brush around the base of wind turbines in the Altamont Pass of California may establish a more open habitat than currently exists that constitutes an "attractive nuisance" for raptors seeking ground-dwelling prey (Smallwood and Thelander 2005).

By far the greatest number of fatalities at onshore wind facilities is songbirds and bats (NWCC 2010). Taller turbines reach higher above the ground than smaller, shorter turbine towers, have much larger rotor sweep areas, and thus further overlap the normal flight heights of nocturnal migrating songbirds and bats (Manville 2009). Larger, taller turbines and their wider and longer blades also produce far greater blade-tip vortices and blade wake turbulence, the potential influence of which on collisions with birds and bats and barotrauma (damage to internal organs from severe changes in air pressure) to bats is uncertain (Manville 2009).

Bats appear to be attracted to wind turbines (Horn, Arnett, and Kunz 2008), but reasons for such attraction are unknown and deserve additional research. Bats are long-lived and have low reproductive rates, making populations susceptible to localized extinction (Barclay and Harder 2003). Bat populations may not be able to withstand the existing rate of wind turbine fatalities (Arnett et al. 2008) or increased fatalities as the wind industry continues to grow. Because North American bat population sizes are poorly known, it is difficult to determine whether bat fatalities at wind facilities represent a significant threat of extinction, although cumulative impacts raise concern and more studies are needed to assess population impacts (Arnett et al. 2008).

The Wildlife Society has noted that fatalities of birds and bats have been reported at wind energy facilities worldwide, but baseline or systematically collected data against which to compare studies of particular sites proposed for development are lacking. Large numbers of raptor kills in California and bat kills in the eastern United States have heightened concern for some species and sites. The Wildlife Society maintains that loss of wildlife habitat due to construction of turbines, access roads, and power transmission networks, the footprint of turbine facilities, and increased human access is an important issue that should be considered in the wind energy development process (Wildlife Society 2008, 1).

Although wind power plants have relatively little impact on the natural environment compared to other conventional power plants, there is increasing concern over noise produced by the rotor blades, aesthetic (visual) impacts, and birds killed by flying into the rotors. On days with a light breeze, a repetitive swoosh, high-pitched whistle, and stroboscopic flicker of light came from 220-foot-tall wind machines located less than 1,500 yards from a home in Maine, stimulating a proposal for a local Dixmont ordinance requiring a one-mile setback from homes (Turkel 2009). Such concerns have stimulated development of new ordinances in hundreds of U.S. communities, often requiring performance bonds and site restoration upon decommissioning and establishing noise standards, setback requirements, and regulation of "shadow flicker," or shadows cast on nearby surfaces by rotating turbine blades (USDOE 2011d).

Offshore Impacts

Similar difficulties attend offshore development of wind resources, where conflicts with commercial fishing interests may influence location decisions so as to avoid entanglements with fishing gear. Since offshore wind installations must be anchored to the seabed, they may create obstacles to migration of marine mammals such as whales. Whether large offshore wind developments that alter the topography of the coastline may have an impact on migration of birds in major flyways is not well understood. Moreover, views of the "open ocean" may not appear so open and natural to boaters and ocean tourists if covered by large numbers of wind turbines, affecting the tourist industry in some areas. According to Christina Jarvis,

> The construction, operation, and decommissioning of offshore wind facilities may have adverse effects on the marine environment and marine wildlife species, increasing habitat fragmentation, sedimentation and turbidity around turbines, levels of underwater noise and vibrations, effects from electromagnetic fields around power cables, navigational hazards, and collisions between birds and turbine blades. Many of the areas proposed for offshore wind development provide habitat for various species of fish, marine mammals, marine turtles, invertebrates, and birds; however, a thorough review of the short-term, long-term, and cumulative impacts of offshore wind facilities on these species has yet to be conducted. (2005, 13–14)

Concern for the lack of data about effects of wind energy development on wildlife is prominent in the few studies that have been published (Lindeboom et al. 2011; Fisher et al. 2010), most of which concern European settings and ecosystems. Some studies that have concluded there are hardly any negative effects on wildlife (Lindeboom et al. 2011) have been based on only a couple of years of observation and were sponsored by proponents of wind energy development. Most important is the lack of baseline data regarding the abundance and distribution of cetacean species in offshore wind development areas (Dolman, Simmonds, and Keith 2003). Lack of experience with offshore wind energy development in U.S. waters makes it impossible to project with precision the likely impacts on North American ecosystems and species, especially whales.

Activities with short-term impacts on marine wildlife, such as those occurring during construction and decommissioning of offshore wind development, include seismic exploration, drilling and dredging operations, increased vessel traffic, and cable-laying activities. Activities with long-term impacts on marine wildlife, such as those occurring during operation of a wind farm, include the physical presence of the structures themselves, noise and vibrations from continuous operation of turbines, generation of electromagnetic fields from cables, and increased vessel traffic (Dolman, Simmonds, and Keith 2003).

According to one study, the risk of avian collisions with turbines is greater at offshore wind farms than land-based wind developments. Birds may be affected by offshore wind development through collisions with turbines, short-term habitat loss during construction activities, long-term habitat loss during maintenance activities, and turbines acting as barriers to flight and to ecological sites such as roosting and feeding grounds. Habitat disturbance and barrier effects of turbines have been identified as the impacts with the greatest potential for conflict with birds (Exo, Hüppop, and Garthe 2003).

Visual Impacts

Utility-scale wind energy facilities require relatively large areas for wind turbines when used to generate electricity on a commercial scale, and large numbers of wind turbines may interfere with aesthetic values associated with the natural terrain. One of the more controversial issues surrounding development of offshore wind facilities is the aesthetic effect of wind turbines on the horizon, as well as on the local communities and residents for whom the facilities will be visible (Jarvis 2005, 13). Many individuals find the aesthetic qualities of wind turbines less attractive than the natural ridgelines and open expanses of ocean horizon on which they are generally located to secure a viable wind energy resource. Although the high-voltage transmission tower was often viewed as the symbol of progress and rural electrification by nearby residents in the 1940s, the wind turbine tower has not acquired a similar cachet in the twenty-first century: rather, it is often viewed by nearby residents as a negative symbol of rural industrialization and degradation, emblematic of continuing loss of pleasant natural surroundings where people can work and play. Wind turbines on towers at elevations of fifty to eighty meters to utilize the most favorable wind resources are visible for great distances and have generally not been made to blend in with their natural surroundings. They may be more attractive to those who receive land rents for their location and operation than they are to nearby residents or others who do not participate in such benefits or who depend on nature-oriented tourism for their livelihoods.

Waste Disposal

Pollutant emissions associated with wind energy are due primarily to raw material extraction and energy consumption during the turbine manufacturing process. As with other industrial applications, waste materials must be disposed of in licensed waste disposal facilities. Thus, the only pollutants associated with use of wind energy are those involved in construction and transportation of its parts.

Dollar Costs of Utilizing Wind Power

The market cost to consumers for wind energy in calendar year 2009 was estimated at almost $6.6 billion, and almost $8.5 billion in 2010 (calculated from USEIA 2011a, Table 8.2c, Table 8.10). Federal subsidies and tax expenditures for wind energy were estimated at almost $5 billion for FY2010 (USEIA 2011b, xviii), all of it for generating electricity.

Wind energy from onshore generators is one of the lowest-priced renewable energy technologies available today, costing between four and six cents per kilowatt-hour, depending upon the wind resource and project financing of a particular project (USDOE 2011b). This is comparable to and in some cases lower than the cost of electricity from conventional technologies (Armaroli and Balzani 2011, 242). Costs would be higher in the absence of government and utility incentives paid for its development. But according to the International Energy Agency, fossil-fuel government subsidies worldwide totaled $312 billion in 2009 compared to only $57 billion for renewables (IEA 2010). Even though the cost of wind power has decreased dramatically in the past ten years, the technology requires a higher initial capital investment than fossil-fueled generators, making it less attractive to some investors. Offshore wind costs have been estimated at $1.95 million/MWe to $2.86 million/MWe, and generating costs range from $80/MWh to $150/MWh. Some developers have released project costs that are much higher: for example, NRG BlueWater Wind estimates that its 450-MWe project off the coast of Delaware will cost approximately $3.5 million/MWe, while FPL Energy's 144-MWe project with Long Island Power Authority is estimated to cost about $5.6 million/MWe (Fisher et al. 2010, note 138). Moreover, because wind resources are available only about 20 to 25 percent of the time (Nersesian 2010, 310), more backup capacity is required for wind power generators than for some other technologies, increasing overall land disturbance and the total dollar costs of using wind substantially.

Energy Management Inc. (EMI), the developer of Cape Wind, is a Massachusetts-based independent power producer with a thirty-year history of engineering, developing, and constructing energy projects. Cape Wind is a proposal to build America's first offshore wind farm on Horseshoe Shoal near the center of Nantucket Sound, about five to six miles off the coast of Cape Cod. Its 130 wind turbines to harness the wind will produce 454 MWe of electricity, with average expected production of about 170 megawatts. The towers, from the surface of the water to the center of the blades, will be 258 feet tall, and the highest blade tip will be 440 feet above the surface of the water, visible for up to twenty-six miles. The base of the wind turbine towers will be sixteen feet in diameter, with a single pole driven eighty feet into the sandy bottom. Estimated capital costs for the project were about $700 million, or about $1.7 million per MWe of gross generating capacity (Energy Management Inc. 2011), but have already increased to over $2.6 billion. Of this amount, it is estimated that federal and state governments will pay about $241 million in subsidies (Kennedy 2005).

Electric utility managers are not enthusiastic about either the cost or the reliability of offshore wind developments, as is evident in the reluctance of NStar, the second-largest utility in Massachusetts, to commit to purchasing electric power from Cape Wind (Associated Press 2011; Kennedy 2011). Even projecting an overly optimistic capacity factor of 37 percent availability, this reflects the low reliability and high cost of electric power from offshore wind projects like Cape Wind, estimated at twenty-four cents per kilowatt-hour (kWh) over fifteen years—about twice the cost of onshore wind power and considerably more than most conventional alternatives (Associated Press 2011).

Wind turbines can be built on farms or ranches, thus benefiting the economy in rural areas, where most of the best onshore wind sites are found. Farmers and ranchers can continue to work their land because wind turbines use only a fraction of the land. Wind power plant owners make rent payments to farmers or ranchers for the use of their land. Good wind sites are often located in remote locations, far from cities where electricity is needed. Transmission lines must be built to bring electricity from the wind farm to the city, adding dollar costs.

The U.S. Department of Energy in 2008 examined the technical feasibility of using wind energy to generate 20 percent of the nation's electricity demand by 2030. The agency examined the costs, major impacts, and challenges associated with producing 300 gigawatts (GW) of wind-generating capacity by that year (USDOE 2008). About 70.8 billion kWh was actually generated by wind in the United States in 2009 (USEIA 2011a, Table 8.2c), or about 1.9 percent of net electricity generation, from about 33.5 GW or 3.4 percent of net summer electrical generating capacity (USEIA 2011a, Table 8.11c), so this would entail a nearly ninefold increase in generating capacity in twenty-two years. DOE concluded that generating 20 percent of the nation's electricity with wind will require building a greatly enhanced transmission infrastructure, streamlined siting and permitting regimes, improved reliability and operability of wind systems, and increased U.S. wind manufacturing capacity. This would entail increasing the number of turbine installations from about 2,000 per year in 2006 to almost 7,000 per year in 2017, requiring a very dramatic increase in the wind turbine manufacturing industry in a relatively short period of time. It would also entail resolving transmission challenges, such as controversial corridor site selection issues and allocation of the costs of new transmission lines, in order to access the best wind resources. Under current deregulation policy concerning production of bulk electric power, utilities have few incentives to make large investments in the expensive, new extra-high-voltage transmission facilities needed for efficient use of wind resources. The DOE report did not provide specifics on how these ambitious and costly goals might be accomplished. Additional discussion of the costs of electricity technologies may be found in Chapter 13 below.

No commercial wind turbines have yet been constructed offshore in U.S. waters, and this lack of experience is viewed as driving up the costs of financing them to the point where finance charges account for roughly half the estimated costs of offshore wind energy (USDOE 2011a, iii). The U.S. Department of Energy in 2011 articulated a goal of deploying fifty-four GW of offshore wind generating capacity by 2030 at a cost of seven cents per kilowatt-hour, with an interim goal of ten GW of capacity deployed by 2020 at a cost of ten cents per kilowatt-hour (USDOE 2011a, iii).

Because of variance in wind speeds, and allowing for maintenance downtime, the average actual output of a commercial wind turbine is only 25 to 40 percent of its rated output (Nersesian 2010, 310). Consequently, 20 to 25 percent may be the maximum contribution wind energy can make to a country's energy demand, considering its low reliability (Nersesian 2010, 307). Relying on a higher percentage of electricity production from wind generators would create an unreliable electrical system.

National Security Costs of Utilizing Wind Power

Wind is a domestic resource. No country or group of countries is able to control supplies or determine price for fuel or materials to construct wind facilities. Wind energy produces no carbon emissions or greenhouse gases other than what is created during the manufacture of wind turbines. Consequently, utilizing wind technologies will not contribute much to climate change or sea level rise. Wind technologies do not produce toxic waste that must be isolated from the human environment for millennia, or other materials useful to terrorists. Consequently, the national security costs of utilizing wind technologies are negligible. Like solar energy, utilization of wind technologies can be conceptualized as having net national security benefits.

SUMMARY OF COSTS

The costs of utilizing wind technologies are summarized in Figure 6.5. Wind energy does not pollute the air like power plants that rely on combustion of fossil fuels such as coal or natural gas, and it will not produce atmospheric emissions that cause acid rain or greenhouse gases. These are substantial environmental benefits of wind energy that are not attendant on use of fossil fuel, and they make wind attractive to a significant part of the domestic population. The environmental costs of producing and using wind technologies are incurred mostly during equipment production, except land use costs of siting and operating wind installations in or near residential areas and the deadly impact of turbine location and operations on wildlife. Lack of public acceptance of the less desirable aspects of living in proximity to large wind turbines has stimulated opposition to wind energy development proposals and changes in local zoning ordinances in many areas of the United States, such that the environmental costs of utilizing wind energy must be considered "moderate" compared to most conventional fuel technologies in use today. The environmental costs for producing electricity from onshore wind power systems are moderately competitive with most conventional fuels in use today, due to the disruption of relatively large acreages of land that are often dedicated to such facilities. The data are not adequate as yet to conclude that the environmental costs of offshore wind power generation are less disruptive to wildlife or aesthetic values than they are onshore.

Dollar costs for decentralized application of onshore wind technologies generating electricity are "moderately high," although nearly competitive today with some conventional fuels in the Great Plains states and some other localities having strong winds, provided subsidies are available from government agencies. Dollar costs for offshore wind generation run to the high end of the "moderate" scale, with lack of experience inflating these costs. Dollar costs for large-scale central-station generation of electricity by wind power plants are generally higher than for smaller decentralized technologies, due to the variability of wind resources and the need for backup capacity. National security costs for wind technologies are very "low" or negligible because the materials for producing them are available in the United States or from friendly nations. This is a very distinct and significant advantage wind technologies hold over other energy technologies

Figure 6.5   **The Costs of Utilizing Wind Technologies**

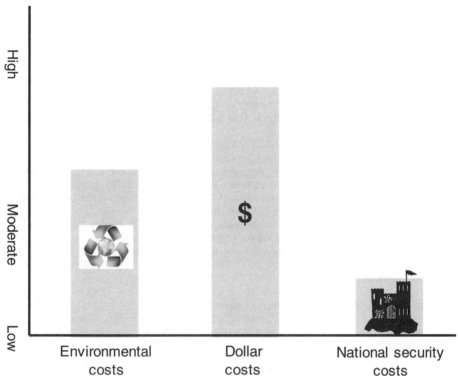

that may have to be acquired from foreign sources, may contribute to global climate change, or may leave a legacy of long-term waste products that are attractive to terrorists.

REFERENCES

Armaroli, Nicola, and Vincenzo Balzani. 2011. *Energy for a Sustainable World*. Weinheim, Germany: Wiley-VCH Verlag.

Arnett, E.B., W.K. Brown, W.P. Erickson, J.K. Fiedler, B.I. Hamilton, T.H. Henry, A. Jain, G.D. Johnson, J. Kerns, R.R. Koford, C.P. Nicholson, T.J. O'Connell, M.D. Piorkowski, and R.D. Tankersly Jr. 2008. "Patterns of Bat Fatalities at Wind Energy Facilities in North America." *Journal of Wildlife Management* 72: 61–78.

Associated Press. 2011. "Utility Is Wild Card in Cape Wind Deal." *Portland Press Herald*, September 26.

AWS Truepower. 2011. "Wind Powering America." Map. www.windpoweringamerica.gov/pdfs/wind_maps/us_windmap_80meters.pdf.

Barclay, R.M.R., and L.M. Harder. 2003. "Life Histories of Bats: Life in the Slow Lane." In *Bat Ecology*, ed. T.H. Kunz and M.B. Fenton. Chicago: University of Chicago Press.

Dolman, S.J., M.P. Simmonds, and S. Keith. 2003. *Marine Wind Farms and Cetaceans*. Cambridge, UK: International Whaling Commission.

Energy Management Inc. 2011. "Project at a Glance." Cape Wind.org. www.capewind.org/article24.htm.

Erickson, Wallace P., Gregory D. Johnson, M. Dale Strickland, David P. Young Jr., Karyn J. Sernka, and Rhett E. Good. 2001. *Avian Collisions with Wind Turbines: A Summary of Existing Studies and Comparisons to Other Sources of Avian Collision Mortality in the United States*. Washington, DC: National Wind Coordinating Committee.

Exo, Klaus-Michael, Ommo Hüppop, and Stefan Garthe. 2003. "Birds and Offshore Wind Farms: A Hot Topic in Marine Ecology." *Wader Study Group Bulletin* 100: 50–53.

Fisher, Curtis, Suraj Patel, Catherine Bowes, and Justin Allegro. 2010. *Offshore Wind in the Atlantic.* Washington, DC: National Wildlife Federation. www.nwf.org/~/media/PDFs/Global-Warming/Reports/NWF-Offshore-Wind-in-the-Atlantic.ashx.

Horn, J.W., E.B. Arnett, and T.H. Kunz. 2008. "Behavioral Responses of Bats to Operating Wind Turbines." *Journal of Wildlife Management* 72: 123–132.

International Energy Agency (IEA). 2010. *"World Energy Outlook 2010* Factsheet." World Energy Outlook 2010. www.iea.org/weo/docs/weo2010/factsheets.pdf.

Jarvis, Christina M. 2005. *An Evaluation of the Wildlife Impacts of Offshore Wind Development Relative to Fossil Fuel Power Production.* Master's thesis, University of Delaware. www.ceoe.udel.edu/windpower/docs/jarvis_thesis05.pdf.

Kennedy, Robert F., Jr. 2005. "An Ill Wind off Cape Cod." *New York Times,* December 16.

———. 2011. "Nantucket's Wind Power Rip-off." *Wall Street Journal,* July 18.

Lindeboom, H.J., H.J. Kouwenhoven, M.J.N. Bergman, S. Bouma, S. Brasseur, R. Daan, R.C. Fijn, D. de Haan, S. Dirksen, R. van Hal, R. Hille Ris Lambers, R. ter Hofstede, K.L. Krijgsveld, M. Leopold, and M. Scheidat. 2011. "Short-Term Ecological Effects of an Offshore Wind Farm in the Dutch Coastal Zone: A Compilation." *Environmental Research Letters* 6 (July–September).

Manville, A.M., II. 2009. "Towers, Turbines, Power Lines, and Buildings: Steps Being Taken by the U.S. Fish and Wildlife Service to Avoid or Minimize Take of Migratory Birds at These Structures." In *Tundra to Tropics: Connecting Habitats and People. Proceedings of the 4th International Partners in Flight Conference,* ed. T.D. Rich, C. Arizmendi, D. Demarest, and C. Thompson. February 13–16, 2008, McAllen, Texas.

National Wind Coordinating Collaborative (NWCC). 2010. "Wind Turbine Interactions with Birds, Bats, and Their Habitats: A Summary of Research Results and Priority Questions." Fact sheet, Spring. www1.eere.energy.gov/wind/pdfs/birds_and_bats_fact_sheet.pdf.

Nersesian, Roy L. 2010. *Energy for the 21st Century,* 2nd ed. Armonk, NY: M.E. Sharpe.

Smallwood, K.S., and C.G. Thelander. 2005. *Bird Mortality at the Altamont Pass Wind Resource Area: March 1998–September 2001.* Golden, CO: National Renewable Energy Laboratory.

Tennessee Valley Authority. 2011. "Wind Turbine Energy." www.tva.gov/greenpowerswitch/wind.htm.

Turkel, Tux. 2009. "Vote May Herald Wind Backlash." *Maine Sunday Telegram,* November 29.

U.S. Department of Energy (USDOE). 2008. *20% Wind Energy by 2030: Increasing Wind Energy's Contribution to U.S. Electricity Supply.* Washington, DC: U.S. Government Printing Office.

———. 2011a. *A National Offshore Wind Strategy.* Washington, DC: U.S. Government Printing Office.

———. 2011b. "How Wind Turbines Work." www1.eere.energy.gov/wind/wind_how.html.

———. 2011c. "Wind Energy Resource Potential." www1.eere.energy.gov/wind/wind_potential.html.

———. 2011d. "Wind Turbine Ordinances." www.windpoweringamerica.gov/policy/ordinances.asp.

U.S. Energy Information Administration (USEIA). 2011a. *Annual Energy Review 2010.* Washington, DC: U.S. Government Printing Office.

———. 2011b. *Direct Federal Financial Interventions and Subsidies in Energy Markets 2010.* Washington, DC: U.S. Government Printing Office.

Wildlife Society. 2008. *Impacts of Wind Energy Development on Wildlife and Wildlife Habitat.* Final Position Statement, March. Bethesda, MD: The Wildlife Society.

7

Geothermal

～～～～～～～～～～～～

Geothermal energy is heat from inside the earth. It is accessed by drilling water or steam wells in a process similar to drilling for oil or natural gas. Geothermal energy is an enormous, underused heat and power resource that emits little or no greenhouse gases, has average system availability of 95 percent, and is a wholly domestic resource.

Geothermal resources range from shallow ground to hot water and rock several miles below the earth's surface and even farther down to extremely hot molten rock called magma. Wells a mile or more deep can be drilled into underground reservoirs to tap steam and very hot water, which can be brought to the surface for use in a variety of applications, but there are currently no commercial applications of magma heat (USDOE 2011).

Where available, hot water near the earth's surface can be piped directly into facilities and used to heat buildings, grow plants in greenhouses, dehydrate onions and garlic, heat water for fish farming, and pasteurize milk (Lienau and Lunis 1991). Some cities pipe hot water under roads and sidewalks to melt snow. District heating applications use networks of piped hot water to heat buildings in entire communities (USDOE 2011).

GEOTHERMAL HEAT PUMPS

The most promising and widespread applications of geothermal energy in the United States involve heat pumps using shallow ground energy to heat and cool buildings. Almost everywhere, the upper ten feet of the earth's surface maintains a nearly constant temperature between 50 and 60°F (10 and 16°C). A geothermal heat pump system consists of a loop of pipes buried in shallow ground or wells drilled near a building; a heat exchanger; and additional pipes for transferring heat into buildings. In winter, heat from the relatively warmer ground goes through a heat exchanger into the house. In summer, hot air from the house is pulled through the heat exchanger into relatively cooler ground. Heat removed during the summer can also be used to heat domestic water. There is a bright future for direct use of geothermal heat pumps in heating and cooling homes and businesses in any location (UCS 2009).

Underground piping loops are made of durable material that allows heat to pass through efficiently. This is important so the pipe does not retard exchange of heat between the earth and fluid in the loop. Loop manufacturers typically use high-density polyethylene, a tough plastic, and some offer up to fifty-year warranties. When installers connect sections of pipe, they heat-fuse the joints, making them stronger than the pipe itself. Fluid in the loop is water or an environmentally safe antifreeze solution that circulates through the pipes in a closed system. The length of a ground loop depends on a number of factors, including the type of loop configuration used, a home's heating and cooling load, soil conditions, local climate, and landscaping. Large homes with large space conditioning requirements generally need larger loops than smaller homes. Homes in climates where temperatures are extreme also generally require larger loops. Geothermal heat pump systems that are too large waste energy and do not provide proper humidity control (GeoExchange 2011).

Most loops for residential systems are installed either horizontally or vertically in the ground or submerged in water in a pond or lake. In most cases, fluid runs through the loop in a closed system, but open-loop systems may be used where local codes permit. Each type of loop configuration has advantages and disadvantages.

Horizontal Closed Loops

For a horizontal closed loop, trenchers or backhoes are used to dig trenches three to six feet below ground level for a series of parallel plastic pipes. The trench is backfilled, taking care not to allow sharp rocks or debris to damage pipes. Fluid runs through the pipes in a closed system. A typical horizontal loop will be 400 to 600 feet long per ton of heating and cooling capacity. This configuration is usually the most cost-effective when adequate yard space is available and trenches are easy to dig. The pipe may be curled into a Slinky shape in order to fit more of it into shorter trenches, but while this reduces the amount of land space needed it may require more pipe. Horizontal ground loops are easiest to install while a home is under construction. However, new types of digging equipment that allow horizontal boring are making it possible to retrofit geothermal heat pump systems into existing homes with minimal disturbance to lawns, at some expense. Horizontal boring machines can even allow loops to be installed under existing buildings or driveways (GeoExchange 2011).

Vertical Closed Loops

For a vertical closed loop, contractors bore vertical holes in the ground 150 to 450 feet deep. Each hole contains a single length of pipe bent double with a U-bend at the bottom. After the pipe is inserted, the hole is backfilled or grouted. Each vertical pipe is then connected to a horizontal pipe, which is also underground. The horizontal pipe then carries fluid in a closed system to and from a geothermal heat pump. This configuration is ideal for homes where yard space is insufficient to permit horizontal loops, for buildings with large heating and cooling loads, when the ground is rocky near the surface, or for retrofit applications where minimum disruption of the landscaping is desired. Vertical loops are generally more expensive to install due to drilling costs, but require less piping than horizontal loops because the earth deeper down is cooler in summer and warmer in winter than the surface (GeoExchange 2011).

Pond Closed Loops

In a pond closed loop, fluid circulates through polyethylene piping in a closed system, just as it does in ground loops. Typically, pipe is run to the water and coils of piping are submerged under water. If a home is near a body of surface water, such as a pond or lake, this loop design may be the most economical. Pond loops are typically used only if the water level above the piping never drops below six to eight feet at its lowest level, assuring sufficient heat-transfer capability. Properly designed pond loops result in no adverse impacts on the aquatic system (GeoExchange 2011).

Open Loop Systems

Open loop systems are the simplest to install and have been used successfully for decades in areas where local codes permit. In this system, groundwater from an aquifer is piped directly from a well to a building, where it transfers its heat to a heat pump. After it leaves the building, the water is pumped back into the same aquifer via a second well—called a discharge well—located at a suitable distance. This loop configuration is used less frequently than others, but may be employed cost-effectively if groundwater is plentiful (GeoExchange 2011).

Standing Column Well Systems

Standing column wells have become an established technology in some regions, especially the northeastern United States. Standing wells are typically six inches in diameter and may be 1,500 feet deep. Temperate water from the bottom of the well is withdrawn, circulated through the heat pump's heat exchanger, and returned to the top of the water column in the same well. Usually, the well also provides potable drinking water. However, groundwater must be plentiful for a standing well system to operate effectively. If a standing well is installed where the water table is too deep, pumping would be prohibitively costly. Under normal circumstances, water diverted for drinking use is replaced by constant-temperature groundwater, which makes the system act like a true open-loop system. If well-water temperature climbs too high or drops too low, water can be bled from the system to allow groundwater to restore well-water temperature to the normal operating range. Permitting conditions for discharging the bleed water vary from locality to locality, but are eased by the fact that quantities are small and the water is never treated with chemicals (GeoExchange 2011).

Fluid circulating in the loop carries ground heat to the home. An indoor geothermal heat pump then uses electrically driven compressors and heat exchangers in a vapor compression cycle, the same principle employed in a refrigerator, to concentrate the earth's energy and release it inside the home at a higher temperature (GeoExchange 2011). Forced air or hot water systems distribute the heat to various rooms.

GEOTHERMAL POWER PLANTS

Geothermal power generation involves harnessing high-temperature, underground reservoirs of geothermal waters or steam and converting the thermal energy to electricity. Geothermal power generation plants, which are typically located adjacent to sources of thermal energy to reduce heat losses from transportation, typically require 0.5 to 3.5 hectares of land per megawatt (IFC 2007, 12). Geothermal heat occurs everywhere under the earth's surface, but the conditions that make water circulate to the surface are found in less than 10 percent of the land area (UCS 2009). Consequently, in the United States most geothermal reservoirs are located in the western states, Alaska, and Hawaii, limiting availability of this energy resource to these areas.

There are two major types of geothermal resources suitable for electric power generation: dry steam and hot water (Duffield and Sass 2003). The basic configuration for a geothermal power plant is illustrated in Figure 7.1. In dry steam resources, the output of producing wells is a dry steam that can be used directly to run turbine-generators. In hot water resources, the well discharge is high-temperature (>180°C) water. For water resources under 180°C, power generation is possible using a binary cycle system involving the use of a secondary fluid (IFC 2007, 12–13).

The following options for geothermal power production are available today:

- Dry steam plants directly use geothermal steam to turn turbines. High-pressure dry steam discharged from production wells is used directly in turbines to generate electricity. After use, lower-pressure, lower-temperature steam may be discharged to the atmosphere or (rarely) reinjected into the geothermal reservoir.

Figure 7.1 **Geothermal Power Plant**

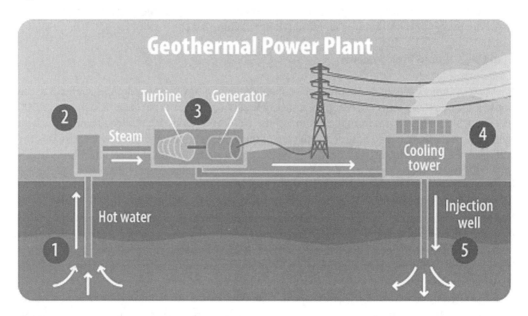

Source: USEPA 2011.

- Flash steam plants pull deep, high-pressure hot water into lower-pressure tanks and use the resulting flashed steam to drive turbines. Steam is separated from a hot water resource and used for power when the temperature of the resource is above 180°C. This allows extraction of some high-pressure steam through "flashing" in steam separators to run the turbine generator. The steam portion is used in turbines and remaining hot water is treated as waste or reinjected into the reservoir (IFC 2007, 13).
- Binary-cycle plants pass moderately hot geothermal water near a secondary fluid with a much lower boiling point than water in a heat exchanger. This causes the secondary fluid to flash to vapor, which then drives a turbine (USDOE 2011). When the resource temperature is below 180°C, a secondary cycle using a low-boiling-point fluid such as isobutene, isopentane, pentafluoropropane, or an ammonia-water mixture is used to exchange heat between the hot geothermal fluids and a turbine (IFC 2007, 13). The two liquids are kept completely separate through use of a heat exchanger, which transfers the heat energy from the geothermal water to the working fluid. The secondary fluid expands into gaseous vapor. The force of the expanding vapor, like steam, turns turbines that power generators (Geothermal Energy Association 2011). Plants that use a closed-loop binary-cycle release no fluids or heat-trapping emissions other than water vapor, which may be used for cooling. With closed-loop systems such as the binary-cycle plant, there are no emissions; everything brought to the surface is returned underground (UCS 2009).
- In some facilities, both flashing and binary processes are used to increase overall efficiency of electricity production (IFC 2007, 13). In this type of plant, the portion of the geothermal water that "flashes" to steam under reduced pressure is first converted to electricity with a backpressure steam turbine and the low-pressure steam exiting the backpressure turbine is condensed in a binary system (Geothermal Energy Association 2011).

Figure 7.2   **The Geothermal Heat Pump Cycle**

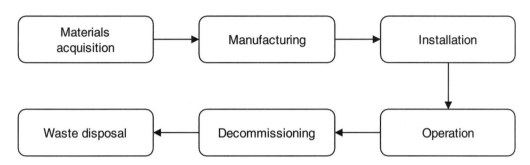

The choice of which design to use is determined by characteristics of a local geothermal resource. If water comes out of a well as steam, it can be used directly, as in the dry steam plant design. If it is hot water of a high enough temperature, a flash steam plant can be used; otherwise it must go through a heat exchanger in a binary-system plant. Since there are more hot water resources than pure steam or high-temperature water sources, there is more growth potential in the binary-system design (UCS 2009).

The technologies discussed above use only a tiny fraction of the total geothermal resource. Several miles everywhere beneath the earth's surface, hot, dry rock is continuously being heated by the molten magma directly below it. Technology is being developed to drill into this rock, inject cold water down a well, circulate it through the hot, fractured rock, and draw off the heated water from another well (USDOE 2011).

COSTS OF UTILIZATING GEOTHERMAL ENERGY

Environmental Costs of Using Geothermal Energy

Because of the diversity of technologies used with geothermal energy, the geothermal energy "fuel cycle" is really two fuel cycles, depending on which technologies one is discussing. A geothermal heat pump fuel cycle is rather similar to the simple solar fuel cycle, involving acquisition of materials, manufacture and installation of geothermal heat pump equipment, operation of geothermal heat pumps, and disposal or recycling of waste materials from manufacturing processes and decommissioning, as illustrated in Figure 7.2. Manufacturing of geothermal heat pumps involves industrial-scale aluminum and sheet metal fabrication of heat pumps, with installation of plumbing, compressors, and electrical components, depending on the specific design utilized. Installation involves some excavation of trenches or drilling of wells near the point of operation, and disposal or recycling of waste materials must be done in licensed facilities as is the case with other industrial manufacturing. Actual operation of geothermal heat pumps entails very low or no environmental costs.

A second, geothermal power plant fuel cycle is rather like the oil and gas fuel cycle, at least in its first and last stages, including exploration, geothermal field development, power plant development, production and transmission of electricity, utilization, reclamation, and disposal of waste by-products, as illustrated in Figure 7.3. The basic components of geothermal power generation facilities include wells to access steam and superheated groundwater, steam turbines, generators, condensers, cooling towers, reinjection pumps, and electrical grid interconnection equipment (IFC

Figure 7.3 **The Geothermal Power Plant Fuel Cycle**

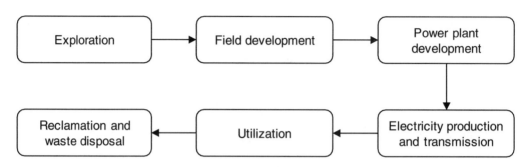

2007, 12). The environmental costs of utility-scale geothermal power plants include significant land disturbance and land use impacts, air emissions, hazardous materials disposal, noise pollution, and potential impacts on water and other resources, depending on the location of the resource and the geothermal technology design employed. The environmental costs of geothermal electric power production are on a par with more conventional technologies for bulk electric power production in use today. Electricity generation using geothermal power plants entails much greater and more concentrated environmental costs than those from geothermal heat pump use, which are less severe and more dispersed.

Exploration

Exploration and reservoir evaluation activities include geological, geophysical, and drilling surveys for exploratory drilling and reservoir testing (IFC 2007, 12). The objective is to locate areas underlain by hot rock; estimate the volume of the reservoir, the temperature of the fluid in it, and the permeability of the formation; predict whether the produce fluid will be dry steam, liquid, or a mixture; define the chemical nature of the fluid; and forecast the electric power potential for a minimum of twenty years. To accomplish this, a survey of published literature, an airborne survey, and surveys of geology, hydrology, geochemistry, and geophysics must be undertaken in a target area (DiPippo 2008, 20–21). Drilling of test wells must be undertaken, with construction of roads, well pads, and pipelines having impacts similar to those described for oil and gas in Chapter 4. Power plant buildings and a substation must be constructed.

Production field development after a geothermal resource has been located and characterized involves drilling steam or hot water production wells and reinjection wells and processing reservoir output for use in a power plant. Drilling continues throughout the life of a project, as production and injection wells need to be periodically renewed to support power generation requirements (IFC 2007, 12).

Air Pollution and Hazardous Waste

Operational activities include operation and maintenance of the geothermal power generating plant, well field monitoring and maintenance, periodic drilling of production and injection wells, geothermal fluid processing, and pipeline maintenance. Superheated geothermal fluids typically contain a number of dissolved metals and gases, including methane, ammonia, hydrogen, and nitrogen (Armaroli and Balzani 2011, 249; Barbier 2002). The main toxic gases are methane, carbon dioxide, and hydrogen sulfide. Carbon dioxide and hydrogen sulfide are denser than air and can collect in pits, depressions, or confined spaces. These gases are a poisonous hazard for people working at geothermal power stations or bore fields. Methane and carbon dioxide are also greenhouse gases, contributing to climate change. Consequently, wastewater effluents and gases are usually reinjected into the reservoir or its periphery to minimize air emissions, potential for subsidence, and surface and groundwater contamination. Construction of cooling and settling ponds with lagoon covers to capture and scrub gases is sometimes necessary for circumstances in which the reinjection of wastewater fluids and gases is not possible (IFC 2007, 12).

Depending on characteristics of the produced water and design of the facility, cooling towers may use geothermal fluids or borrow from surface water sources for circulation. Hazardous solid waste may be generated from sulfur precipitates in the condensate which must be removed and properly stored on site before disposal (IFC 2007, 12). Sometimes the resulting elemental sulfur can then be used as a nonhazardous soil amendment and fertilizer feedstock (DiPippo 2008, 152; Kagel, Bates, and Gawell 2007).

Scrubbers reduce air pollution emissions but produce a watery sludge high in sulfur and vanadium, a heavy metal that can be toxic in high concentrations. Additional sludge is generated when hot water steam is condensed, causing dissolved solids to precipitate out. This sludge is generally high in silica compounds, chlorides, arsenic, mercury, nickel, and other toxic heavy metals (Brower 1992, 151).

Usually the best disposal method is to inject liquid wastes back into a porous level of a geothermal well. Although this technology is more expensive than conventional open-loop systems, in some cases it may reduce scrubber and solid waste disposal costs enough to provide a significant economic advantage. This technique is especially important at geopressured power plants because of the sheer volume of wastes they produce each day. Wastes must be injected well below fresh water aquifers to make certain there is no transport between usable water and waste-water strata. Leaks in well casings at shallow depths must also be prevented (Reed and Renner 1994, 19–23; Brower 1992, 152).

Depletion of Geothermal Resources

The largest geothermal electric power generating system in operation in the United States is a steam-driven plant north of San Francisco in an area called the Geysers. The first well for power production was drilled in 1924, but significant development did not occur until the 1970s and 1980s. By 1990 twenty-six power plants had been built, with a combined capacity of more than 2,000 MWe (UCS 2009). The process of extracting geothermal fluids (which include gases, steam, and water) for power generation typically removes heat from natural reservoirs at over ten times their rate of replenishment. This imbalance may be partially improved by injecting waste fluids back into the geothermal reservoir. It is particularly difficult at dry steam reservoirs, where there is little to reinject after the steam has been utilized (DiPippo 2008, 291).

Because of rapid development in the 1980s, and the technology used, the steam resource was significantly depleted after 1988. Today, it has a net operating capacity of 725 MWe. Plants at the Geysers use an evaporative water-cooling process to create a vacuum that pulls steam through a turbine, producing power more efficiently than some other geothermal plants. However, this process loses 60 to 80 percent of the steam to the air, without reinjecting it underground. To remedy the situation, in 2003 various stakeholders partnered to create the Santa Rosa Geysers Recharge Project, which involves transporting 11 million gallons per day of treated wastewater from neighboring communities through a forty-mile pipeline and injecting it into the geothermal reservoir to provide more steam (UCS 2009). One concern with open systems like the Geysers is that they emit to the air hydrogen sulfide—a toxic gas with a highly recognizable "rotten egg" odor—along with ammonia, methane, carbon dioxide, trace amounts of arsenic, and other minerals. At hydrothermal plants carbon dioxide is expected to make up about 10 percent of the gases trapped in geopressurized brines (Brower 1992, 151).

Land Subsidence

In addition to providing safe waste disposal, injection may also help prevent land subsidence. Extracting geothermal fluids at rates greater than recharge can reduce the pressure in underground reservoirs and cause the land to sink (DiPippo 2008, 104). The largest geothermal subsidence on record is at Wairākei, New Zealand, where wastes and condensates were not injected for many years. The center of the subsidence bowl is sinking at a rate of almost half a meter every year. One area sank 7.5 meters since 1958. In 2005 the ground surface was fourteen meters lower than it was before the power station was built. As the ground sinks, it also moves sideways and tilts toward the center (Stewart 2009). It is projected that subsidence should increase by an additional twenty meters by 2050 (DiPippo 2008, 397). Subsidence puts a strain on bores and pipelines, may damage buildings and roads, and can alter surface drainage patterns (Stewart 2009). Land subsidence has not yet been detected at other hot water plants in long-term operation. In the United States, because geopressurized brines are primarily found along the Gulf of Mexico coast, where natural land subsidence is already a problem, even slight settling could have major implications for flood control and hurricane damage (Brower 1992, 152).

Damage to Unique Natural Resources

Development of hot water geothermal energy faces a special problem. Many hot water reservoirs in the United States are located in or near wilderness areas of great natural beauty such as Yellowstone National Park or the Cascade Mountains. Proposed developments in such areas have aroused intense opposition (Brower 1992, 152–153). Natural features such as hot springs, mud pools, sinter terraces, geysers, fumaroles (steam vents), and steaming ground can be easily, and irreparably, damaged by geothermal development. Beowawe and Steamboat Springs in Nevada both had natural geysers before they were extinguished by geothermal power plant development (DiPippo 2008, 106). When the Wairākei geothermal field in New Zealand was tapped for power generation in 1958, withdrawal of hot fluids from the underground reservoir caused long-term changes to the famous Geyser Valley, the nearby Waiora Valley, and the mighty Karapiti blowhole. The ground sagged three meters in some places, and hot springs and geysers declined and died as the supply of steaming water from below was depleted (Stewart 2009).

In Geyser Valley, one of the first features to vanish was the great Wairākei geyser, which used to rise to a height of forty-two meters. Subsequently, the famous Champagne Pool, a blue-tinted boiling spring, dwindled away to a faint wisp of steam. In 1965 the Tourist Hotel Corporation tried to restore it by pumping in some three million liters of water, but without success. Geyser Valley continued to deteriorate, and in 1973 it was shut down as a tourist spectacle. This story has been repeated many times where there has been geothermal development (Stewart 2009). Geothermal electric power development is unlikely to expand much further in the United States without risking damage to unique natural resources, many of which are of sufficient value that nearby geothermal resources should probably never be developed (DiPippo 2008, 104).

Water Usage

Most geothermal power plants require a large amount of water for cooling towers or other purposes (DiPippo 2008, 104). In places where water is in short supply, this need could raise conflicts with other users for water resources (Brower 1992). Geothermal fluids contain elevated levels of arsenic, mercury, lithium, and boron because of underground contact between hot fluids and rocks. If waste is released into rivers or lakes instead of being injected into the geothermal field, these pollutants can damage aquatic life and make the water unsafe for drinking or irrigation (Stewart 2009). Geothermal plants of all types discharge more waste heat per unit of power output than other thermal power plants (DiPippo 2008, 183), so it is imperative that some beneficial use, such as greenhouse heating, should be found for the waste heat; alternatively, cooling towers could be used or the waste fluids could be reinjected into the geothermal reservoir.

Noise Pollution

Drilling and well testing, which requires periodic venting of geothermal steam and gases directly to the atmosphere, generate loud hissing and whistling noises on-site, which may be irritating to nearby residents, livestock, and wildlife. This noise pollution must be controlled using mechanical means (DiPippo 2008, 104).

Future Developments

A new approach to capturing the heat in dry areas is known as enhanced geothermal systems (EGS) or "hot dry rock." Hot dry rock reservoirs, typically at greater depths below the earth's surface than conventional sources, are first broken up by pumping high-pressure water through them. More water is then pumped through the broken hot rocks, where it heats up, returns to the surface as steam, and powers turbines to generate electricity. Water is returned to the reservoir through injection wells to complete the circulation loop (UCS 2009).

The U.S. Department of Energy, several universities, the geothermal industry, and venture capital firms (including Google) are collaborating on research and demonstration projects to harness the potential of hot dry rock. DOE, which has funded several demonstration projects, hopes to have EGS ready for commercial development by 2015 (UCS 2009). One cause for careful consideration with EGS is the possibility of induced seismic activity that might occur from hot dry rock drilling and development. This risk is similar to that associated with hydraulic fracturing (fracking), an increasingly used, controversial method of oil and gas drilling, and with carbon dioxide capture and storage in deep saline aquifers (UCS 2009). There is sound evidence that the frequency of local earthquakes can be increased by injection of fluids in deep wells (Scanlon 1992, 6; Hsieh and Bredehoeft 1981).

Oil and gas fields already in production represent another large potential source of geothermal energy. In many existing oil and gas reservoirs, a significant amount of high-temperature water or suitable high-pressure conditions are present, which could allow for production of electricity with oil or gas at the same time. In some cases, exploiting these resources may enhance extraction of oil and gas (UCS 2009). An MIT study estimated that the United States has the potential to develop 44,000 MWe of geothermal capacity by 2050 by coproducing geothermal electricity, oil, and natural gas at oil and gas fields—primarily in the Southeast and southern Plains states. The study projects that such advanced geothermal systems could supply 10 percent of U.S. baseload electricity by that year, given research and development and related deployment in the interim (Tester et al. 2006).

Dollar Costs of Utilizing Geothermal Energy

Geothermal heat pump technology is widely available commercially today, with some producers claiming savings of 30 to 70 percent over conventional heating options, and 20 to 50 percent over other cooling systems (ClimateMaster 2011; Excel Energy Solutions 2011; Smithfield Construction 2011). This technology is competitive with other conventional heating and cooling systems for residential, commercial and industrial buildings. Geothermal heating and cooling systems are much more efficient than competing fuel technologies when all losses in the fuel cycle, including waste heat at power plants during generation of electricity, are accounted for. High-efficiency geothermal heat pump systems are on average 48 percent more efficient than the best gas furnaces and more than 75 percent more efficient than oil furnaces. The best geothermal heat pump systems even outperform the best gas technology, natural gas heat pumps, by an average of 36 percent in the heating mode and 43 percent in the cooling mode (L'Ecuyer, Zoi, and Hoffman 1993).

In regions with temperature extremes, such as the northern United States in winter and the southern United States in summer, geothermal heat pumps are the most energy-efficient and environmentally clean heating and cooling system available. Far more efficient than electric heating and cooling, these systems can move as much as three to five times the energy they use. The U.S. Department of Energy found that geothermal heat pumps can save a typical home hundreds of dollars in energy costs each year, with the system typically paying for itself in eight to twelve years. Tax credits and other incentives can reduce the payback period to five years or less (Hughes 2008).

In 2008 more than 600,000 ground-source heat pumps supplied climate control in U.S. homes and other buildings, with new installations occurring at a rate of about 60,000 per year. While this is significant, it is still only a small fraction of the U.S. heating and cooling market. Several barriers to greater penetration into the market remain. Despite their long-term savings, geothermal heat pumps have higher up-front costs than conventional alternatives. Installing them in existing homes and businesses can be difficult because it involves digging up areas around a building's structure. Finally, many heating and cooling installers are not familiar with the technology (Hughes 2008).

Geothermal heat pumps are highly reliable, require little maintenance, and are built to last for decades. They add considerably to the value of homes. Many financial institutions also now allow home buyers to qualify for larger mortgages if they purchase a house that utilizes a geothermal heat pump system (GeoExchange 2011). Recent policy developments offer strong incentives for homeowners to install these systems. The Emergency Economic Stabilization Act of 2008 included an eight-year extension (through 2016) of the 30 percent investment tax credit, with no upper limit, to all home installations of EnergyStar certified geothermal heat pumps (UCS 2009). Under the American Recovery and Reinvestment Act of 2009, $400 million of new funding was allocated to DOE's Geothermal Technologies Program. Of this, $90 million is expected to go toward up to ten demonstration projects to prove the feasibility of EGS technology. Another $50 million will fund up to twenty demonstration projects for other new technologies, including coproduction with oil and gas and low-temperature geothermal. The remaining funds will go toward improving exploration technologies, expanding deployment of geothermal heat pumps, and other uses. These investments will very likely produce great net benefits for consumers in the future (Jennejohn 2009, 19).

Electrical generation from geothermal power plants is one of the few renewable energy technologies that—like fossil fuels—can supply continuous baseload electrical power twenty-four

Figure 7.4 **The Costs of Utilizing Geothermal Heat Pump Technologies**

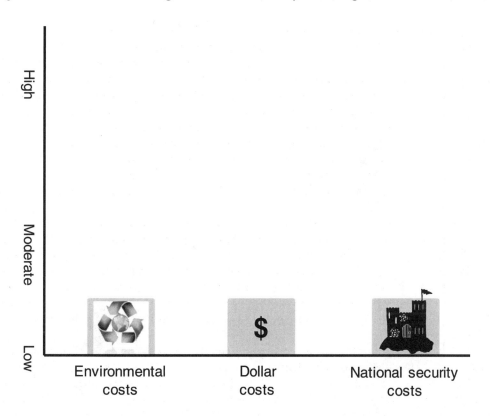

hours per day. The market cost to consumers for electricity generated by geothermal energy in calendar year 2009 was estimated at a bit over $1.4 billion (calculated from USEIA 2011a, Table 8.2c, Table 8.10). Federal subsidies and tax expenditures for geothermal energy were estimated at about $273 million for FY2010, including about $200 million for electricity production (USEIA 2011b, xiii, xviii). The costs for electricity from geothermal facilities are declining. Some geothermal electric power facilities have realized at least 50 percent reductions in the price of their electricity since 1980. A considerable portion of potential geothermal resources in California will be able produce electricity for as little as eight cents per kilowatt-hour (including a production tax credit), competitive with new conventional fossil fuel-fired power plants (California Energy Commission 2003). But the potential usefulness of geothermal electric power production is limited to areas where significant undeveloped geothermal reservoirs are found, which are mostly in the western states, especially California, Alaska, and Hawaii.

National Security Costs of Utilizing Geothermal Energy

The heat of the earth is available everywhere, and access to it is not dependent upon the actions of any government other than our own. As a domestic resource, no nation-state or other organization is able to control supplies or determine price. Geothermal energy produces almost no atmospheric emissions or greenhouse gases, and what little it does produce is generated during

Figure 7.5 **The Costs of Utilizing Geothermal Power Plant Technologies**

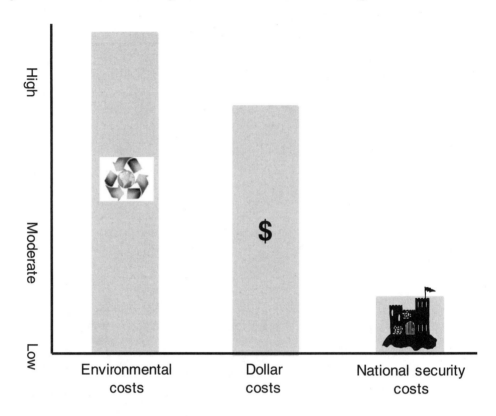

the manufacture of industrial equipment, not during ongoing operations. Consequently, utilizing geothermal technologies will not produce climate change or a rise in sea level. Geothermal technologies do not produce substantial amounts of toxic waste that must be isolated from the human environment for millennia. Geothermal energy utilization does not produce materials or targets useful to terrorists. Consequently, the national security costs of utilizing geothermal technologies are nil. As compared to other energy technologies, utilization of geothermal technologies can be conceptualized as having net national security benefits.

SUMMARY OF COSTS

The costs of utilizing geothermal heat pump technologies are summarized in Figure 7.4 (see page 141). Overall, the environmental costs for producing and using geothermal heat pump technologies are incurred mostly during production of equipment and are "low" compared to most conventional fuel technologies in use today.

The costs of utilizing geothermal power plant technologies are summarized in Figure 7.5. The environmental costs for producing electricity from geothermal power plants are competitive with most conventional fuels in use today and are therefore "high." Special attention must be paid to effective disposal of hazardous wastes produced during power production.

Dollar costs for dispersed application of geothermal heat pumps for heating residential, commercial, and industrial buildings are "low" and competitive with conventional heating and cooling options. Geothermal power plants are severely restricted by the location of high-temperature steam and water resources. Dollar costs for central-station generation of electricity by geothermal power plants are almost competitive with conventional fuels for central-station generation of electricity and are "moderately high." National security costs for all geothermal technologies are very "low" or negligible because geothermal resources are a domestic resource. This is a significant advantage geothermal technologies hold over other energy technologies that may be acquired from foreign sources, may contribute to global climate change, or may leave a legacy of long-term waste products attractive to terrorists.

Geothermal heat pump technologies do not produce much hazardous waste. Geothermal power is also environmentally advantageous because its energy supply will never run out and cannot be controlled by any combination of foreign governments. For the foreseeable future, geothermal resources will always be available on this planet, providing energy that geothermal technologies can exploit. Creating the components of geothermal technology is extremely easy, does not require mining or drilling in a politically dangerous locale, and can be acquired without involvement of unreliable political allies. Of the various geothermal technologies, geothermal heat pumps hold the greatest promise for rapid market penetration utilizing recent innovations in financing, installation, and ownership arrangements.

REFERENCES

Armaroli, Nicola, and Vincenzo Balzani. 2011. *Energy for a Sustainable World*. Weinheim, Germany: Wiley-VCH Verlag.
Barbier, E. 2002. "Geothermal Energy Technology and Current Status: An Overview." *Renewable and Sustainable Energy Review* 6 (1–2): 3–65.
Brower, Michael. 1992. *Cool Energy: Renewable Solutions to Environmental Problems*. Cambridge, MA: MIT Press.
California Energy Commission. 2003. *Comparative Cost of California Central Station Electricity Generation Technologies. Final Staff Report*. Sacramento: California Energy Commission.
ClimateMaster. 2011. "Geothermal Applications." www.climatemaster.com/commercial-geothermal.
DiPippo, Ronald. 2008. *Geothermal Power Plants: Principles, Applications, Case Studies and Environmental Impact*, 2nd ed. New York: Elsevier.
Duffield, W.A., and J.H. Sass. 2003. *Geothermal Energy: Clean Power from the Earth's Heat*. Circular 1249. Washington, DC: U.S. Geological Survey.
Excel Energy Solutions Inc. 2011. "Geothermal Heating and Cooling: Introduction to Geothermal." www.excelenergysolutions.com/geothermal-heating-cooling-main.html.
GeoExchange. 2011. "Geothermal Heat Pumps." www.geoexchange.org/index.php?option=com_content&view=article&id=48:geothermal-heat-pumps&catid=375:geothermal-hvac&Itemid=32.
Geothermal Energy Association. 2011. "Basics." http://geo-energy.org/Basics.aspx.
Hsieh, Paul A., and John D. Bredehoeft. 1981. "A Reservoir Analysis of the Denver Earthquakes: A Case of Induced Seismicity." *Journal of Geophysical Research* 86 (B2): 903–920.
Hughes, Patrick J. 2008. *Geothermal (Ground-Source) Heat Pumps: Market Status, Barriers to Adoption, and Actions to Overcome Barriers*. Oak Ridge: Oak Ridge National Laboratory. www1.eere.energy.gov/geothermal/pdfs/ornl_ghp_study.pdf.
International Finance Corporation (IFC). 2007. *Environmental, Health, and Safety Guidelines: Geothermal Power Generation*. Washington, DC: International Finance Corporation.
Jennejohn, Jan. 2009. *U.S. Geothermal Power Production and Development Update*. Report, September. Washington, DC: Geothermal Energy Association. http://geo-energy.org/pdf/reports/US_Geothermal_Industry_Update_Sept_29_2009_Final.pdf.
Kagel, Alyssa, Diana Bates, and Karl Gawell. 2007. *A Guide to Geothermal Energy and the Environment*. Report, April (update). Washington, DC: Geothermal Energy Association.
L'Ecuyer, Michael, Cathy Zoi, and John S. Hoffman. 1993. *Space Conditioning: The Next Frontier*. Report No. EPA 430-R-93-004, April. Washington, DC: U.S. Environmental Protection Agency.

Lienau, Paul J., and Ben C. Lunis, eds. 1991. *Geothermal Direct Use Engineering and Design Guidebook.* Klamath Falls: Oregon Institute of Technology.

Reed, Marshall J., and Joel L. Renner. 1994. "Environmental Compatibility of Geothermal Energy." In *Alternative Fuels and the Environment*, ed. Frances S. Sterrett, 19–27. Ann Arbor, MI: Lewis.

Scanlon, Bill. 1992. "Twenty-Five Years Ago, the Ground Shook Around Denver." *Rocky Mountain News*, November 27.

Smithfield Construction. 2011. "Earth Power . . ." www.smithfieldconstruction.com/geothermal.htm.

Stewart, Carol. 2009. "Story: Geothermal Energy. Page 5—Effects on the Environment." *Te Ara: The Encyclopedia of New Zealand.* Wellington, New Zealand: Manatū Taonga Ministry for Culture and Heritage. www.teara.govt.nz/en/geothermal-energy/5.

Tester, J., B. Anderson, A. Batchelor, D. Blackwell, R. DiPippo, E. Drake, J. Garnish, B. Livesay, M. Moore, K. Nichols, S. Petty, M. Toksöz, and R. Veatch. 2006. *The Future of Geothermal Energy: Impact of Enhanced Geothermal Systems (EGS) on the United States in the 21st Century.* Cambridge: Massachusetts Institute of Technology and Idaho National Laboratory. http://geothermal.inel.gov/publications/future_of_geothermal_energy.pdf.

Union of Concerned Scientists (UCS). 2009. "How Geothermal Energy Works." December 16. www.ucsusa.org/clean_energy/technology_and_impacts/energy_technologies/how-geothermal-energy-works.html.

U.S. Department of Energy (USDOE). 2011. "Geothermal Overview." www1.eere.energy.gov/geothermal/geothermal_basics.html.

U.S. Energy Information Administration (USEIA). 2011a. *Annual Energy Review 2010.* Washington, DC: U.S. Government Printing Office.

———. 2011b. *Direct Federal Financial Interventions and Subsidies in Energy Markets 2010.* Washington, DC: U.S. Government Printing Office.

U.S. Environmental Protection Agency (EPA). 2011. "A Student's Guide to Global Climate Change: Geothermal Energy." April 13. www.epa.gov/climatechange/kids/solutions/technologies/geothermal.html.

8

Hydroelectricity

Rainfall, like wind, is common but is unevenly distributed across the surface of the earth. Hydroelectric energy technologies, which in a sense use water for "fuel," depend on rainfall to create flowing water that, when falling due to the gravitational pull of the earth, may be used to generate mechanical power to grind flour, motivate other machinery, or produce electricity. Thus, hydroelectric energy is produced by the force of falling water (USGS 2011). The movement of water as it flows downstream creates energy that can be converted into electricity. A hydroelectric power plant converts this energy into electricity by running water, often held in a reservoir behind a dam, through a hydraulic turbine connected to a generator. Water exits the turbine and is returned to a stream or riverbed below the reservoir (USEPA 2011).

The capacity to produce hydroelectric energy is dependent on both the available flow and the height from which it falls. Building up behind a dam, water accumulates potential energy. The amount of power that may be extracted from water depends on the volume and the difference in height between the source and the turbine. This height difference is called head. The amount of potential energy in water is proportional to the head. Falling water is used to turn a turbine, as illustrated in Figure 8.1. The turbine's rotation spins electromagnets that generate current in stationary coils of wire. Finally, the current is put through a transformer where voltage is increased for long-distance transmission over power lines (USGS 2011). Thus, hydropower is mostly dependent upon precipitation and elevation changes; high precipitation levels and large elevation changes are necessary to generate significant quantities of electricity. An area such as the mountainous Pacific Northwest has more head and more productive hydropower plants than an area such as the Gulf Coast, which might have large amounts of precipitation but is comparatively flat (USEPA 2011).

LARGE HYDRO

Facilities with a few hundred megawatts to more than 10,000 MWe are generally considered to be large hydroelectric facilities. Large hydroelectric facilities attempt to maximize the capture of seasonal runoff and store it until it is needed for irrigation or power generation, so they attempt to impound an entire year's worth of water in large reservoirs. Grand Coulee Dam on the Columbia River in Washington State is the largest single electric power facility in the United States (USEIA 2011c), at 550 feet (168 meters) high and 5,223 feet (1,592 meters) long, with installed generating capacity of over 6,800 MWe and reservoir capacity of over 9.5 million acre-feet of water (U.S. Bureau of Reclamation 2011a). In addition to generating electric power, Grand Coulee provides water for approximately 600,000 acres of irrigated farmland in the Columbia River Basin and is a primary factor in controlling floods on the Columbia River. Hoover Dam, southeast of Las Vegas, Nevada, is the tallest solid concrete dam in the United States at 726 feet (221.3 meters) high and 1,244 feet (379.2 meters)long, although its installed generating capacity is a bit less than 2,100 MWe. Hydroelectric plants with greater generating capacity

145

Figure 8.1 **Hydroelectric Dam**

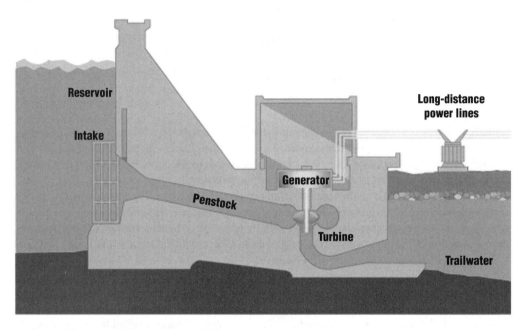

Source: Tennessee Valley Authority 2011.

than Grand Coulee Dam are found in China, Brazil, and Venezuela. Large-scale hydroelectric power stations are commonly seen as the largest power-producing facilities in the world (U.S. Bureau of Reclamation 2011b).

SMALL HYDRO

Generating capacity of up to thirty MWe is generally accepted as the upper limit of what can be termed small hydro in the United States (USDOE 2003, 5), for development of water power on a scale serving a small community or industrial plant. Small hydro plants may be connected to conventional electrical distribution networks as a source of low-cost renewable energy, built in isolated areas that would be uneconomic to serve from a network, or built in areas where there is no electrical distribution network. Because small hydro projects usually have minimal reservoirs and civil construction work, they are often seen as having relatively low environmental impact compared to large hydro. However, this decreased environmental impact depends strongly on the balance between stream flow and power production.

MICRO HYDRO

Micro hydro is a term used for small hydro installations that typically produce up to 100 kilowatts of power (USDOE 2003, 5). These installations can provide power to isolated homes or a small community and are sometimes connected to electric power networks. Micro hydro systems may be designed either with or without battery storage or a grid connection (Cunningham and Woofenden 2011). Micro hydro systems often complement photovoltaic solar energy systems because in many areas water flow, and thus available hydropower, is highest in the winter when solar energy is least.

Micro hydro facilities may be constructed with either little or no reservoir capacity, so that water coming from upstream must be used for generation at that moment, or allowed to bypass the generator. Hydroelectric stations constructed with little or no reservoir capacity are known as "run-of-the-river" facilities. A run-of-the-river project uses water within the natural flow range of the river, requiring little or no impoundment (USDOE 2003, 4). A plant with no reservoir has no storage and is therefore subject to seasonal river flows and may serve only as a peaking power plant, while a plant with a reservoir can regulate water flow and serve either as a peaking or base load power plant. Although most run-of-the-river hydro facilities would be considered small hydro or micro hydro projects, a few large ones have been designed with up to about 1,000 MWe generating capacity. An example of a micro hydro run-of-the-river technology is the barge-mounted floating power station developed by Eco Hydro Energy Limited:

> The floating power station consists of an electricity generating device which is anchored in an existing river system. Flexible rotor blades are mounted on an axis which rotates, providing a turbine effect. Rotor blades are distanced from each other and are arranged along the rotor axle in staggered rows. The rotating assembly directly drives conventional electromagnetic generators, providing electric power for immediate local consumption or for transmission to an existing distribution grid.
>
> The Eco Hydro system provides a low cost opportunity for power generation. As opposed to traditional hydro-electric plants, there is no requirement for highly invasive construction processes as the entire system can be towed into position and its location can be quickly changed as required.
>
> There is no population displacement, no loss of traditional lands. The activity of the flexible rotor blades provides oxygenation of the river, which can repair damage done to a river's chemistry and physiology by other human activity. This is beneficial for fish populations, the organisms upon which they depend for food and aquatic plant life. The system's operators benefit from both low capital and operation costs. There are no land-based construction costs.
>
> Manufacture of the equipment occurs in a manufacturing plant distant from the power generating location. Once operational, the Eco Hydro system does not require the purchase and transportation of expensive carbon fuel, nor does it require maintenance of a land-based infrastructure. The scale of power generation can be increased simply through addition of system units, limited only by available water flow. (Eco Hydro Energy Limited 2005)

The floating power station is available in units ranging from 250 KWh to 150 MWh generating capacity (Eco Hydro Energy Limited 2005). It may also be used in estuaries to generate electricity from tidal currents.

PICO HYDRO

Pico hydro is a term used for very small hydro generation of under five kilowatts, comparable to the output of the portable gasoline generators often in use in the United States today. It is useful in small, remote communities that require only a small amount of electricity to power one or two fluorescent lightbulbs and a TV or radio for a few homes (University of Nottingham. 2011). Even smaller turbines of 200 to 300 watts may power a single home in a developing country with a drop of only one meter (Williams 2007). Pico-hydro setups typically are run-of-the-river, meaning that dams are not used, but pipes divert some of the flow, dropping it down a gradient and through a turbine before returning it to a stream (University of Nottingham 2011). Pico hydro is of greatest interest to persons concerned with rural electrification in developing countries and with very small, remote off-grid applications in the United States.

PUMPED STORAGE

Pumped storage projects differ from conventional hydroelectric projects. They normally pump water from a lower reservoir to an upper reservoir when demand for electricity is low. Water is stored in an upper reservoir for release to generate power during periods of peak demand. At times of low electrical demand, excess generation capacity is used to pump water from a lower elevation to a higher reservoir. When there is higher demand, water is released from the higher reservoir through a turbine back into the lower reservoir (USDOE 2003, 4). Pumped storage facilities currently provide the most commercially important means of large-scale storage and improve the daily capacity factor of hydroelectric generation. These projects are uniquely suited for generating power when demand for electricity is high and for supplying reserve capacity to complement the output of large fossil-fueled and nuclear steam-electric plants. Start-up of this type of generation is almost immediate, thus serving peak demand for power better than fossil-fueled plants that require significantly more start-up time. Like conventional projects, they use falling water to generate power, but they use reversible turbines to pump the water back to the upper reservoir. Because they are designed to meet only peak demand, pumped storage reservoirs are much smaller than those designed to provide base load power and therefore have lesser environmental costs than large hydro reservoirs. Pumped storage facilities in the United States range from less than 100 MWe to almost 1,600 MWe in generating capacity (USFERC 2010).

Because projects with a small reservoir surface area minimize natural habitat losses and human resettlement needs, pumped storage facilities entail lower environmental costs than do large hydro facilities.

COSTS OF HYDROPOWER UTILIZATION

Environmental Costs of Utilizing Hydropower

The "fuel cycle" for hydropower involves exploration, power plant construction, generation and transmission of electricity, decommissioning, and reclamation of the generating site, as illustrated in Figure 8.2. The basic components of hydroelectric power generation facilities include a dam and reservoir for large hydro, a powerhouse with hydraulic generators, turbines, and electrical grid interconnection equipment. Small hydro may or may not require a dam and reservoir, and connection to a high-voltage transmission network. Riverine areas and geologic depressions must be evaluated, dams and reservoirs constructed, generating facilities operated, and eventually dams, reservoirs, and generating equipment must be decommissioned. Potential environmental costs of using hydroelectric technologies include alteration of landscapes through formation of reservoirs; land disturbance and major ecosystem changes; alteration of aquatic and streamside habitats; effects on water quality and quantity; climate-changing air emissions; displacement of human, fish, or wildlife populations; interruption of migratory patterns for fish; injury or death to fish passing through turbines; and risk of catastrophic failure of a dam, depending on the design and scale of the technology employed.

Figure 8.2 **The Hydroelectric Fuel Cycle**

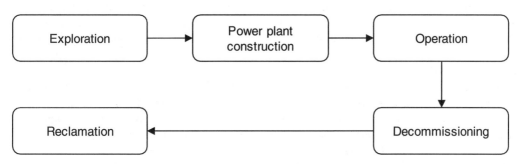

Exploration

The most effective way to mitigate environmental costs is good site selection, to ensure that a proposed dam will cause relatively little damage. Projects with a small reservoir surface area (relative to amount of power generation) tend to be most desirable from an environmental standpoint because they minimize natural habitat losses and human resettlement needs. In general, the most environmentally benign hydroelectric dam sites are on upper tributaries, while the most problematic ones are on large main stems of rivers (Ledec and Quintero 2003).

Identification of an appropriate site for a new hydroelectric generating facility involves finding an area along a river or stream where a structure can be built which will have adequate head and water flow to make a project economically viable for at least twenty years. The location of a large hydro dam must have a geologic formation that is relatively nonporous and able to support substantial weight, so a heavy concrete structure built upon it will have a stable footing and not leak. Rock that crumbles or fractures easily will not suffice. Major fault zones and fractures are weak zones where dams should not be built (Mah 2011). These requirements made the deep canyons of some rivers in the western United States particularly attractive for hydro development, and it is there that most of the existing large hydroelectric generating capacity has been constructed in this country.

The initial stage of exploration consists of gathering available information about an area from library sources, state and local government agencies, previous mining activities, and oil, gas, and water well records. This is followed by a site visit with field geologists, core drilling, and logging of boreholes, which provide more detail on the depth, structure, thickness, and hardness of various rock strata. This information will determine the structural suitability of a site for hydroelectric development.

Exploration and evaluation activities include geological, geophysical (seismic, magnetic, or gravity), and small diameter core drilling surveys at the location of a prospective dam and power facilities to determine the characteristics of local geology and hydrology (B.C. Hydro 1981, 3). Data must be obtained concerning water drainage patterns, terrain conditions, soil materials and glacial transport, and surface and subsurface structures for the planning of a dam, reservoir, and hydroelectric transmission corridors, for bedrock mapping and forest inventory, and for land capability studies. After a survey of published literature, an airborne survey using remote sensing techniques, and surveys of geology, hydrology, and soils must be undertaken in a target area (U.S. Army Corps of Engineers 1967). These surveys involve much drilling to determine depth and characteristics of subterranean geologic structures and groundwater, especially to provide information on the approximate profile of the bedrock surface where it is overlain by overburden, and the location and nature of any major faults or weak zones in the foundations and abutments (B.C. Hydro 1981, 3). Although equipment required for geophysical surveys and small-bore core drilling can be transported to remote areas by helicopter, tunneling and heavy drilling equipment is too heavy and must be moved by ground transport. Consequently, the most significant environmental costs of hydroelectric site selection often attend construction of new roads in roadless areas and core drilling for samples, having impacts similar to those described for coal exploration in Chapter 2. Exploration causes soil and vegetation impacts that disturb wildlife habitat, possibly including endangered species, in addition to noise generated from drills and heavy equipment. Areas of greatest disturbance include drill sites, helipads, camps, and adit portal (tunnel) areas where ground disturbance occurs (B.C. Hydro 1981, 11).

Extensive exploration is also required to determine the source, nature, and extent of natural construction materials such as gravel, sands, silts, and clays, undertaken with small trenching equipment, backhoes, augers, or hammer drills where deposits are deep. Continuous samples of coarse-grained soils in deep overburden deposits are required to determine the grain size distribution of the material and assess its suitability for construction purposes and its strength as foundation material (B.C. Hydro 1981, 4).

Construction

Construction of a new hydroelectric generating facility generally involves use of bulldozers, trucks, and shovels to rearrange the terrain in a manner that exposes bedrock upon which concrete footings may be poured. This displaces or destroys potential archeological sites, wildlife, and habitat, alters current land uses, and permanently changes the general topography of the area. Trees and other vegetation must be removed from the entire area of a reservoir or they will create problems for boat navigability in shallows after inundation, and their decomposition may constitute a major source of methane emissions, which contribute to climate change (IEA 2011; Bergerson and Lave 2002). During construction, roads are built to handle heavy equipment, increasing dust particulate emissions that may impair air quality. In addition to the dam and reservoir, power plant buildings and an electrical substation must be constructed, usually near the base of any impoundment structure. Operation of bladed Caterpillar tractors, drill rigs, and backhoes can have a severe and irreversible effect on any previously unidentified archaeological resources (B.C. Hydro 1981, A-3).

Construction of hydroelectric power generating dams requires the use of tremendous quantities of concrete and steel, which are manufactured at other locations from limestone and iron ore mined elsewhere. Combustion of fossil fuels is required during production processes for heating limestone to make concrete and steel components of dams and generating equipment, on a par with manufacturing processes for preparing materials to construct large buildings and other structures.

Operation

Impoundment dams and powerhouse operations essential to hydropower plants cause the greatest costs to the environment. Changes in river conditions and land and vegetation bordering water bodies caused by dams and powerhouse turbines may significantly affect fish and wildlife populations. The impacts of large dams are wide-ranging, but even small dams can have large detrimental effects on the health of regional fish populations. The impacts of any hydroelectric dam depend upon many factors, including location of the dam, facility design, sensitivity of the local environment to effects of a hydropower facility, and steps taken to modify design and operation of each facility to mitigate potential impacts (Power Scorecard 2011).

Construction of hydropower plants can alter large portions of land when dams are constructed and lakes are created, flooding land that may have served as wildlife habitat, farmland, and recreational areas (Armaroli and Balzani 2011, 234). Large reservoirs result in submersion of extensive areas upstream of dams, destroying biologically rich and productive lowland and riverine valley forests, marshland, and grasslands. Reservoirs cause wildlife habitat fragmentation of surrounding areas, and may disrupt migration patterns of fish, mammals, and birds encountering unfamiliar terrain.

Stratification. Reservoirs can significantly slow the rate at which water moves downstream. Surface temperatures tend to become warmer as the slower-moving or "slack" water absorbs heat from the sun. Colder water sinks toward the bottom because of its higher density. This causes a layering effect called stratification. The bottom layer is the coldest and the top layer the warmest, and they tend not to mix. When stratification occurs, colder water that sinks toward the bottom contains reduced oxygen levels. At some sites when water is released through a dam from the colder, oxygen-depleted depths, downstream habitat conditions change because of reduced oxygen in the water (FWEE 2011). Many fish that are adapted to stream conditions do not survive in lakes. Often, water at the bottom of a lake created by a dam is inhospitable to fish because it is much colder and oxygen-poor compared with water at the top. When this colder, oxygen-poor water is released into the river, it can kill fish living downstream that are accustomed to warmer, oxygen-rich water (USEPA 2011).

Changing Water Levels. Building a storage project can raise the water level behind a dam from a few feet to several hundred feet. When stream banks and riparian areas become inundated by a reservoir's higher water level, habitat conditions change permanently. As this occurs, a different set of dynamics begin impacting species that traditionally grow, nest, feed, or spawn in these areas. Once built, storage projects can also raise and lower the level of water in a reservoir on a daily, weekly, or seasonal basis to produce electricity. In a riparian zone, where moist soils and plants exist next to a body of water, this may result in shoreline vegetation not being effectively reestablished (FWEE 2011). Some dams withhold water and then release it all at once, causing the river downstream to flood suddenly. This action can disrupt plant and wildlife habitats and affect drinking water supplies (USEPA 2011). Humans living on the shores of such a reservoir may find it is not always pleasant, with vast expanses of recently inundated land exposed to the air for months at a time, bearing the smell of decaying fish and other organic matter. And it may not be visually attractive.

Generation of hydroelectric power changes the downstream river environment. Water exiting a turbine usually contains little suspended sediment, lack of which can lead to scouring of downstream riverbeds and loss of riverbanks. Since turbine gates are often opened intermittently, rapid or even daily fluctuations in river flow are observed, with cyclic flow variation contributing to erosion of downstream sandbars. Dissolved oxygen content of water may change from preconstruction conditions. In some cases, an entire river may be diverted, leaving a dry riverbed.

Erosion. Hydroelectric projects can be disruptive to surrounding aquatic ecosystems both upstream and downstream of a plant site. Changing water levels and a lack of streamside vegetation can lead to increased erosion. Hydroelectric dams can cause erosion along the riverbed upstream and downstream, which can disturb wildlife ecosystems and fish populations (USEPA 2011). Lack of vegetation along a shoreline means that a river or reservoir can start cutting deeply into its banks.

This can result in further changes to a riparian zone and the species that it can support. Increases in erosion can also increase the amount of sedimentation behind a dam (FWEE 2011).

Siltation. Flowing water transports particles heavier than itself downstream. Sediments, which are fine organic and inorganic materials that are typically suspended in the water, can collect behind a dam. Human-made and natural erosion of lands adjacent to a reservoir can lead to sediment buildup behind a dam. This buildup can vary based on the ability of a river to flush sediments past a dam (FWEE 2011).

When sediments collect, an ecosystem can be affected in two ways. First, downstream habitat can decline because these sediments no longer provide important organic and inorganic nutrients. Second, where sediment builds up behind a dam, the supply of oxygen may be depleted. This happens because more nutrients are available, and more organisms populate the area to consume the nutrients. As these organisms consume nutrients, more oxygen is used, depleting the supply of oxygen in the reservoir. Gravel can be trapped behind a dam in the same way as sediment. In cases where the movement of gravel downstream is part of establishing spawning areas for fish, important habitat conditions can be affected (FWEE 2011).

This has a negative effect on dams and subsequently their power stations, particularly those on rivers or within catchment areas with high siltation, which can fill a reservoir, reduce its capacity to control floods, and cause additional horizontal pressure on upstream portions of a dam (Chanson and James 1998; Sentürk 1994, 375). Eventually, some reservoirs can become completely full of sediment and useless, or they allow water to flow over the top of accumulated sediment during a flood and fail.

Low Flows. Changes in the amount of river flow correlate with the amount of energy produced by a dam. Lower river flows because of drought, climate change, or upstream dams and diversions will reduce the amount of storage in a reservoir, thereby reducing the amount of water that can be used for hydroelectric generation. The result of diminished river flow can be power shortages in areas that depend heavily on hydroelectric power. The risk of low flows may increase as a result of climate change (Urban and Mitchell 2011).

Wildlife. Riparian vegetation and its bordering waters provide critical habitat for birds, waterfowl, and small and large mammals. When a hydroelectric project results in inundation of a free-flowing river, the nesting, forage, and cover provided by these areas is temporarily or permanently lost.

When habitat is lost, animals are forced to move to higher ground or other areas where habitat conditions may be less suitable, predators are more abundant, or the territory is already occupied. As an example, ground birds like pheasant and grouse require cover and cannot successfully move to higher, more open, ground. In cases where water levels stabilize at a new height, vegetation in riparian zones can reemerge and species can repopulate an area. With storage projects, the riparian zone that reemerges has conditions that reflect those of a reservoir or lake rather than a free-flowing river. When such conditions occur, certain species will decline, others will become more abundant, and some will populate these areas for the first time.

Ducks and geese are examples of waterfowl that are strongly attracted to habitat conditions found in reservoirs. For some of these species, reservoirs are providing an important alternative to the wetland areas that they formerly occupied. Canada geese, for example, now frequent reservoirs as part of their migration pattern (FWEE 2011).

Hydroelectric power plants affect various fish populations in different ways. Dams along the

Atlantic and Pacific coasts of the United States have reduced salmon populations by preventing their access to spawning grounds upstream. Salmon spawn are also harmed on their migration downstream when they must pass through turbines. When young salmon travel downstream toward the ocean, they may be killed by turbine blades at hydropower plants. When adult salmon attempt to swim upstream to reproduce, they may not be able to get past the dams (USEPA 2011). Moreover, lake species often replace river species of fish in reservoirs, either naturally or with artificial stocking for sports fishing. Hydropower facilities can damage fish, restrict or delay migration, increase predation, and degrade water quality (Schilt 2007).

Supersaturation. Supersaturation occurs when air becomes trapped in water spilled over a dam as it hits a pool below, creating turbulence. Because air is comprised of 78 percent nitrogen, the level of nitrogen dissolved in water can increase dramatically. Affected water does not lose the excess nitrogen quickly. Supersaturated water can enter tissues of fish and other species. If fish swim from an area supersaturated with nitrogen to a lower pressure area, a condition similar to "the bends" in scuba divers can occur. This effect causes injury and can cause death to fish (FWEE 2011).

Methane Emissions. Hydroelectricity generation has different impacts on climate change, depending on the climate where a hydro project is located. Decaying plant matter from flooded areas releases methane and carbon dioxide (Guerin et al. 2006). Hydro facilities located in tropical climates may produce substantial amounts of methane and are therefore likely to have more severe impacts on climate change than facilities located in temperate climates, which may actually sequester methane (FWEE 2011).

Water Quality. Mercury is mobilized and released into the environment for twenty to thirty years by decaying organic matter undergoing anaerobic decomposition in reservoirs (Dillon 2010). A fivefold to sixfold increase in mercury concentrations has been observed in fish in hydroelectric impoundments as compared to natural reservoirs (Tremblay, Lucotte, and Hillaire-Marcel 1993). Mercury is picked up by fish that humans like to catch and eat, and it bioaccumulates in both fish and human body tissues. Too much mercury is especially harmful to development of the nervous systems of small children (Dillon 2010).

Dam Failures. Because large dams hold back large volumes of water, a failure due to poor construction, earthquakes (Armaroli and Balzani 2011, 234), terrorism, or other causes can be catastrophic to downriver settlements. In an unstable political world, large dams upstream of population centers constitute attractive targets for terrorism. Sound design and construction are not adequate guarantees of safety. Smaller dams and micro hydro facilities create less risk, but may constitute continuing hazards even after being decommissioned. Small dams can fail many years after decommissioning, causing death and property destruction downstream.

Multiple Uses of a Reservoir. Reservoirs created by hydroelectric schemes often provide facilities for water sports and sport fishing, becoming tourist attractions. Multiple-use dams serve multiple goals of providing water for agricultural irrigation, municipal water supply, and flood control to protect people and property downstream (FWEE 2011).

Cultural Impacts. Large dam construction may require relocation of human populations from a reservoir area and destruction of archeological and cultural resources of value to local populations. In many cases, no amount of compensation can replace ancestral and cultural attachments to places that have spiritual value to a displaced population. Historically and culturally important sites can be flooded and lost. Some of these may have religious significance (Armaroli and Balzani 2011, 234).

Decommissioning

Decommissioning of a hydroelectric facility involves removal of the dam structure and powerhouse from the river on which it was built. For small hydro facilities, this can generally be accomplished through use of bulldozers, trucks, and shovels similar to those used in road construction. Somewhat durable in construction, no large hydro power plant has ever been decommissioned in the United States, so cost estimates for large facilities are not available.

Hydroelectric facilities must be licensed and relicensed by the U.S. Federal Energy Regulatory Commission (FERC) every fifty years. Since the 1980s, the environmental amenities of many existing small hydroelectric generating sites have increasingly been viewed by the public as more valuable than the small amount of electricity they generate. This stimulated public participation in FERC relicensing proceedings and demands for removal or substantial alteration of numerous dams and reservoirs. The vision of a free-running river, interruption of migratory patterns for fish such as salmon—some of which are endangered species—and injury or death to fish passing through turbines attracted the attention of sports fishing enthusiasts and recreational users of rivers, who pushed for removal of some small dams and installation of fish ladders at others.

In the early 1980s, the state of Maine adopted a comprehensive plan for the lower Kennebec River that established a goal of restoring several species of migratory fish to the lower Kennebec and specifically called for removal of the Edwards Dam, a small hydro facility. In 1986, Congress amended the Federal Power Act, which governs FERC's licensing of hydropower dams, by requiring "equal consideration" of power and nonpower values such as fish and wildlife and recreation. Coupled with FERC's obligation to license projects "consistent with comprehensive plans," this change in law opened the way for a new type of environmental advocacy focused on restoration of America's rivers (Fahlund 2011).

The Kennebec River was once home to all ten species of migratory fish native to Maine—including Atlantic salmon, American shad, several species of herring, alewife, and shortnose and Atlantic sturgeon—along with several thriving commercial fisheries. Damming the river transformed the natural landscape and ushered in an era of industrialization and pollution (Fahlund 2011).

> Built in 1837, the Edwards Dam was 25 feet high and 917 feet wide, with an 850-foot spillway. The timber and concrete structure rose approximately 20 feet above the water, creating a 1,143-acre reservoir that extended 17 miles upstream to the next dam in Waterville. Sitting just at the far reaches of tidal influence, the Edwards Dam was the first, and therefore most devastating, obstruction encountered by large populations of sea-run fish on the way to their upstream spawning grounds, especially Atlantic salmon, striped bass, river herring, and sturgeon. (American Museum of Natural History 2011)

The Edwards Dam generated only 3.5 MWh of electricity in 1995 (Fahlund 2011).

The Federal Energy Regulatory Commission's 1997 decision to order removal of Edwards Dam was nationally significant because the federal government recognized that a free-flowing, healthy river teeming with life can be more valuable than the electric power and private profit it produces (Maine State Planning Office 2011). This was the first time that FERC ordered dam removal when the dam owner wanted to keep running it (Goldberg 1997). During the following decade, more than 430 outdated dams were removed nationwide, and the number of recorded dam removals grew each year (Fahlund 2011). Recently decommissioned small hydro facilities include the 13.7 MWe Condit Dam in south-central Washington on the White Salmon River scheduled to be breached in October 2011 (Pacificorp 2011), the 22 MWe Marmot Dam on the Sandy River in Oregon (Romey 2007), the Smelt Hill Dam on the Presumpscot River in 2002, Brownville Dam on the Pleasant River, Souadabscook Dam on the Penobscot River, and the East Machias Dam on East Machias River (Griset 2010), all in Maine.

Reclamation

After the artificial structures have been removed, reclamation of rivers is largely a matter of getting out of the way so nature can move in and take over the exposed land. Some reseeding may be necessary to stabilize steep slopes on the sides of former reservoirs and prevent erosion from heavy rainfall, and some desired fish species may be restocked to speed their reoccupation of remote reaches of former reservoirs, but if the rivers below a former reservoir are unobstructed by other dams, the fish will generally find their way upstream in large numbers within a year or two, so the costs of reclamation are generally very low.

Dollar Costs of Utilizing Hydropower

The major advantage of hydroelectricity over other electricity-generating technologies is elimination of the cost of fuel. The cost of operating a hydroelectric plant is nearly immune to increases in the cost of fossil fuels such as oil, natural gas, and coal, and no imported fuels are needed. Hydroelectric plants have long economic lives, with some plants still in service after fifty or even a hundred years. Operating labor cost is also usually low, as plants are automated and have few personnel on site during normal operation. Although numerous small hydro plants have been dismantled, no large hydro power plant has ever been decommissioned in the United States, so cost estimates for decommissioning large facilities are not available. The costs of reclamation are generally very low.

The market cost to consumers for hydroelectric energy consumed in calendar year 2009 was estimated at a bit over $24.2 billion, and $22.8 billion in 2010 (calculated from USEIA 2011a, Table 8.2c, Table 8.10). Federal subsidies and tax expenditures for hydroelectric energy were estimated at $216 million for FY2010, of which $215 million was for producing electricity (USEIA 2011b, xiii, xviii). The dollar costs of hydroelectricity can be broken down into two categories, capital investment costs and operating costs. Capital investment costs are the largest, accounting for almost 75 to 80 percent of the total lifecycle costs of a hydro power station. Operating costs of hydroelectric power generation are considerably lower as hydro does not require any fuel except for water, which is freely available. However, all mechanical equipment requires periodic maintenance. The total dollar cost of a hydroelectric power plant is two to five cents per kilowatt/hour, while that of small hydro power turbines is three to ten cents per kilowatt/hour. These costs are comparable to the lowest fossil fuel and nuclear power generating technologies (Green World Investor 2011).

Where a dam already serves multiple purposes such as flood control, irrigation, and provision of municipal drinking water, a hydroelectric plant may be added with relatively low construction cost, providing a useful revenue stream to offset the costs of dam operation. For purposes of evaluating energy technologies to develop future energy policies, it is worth noting that most of the economically viable hydro sites in the United States were developed long ago and already play a role in providing our electrical power (USDOI et al. 2007).

Hydroelectric power in 2003 was generated at more than 2,000 facilities in fifty states and Puerto Rico, contributing approximately 80,000 megawatts of generating capacity, representing about 10 percent of total U.S. electrical generating capability. In the Pacific Northwest alone, hydropower provides about two-thirds of the region's electricity supply (USEPA 2011). According to an assessment conducted by the U.S. Department of Energy (DOE), the estimated average available hydropower at undeveloped sites in the United States is 170,000 MWe, not counting areas excluded from development by federal statutes and policies. The Alaska Region contains the largest available potential with slightly less than 45,000 MWe. The Pacific Northwest Region has the second highest amount of available potential with almost 40,000 MWe. Together these two regions contain about half of the estimated undeveloped U.S. hydropower potential (USDOE 2003, 15).

Run-of-the-river resources with less than 1 MWe of power make up about 50,000 MWe of the total available potential. These resources could be captured using technologies not requiring the use of dams, thus avoiding many environmental impacts. Development of about 30 percent of these resources would require unconventional systems or micro hydro technologies. Partial use of the remaining available potential of approximately 120,000 MWe of resources greater than or equal to 1 MWe represents an additional source of power potential that could be captured using conventional turbine technology in configurations offering the same low impact environmental benefits (USDOE 2003, 15). Beyond these undeveloped resources, the National Hydropower Association estimates that more than 4,300 MWe of additional or "incremental" hydropower capacity could be brought on line by upgrading or augmenting existing facilities (USDOE 2003, 2–3).

A more recent multi-agency study of the potential for increasing electric power production at federally owned or operated water regulation, storage, and conveyance facilities examined 871 existing federal facilities, with and without hydroelectric generating capability, assessing their physical capacity for generation or generation expansion and their economic viability based on comparisons with regional electric power rates. Based on economic conditions in 2006, the report found a total of sixty-four potentially viable sites at federal facilities managed by the Bureau of Reclamation and Army Corps of Engineers that could demonstrate both physical and economic conditions sufficient to warrant further exploration for additional hydropower development. The total additional capacity at these sites was estimated at 1,230 MWe. Additional opportunities for refurbishment of some facilities with existing hydropower could result in the addition of approximately 1,283 MWe of generating capacity. These are not large numbers. It is unlikely hydropower will ever contribute a larger portion of national energy supply than it does today, and the portion will probably shrink as energy demand increases with population growth in future.

National Security Costs of Utilizing Hydropower

Rainfall, changes in elevation, and steel and limestone, from which concrete is made, are common in the United States. Thus, production of hydroelectric energy depends upon domestic resources, and no country or group of countries is able to control supplies or determine price.

Outside the tropics, hydroelectric reservoirs produce almost no carbon emissions or greenhouse gases. Consequently, utilizing hydroelectric power technologies will not contribute much to climate change or sea level rise. Hydro technologies do not produce substantial amounts of

Figure 8.3   **The Costs of Utilizing Hydroelectric Technologies**

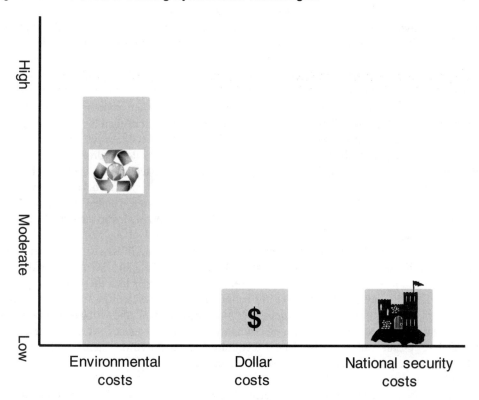

toxic waste that must be isolated from the human environment for millennia, and therefore do not produce materials useful to terrorists. The only national security risk from hydroelectricity is that presented by large dams upstream of substantial population concentrations, which are few in the United States and probably more difficult and less desirable targets to hit with a large airplane than a tall building in a major city. Consequently, the national security costs of utilizing hydroelectric technologies are very low.

SUMMARY OF COSTS

The costs of utilizing hydroelectric energy technologies are summarized in Figure 8.3. Overall, the environmental costs for producing and using hydroelectric technologies are "moderately high" compared to most conventional fuel technologies in use today. The environmental costs for producing electricity from power plants depending on large reservoirs are substantial, due to the high costs of disruption of relatively large acreages of land that must be dedicated to such facilities. Environmental costs for utilization of small hydro are much lower, but these technologies appear to be on their way out, as older river dams are increasingly being removed to allow return of fishing and recreational opportunities throughout the United States.

Dollar costs for decentralized application of hydroelectricity are "low" and quite competitive today with other conventional fuels, but most of the available large hydro sites are already in use or off limits due to previous policy decisions. Because the larger hydro facilities were mostly built by the national government at lower construction costs than are available today, it seems unlikely that any large hydro facility proposed today would share the low dollar costs of previous generations of hydro plants. National security costs for all hydro technologies are very "low" or negligible because the materials for producing them are all available in the United States. This is a distinct advantage hydro technologies hold over other energy technologies that may be acquired from foreign sources, contribute to global climate change, or leave a legacy of long-term waste products that are attractive to terrorists.

Hydroelectric technologies do not produce much hazardous waste, are environmentally advantageous because the "fuel" supply will never run out, and cannot be controlled by any combination of hostile foreign governments. For the foreseeable future, rainfall will always fall upon at least portions of this planet and, as long as it does, it will provide energy that hydro technologies can exploit. This means that creating the components of hydroelectric technology is extremely easy, does not require mining or drilling in a politically dangerous locale, and can be acquired without involvement of unreliable political allies. Because fewer resources are expended in the acquisition and utilization of concrete, the overall effect on ecosystems of utilizing hydro technologies is less than for other fuel sources except solar.

To capture appreciable amounts of energy, hydroelectric facilities require either large reservoirs or a large number of small generators. Large reservoirs can take up a considerable amount of space and destroy entire ecosystems, but small generators lack these costs. A practical solution to this issue is to decentralize utilization of hydropower, using small hydro located near electricity consumers, thereby reducing the inundation of land and wildlife habitat while using the water resource with minimum electrical transmission distances, which are described in Chapter 13. Of the various hydroelectric technologies, small hydro systems hold the greatest promise for dispersed market penetration utilizing recent technological developments and financial innovations.

We need to be aware that when we buy electricity from distant generators, we export the environmental impacts of our energy demand. There are people and other living things at the other end of the electric wires. The electricity we use is being generated somewhere else, and when we sign purchase contracts for electricity there are going to be long-term environmental consequences and not just long-term price stability.

REFERENCES

American Museum of Natural History. 2011. "A Historic Fishing Grounds." BioBulletin. www.amnh.org/sciencebulletins/biobulletin/biobulletin/story1204.html.

Armaroli, Nicola, and Vincenzo Balzani. 2011. *Energy for a Sustainable World*. Weinheim, Germany: Wiley-VCH Verlag.

B.C. Hydro. 1981. *Stikine-Iskut Hydroelectric Development Exploration Program and Access Requirements*. Vancouver: B.C. Hydro.

Bergerson, Joule, and Lester Lave. 2002. *A Life Cycle Analysis of Electricity Generation Technologies: Health and Environmental Implications of Alternative Fuels and Technologies*. Report, November. Pittsburgh: Carnegie Mellon Electricity Industry Center.

Chanson, Hubert, and D. Patrick James. 1998. "Teaching Case Studies in Reservoir Siltation and Catchment Erosion." *International Journal of Engineering Education* 14 (4): 265–275.

Cunningham, Paul, and Ian Woofenden. 2011. "Microhydro Electricity Basics." *Home Power Magazine*. http://homepower.com/basics/hydro/.

Dillon, John. 2010. "Big Hydro: Environmental Impacts." Vermont Public Radios News, August 18. www.vpr.net/news_detail/88654/.

Eco Hydro Energy Limited. 2005. "Introduction to Eco Hydro Energy Ltd. FPS—Floating Power Station." www.ecohydroenergy.net/about.html.

Fahlund, Andrew. 2011. "River Rebirth: Removing Edwards Dam on Maine's Kennebec River." National Geographic Online. http://environment.nationalgeographic.com/environment/freshwater/lessons-from-the-field-edwards-dam-removal-maine/.

Foundation for Water and Energy Education (FWEE). 2011. "How a Hydroelectric Project Can Affect a River." www.fwee.org/hpar.html.

Goldberg, Carey. 1997. "For a Change, the Fish Win." *New York Times*, November 30.

Green World Investor. 2011. "Hydroelectricity Costs—Not as Simple as Dollars per Kilowatthour." March 31. www.greenworldinvestor.com/2011/03/31/hydroelectricity-costs-not-as-simple-as-dollars-per-kilowatthour/.

Griset, Todd. 2010. "Removing Maine Dams, or Not." Energy Policy Update, October 27. http://energypolicyupdate.blogspot.com/2010/10/october-27-2010-removing-maine-dams-or.html.

Guerin, F., G. Abril, S. Richard, B. Burban, C. Reynouard, P. Seyler, and R. Delmas. 2006. "Methane and Carbon Dioxide Emissions from Tropical Reservoirs: Significance of Downstream Rivers." *Geophysical Research Letters* 33, L21407.

International Energy Agency (IEA). 2011. *Environmental and Health Impacts of Electricity Generation: A Comparison of the Environmental Impacts of Hydropower with Those of Other Generation Technologies.* Paris: IEA.

Ledec, George, and Juan David Quintero. 2003. *Good Dams and Bad Dams: Environmental Criteria for Site Selection of Hydroelectric Projects.* Latin America and Caribbean Region Sustainable Development Working Paper 16. Washington, DC: World Bank. http://siteresources.worldbank.org/LACEXT/Resources/258553-1123250606139/Good_and_Bad_Dams_WP16.pdf.

Mah, Abdullah. 2011. "Remote Sensing Techniques for Hydro Power Site Selection." Geospatial World. www.geospatialworld.net/index.php?option=com_content&view=article&id=16446%3Aremote-sensing-techniques-for-hydro-power-site-selection&catid=164%3Autility-power&Itemid=41.

Maine State Planning Office. 2011. "The River Runs Free. . . ." Edwards Dam Removal Update. Augusta: Maine State Planning Office. www.maine.gov/spo/specialprojects/docs/edwsdam_theriverrunsfree.pdf.

Pacificorp. 2011. "Condit: Project Overview." www.pacificorp.com/es/hydro/hl/condit.html.

Power Scorecard. 2011. Electricity from Hydro. www.powerscorecard.org/tech_detail.cfm?resource_id=4.

Romey, Bernard T. 2007. *Bull Run Hydroelectric Project Turbidity Monitoring & Evaluation.* Brightwood, OR: Romey Associates.

Schilt, C.R. 2007. "Developing Fish Passage and Protection at Hydropower Dams." *Applied Animal Behavior Science* 104 (3): 295–325.

Sentürk, Fuat. 1994. *Hydraulics of Dams and Reservoirs.* Highlands Ranch, CO: Water Resources Publications.

Tennessee Valley Authority. 2011. "Hydroelectric Power." www.tva.gov/power/hydro.htm.

Tremblay, Alain, Marc Lucotte, and Claude Hillaire-Marcel. 1993. *Mercury in the Environment and in Hydroelectric Reservoirs*, trans. Shirley Péloquin. Montreal: Great Whale Public Review Support Office.

Urban, Frauke, and Tom Mitchell. 2011. *Climate Change, Disasters and Electricity Generation.* Strengthening Climate Resilience Discussion Paper 8. London: Overseas Development Institute and Institute of Development Studies.

U.S. Army Corps of Engineers. 1967. *Dickey-Lincoln School Lakes, Maine, U.S.A. and Quebec, Canada: Design Memorandum.* Waltham, MA: U.S. Army Corps of Engineers.

———. 2011a. "Grand Coulee Dam." www.usbr.gov/pn/grandcoulee/.

U.S. Bureau of Reclamation. 2011b. "Hoover Dam." www.usbr.gov/projects/Facility.jsp?fac_Name=Hoover+Dam&groupName=Overview.

U.S. Department of Energy (USDOE). 2003. *Hydropower: Setting a Course for Our Energy Future.* Report. Springfield, VA: National Technical Information Service.

U.S Department of the Interior, U.S. Corps of Engineers, and U.S. Department of Energy (US DOI et al.) 2007. *Potential Hydroelectric Development at Existing Federal Facilities.* Washington, DC: U.S. Government Printing Office.

U.S. Energy Information Administration (USEIA). 2011a. *Annual Energy Review 2010.* Report DOE/EIA-0384 (2010), October. Washington, DC: U.S. Government Printing Office.

———. 2011b. *Direct Federal Financial Interventions and Subsidies in Energy Markets 2010.* Washington, DC: U.S. Government Printing Office.

———. 2011c. "What Are the Different Types of Renewable Energy?" www.eia.gov/energyexplained/index. cfm?page=renewable_home#tab2.

U.S. Environmental Protection Agency (USEPA). 2011. "Hydroelectricity: Electricity from Hydropower." www.epa.gov/cleanenergy/energy-and-you/affect/hydro.html.

U.S. Federal Energy Regulatory Commission (USFERC). 2010. "Pumped Storage Projects." www.ferc.gov/industries/hydropower/gen-info/licensing/pump-storage.asp#skipnav.

U.S. Geological Service (USGS). 2011. "Hydroelectric Power Water Use." http://ga.water.usgs.gov/edu/wuhy.html.

University of Nottingham. 2011. "What Is Pico Hydro?" www.picohydro.org.uk.

Williams, Arthur. 2007. "Pico Hydro for Cost Effective Lighting." *Boiling Point Magazine* 53 (May). www.hedon.info/PicoHydroForCost-effectiveLighting?bl=y.

9

Biomass

~~~~~~~~~~~~~~~~~~

Whether crop or forest residues, urban and mill wastes, or energy crops, energy in the form of organic materials—biomass—of one kind or another is available in most areas of the United States. Plant material and animal waste are the raw materials of biomass energy, which can be used with a variety of technologies to either generate electricity or provide fuel for transportation and other uses. Generally we refer to biomass generation of electricity as biopower, and biomass fuel for other uses such as transportation as biofuels. Biomass ultimately is another form of solar energy, stored in plants in the form of carbohydrates through the process of photosynthesis, and released through various technologies. In effect, biomass functions as a sort of natural battery for storing solar energy (UCS 2010). A study done for the U.S. Department of Energy in 2005 found that the United States has the technical potential to produce more than 1 billion tons of biomass per year for energy use, which could have met about 42 percent of our electricity needs in 2007 (Perlack et al. 2005).

BIOPOWER

Biomass can be processed in a variety of ways to produce solid, gaseous, or liquid fuels that may be used to generate electricity. Biomass fuels suitable for generation of electricity include forest harvest residues such as tree tops and branches; bark, sawdust, "black liquor," and other by-products of milling timber and making paper; shavings produced during manufacture of wood products, often in the form of wood chips; bagasse, the fibrous matter that remains after sugarcane or sorghum stalks are crushed to extract their juice; corn stover residue of corn cultivation; prairie grasses; dried manure; urban wood waste such as tree trimmings, shipping pallets, and clean, untreated, leftover construction wood; rice hulls; oat hulls; barley malt dust from brewing of beer; the clean, biodegradable portion of municipal garbage such as unrecycled paper; and woody yard waste (Brower 2002). Methane can be captured from landfills or produced in the operation of sewage treatment plants. All are routinely used to generate electricity, although wood chips account for the greatest portion by far of biomass energy production in the United States.

Direct combustion of biomass produces heat that can be used to heat buildings, for industrial processes, and to produce steam for turbine generation of electricity. Forest and crop residues, switchgrass, and urban wood residues can be made into pellets and sold for residential wood stove combustion or burned directly in power plants to generate electricity. Biomass can be mixed with coal and burned at a power plant designed for coal—a process known as cofiring (UCS 2010).

BIOFUELS

Biomass can be converted into liquid fuels or cooked in a process of gasification to produce combustible gases, which reduces some emissions from combustion, especially particulates. By heating biomass in the presence of a carefully controlled amount of oxygen under pressure, it

161

can be converted into synthetic gas (syngas), a mixture of hydrogen and carbon monoxide. Microorganisms can break down biomass from human sewage, animal manure, or poultry litter in anaerobic digesters to produce methane and carbon dioxide (UCS 2010).

Through gasification, biomass can also be cofired at natural gas–powered electric generating plants. Syngas is often refined to remove contaminants and carbon dioxide and can then be burned directly in a gas turbine or burned in a steam turbine to produce electricity. Biomass gasification is generally cleaner and more efficient than direct combustion. Syngas can also be further processed to make liquid biofuels or other useful chemicals (UCS 2010). Liquid biofuels have great potential to help supply our transportation needs (Luque et al. 2008).

To assess the global warming impact of transportation fuels, we must measure their full life cycle emissions per unit of energy delivered. Emissions vary depending on the feedstock and refining process. A study by the Union of Concerned Scientists found that liquid coal (gasoline or diesel made from coal) may produce emissions more than 80 percent greater than conventional gasoline. Gasoline produced from tar sands may produce emissions about 14 percent greater than conventional gasoline, depending on the feedstock and refining process used. Corn ethanol can produce higher emissions than conventional gasoline or cut emissions more than 50 percent, depending on how it is processed. Cellulosic ethanol, which is made from woody plants, may be able to reduce emissions more than 85 percent, as compared to conventional gasoline (UCS 2007). The range of findings suggests great caution is warranted when analyzing the environmental costs of biomass technologies.

COSTS OF BIOMASS UTILIZATION

Environmental Costs of Utilizing Biomass

The fuel cycle for biomass is twofold, depending on whether one wishes to use it for biopower or biofuel. The fuel cycle for biopower includes growing and harvesting the fuel, transportation, processing, combustion in a power plant, decommissioning and reclamation of the generating site, and disposal of waste by-products, as illustrated in Figure 9.1. The basic components of biopower generation facilities include a nearby source for fuel, a processing facility, a combustion turbine, and electrical grid interconnection equipment. Suitable areas must be evaluated, processing and generating facilities constructed and operated, and eventually generating equipment must be decommissioned. Potential environmental costs of using biopower technologies include land disturbance and major ecosystem changes, adverse effects on water quality and quantity, and climate-changing air emissions.

The fuel cycle for biofuels includes growing and harvesting the fuel, processing, transportation, combustion, decommissioning and reclamation of the processing site, and disposal of waste by-products, as illustrated in Figure 9.2. The basic components of biofuels production and consumption include a nearby source for fuel, processing equipment, and combustion. Suitable areas must be evaluated, processing facilities constructed and operated, and eventually processing equipment must be decommissioned. Potential environmental costs of using biofuels include land disturbance and major ecosystem changes, adverse effects on water quality and quantity, and climate changing air emissions.

Biomass can be grown and harvested in ways that protect soil quality, avoid erosion, and maintain wildlife habitat. However, biomass for energy can also be harvested at unsustainable rates, damage ecosystems, produce harmful air pollution, consume large amounts of water, and produce increased net greenhouse emissions, affecting climate change. The Union of Concerned Scientists main-

Figure 9.1 **The Biopower Fuel Cycle**

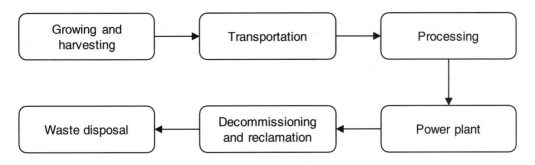

Figure 9.2 **The Biofuels Fuel Cycle**

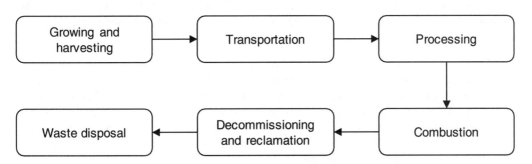

tains that the environmental costs and benefits of using biomass depend on developing beneficial biomass resources and avoiding harmful resources. Because biomass markets may involve new or additional removals of residues, crops, or trees, care must be taken to minimize impacts from whatever additional demands biomass growth or harvesting makes on the land (UCS 2010).

Beneficial Biomass

Some biomass resources are clearly beneficial in their potential to reduce net carbon emissions. These beneficial resources exist in substantial quantities and can support increasing production of biopower and biofuels. A wide range of biomass resources are beneficial because their use will clearly reduce overall carbon emissions and provide other benefits. Beneficial biomass includes:

- energy crops that do not compete with food crops for land
- portions of crop residues such as wheat straw or corn stover
- sustainably harvested wood and forest residues
- clean municipal and industrial wastes. (Tilman et al. 2009)

Utilization of other biomass resources may be harmful if their use will increase overall carbon emissions or entail other severe environmental costs.

Harmful Biomass

Harmful biomass resources and practices include clearing forests, savannas, or grasslands to grow energy crops, and displacing food production for energy production that ultimately leads to the clearing of carbon-rich ecosystems elsewhere to grow food (Tilman et al. 2009). Moreover, harmful biomass adds net carbon to the atmosphere by either directly or indirectly decreasing the overall amount of carbon stored in plants and soils. Biofuels made from most food crops do not significantly reduce greenhouse gas emissions—and, in many cases, cause additional forests to be destroyed to grow more food, creating more net carbon-dioxide emissions than fossil fuels (Lomborg 2011). There can be an indirect land-use effect when corn and soy are taken out of the market for food and animal feed. This increases corn and soy prices, stimulating land conversion in other parts of the world (UCS 2008).

The United States spends about $6 billion a year on federal support for ethanol production through tax credits, tariffs, and other programs. Thanks to this financial assistance, one-sixth of the world's corn supply is burned in American cars. That is enough corn to feed 350 million people for an entire year (Lomborg 2011). Increasing production of food-based fuels may cause more people to suffer from hunger and add to global political instability (Goldemberg 2008). As Lester Brown (2006) notes,

> As the price of oil climbs, it becomes increasingly profitable to convert farm commodities into automotive fuel—either ethanol or biodiesel. U.S. investment in biofuel production in response to runaway oil prices is spiraling out of control, threatening to draw grain away from the production of beef, pork, poultry, milk and eggs. And, most seriously, the vast number of distilleries in operation, under construction and in the planning stages threaten to reduce the amount of grain available for direct human consumption. Simply put, the stage is being set for a head-on collision between the world's 800 million affluent automobile owners and food consumers.

For the 2 billion poorest people in the world, many of whom spend half or more of their income on food, rising grain prices can quickly become life-threatening. Rising food prices could spread hunger and generate political instability in low-income countries that import grain, such as Indonesia, Egypt, Nigeria, and Mexico (Brown 2006). In these countries, which are all friends of the United States, instability may directly impact our national security interests.

Marginal Biomass

The carbon benefits and risks of using biomass resources vary widely, depending on how and where they are harvested, how efficiently they are converted to energy, and what fossil fuels they replace. These resources might be beneficial or harmful depending on specific situations. For example, harvesting trees especially for energy use that quickly regrow to displace more carbon-intensive fossil fuels may be beneficial. But using trees that grow slowly or may not be fully replaced or may displace less carbon-intensive fuels may not be beneficial. Therefore, marginal biomass resources should be used only when their use can be demonstrated to reduce net carbon emissions (UCS 2010).

Land Use Changes

Increased forest harvesting and large scale conversion of forests, wetlands, and other relatively natural areas to energy crops could result in loss of habitat for native wildlife, including endangered species. Coarse woody material that could be removed from a forest for biomass energy provides crucial wildlife habitat for birds and small mammals; snags, den trees, and large downed woody material are important to the well-being of many wildlife species (UCS 2010). Fuels made from biomass waste products or native perennials grown on land not currently used for or well suited to food crops can be produced without harmful changes in land use. Some types of land should not be used for biofuel production, especially forests high in stored carbon and rich in biodiversity. Cutting down rain forest in Indonesia to create palm oil plantations for manufacture of biofuels is one example of biomass cultivation reducing biodiversity.

Biofuels that use land more efficiently, such as those derived from agricultural, forest-product, and municipal waste streams, are more beneficial than food-based biofuels from a land-use perspective. Bioenergy crops that improve land currently considered unsuitable for agriculture are likely to be the most beneficial of all (UCS 2008). Cultivating switchgrass on marginal agricultural lands in the United States for production of biofuels is one example of this.

Water Quality

When crop-based biofuels contribute to deforestation or other damaging land conversions, environmental costs can be high, potentially producing a net increase in pollution (UCS 2008). Cultivation of bioenergy crops may increase sediment yield, nitrogen, and total phosphorous losses in runoff from agricultural land (Nyakatawa et al. 2006). Phosphorous is particularly important because it is often the critical nutrient triggering algae blooms in downstream lakes and other slow-moving waters.

Similarly, excessive removal of crop residues may adversely impact water quality by increasing transport of sediment, nitrogen, and phosphorous to downstream water bodies. Crop residues are essential to conserve soil and water and improve crop production. Crop residue mulch increases water infiltration and reduces the amount of rainfall runoff. It filters pollutants from runoff and increases soil organic matter, which is essential for adsorbing and retaining pollutants (Dreiling 2009). Leaving crop residue on the soil surface is the best and simplest way of reducing water and wind erosion. Widespread crop residue removal for use as biofuels may accelerate soil erosion and increase loss of sediments, nutrients, and pesticides in runoff water. Sediment and nutrients leaching into runoff are the main culprits of nonpoint source pollution flowing into downstream water bodies (Dreiling 2009). In some semiarid regions of the United States, not enough crop residue is produced in most years to protect soil from water and wind erosion and maintain adequate levels of organic matter in the soil. Crop residue mulch plays a beneficial role in plowed and no-till soils in reducing runoff transport of nonpoint source pollutants. In some watersheds, only a fraction of crop residue may be available for removal without negatively affecting water quality (Dreiling 2009). Soil organic carbon is essential to increase the soil's ability to absorb and filter nonpoint source pollutants and maintain productivity of the soil (Dreiling 2009). Increases in soil carbon storage occur on sites planted to woody or herbaceous species for biomass production (Tolbert et al. 2002). But removing crop residue after harvest reduces soil carbon, total nitrogen, and phosphorous (Dreiling 2009).

Crop residues are essential to reduce sediment, soil organic carbon, and nutrient loss in runoff, regardless of tillage system. Crop residue left on the soil surface protects soil against impacting raindrops, helps maintain the integrity of soil aggregates, and improves rainwater infiltration. Only about 25 percent of crop residue may be available for removal for biomass energy production from no-till soils, and less from intensively tilled soils, without degradation (Dreiling 2009).

Air Emissions

Combustion of biomass produces carbon monoxide, nitrogen oxides, and particulates such as soot and ash. The amount of pollution emitted per unit of energy generated varies widely by technology, with wood-burning stoves and fireplaces generally the worst offenders. Newer, enclosed fireplaces and wood stoves pollute much less than older, open fireplaces because they are more efficient. Emissions from biomass power plants are generally similar to emissions from coal-fired power plants, except biomass facilities produce little sulfur dioxide or toxic metals because most biomass resources and natural gas contain far less sulfur and heavy metals than coal (Bain et al. 2003). Their most serious problem is particulate emissions, which must be controlled with special air pollution control equipment (Brower 1992, 106).

Facilities that burn raw municipal waste present special pollution-control problems. Municipal garbage often contains heavy metals, chlorinated compounds, and plastics, which generate harmful emissions. This problem is much less severe in facilities burning refuse-derived fuel (RDF) from which most inorganic material has been removed, leaving mostly shredded paper and paperboard (Brower 1992, 107). However, RDF has considerably lower heat content than waste which has not had high-Btu inorganic materials such as plastics removed. In general, the more one recycles from municipal solid waste, the lower the heat content of remaining fuel.

Using methanol and ethanol distilled from biomass as vehicle fuels instead of conventional gasoline could substantially reduce air pollution from automobiles. Both methanol and ethanol evaporate more slowly than gasoline, reducing evaporative emissions of volatile organic compounds (VOCs), which react with heat and sunlight to generate ground-level ozone, a component of smog. In cars specifically designed to burn pure methanol or ethanol, VOC emissions from the tailpipe could be reduced 85 to 95 percent, while carbon monoxide emissions could be reduced 30 to 90 percent. Using blends of gasoline and ethanol reduces most air emissions by proportionate amounts. However, emissions of nitrogen oxides, a source of acid precipitation, would not change significantly compared to gasoline-powered vehicles without ethanol (Brower 1992, 107).

Some studies have indicated that use of fuel alcohol increases emissions of formaldehyde and other aldehydes, which are potential carcinogens. Other studies counter that these results consider only tailpipe emissions, where VOCs, another significant pathway of aldehyde formation, are much lower in alcohol-burning vehicles (Alson 1990). On balance, methanol vehicles would therefore decrease ozone levels (Brower 2002). Thermochemical conversion of biomass using gasification, liquefaction, and pyrolysis can produce carbon monoxide and VOCs. Standard pollution control technology can neutralize or remove most of these before release into the atmosphere. Pyrolysis and liquefaction also generate liquid and solid hazardous wastes such as residual tars, catalysts, acids, char, and ash that must be disposed of properly, at some expense. More research is needed on the environmental costs of controlling these air pollutants from biomass conversion (Brower 1992, 100, 108).

Greenhouse Gases

A major benefit of substituting biomass for fossil fuels is that, if done in a sustainable fashion, it would greatly reduce emissions of greenhouse gases. The amount of carbon dioxide released when biomass is burned is very nearly the same as the amount required to replenish the plants grown to produce the biomass (Brower 2002). Thus, in a sustainable fuel cycle, there would be no net emissions of carbon dioxide, although some fossil-fuel inputs may be required for planting, harvesting, transporting, and processing biomass. If efficient cultivation and conversion processes are used, the resulting emissions should be small, about 20 percent of the emissions created by fossil fuels alone. And if the energy needed to produce and process biomass came from renewable sources like wind, hydro, or solar energy, the net contribution to global warming would be zero (Brower 1992, 108). Similarly, if biomass wastes such as crop residues or municipal solid wastes are used for energy production, there should be no net increase in greenhouse gas emissions. Biomass power plants divert wood waste from landfills, which reduces the production and atmospheric release of methane. There might even be a slight greenhouse benefit in some cases, because if wastes are burned to produce electricity, some of the methane otherwise formed through anaerobic decay of biomass in landfills would not be created, and methane is a more potent greenhouse gas than carbon dioxide (Brower 1992, 108).

In sum, growing trees and other plants for energy might benefit soil quality and farm economies. Energy crops could provide a steady supplemental income for farmers or allow them to work unused land without requiring much additional equipment. Moreover, energy crops could be used to stabilize cropland or rangeland prone to erosion and flooding. Trees would be grown for several years before being harvested, and their roots and leaf litter could help stabilize the soil. Perennial grasses harvested like hay would minimize the need for disruptive tilling and planting; soil losses with a crop such as switchgrass, for example, would be negligible compared to annual crops such as corn, because it can be harvested for many years before replanting (Tyson 1990).

If improperly managed, however, energy farming could have harmful environmental impacts. Although energy crops can be grown with less pesticide and fertilizer than conventional food crops, large-scale energy farming could lead to increases in chemical use simply because more land would be under cultivation. It could also reduce biodiversity through destruction of habitats, especially if forests are more intensively managed than previously. If agricultural or forestry wastes and residues are used for fuel, soils may be depleted of organic content and nutrients unless care is taken to leave an appropriate portion of wastes behind on the land (Brower 1992, 109).

Dollar Costs of Utilizing Biomass

Unprocessed biomass typically cannot be cost-effectively shipped more than fifty to a hundred miles by truck before it is converted into fuel or energy (UCS 2010). Consequently, all prices for biopower and biofuels must be considered local, and there is substantial variation between locales. The cost of energy produced from biomass depends on the type of biomass being utilized, the type of energy being produced (heat, electricity, or fuel), the technology used, and the size of the plant producing or using it.

In the United States, almost 57 billion kilowatt-hours of electricity were generated from biomass, providing nearly 1.4 percent of total electric sales, in 2010 (USEIA 2011a, Table 8.2a). Using conventional combustion technology, the estimated cost to generate electricity from biomass ranges from 5.2 to 6.7 cents per kilowatt-hour in Oregon and the Pacific Northwest, competitive with other conventional fuels. Actual costs would vary depending on financing, location, system design, and fuel cost. Power plants that burn biomass directly can generate electricity at a cost of seven to nine cents per kilowatt-hour. In contrast, the estimated cost of generating electricity from a new natural gas-fired, combined-cycle power plant is 2.8 cents per kilowatt-hour (NRDC 2011). In states such as Oregon, generating electricity from landfill gas is cost-competitive with natural gas power generation. The estimated cost is 2.9 to 3.6 cents per kilowatt-hour (Oregon Department of Energy 2007). Dollar costs in Oregon are roughly comparable to those in the rest of the United States.

The cost of producing ethanol varies with the cost of the feedstock used and the scale of production. Approximately 85 percent of ethanol production capacity in the United States relies on corn feedstock. The cost of producing ethanol from corn is estimated to be about $1.10 per gallon. Although there is currently no commercial production of ethanol from cellulosic feedstocks such as agricultural wastes, grasses, and wood, the estimated production cost using these feedstocks is $1.15 to $1.43 per gallon (Oregon Department of Energy 2007).

Because a gallon of ethanol contains less energy than a gallon of gasoline, the production cost of ethanol must be multiplied by a factor of 1.5 to make an energy-cost comparison with gasoline. This means that if ethanol costs $1.10 per gallon to produce, then the effective cost per gallon to equal the energy contained in a gallon of gasoline is $1.65. The federal motor fuel excise tax on gasohol, a blended fuel of 10 percent ethanol and 90 percent gasoline, is 5.4 cents less per gallon than the tax on straight gasoline. In other words, the federal subsidy is fifty-four cents per gallon of ethanol when ethanol is blended with gasoline. The subsidy makes ethanol-blended fuel competitive in the marketplace and stimulates growth of an ethanol production and distribution infrastructure (Oregon Department of Energy 2007).

A major hurdle facing commercial biodiesel production is the cost of producing the fuel. Vegetable oil seed procurement, transport, storage, and oil extraction accounts for at least 75 percent of the cost of producing biodiesel. The cost varies depending on the feedstock used. For example, based on the market price for industrial rapeseed grown in Washington and Idaho, the estimated cost of producing biodiesel is $2.56 per gallon of rapeseed methyl ester. Recent estimates put the cost of production in the range of $1.30 per gallon (using waste grease feedstock) to $2.00 or more per gallon using soybean oil (Oregon Department of Energy 2007).

The market cost to consumers for biomass energy consumed in calendar year 2009 was estimated at a bit over $5 billion, and a little over $6.9 billion in 2008, not including fuel ethanol or biodiesel (USEIA 2011a, Table 3.5). Federal subsidies and tax expenditures for biomass and biofuels were estimated at $7.76 billion for FY2010 (USEIA 2011b, xiii), including about $114 million for biomass municipal solid waste and landfill gas used to generate electricity (USEIA 2011b, xviii). The rest was for ethanol production to be blended with liquid fuels.

National Security Costs of Utilizing Biomass

As a domestic resource, no nation-state or other organization is able to control supplies or determine price of biomass energy supplies. Access to it is not dependent upon the actions of any government other than our own. Growing fuels at home reduces the need to import fossil fuels from other nations, reducing our expenses and exposure to disruptions of supply (UCS 2010). Moreover, the diversity of sources of biomass energy, and the variety of technologies available to use it, make it unlikely the United States would ever become dependent on one source or one technology for its exploitation.

Beneficial biopower or biofuels production results in no net emissions of uncontrolled atmospheric emissions or greenhouse gases. Consequently, utilizing beneficial biomass technologies will not produce climate change or a rise in sea level. Biomass technologies do not produce substantial amounts of toxic waste that must be isolated from the human environment for millennia. Utilization of biomass reduces organic waste streams to the environment, reducing demand for landfill space. The utilization of biomass energy does not produce materials or targets useful to terrorists. Consequently, the national security costs of utilizing biomass technologies are nil. Like solar power and wind, as compared to other conventional energy technologies, utilization of biomass can be conceptualized as having net national security benefits.

Figure 9.3   **The Costs of Utilizing Beneficial Biomass Technologies**

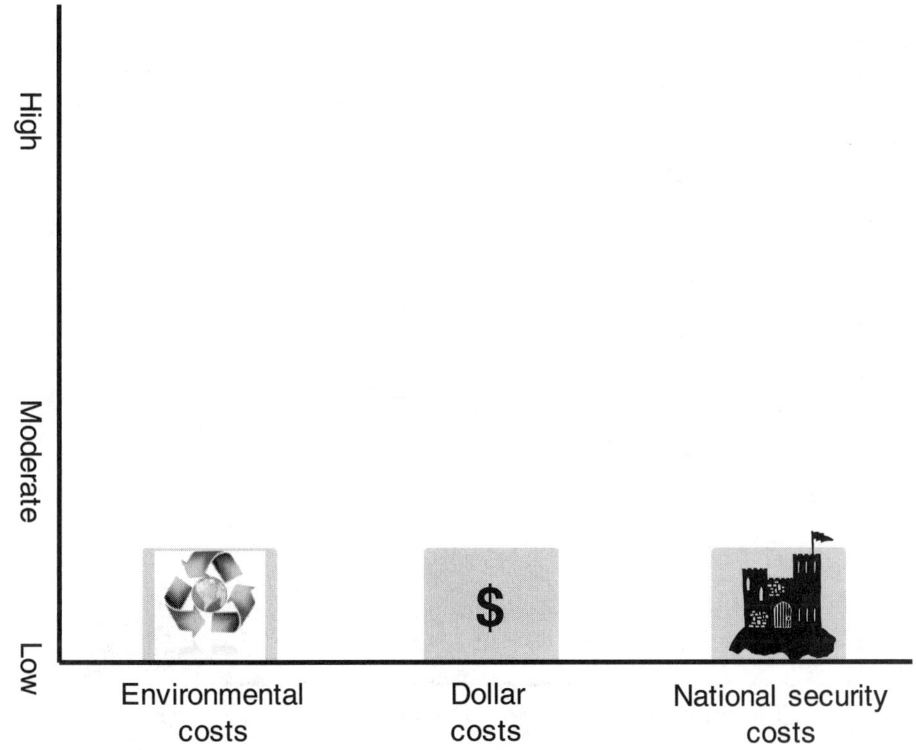

SUMMARY OF COSTS

The costs of utilizing beneficial biomass technologies are summarized in Figure 9.3. Overall, the environmental costs for producing and using beneficial biomass technologies are "low" compared to most conventional fuel technologies in use today because they reduce overall carbon emissions to the atmosphere and do not compete with food crops for land, instead using portions of crop residues, sustainably harvested wood and forest residues, and clean municipal and industrial wastes.

The costs of utilizing harmful biomass technologies are summarized in Figure 9.4. The environmental cost of using harmful biomass technologies is "high" because they add net carbon to the atmosphere; involve clearing forests, savannas, or grasslands to grow energy crops; and displace food production for energy production that ultimately leads to the clearing of carbon-rich ecosystems elsewhere to grow food, or due to the high costs of disruption of relatively large acreages of land that would be dedicated to growing energy crops. Producing biopower and biofuels through use of beneficial biomass resources and practices such as agricultural and forest waste materials is clearly less environmentally damaging than through exploitation of harmful biomass resources such as food crops for fuel.

Dollar costs for biomass technologies generating electricity and biogas are generally "low" and competitive today with conventional fuel technologies. High gasoline prices and federal subsidies have made the dollar costs for biomass used to produce liquid fuels such as ethanol-blended fuel and biodiesel competitive with other fuels.

National security costs for all biomass technologies are very "low" or negligible because the

Figure 9.4 **The Costs of Utilizing Harmful Biomass Technologies**

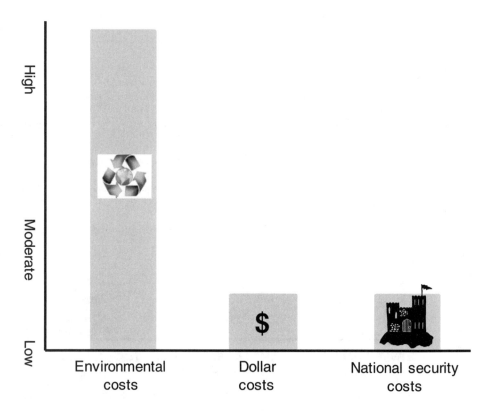

materials for using them are all readily available in the United States, often as wastes from other economic activities. Use of beneficial biomass technologies results in no net increase in emissions of greenhouse gases, will not produce climate change or sea level rise, and does not produce materials or targets useful to terrorists. This is a significant advantage biomass holds over energy fuels or technologies that may be acquired from foreign sources, may contribute to global climate change, or may leave a legacy of long-term waste products or facilities that are attractive to terrorists.

Any national energy policy commitment to biofuels must be tempered by realistic expectations about the scope of future biomass production. Biofuels derived from many resources can play a role in reducing pollution contributing to climate change, while providing domestic substitutes for petroleum feedstocks and fuels obtained from foreign sources. The federal Renewable Fuel Standard calls for 21 billion gallons of advanced ethanol, which would require about 300 million tons of biomass per year. Based on current estimates, this amount of biomass can be obtained from waste products such as agricultural residues, forestry residues, and municipal and construction waste (Perlack et al. 2005), without reliance on cultivation of food crops as energy crops, or exploitation of new energy crops other than cellulosic biomass like switchgrass. Any significant expansion beyond this level, however, must be based on a scientific determination that the required volume of biomass can be produced in a sustainable manner. Biofuels will have to compete for biomass with electric power generation, biogas and chemical production, and traditional agricultural uses such as food, feed, and fiber. Unexploited biomass resources such as forests and prairies provide natural environmental services including water purification, carbon sequestration, nutrient cycling, biodiversity, and recreation. If these resources are overutilized to make fuel, a potential solution to our fuel challenges may be transformed into a major problem concerning provision of adequate food supplies and necessary environmental services. We need to ensure that renewable resource policies account for this risk and strike an appropriate balance (UCS 2008) in national energy policy.

REFERENCES

Alson, Jeffrey. 1990. "The Methanol Debate: Clearing the Air." In *Methanol as an Alternative Fuel Choice: An Assessment*, ed. Wilfred L. Kohl. Washington, DC: Johns Hopkins Foreign Policy Institute.

Bain, Richard, Wade A. Amos, Mark Downing, and Robert L. Perlack. 2003. *Biopower Technical Assessment: State of the Industry and the Technology*. Springfield, VA: National Technical Information Service. www.fs.fed.us/ccrc/topics/urban-forests/docs/Biopower_Assessment.pdf.

Brower, Michael. 1992. *Cool Energy: Renewable Solutions to Environmental Problems*, rev. ed. Cambridge: MIT Press.

———. 2002. *Environmental Impacts of Renewable Energy Technologies*. Union of Concerned Scientists Briefing Paper, October 26. www.ucsusa.org/clean_energy/technology_and_impacts/impacts/environmental-impacts-of.html.

Brown, Lester. 2006. "Starving for Fuel: How Ethanol Production Contributes to Global Hunger." *The Globalist*, August 2.

Dreiling, Larry. 2009. "Study Examines Biomass Harvesting, Water Quality." *High Plains/Midwest Ag Journal*, March 17. www.hpj.com/archives/2009/mar09/mar16/Studyexaminesbiomassharvest.cfm.

Goldemberg, J. 2008. "The Challenge of Biofuels." *Energy and Environmental Science* 1: 523–525.

Lomborg, Bjørn. 2011. "Biofuels Aggravate Global Warming and Cause Hunger. Why Won't the U.S. Stop Subsidizing Them?" *Slate*, March 10.

Luque, Rafael, Lorenzo Herrero-Davila, Juan M. Campelo, James H. Clark, Jose M. Hidalgo, Diego Luna, Jose M. Marinas, and Antonio A. Romero. 2008. "Biofuels: A Technological Perspective." *Energy and Environmental Science* 1: 542–564.

Natural Resources Defense Council (NRDC). 2011. "Renewable Energy for America: Biomass Energy and Cellulosic Ethanol." www.nrdc.org/energy/renewables/biomass.asp.

Nyakatawaa, E.Z., D.A. Mays, V.R. Tolbert, T.H. Green, L. and Bingham. 2006. "Runoff, Sediment, Nitrogen, and Phosphorus Losses from Agricultural Land Converted to Sweetgum and Switchgrass Bioenergy Feedstock Production in North Alabama." *Biomass and Bioenergy* 30: 655–664.

Oregon Department of Energy. 2007. "Biomass Energy: Cost of Production." www.oregon.gov/ENERGY/RENEW/Biomass/Cost.shtml.

Perlack, Robert D., Lynn L. Wright, Anthony F. Turhollow, Robin L. Graham, Bryce J. Stokes, and Donald C. Erbach. 2005. *Biomass as Feedstock for a Bioenergy and Bioproducts Industry: The Technical Feasibility of a Billion-Ton Annual Supply*. Springfield, VA: U.S. Department of Commerce.

Tilman, David, Robert Socolow, Jonathan A. Foley, Jason Hill, Eric Larson, Lee Lynd, Stephen Pacala, John Reilly, Tim Searchinger, Chris Somerville, and Robert Williams. 2009. "Beneficial Biofuels: The Food, Energy and Environment Trilemma." *Science* 325 (July 17): 270–271.

Tolbert, V.R., D.E. Todd, L.K. Mann, C.M. Jawdy, D.A. Mays, R. Malik, W. Bandaranayake, A. Houston, D. Tyler, and D.E. Pettry. 2002. "Changes in Soil Quality and Below-Ground Carbon Storage with Conversion of Traditional Agricultural Crop Lands to Bioenergy Crop Production." *Environmental Pollution* 116: S97–S106.

Tyson, K. Shaine. 1990. *Biomass Resource Potential of the United States*. Golden, CO: National Renewable Energy Laboratory.

U.S. Energy Information Administration (USEIA). 2011a. *Annual Energy Review 2010*. Washington, DC: U.S. Government Printing Office.

———. 2011b. *Direct Federal Financial Interventions and Subsidies in Energy Markets 2010*. Washington, DC: U.S. Government Printing Office.

Union of Concerned Scientists (UCS). 2007. *Biofuels: An Important Part of a Low-Carbon Diet*. Cambridge, MA: Union of Concerned Scientists.

———. 2008. "Land Use Changes and Biofuels: The Changing Landscape of Low Carbon Fuel Risks and Rewards." www.ucsusa.org/assets/documents/clean_vehicles/Indirect-Land-Use-Factsheet.pdf.

———. 2010. "How Biomass Energy Works." October 29. www.ucsusa.org/clean_energy/technology_and_impacts/energy_technologies/how-biomass-energy-works.html.

10

Conservation and Efficiency

Energy conservation refers to efforts made to reduce energy consumption. Energy conservation can be achieved through simply reducing the amount of energy used to perform some task, possibly also reducing the amount of the task completed, or by increasing the efficiency of energy use, if this produces decreased energy consumption without reducing the amount of the task completed. Energy efficiency is using less energy to provide the same service (Lawrence Berkeley National Laboratory 2011), while energy conservation is any reduction in use of energy. Energy can be conserved or reduced without improving energy efficiency, but energy efficiency cannot be improved without reducing the amount of energy required to perform a task. Thus, energy conservation and energy efficiency are related, but are not the same. This often leads to some confusion. Energy conservation is broader than energy efficiency because it includes efforts to decrease energy consumption through behavioral change, in addition to using energy more efficiently. Examples of conservation without efficiency improvements are heating a room less in winter, using the car less, or enabling energy saving modes on a computer. Examples of improving energy efficiency include replacing an appliance, such as a refrigerator or clothes washer, with a model that provides the same service, but uses less energy.

Improvements in energy efficiency are most often achieved by adopting a more efficient technology or production process (Diesendorf 2007, 86). Because the existing stock of energy-using appliances and other equipment is so huge in the American economy, energy conservation and efficiency can be thought of as energy resources that can be used to meet human needs. The notion of a "soft energy path," with a strong focus on improving energy efficiency, was popularized with the term "negawatts," or meeting energy needs by increasing efficiency instead of increasing energy production (Lovins 1977). Perhaps the term was too cute to catch on, but the general idea has been increasingly accepted over the objections of some electric utility managers, who insisted that energy efficiency measures were "one-time" measures that, after implementation, would not be available in future.

This "one-time" view ignored the enormous number of washing machines already in use, the fact that the number seems always to be increasing, that existing washing machines age and must be replaced, that they cannot possibly be replaced all at once, and that technological advances have continued to make them more energy-efficient over time. Moreover, this is true with all types of appliances currently in use, as it is with housing stock, factory buildings and processes, commercial establishments, automobiles, and other energy-using devices. Everything eventually wears out and can be replaced with something more energy-efficient. Consequently, the opportunities for improving energy efficiency and increasing energy conservation are so numerous in the American economy that they are actually increasing with the pace of technological innovation rather than being "one-time" measures that decrease in the aggregate over time. Thus, energy conservation and efficiency may be conceived of as energy resources comparable to oil, natural gas, or coal.

National energy use can be conceived as comprising four broad sectors: transportation, residential, commercial, and industrial, as illustrated in Figure 10.1.

Figure 10.1 **Energy Consumed by Sector, 2010**

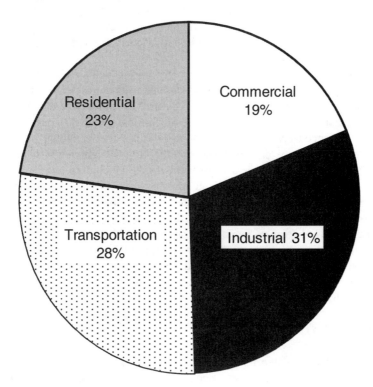

Source: USEIA 2011a.

TRANSPORTATION

The transportation sector includes all vehicles that transport people or goods, such as cars, trucks, buses, motorcycles, trains, subways, aircraft, boats, barges, and even hot air balloons, accounting for about 28 percent of total U.S. energy consumption in 2010 (USEIA 2011a, 38).

Of the energy used in this sector, approximately 63 percent is consumed by gasoline-powered vehicles. Diesel-powered transport (trains, merchant ships, heavy trucks) consumes about 24 percent, and aircraft consume most of the remaining 13 percent (USEIA 2011b, 118).

Two measures have increased the energy efficiency of motor vehicles by boosting fuel economy and hold some promise for further improvements: corporate average fuel economy (CAFE) standards and greenhouse gas emissions standards. After the introduction of corporate CAFE standards in 1978, the fuel economy for all light-duty vehicles increased from 19.9 miles per gallon (mpg) in 1978 to 26.2 in 1987. However, increased sales of light trucks with lower miles per gallon worked against this trend. Despite continued technological improvements, fuel economy fell to between 24 and 26 mpg over the next two decades, as sales of light trucks increased from about 20 percent of new light-duty vehicles sales in 1980 to 55 percent in 2004. From 2004 to 2008, fuel prices increased, sales of light trucks slowed, and tighter fuel economy standards for light-duty trucks were introduced. As a result, average fuel economy for light-duty vehicles rose to 28.0 mpg in 2008 (USEIA 2011b).

The National Highway Traffic Safety Administration (NHTSA) introduced new CAFE standards for model year 2011 light-duty vehicles in 2009, and in 2010 NHTSA and the U.S. Environmental Protection Agency jointly announced CAFE and greenhouse gas emissions standards for model years 2012 to 2016. Light-duty vehicles are required to reach an average fuel economy of 35 mpg by model year 2020 (USEIA 2011b).

Market adoption of advanced technologies in conventional vehicles is expected to improve fuel economy through model year 2020 and reduce fuel costs thereafter, due in part to greater penetration of unconventionally fueled (electric, hybrid, natural gas, hydrogen) vehicles and in part to the addition of new technologies in conventional vehicles. These advanced technologies include advanced drag reduction, which provides fuel economy improvements by reducing vehicle air resistance at higher speeds; adoption of lightweight materials through material substitution; advanced transmission technologies, including aggressive shift logic, continuously variable, automated manual, and six-speed transmissions; cylinder deactivation and turbocharging; and electrification of accessories such as pumps and power steering (USEIA 2011b). It is both technically feasible and cost-effective to raise the average fuel economy of new passenger cars and light trucks even if gas drops back to $2.50 a gallon. Using continuously evolving conventional technologies, automakers could produce a fleet of cars and light trucks that achieve over 35 mpg by 2020. Hybrid, fuel cell, and other advanced technologies could be used to make vehicles even more efficient while maintaining, if not improving, vehicle safety and performance (UCS 2007).

RESIDENTIAL SECTOR

The residential sector includes all private residences, including single-family homes, apartments, manufactured homes, and condominiums, accounting for about 23 percent of total U.S. energy consumption in 2010 (USEIA 2011a, 38). Energy use in this sector varies significantly across the country, due to regional climate differences and different regulations. On average, about 60 percent of the energy used in U.S. homes is expended on space conditioning (heating and cooling) (USEIA 2011b, 34).

How energy is used in American homes has changed substantially over the past three decades. U.S. homes on average have become larger, have fewer occupants, and are more energy-efficient, due in part to building code and appliance standards with strict efficiency requirements. In 2005 energy use per household was 95 million British thermal units (Btu) of energy compared with 138 million Btu per household in 1978, a drop of 31 percent. In 2009, 58 percent of housing units had energy-efficient, multipane windows, up from 36 percent in 1993. Multipane windows are much more prevalent in newer homes. About 80 percent of houses built since 2000 have double- or triple-pane energy-efficient windows, up from only 52 percent of homes constructed before 1990. Over 40 million householders have used caulking or weather-stripping to seal cracks and air leakages around their home, 26 million have added insulation, and 68 million have at least some energy-efficient compact fluorescent (CFL) or light-emitting diode (LED) lights. Appliances (refrigerators, freezers, ovens, stoves, dishwashers, clothes washers, and clothes dryers), heating, and cooling equipment now use less energy. In addition, less heat passes through the walls, roofs, and windows of homes because of better insulation and construction. At the same time, however, many homes contain more energy-consuming devices. The type and number of home electronics have increased significantly over the past thirty years (USEIA 2011b).

Figure 10.2 **Energy Consumed in Commercial Buildings**

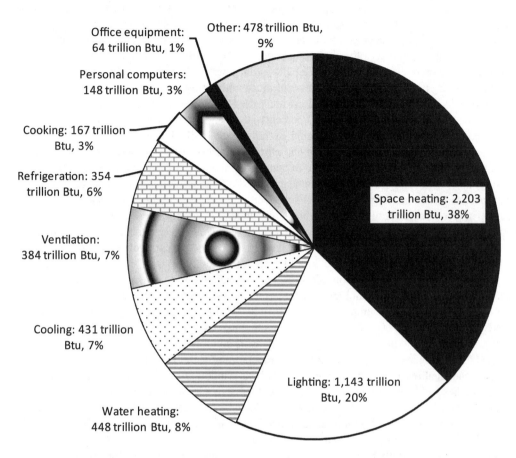

Office equipment: 64 trillion Btu, 1%

Other: 478 trillion Btu, 9%

Personal computers: 148 trillion Btu, 3%

Cooking: 167 trillion Btu, 3%

Refrigeration: 354 trillion Btu, 6%

Ventilation: 384 trillion Btu, 7%

Space heating: 2,203 trillion Btu, 38%

Cooling: 431 trillion Btu, 7%

Lighting: 1,143 trillion Btu, 20%

Water heating: 448 trillion Btu, 8%

Source: USEIA 2003, Table E1.

COMMERCIAL SECTOR

The commercial sector includes business and public buildings such as offices, malls, stores, schools, hospitals, hotels, warehouses, restaurants, places of worship, and other workplaces, accounting for about 19 percent of total U.S. energy consumption in 2010 (USEIA 2011a, 38). Energy consumed by various uses in nonmall commercial buildings is illustrated in Figure 10.2. Space heating and lighting provide the largest potential for reducing energy use in this sector.

While growth in commercial floor space (1.2 percent per year) is faster than growth in population (0.9 percent per year), energy use per capita remains relatively steady due to efficiency improvements in equipment and building shells. Efficiency standards and the addition of more efficient technologies account for a large share of the improvement in the efficiency of end-use services, notably in space cooling, refrigeration, and lighting (USEIA 2011b).

Energy in this sector has the same basic end uses as the residential sector, in slightly different proportions. Delivered energy consumption for core space heating, ventilation, air conditioning, water heating, lighting, cooking, and refrigeration, uses which frequently have been targets of energy efficiency standards, accounted for just over 60 percent of commercial delivered energy demand in 2009 and are projected to fall to 55 percent of delivered energy in 2035 (USEIA 2011b).

Lighting is a significant consumer of energy in commercial buildings. More electricity is consumed by lighting than any other individual end use. One-fifth of total site energy is consumed by lighting in commercial buildings (EESI 2006a, 1). Nearly all commercial buildings have some type of lighting (91 percent). The majority of those without lighting are warehouses and vacant buildings. Standard fluorescent lamps are widely used—85 percent of commercial buildings use these lamps. Nearly half of buildings (47 percent) use incandescent lamps and just under one-third (30 percent) use compact fluorescent lamps. Lighting is generally the most wasteful component of commercial use. More efficient lighting and elimination of overillumination can reduce lighting energy use by approximately 50 percent in many commercial buildings (USEIA 2011b).

Lighting continues to have the largest and most cost-effective energy-saving potential in existing commercial buildings. Improvements in refrigeration systems and components are the second-largest source of savings potential. A reasonable range of economic savings potential in existing commercial buildings is between 10 and 20 percent of current energy use. Building sensors and controls—excluding those associated with lighting—have the potential of reducing commercial building energy use by an additional 5 to 20 percent (Belzer 2009).

Traditional windows waste about 30 percent of the energy used to heat and cool a building. Advanced dynamic window technologies, or "smart windows," could save more than 1 percent of the nation's annual energy consumption, or more than $10 billion in annual energy costs (Risser 2011). For example, Pleotint LLC has developed a glass film that uses sunlight to prevent excess heat and light from coming into homes and buildings, increasing comfort and reducing the amount of energy needed for heating and cooling. Pleotint's "thermochromic" technology harnesses the sun's heat to cause a chemical reaction that automatically darkens window tint as the sun gets hotter. Pleotint estimates these self-tinting windows could pay for themselves in five to seven years through reduced energy costs (Risser 2011). SAGE Electrochromics has created SageGlass, which uses a small electric charge to switch between clear and tinted, depending on heat and light conditions. These "electrochromic" windows can be programmed to respond to specific temperature and sunlight levels or can be regulated manually by the click of a button. SAGE estimates its tinted-window technology can reduce a building's energy consumption substantially (Risser 2011).

INDUSTRIAL SECTOR

The industrial sector represents production and processing of goods, including facilities and equipment used for manufacturing, agriculture, mining, and construction, accounting for about 30 percent of total U.S. energy consumption in 2010 (USEIA 2011a, 38). Since 1990, a growing share of U.S. output has come from less energy-intensive services. In 1990, 68 percent of the total value of output came from services, 8 percent from energy-intensive manufacturing industries, and the balance from non-energy-intensive manufacturing and the nonmanufacturing industries (e.g., agriculture, mining, and construction). In 2009 services accounted for 76 percent of total output and energy-intensive industries only 6 percent. Services are expected to continue to play a growing role in the future, accounting for 79 percent of total output in 2035, with energy-intensive manufacturing accounting for less than 5 percent of output (USEIA 2011b). U.S. agriculture has almost doubled farm energy efficiency in the last twenty-five years (Morris and Grubinger 2010).

From 1949 to 2010, primary energy consumption in the United States tripled. A sharp reversal of this historical trend occurred in 2009, in part due to the recession. Real gross domestic product (GDP) fell 2 percent compared to 2008, and energy consumption declined by nearly 5 percent. Decreases occurred in all four major end-use sectors: residential, 2 percent; commercial, 1 percent; industrial, 9 percent; and transportation, 4 percent. Consumption decreased the most in the industrial sector, which was particularly hard-hit by the recession. Real value added for the manufacturing sector fell by 6 percent. Total energy consumption in the transportation sector fell by about 4 percent in 2009, as fewer goods were shipped. However, the previous historical trend for annual increases in energy consumption resumed in 2010 as the U.S. economy improved. Total energy consumption increased by about 4 percent over 2009. Increases occurred in all sectors: residential, 5 percent; commercial, 2 percent; industrial, 6 percent; and transportation, 2 percent (USEIA 2011a).

Many opportunities have been identified where industry might conserve energy or improve energy efficiency, thereby reducing environmental and dollar costs. Many large industrial firms generate their own electricity. When electricity is generated, heat produced as a by-product can be captured and used for process steam, space heating, or other industrial purposes. Conventional electricity generation is about 30 percent efficient, whereas combined heat and power (cogeneration) converts up to 90 percent of the fuel into usable energy. Moreover, advanced boiler and furnace technologies can operate at higher temperatures while burning less fuel. These technologies are more efficient and produce fewer pollutants (EESI 2006b, 1).

Over 45 percent of fuel used by U.S. manufacturers is combusted to make steam. A typical industrial facility can reduce this energy usage 20 percent by insulating steam and condensate return lines, stopping steam leakage, and maintaining steam traps (EESI 2006b, 1).

Electric motors usually run at a constant speed, but a variable speed drive allows a motor's energy output to match the required load, achieving energy savings ranging from 3 to 60 percent, depending on how the motor is used. Motor coils made of superconducting materials can also reduce energy losses (EESI 2006b, 1).

Industry uses a large number of pumps and compressors of all shapes and sizes and in a wide variety of applications. The efficiency of pumps and compressors depends on many factors but often improvements can be made by implementing better process control and maintenance practices. Compressors are commonly used to provide compressed air used for sand blasting, painting, and other power tools. Optimizing compressed air systems by installing variable speed drives, along with preventive maintenance to detect and fix air leaks, can improve energy efficiency 20 to 50 percent (EESI 2006b, 1).

The U.S. economy has the potential to reduce annual nontransportation energy consumption by roughly 23 percent by 2020, eliminating more than $1.2 trillion in waste—well beyond the $520 billion up-front investment that would be required. This reduction in energy use would also result in abatement of 1.1 gigatons of greenhouse-gas emissions annually—the equivalent of taking the entire U.S. fleet of passenger vehicles and light trucks off the roads. Recommended measures include turning off or switching to standby mode all computers in U.S. office buildings at night and sealing all heating and cooling ducts to reduce air leaks. Replacement of old appliances is one of the most efficient global measures to reduce emissions of greenhouse gases (Granade et al. 2009).

COSTS OF ENERGY CONSERVATION AND EFFICIENCY

Environmental Costs of Conservation and Efficiency

The energy conservation and efficiency technology "fuel cycle" is a bit abstract, involving the identification, manufacture, installation and operation of a tremendous variety of technologies,

Figure 10.3 **The Energy Conservation and Efficiency Fuel Cycle**

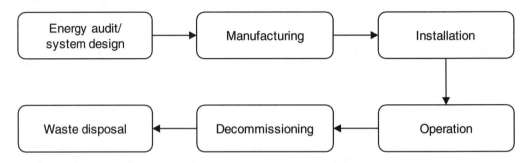

some quite simple like duct tape to seal joints in heating, ventilation, and air conditioning (HVAC) ducts, others quite sophisticated like programmable residential thermostats. In each case, the fuel cycle starts with some previously utilized technology and attempts to make improvements in energy efficiency or otherwise reduce energy usage. In new construction, designers must plan more energy-efficient deviations from previous conventional approaches to energy end-use technologies. This involves manufacturing processes and eventually the decommissioning of facilities, as illustrated in Figure 10.3. Manufacturing may involve industrial-scale fabrication of equipment and energy-conserving materials like insulation, plumbing, and electrical components, depending on the specific technology utilized. Where housing or other buildings are involved, decommissioning may occur after a very long time, potentially fifty or even a hundred years. Disposal or recycling of waste materials follows manufacturing and construction of the components and completion of each project.

Environmental costs of energy conservation and efficiency improvements include a wide variety of conventional land disturbance and land use impacts attending manufacture of goods, possible hazardous materials disposal, and potential impacts on water and other resources, depending again on physical characteristics of the technology employed. These costs generally are no greater than the environmental costs of producing other goods in the U.S. economy and are subject to the same environmental regulations as other products.

Some have suggested that using energy more efficiently might not be as effective at tackling climate change as people think, hypothesizing the occurrence of so-called rebound effects, where efficiency improvements would be offset by behavior changes, such as increasing demands for cheaper energy, which could potentially slash future carbon and energy savings by half (Jha 2009). It has been suggested that, if the International Energy Agency's (IEA) recommendations for efficiency measures are followed in full in the next few decades, the total rebound effect—the proportion of potential energy savings offset by changes in consumer and industry behavior—could be 31 percent by 2020 and about 52 percent around the world by 2030 (Barker and Dagoumas 2009). Others suggest that for household heating, household cooling, and personal automotive transport in developed countries, the direct rebound effect is likely to be less than 30 percent and may be closer to 10 percent for transport. Direct rebound effects are likely to be smaller where energy forms a relatively small proportion of total costs and has little influence on operating decisions (Sorrell 2007).

Direct rebound effects might include people who would drive more regularly because their fuel-efficient cars are cheaper to run. It is suggested that more fuel-efficient cars burning less gasoline per mile, and costing less to fill up at the pump, encourage extra driving. An indirect rebound effect is hypothesized as drivers use the money they save on gasoline to buy other things that produce greenhouse emissions, like new electronic gadgets or vacation trips on fuel-burning airplanes (Tierney 2011, D1). Efficiency improvements in industry might lead to indirect rebound effects: cheaper steel manufactured with more efficient energy use might increase the amount of steel produced and, therefore, the number of construction projects in which it could be used. Across society, cheaper electricity bills overall might mean consumers have more money to spend on other activities, such as holidays or entertainment, again potentially raising their overall carbon footprint (Jha 2009).

There are difficulties with the rebound effect hypothesis. It assumes that savings from increased energy efficiency will be spent on energy-using activities or products, but this is not proven. The assumed causal linkage is tenuous, at best. Savings might as easily be invested (not spent), used to pay off existing debt, or perhaps spent on things that use less or no energy. Thus, the rebound effect assumes a causal relationship where there may be none.

Moreover, it is not energy efficiency that stimulates increased energy use, but latent demand for products or activities. That demand would exist (or not) regardless of improvements in energy efficiency. That is, people do not drive more because of increased fuel efficiency. People drive mostly (with the possible exception of teenagers with new licenses) because they have some place they need to go. Contrary to the rebound effect hypothesis, vehicle miles traveled began to plateau in 2004 and dropped between 2007 and 2010 for the first time since 1980 (Puentes and Tomer 2008), during the same period that fuel efficiency measured in miles per gallon increased (Young 2010). Vehicle miles traveled appear to be more responsive to volatility in gas prices and national economic performance (recession) than to increases in vehicle energy efficiency. The most valuable contribution made by the literature on the rebound effect may be verification that energy efficiency policies lead to economic growth and consequently to an increase in employment (Barker and Dagoumas 2009).

Dollar Costs of Conservation and Efficiency

In most cases, energy efficiency measures will pay for themselves over time in the form of lower energy bills. Most energy efficiency measures are cheaper, and therefore pay for themselves faster, than most kinds of energy generation (Lawrence Berkeley National Laboratory 2011). With energy efficiency improvements, electricity use in U.S. buildings can be reduced by approximately one-third at a cost of 2.7 cents per kWh in 2007 dollars, resulting in national annual energy-bill savings in 2030 of nearly $170 billion. To achieve these savings, the cumulative capital investment needed between 2010 and 2030 is about $440 billion, which translates to a 2.5 year simple payback period. Savings over the life of these energy efficiency measures would be nearly 3.5 times larger than the investment required, providing a benefit-cost ratio of 3.5 (Brown et al. 2008). This makes the cost of energy conservation extremely competitive with conventional fuels capable of providing the same services. Federal subsidies and tax expenditures for energy conservation and efficiency improvements were estimated at almost $6.6 billion for FY2010 (USEIA 2011c, xiii), up substantially from about $369 million in FY2007 (USEIA 2011c, xviii)

Moreover, use of energy conservation and efficiency improvements slows the rate of growth in electricity demand, resulting in less new construction of electric power plants than would otherwise occur and allowing capital saved to be expended on other economic activities. Lower demand for capital may result in lower interest rates charged on money borrowed to do other things. Energy conservation and efficiency improvements may also produce savings in disaster relief expenditures to deal with natural disasters exacerbated by climate change (hurricanes, drought) and reduce expenditures on health impacts associated with use of other fuels and technologies (e.g., emphysema, asthma). Energy conservation and efficiency policies to reduce domestic demand can also reduce the world oil price, thereby benefiting the nation through lower prices on the remaining oil it imports (NRC 2010, 20).

National Security Costs of Conservation and Efficiency

Anywhere energy is used, there are opportunities to increase efficiency. Energy conservation and improvements in energy efficiency can be implemented without dependence on politically unstable areas such as the Middle East. No country or group of countries is able to control supplies or determine price for fuel or materials to implement energy conservation or efficiency measures. Energy conservation and efficiency measures produce almost no carbon emissions or greenhouse gases, and what little they do produce is generated during the manufacture of equipment, not during ongoing operations. Consequently, utilizing energy conservation and efficiency technologies will not produce climate change or a rise in sea level. Energy conservation and efficiency technologies do not produce substantial amounts of toxic waste that must be isolated from the human environment for millennia. Utilization of energy conservation and efficiency measures does not produce materials useful to terrorists. Consequently, the national security costs of utilizing energy conservation and efficiency technologies are nil. As compared to other energy technologies, utilization of energy conservation and efficiency improvement technologies can be conceptualized as having net national security benefits.

SUMMARY OF COSTS

The costs of utilizing energy conservation and efficiency technologies are summarized in Figure 10.4. Overall, the environmental costs of producing and using these technologies are incurred mostly during production of materials and equipment and are "low" compared to most conventional fuel technologies in use today. Dollar costs for application of energy conservation and efficiency improvements for heating residential, commercial, and industrial hot water, for some space heating applications, and for lighting are "low" and competitive today with conventional fuels in most situations. Dollar costs for fuel efficiency improvements to vehicles are being phased in slowly and appear to be affordable. National security costs for all energy conservation and efficiency improvements are very "low" or negligible because the materials for producing them are available in the United States or from friendly nations. This is a distinct advantage energy conservation and efficiency technologies hold over other energy technologies that may be acquired from foreign sources, contribute to global climate change, or leave a legacy of long-term waste products that are attractive to terrorists.

Energy conservation and efficiency improvements do not produce much hazardous waste, and the probability of an environmentally devastating accident from using them is nil. Energy conservation and efficiency improvements are also environmentally advantageous because they will probably never be exhausted and cannot be controlled by any combination of foreign governments. For the foreseeable future, anywhere energy is used, there will be opportunities to increase efficiency of its use. Creating the components of energy conservation and efficiency technologies is often extremely easy, does not require mining or drilling in a dangerous locale, and can be accomplished without involvement of unreliable political allies. As a largely decentralized group of technologies, energy conservation and efficiency improvement measures can usually be retrofitted by home improvement enthusiasts or included in original building construction by local contrac-

Figure 10.4   **The Costs of Energy Conservation and Efficiency Technologies**

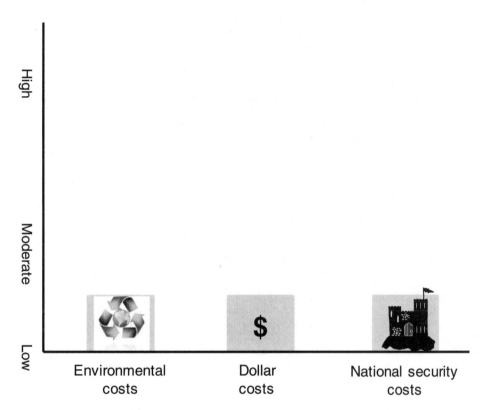

tors, often without large capital investments. Every individual can take part and reap the benefits, from making very small changes to large ones.

REFERENCES

Barker, Terry, and Athanasios Dagoumas. 2009. "The Global Macroeconomic Rebound Effect of Energy Efficiency Policies." PowerPoint presentation, Cambridge Energy Forum and 4CMR Seminar on the Rebound: Could Energy Efficiency Improvements Backfire?, Cambridge, UK, May 14.

Belzer, D.B. 2009. *Energy Efficiency Potential in Existing Commercial Buildings: Review of Selected Recent Studies*. Richland, WA: Pacific Northwest National Laboratory.

Brown, Rich, Sam Borgeson, Jon Koomey, and Peter Biermayer. 2008. *U.S. Building-Sector Energy Efficiency Potential*. Berkeley, CA: Lawrence Berkeley National Laboratory.

Diesendorf, Mark. 2007. *Greenhouse Solutions with Sustainable Energy*. Sydney: University of New South Wales Press.

Environmental and Energy Study Institute (EESI). 2006a. "Energy-Efficient Buildings: Using Whole Building Design to Reduce Energy Consumption in Homes and Offices." Washington, DC: Environmental and Energy Study Institute.

———. 2006b. "Industrial Energy Efficiency: Using New Technologies to Reduce Energy Use in Industry and Manufacturing." Washington, DC: Environmental and Energy Study Institute.

Granade, Hannah Choi, Jon Creyts, Anton Derkach, Philip Farese, Scott Nyquist, and Ken Ostrowski. 2009. *Unlocking Energy Efficiency in the U.S. Economy*. Executive summary, July. Atlanta, GA: McKinsey and Company.

Jha, Alok. 2009. "Rebound Effects of Energy Efficiency Could Halve Carbon Savings, Says Study." *The Guardian*, May 14.

Lawrence Berkeley National Laboratory. 2011. "What Is Energy Efficiency?" Berkeley, CA: Lawrence Berkeley National Laboratory. http://eetd.lbl.gov/ee/ee-1.html.

Lovins, Amory. 1977. *Soft Energy Paths: Toward a Durable Peace*. San Francisco: Friends of the Earth International.

Morris, Mike, and Vern Grubinger. 2010. "Introduction to Energy Efficiency and Conservation on the Farm." Cornell University, Cooperative Extension, November 4.Orono: University of Maine Cooperative Extension. www.extension.org/pages/26607/introduction-to-energy-efficiency-and-conservation-on-the-farm.

National Research Council (NRC). 2010. *Hidden Costs of Energy: Unpriced Consequences of Energy Production and Use*. Washington, DC: National Academies Press.

Puentes, Robert, and Adie Tomer. 2008. *The Road . . . Less Traveled: An Analysis of Vehicle Miles Traveled Trends in the U.S.* Washington, DC: Brookings Institution.

Risser, Roland. 2011. "Making Smart Windows Smarter." Energy.gov, April 5. http://energy.gov/articles/making-smart-windows-smarter.

Sorrell, Steve. 2007. *The Rebound Effect: An Assessment of the Evidence for Economy-Wide Energy Savings from Improved Energy Efficiency*. Brighton, UK: Sussex Energy Group.

Tierney, John. 2011. "When Energy Efficiency Sullies the Environment." *New York Times*, March 8.

Union of Concerned Scientists (UCS). 2007. "Fuel Economy Basics." November 26. www.ucsusa.org/clean_vehicles/solutions/cleaner_cars_pickups_and_suvs/fuel-economy-basics.html.

U.S. Energy Information Administration (USEIA). 2003. *2003 Commercial Buildings Energy Consumption Survey*. Washington, DC: U.S. Government Printing Office.

———. 2011a. *Annual Energy Review 2010*. October. Washington, DC: U.S. Government Printing Office.

———. 2011b. *Annual Energy Outlook 2011*. Washington, DC: U.S. Government Printing Office.

———. 2011c. *Direct Federal Financial Interventions and Subsidies in Energy Markets 2010*. Washington, DC: U.S. Government Printing Office.

Young, Peg. 2010. "Upward Trend in Vehicle-Miles Resumed During 2009: A Time Series Analysis." Washington, DC: U.S. Department of Transportation, Bureau of Transportation Statistics.

11

Ocean

~~~~~~~~~~~~~~~~~~~~~

Almost three-fourths of the surface of the earth is covered by water, most of it in oceans. Technologies for deriving electrical power from the ocean include tidal power, wave power, ocean thermal energy conversion, and ocean currents. Of these, the three most well-developed technologies are tidal power, wave power, and ocean thermal energy conversion. All of them require construction of onshore substations, transmission lines, and submersible electric cables to transport electrical current to shore for incorporation into an electrical grid.

TIDAL ENERGY TECHNOLOGIES

Some of the oldest ocean energy technologies use tidal power. All coastal areas experience two high tides and two low tides over a period of slightly more than twenty-four hours. For those tidal differences to be harnessed as electricity, the difference between high and low tides must be more than sixteen feet (or at least five meters). However, there are only about forty sites on earth with tidal ranges of this magnitude, so the utility of tidal power may be geographically limited. Currently, there are no tidal power plants in the United States, but conditions are favorable for tidal power generation in the Pacific Northwest and the Atlantic Northeast regions (USDOI 2011a). Tidal energy technologies include barrages or dams, tidal fences, and tidal turbines.

Barrages or Dams

A barrage or dam is typically used to convert tidal energy into electricity by capturing tidal flows behind a stationary structure and forcing water through turbines, which drive a generator. Gates and turbines are installed along a dam. When tides produce an adequate difference in the level of water on opposite sides of the dam, the gates are opened and water flows through the turbines, turning an electric generator to produce electricity (USDOI 2011a).

Tidal Fences

Tidal fences look like giant turnstiles. They can reach across channels between small islands or across straits between the mainland and an island. The turnstiles turn and pivot slowly around a central point containing a generator using tidal currents typical of coastal waters. Some of these currents run at five to eight knots (5.6 to 9 miles per hour) and generate as much energy as winds of much higher velocity (USDOI 2011a).

Tidal Turbines

Tidal turbines usually look like wind turbines. They may be moored to the bottom and arrayed underwater in rows, similar to some wind farms. The turbines function best where coastal currents

Figure 11.1 **TidGen™ Power System**

Source: Ocean Renewable Power Company 2011c.

run between 3.6 and 4.9 knots (4 to 5.5 mph). In currents of that speed, a 49.2-foot (15-meter) diameter tidal turbine can generate as much energy as a 197-foot (60-meter) diameter wind turbine. Ideal locations for tidal turbine farms are close to shore in water 65.5 to 98.5 feet (20 to 30 meters) deep (USDOI 2011a).

A recent innovation is a tidal turbine that uses rotating foils with the appearance of a manual reel lawn mower, as illustrated in Figure 11.1, manufactured by Ocean Renewable Power Company (Sharp 2010). A sixty-kilowatt prototype tidal power generator mounted on a barge was successfully tested in tidal currents at Eastport, Maine, by Ocean Renewable Power Company (ORPC) in 2010. In the TidGen™ Power System, each side of a central hub features four helix-shaped foils wrapped around spacing rings and pierced by the turbine shaft. The turbines turn slowly, roughly sixty revolutions per minute in a seven-mph current. The slow speed and wide foil spacing are intended to allow marine life to move through the turbine unharmed (Turkel 2010). The ORPC design may also be useful in rivers and estuaries and possibly even using large ocean currents described below.

Dams used with hydroelectric facilities and other energy technologies often cause considerable harm to fish and ocean mammals, and silt builds up behind them. Because it does not require use of a dam, the ORPC unit does not entail ecosystem change from buildup of silt behind a dam. The TidGen™ Power System unit tested in 2010 produced grid-compatible electricity; underwater video cameras and sensors indicated there was no harm to fish, which appeared to go out of their way to avoid the unit (Sharp 2010).

The ORPC TidGen™ Power System unit self-starts when the current reaches two knots and produces increasing amounts of electricity as tidal currents reach six knots. All told, the unit produces power for twenty to twenty-one hours per day as the tides come in and go out. ORPC's design consists of stackable power units tethered to the ocean floor, where ship traffic may pass overhead without harm (Sharp 2010).

ORPC plans to install a larger, 150-kilowatt unit off eastern Maine that will deliver power to Bangor Hydro Electric Company's grid, with additional future units increasing capacity to 3.2 megawatts by the end of 2014 (ORPC 2011b; Sharp 2010). Additional units to be installed by 2015 will bring capacity to a total of more than five megawatts (Woodard 2011). ORPC has permits for three sites off Eastport, one of the world's best tidal sites, where twice a day the tide rises and falls about twenty feet (Sharp 2010). ORPC is developing tidal power sites in Maine, Alaska, and Nova Scotia, with combined potential to generate more than 300 megawatts (ORPC 2011a).

Tidal power is appealing because seawater's greater density, compared with wind, means fewer turbines are needed to create the same amount of power (USDOI 2011a). Water is more than 800 times denser than air, so for the same surface area, water moving twelve miles per hour exerts about the same amount of force as a constant 110 mph wind (USDOI 2006a). And tides, unlike the wind, are predictable. But perhaps the greatest advantage is that the underwater equipment is hidden, unlike wind turbines, so there are no complaints from the public about aesthetics. According to Paul Jacobson, water power manager for the Electric Power Research Institute, the largest obstacle to development of tidal power is lack of funding for further development of technology and for permitting and licensing of demonstration projects (Sharp 2010).

OCEAN WAVE ENERGY

Waves are caused by friction between air and water from wind blowing over the surface of the ocean. In many areas of the world, the wind blows with enough consistency and force to provide continuous waves. There is tremendous energy in ocean waves. Wave power devices extract energy directly from the surface motion of ocean waves or from pressure fluctuations below the surface (USDOI 2011b).

Wave power varies considerably in different parts of the world, and wave energy cannot be harnessed effectively everywhere. Wave-power-rich areas of the world include coasts of the northwestern United States, western Scotland, northern Canada, southern Africa, and Australia. Wave energy resources in the United States are quite limited. In the Pacific Northwest, it is possible that wave energy could produce forty to seventy kilowatts per meter (3.3 feet) of western coastline (USDOI 2011b).

A variety of technologies have been proposed to capture the energy from waves, with some demonstration testing at commercial scales. Wave technologies have been designed for installation in nearshore, offshore, and far offshore locations. Offshore systems are situated in deep water, typically more than forty meters (131 feet) (USDOI 2011b). While all wave energy technologies are intended to be installed at or near the water's surface, they differ in their orientation to the waves with which they are interacting and in the manner in which they convert wave energy into other energy forms, usually electricity. Wave energy conversion technology is not commercially available in the United States.

Terminator devices extend perpendicular to the direction of wave travel and capture or reflect the power of waves. These devices are typically onshore or nearshore, but floating versions have been designed for offshore applications. The Oscillating Water Column is a terminator device in which water enters through a subsurface opening into a chamber with air trapped above it. Wave action causes the captured water column to move up and down like a piston and forces air though an opening connected to a turbine, such that the air turns the turbine (USDOI 2011b).

A point absorber is a floating structure with components that move relative to each other due to wave action (e.g., a floating buoy inside a fixed cylinder). The relative motion is used to drive electromechanical or hydraulic energy converters that generate electricity (USDOI 2011b).

Attenuators are long multisegmented floating structures oriented parallel to the direction of the waves. Differing heights of waves along the length of the device cause flexing where the segments connect, and this flexing is connected to hydraulic pumps or other converters that generate electricity (USDOI 2011b).

Overtopping devices have reservoirs filled by incoming waves to levels above the surrounding ocean. When waves recede, water is released and gravity causes it to fall back toward the ocean surface. The energy of falling water is used to turn hydroelectric turbines. Specially built seagoing vessels can also capture the energy of offshore waves. These floating platforms create electricity by funneling waves through internal turbines and then back into the sea (USDOI 2011b).

OCEAN THERMAL ENERGY CONVERSION

A process called ocean thermal energy conversion (OTEC) uses heat energy stored in the oceans to generate electricity. OTEC works best when the temperature difference between the warmer, top layer of the ocean and the colder, deep ocean water is about 36°F (20°C). These conditions exist in tropical coastal areas, roughly between the Tropic of Capricorn and the Tropic of Cancer. To bring cold water to the surface, ocean thermal energy conversion plants require an expensive, large-diameter intake pipe, submerged a mile or more into the ocean's depths. Some energy experts believe that if ocean thermal energy conversion can become cost-competitive with conventional power technologies, it could be used to produce billions of watts of electrical power (USDOE 2011). It has a long way to go before this happens. There are three kinds of OTEC systems: closed-cycle, open-cycle, and hybrid.

Closed-Cycle OTEC

Closed-cycle systems use fluids with a low boiling point, such as ammonia, to rotate a turbine and generate electricity. Warm surface seawater is pumped through a heat exchanger, where a low-boiling-point fluid is vaporized. Expanding vapor turns a turbo-generator. Cold, deep seawater—pumped through a second heat exchanger—then condenses the vapor back into a liquid that is recycled through the system (Robinson 2006; Avery and Wu 1994).

In 1979 the Natural Energy Laboratory and several private-sector partners developed a mini OTEC experiment that achieved the first successful at-sea production of net electrical power from closed-cycle OTEC. The mini OTEC vessel was moored 1.5 miles (2.4 kilometers) off the Hawaiian coast and produced enough net electricity to illuminate the ship's light bulbs and run its computers and televisions. In 1999 the Natural Energy Laboratory successfully tested a 250-kilowatt pilot OTEC closed-cycle plant, the largest such plant ever put into operation (USDOE 2011).

Open-Cycle OTEC

Open-cycle systems use the tropical oceans' warm surface water to make electricity, producing fresh water as a by-product. When warm seawater is placed in a low-pressure container, it boils. The expanding steam drives a low-pressure turbine attached to an electrical generator. The steam, which has left its salt behind in the low-pressure container, is almost pure, fresh water. It is condensed back into a liquid by exposure to cold temperatures from deep-ocean water (Avery and Wu 1994).

Hybrid OTEC

Hybrid systems combine the features of closed- and open-cycle OTEC systems. In a hybrid system, warm seawater enters a vacuum chamber where it is flash-vaporized into steam, similar to the open-cycle evaporation process. The steam vaporizes a low-boiling-point fluid (in a closed-cycle loop) that drives a turbine to produce electricity (Avery and Wu 1994). An advantage of open or hybrid-cycle OTEC plants is the production of fresh water from seawater. Theoretically, an OTEC plant that generates 2 megawatts of net electricity could produce about 14,118 cubic feet (4,300 cubic meters) of desalinated water each day (USDOE 2011).

OCEAN CURRENT ENERGY

Ocean waters are constantly on the move. Ocean currents flow in complex patterns affected by wind, water salinity and temperature, topography of the ocean floor, and the earth's rotation. They are driven by wind and solar heating of waters near the equator, though some ocean currents result from density and salinity variations of water. These currents are relatively constant and flow in one direction only, in contrast to tidal currents closer to shore. Some examples of ocean currents are the Gulf Stream, Florida Straits Current, and California Current (USDOI 2006a).

While ocean currents move slowly relative to typical wind speeds, they carry a great deal of energy because of the density of water. Ocean currents thus contain an enormous amount of energy that may be captured and converted to a usable form. It has been estimated that taking just one-thousandth of the available energy from the Gulf Stream would supply Florida with 35 percent of its electrical needs (USDOI 2006a).

Technology for utilization of large-scale ocean current energy is at a very early stage of development. There are no commercial grid-connected turbines currently operating in the United States, and only a small number of prototypes and demonstration units have been tested (USDOI 2006a). According to the U.S. Minerals Management Service, under the most likely commercial development scenario, energy would be extracted from ocean currents by using submerged water turbines similar to wind turbines. These turbines would have rotor blades, a generator for converting rotational energy into electricity, and a means of transporting electrical current to shore for incorporation into an electrical grid. There would need to be a way to anchor turbines in a stationary position, such as posts or cables anchored to the sea floor. In large open areas with fast currents, it might be possible to install water turbines in groups or clusters to make up an ocean current "farm," with a predicted density of up to 37 turbines per square kilometer. Space would be needed between the water turbines to eliminate wake-interaction effects and allow access by maintenance vessels (USDOI 2006a).

COSTS OF OCEAN ENERGY UTILIZATION

Environmental Costs of Utilizing Ocean Energy Technologies

The ocean energy technology "fuel cycle" involves acquisition of materials, manufacture and installation of generating and transmission equipment, operation of this equipment, and disposal or recycling of waste materials from manufacturing processes and decommissioning, as illustrated in Figure 11.2. Manufacturing involves industrial-scale piping and sheet metal fabrication of generators, with installation of turbine and electrical components, depending on the specific technology utilized. Utility-scale ocean energy environmental costs include disturbance of the marine environment, visual impacts, hazardous materials disposal, and potential impacts on water and other resources, depending on the technology employed.

Tidal power plants that dam estuaries can impede migration of marine life, and silt builds up behind dams, altering marine ecosystems. Tidal fences may also disturb migration of sea life (USDOI 2011a). Tidal barrages alter marine ecosystems by changing the flow of saltwater into and out of estuaries (Armaroli and Balzani 2011, 244). Newly developed tidal turbines like the TidGen™ Power System of the Ocean Renewable Power Company may ultimately prove to be the least environmentally damaging of the tidal power technologies because they do not block migratory paths, facilitate buildup of silt, or induce ecosystem change (ORPC 2011a; Sharp 2010).

Potential environmental costs of wave energy development include adverse impacts on marine habitat (depending on the nature of associated submerged surfaces, above-water platforms, and changes in the seafloor); toxic releases from leaks or accidental spills of hydraulic fluids; visual and noise impacts above and below the water surface; and conflict with other ocean users, such as commercial shipping, recreational boating (USDOI 2011b; Nelson 2008; Previsic 2004), and

Figure 11.2 **The Ocean Energy Fuel Cycle**

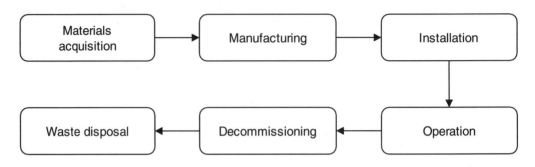

commercial fishing. A better understanding of the impacts of wave energy technology on the shoreline is also needed (California Energy Commission 2011). Careful site selection is the key to keeping the environmental effects of wave power systems to a minimum. Wave energy system planners can choose sites that preserve scenic shorefronts and avoid areas where wave energy systems can significantly alter flow patterns of sediment on the ocean floor (USDOI 2006b). Also essential is a demonstration of the ability of the equipment to survive the salinity and pressure environments of the ocean as well as weather effects over the life of the facility (California Energy Commission 2011). With some technologies in some locations near shipping lanes, there is a risk of collision due to the low free board of wave-energy devices, which makes them undetectable either by eyesight or by radar (Shaw 1982, 170). An oil tanker striking a wave energy generator could produce catastrophic results.

For ocean current energy to be utilized successfully at a commercial scale, a number of potential technical challenges need to be addressed to minimize environmental costs, including prevention of marine growth buildup and resistance to corrosion without degradation of the marine environment (Armaroli and Balzani 2011, 244; Mueller and Wallace 2008), and protection of fish and marine species from injury from turning turbine blades. These are environmental costs of all ocean technologies, except as noted above. Other uses of the ocean environment for shipping routes, commercial fishing, and present recreational uses, such as sport fishing and diving, will need to be considered when siting turbines. Other environmental costs include potential large-scale risks of slowing a current flow by extracting energy. Local effects, such as changes of estuary mixing that result in potential temperature and salinity modifications, might affect species in estuaries (USDOI 2006a).

Appropriate spacing of OTEC plants in tropical oceans will be necessary to mitigate potential negative environmental costs on ocean temperatures and marine life (USDOE 2011). The environmental costs of discharges of large volumes of both warm and cold water from OTEC power plants into the ocean are not well known (Trenka 1994, 16), but have been found problematic when associated with other technologies (*Calvert Cliffs Coordinating Committee v. AEC* 1971). There is also a risk of discharge of low-boiling-point fluids such as ammonia or freon to the environment from leaks. OTEC power plants may conflict with other uses of the ocean, such as commercial shipping, recreational boating, and commercial fishing (Trenka 1994, 16).

Dollar Costs of Utilizing Ocean Energy Technologies

Operating costs of tidal power plants are very low, but their initial capital construction costs are high, which lengthens payback periods. As a result, the cost per kilowatt-hour of tidal power is generally not competitive with conventional fossil-fueled power. Recent innovations like the tidal turbine made by Ocean Renewable Power Company are, however, competitive in dollar costs with wind energy (ORPC 2011a; Sharp 2010).

Wave power systems have high capital costs and a hard time competing with traditional power sources for price, although these dollar costs appear to be coming down. Some European experts predict that wave power devices will find lucrative niche markets. Once built, they have low operation and maintenance costs because their fuel—seawater—is free (USDOI 2006b).

OTEC power plants require substantial capital investment up front. Private sector firms may be unwilling to make substantial initial investments required to build large-scale OTEC plants until the price of fossil fuels increases dramatically or national governments provide financial incentives. A major factor hindering commercialization of OTEC is that there are only a few hundred land-based sites in the tropics where deep-ocean water is close enough to shore to make transmission of electricity from OTEC plants to consumers feasible. This will greatly limit the utility of OTEC plants in the United States for areas outside Hawaii.

National Security Costs of Utilizing Ocean Energy Technologies

Ocean energy technologies can be implemented without dependence on politically unstable areas such as the Middle East. No country or group of countries is able to control supplies or determine price for fuel or materials to implement ocean energy technologies. These technologies produce limited carbon emissions and greenhouse gases from fabrication and manufacturing of equipment. Consequently, ocean energy technologies will not produce climate change or a rise in sea level. Ocean energy technologies do not produce substantial amounts of toxic waste that must be isolated from the human environment for millennia. Utilization of ocean energy technologies does not produce materials useful to terrorists. Consequently, the national security costs of utilizing ocean energy technologies are nil. As compared to other energy technologies, utilization of ocean energy technologies can be conceptualized as having net national security benefits.

SUMMARY OF COSTS

The costs of utilizing ocean energy technologies are summarized in Figure 11.3. Overall, the environmental costs for producing and using these technologies are incurred mostly during production of materials and equipment, with some local disruption due to construction and placement of equipment in marine ecosystems, so they are "moderately low" compared to most conventional fuel technologies in use today. Dollar costs for application of ocean energy technologies are "high" and not competitive today with conventional fuels. Tidal power generation and wave energy may be competitive with wind energy, but not with conventional fuels. National security costs for all ocean energy technologies are very "low" or negligible because the materials for producing them are available in the United States or from friendly nations. This is an advantage ocean energy technologies hold over other energy technologies that may be acquired from foreign sources, contribute to global climate change, or leave a legacy of long-term waste products attractive to terrorists.

Figure 11.3 **The Costs of Ocean Energy Technologies**

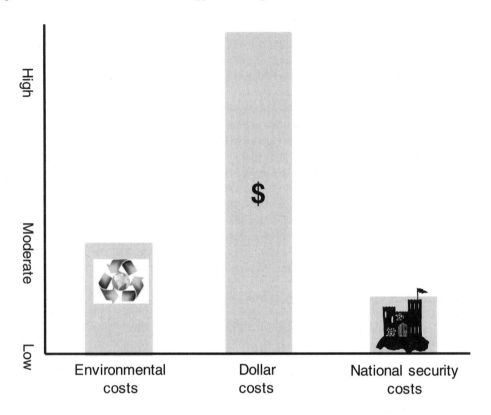

Tidal power requires large tidal differences which, in the United States, occur only in Maine and Alaska. Ocean thermal energy conversion is limited to tropical regions, such as Hawaii. Wave energy has a more general application, along many coastal areas. Ocean current energy technology is in the earliest stages of development. Consequently, the different technologies have widely varying utility in the United States and collectively are unlikely to contribute a significant portion of energy required in the near future.

REFERENCES

Armaroli, Nicola, and Vincenzo Balzani. 2011. *Energy for a Sustainable World*. Weinheim, Germany: Wiley-VCH Verlag.

Avery, W.H., and C. Wu. 1994. *Renewable Energy from the Ocean: A Guide to OTEC*. New York: Oxford University Press.

California Energy Commission. 2011. "Ocean Energy." CA.gov, February 17. Sacramento: California Energy Commission.

Calvert Cliffs Coordinating Committee v. U.S. Atomic Energy Commission (AEC). 449 F.2d 1109 (D.C. Cir. 1971).

Mueller, M., and R. Wallace. 2008. "Enabling Science and Technology for Marine Renewable Energy." *Energy Policy* 36 (12): 4376–4382.

Nelson, Peter A. 2008. *Developing Wave Energy in Coastal California: Potential Socio-Economic and Environmental Effects*. Sacramento: California Energy Commission.

Ocean Renewable Power Company (ORPC). 2011a. "About Us." www.orpc.co/aboutorpc_company_abou-tus.aspx.

———. 2011b. "Projects: Maine." www.orpc.co/content.aspx?p=h3jCHHn6gcg%3d.

———. 2011c. "TidGen™ Power System." www.orpc.co/orpcpowersystem_tidgenpowersystem.aspx.

Previsic, Mirko. 2004. *E2I EPRI Assessment: Offshore Wave Energy Conversion Devices*. Palo Alto: Electric Power Research Institute.

Robinson, Michael C. 2006. *Ocean Energy Technology Development*. Golden, CO: National Renewable Energy Laboratory.

Sharp, David. 2010. "Maine Tidal Power Prototype Passes All Tests." *Portland Press Herald*, March 8.

Shaw, Ronald. 1982. *Wave Energy: A Design Challenge*. Chichester, UK: Ellis Horwood.

Trenka, Andrew R. 1994. "Ocean Thermal Energy Conversion (OTEC): A Status Report on the Challenges." In *Alternative Fuels and the Environment*, ed. Frances S. Sterrett, 1–17. Ann Arbor, MI: Lewis.

Turkel, Tux. 2010. "Tide Effects: A Lot of Hopes Are Riding on the Final Demonstration of a Turbine Designed to Tap the Powerful Tides off Eastport." *Portland Press Herald*, February 22.

U.S. Department of Energy (USDOE). 2011. "Ocean Thermal Energy Conversion." www.eere.energy.gov/basics/renewable_energy/ocean_thermal_energy_conv.html.

U.S. Department of the Interior (USDOI). 2006a. *Technology White Paper on Ocean Current Energy Potential on the U.S. Outer Continental Shelf*. Washington, DC: U.S. Department of the Interior, Minerals Management Service.

———. 2006b. *Technology White Paper on Wave Energy Potential on the U.S. Outer Continental Shelf*. Washington, DC: U.S. Department of the Interior, Minerals Management Service.

———. 2011a. "Ocean Wave Energy." http://ocsenergy.anl.gov/guide/wave/index.cfm.

———. 2011b. "OCS Alternative Energy and Alternative Use Programmatic EIS." Washington, DC: U.S. Department of the Interior, Bureau of Ocean Energy Management. http://ocsenergy.anl.gov/guide/ocean/index.cfm.

Woodard, Colin. 2011. "Tidal Turbines: New Sparks of Hope for Green Energy from Beneath the Waves." *Christian Science Monitor*, May 16.

12

Hydrogen

Hydrogen is the lightest and most abundant chemical element in the universe, constituting roughly 75 percent of chemical elemental mass. It is an invisible, nontoxic, light gas that can be used to power nearly every end-use energy need. Hydrogen has high energy content compared to gasoline, and its small molecules can diffuse through most materials and make steel brittle. This creates some difficulties in handling it, discussed below. Hydrogen is used as a feedstock in the chemical and petroleum industries, principally to produce ammonia, upgraded fossil fuels, and a variety of chemicals. It is rarely used today as a transportation fuel (Armaroli and Balzani 2011, 280–281).

THE HYDROGEN ENERGY PROCESS

The hydrogen energy fuel cycle includes hydrogen production, manufacturing of fuel cells, storage, transportation, distribution, and utilization of hydrogen, as illustrated in Figure 12.1. The fuel cycle for hydrogen includes producing hydrogen by conversion from other fuels or water, transportation to decentralized fueling stations, and utilization in fuel cells. The basic components of central-station generation facilities are the same except generation of electricity is at a much larger scale and access to the electric power network is required. Suitable areas must be evaluated, production and generating facilities must be constructed and operated, and eventually generating equipment must be decommissioned.

Hydrogen Production

Although plentiful, hydrogen does not exist naturally on earth in its elemental form. Pure hydrogen stores and delivers energy in a usable form, but it must be produced from hydrogen-rich compounds, such as fossil fuels or water. Hydrogen can be produced from diverse domestic resources,

Figure 12.1 **The Hydrogen Fuel Cycle**

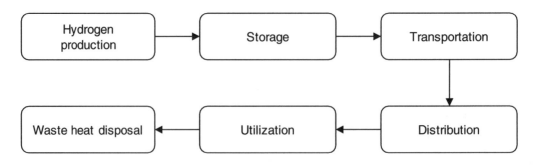

including fuels, such as coal, natural gas, and biomass, or by using nuclear energy and renewable energy sources, such as wind, solar, geothermal, and hydroelectric power to split water. More than 95 percent of hydrogen is produced from fossil fuels, in a variety of processes, some of which generate carbon dioxide in addition to hydrogen. Only about 4 percent of hydrogen is produced by electrolysis of water, a much more expensive process used only when high-purity hydrogen is needed (Armaroli and Balzani 2011, 281).

Hydrogen can be produced almost anywhere, at large central plants, or in small distributed units located at or near the point of use, such as at gasoline refueling stations or stationary power sites. It can even be produced onboard a transportation vehicle. A wide range of technologies is being developed to produce hydrogen economically from a variety of resources (USDOE 2006).

Natural Gas Reforming

Hydrogen can be produced from the methane in natural gas using high-temperature steam. Steam methane reforming accounts for about 95 percent of the hydrogen used today in the United States. In steam-methane reforming, methane reacts with heated steam (700°C–1000°C) under pressure in the presence of a catalyst to produce hydrogen, carbon monoxide, and a small amount of carbon dioxide. Subsequently, in what is called a water-gas shift reaction, the carbon monoxide and steam are reacted using a catalyst to produce carbon dioxide and more hydrogen. In a final process step called pressure-swing adsorption, carbon dioxide and other impurities are removed from the gas stream, leaving essentially pure hydrogen (USDOE 2006). Steam methane reforming is considered the least expensive way to produce hydrogen (Ekins, Hawkins, and Hughes 2010, 31).

Biofuel Reforming

Biomass can be processed to make renewable liquid fuels, such as ethanol or bio-oil, which are relatively convenient to transport and can be reacted with high-temperature steam to produce hydrogen at or near the point of use. A variation of this technology is known as aqueous-phase reforming (USDOE 2006).

Electrolysis

Electrolysis uses an electric current to separate water into hydrogen and oxygen. Required electricity can be generated using any of a number of resources. However, to minimize greenhouse gas emissions, electricity generation using renewable energy technologies, such as wind, solar photovoltaics, geothermal, or hydroelectric power might be preferred (USDOE 2006). A well-to-wheels energy use study showed hydrogen produced by wind-powered electrolysis, from coal with CO_2 sequestration, and from natural gas with CO_2 sequestration generates very low amounts of greenhouse gas emissions compared to advanced internal combustion engine vehicles and hybrid vehicles (Ogden 2004, 81). Carbon sequestration is a risky, expensive technology with which there has not been much experience (White et al. 2003). Presumably hydrogen produced with electrolysis powered by solar photovoltaics, geothermal, or hydroelectric power would produce comparably low emissions of greenhouse gases, without the expense and risks of sequestration. Moreover, carbon sequestration for the purpose of emissions reduction has not yet been demonstrated on a commercial scale, so its costs and long-term viability remain speculative (Ekins, Hawkins, and Hughes 2010, 31).

In 2009 ITM Power, a British company, announced it had produced hydrogen at a commercially competitive price using small-scale water electrolysis without the usual platinum catalyst, using significantly lower-cost membrane materials and a new one-step assembly process that facilitates mass production. Development of cost-competitive small-scale, residential electolyzers could be a game-changer, because it may allow hydrogen to be widely used without the need for major new transportation and distribution infrastructure (Ekins, Hawkins, and Hughes 2010, 35).

Nuclear High-Temperature Electrolysis

Heat from a nuclear reactor can be used to improve the efficiency of water electrolysis to produce hydrogen. By increasing the temperature of the water, less electricity is required to split it into hydrogen and oxygen, which reduces total energy required (USDOE 2006). Nuclear reactors operate at higher temperatures than most electric generators and produce substantial excess heat that can be used in this manner.

High-Temperature Thermochemical Water-Splitting

Another water-splitting method uses high temperatures generated by solar concentrators (mirrors that focus and intensify sunlight) (Rand and Dell 2008, 124) or nuclear reactors to drive a series of chemical reactions to split water into hydrogen and oxygen. All intermediate process chemicals are recycled within this process (USDOE 2006). This process allows utilization of what would otherwise be considered waste heat from solar power plants or nuclear reactors. Advanced nuclear-fueled thermochemical processes are currently unproven, but may provide low per-unit production costs for hydrogen production in the future (USEIA 2008b).

Gasification

Gasification is a process in which coal or biomass is converted into gaseous components by applying heat under pressure in the presence of oxygen and steam, producing hydrogen and carbon monoxide. This syngas can be used directly in electric power production, as a chemical feedstock for production of synthetic chemicals and fuels, or for hydrogen production. If used for hydrogen production, the syngas is chemically cleaned to remove hydrogen sulfide, coal ash, and other impurities before a water-gas shift reaction is used to produce hydrogen and carbon dioxide. Carbon dioxide is removed using pressure-swing adsorption, leaving virtually pure hydrogen. In commercial hydrogen production, CO_2 is usually vented to the atmosphere (Ekins, Hawkins, and Hughes 2010, 32). With carbon capture and storage, hydrogen might be produced directly from coal with near-zero greenhouse gas emissions. Since growing biomass removes carbon dioxide from the atmosphere, producing hydrogen through biomass gasification releases near-zero net greenhouse gases (USDOE 2006). Biomass gasification can use a variety of feedstocks, including nonfood fuel crops like willow and switch grass or biomass residues like peanut shells and sugarcane waste (Ekins, Hawkins, and Hughes 2010, 32).

Biological

Certain microbes, such as green algae and cyanobacteria, produce hydrogen by splitting water in the presence of sunlight as a by-product of their natural metabolic processes. Other microbes can extract hydrogen directly from biomass (USDOE 2006). Hydrogen produced by electrohydrogenesis may be able to achieve greater efficiencies than other biological hydrogen production processes while reducing solids in municipal wastewater treatment facilities at competitive costs (Ekins, Hawkins, and Hughes 2010, 36).

Photo-Electrochemical

Hydrogen can be produced directly from water using sunlight and a special class of semiconductor materials. These highly specialized semiconductors absorb sunlight and use light energy to completely separate water molecules into hydrogen and oxygen (USDOE 2006).

Hydrogen production technologies are in various stages of development. Some technologies, such as steam methane reforming, are well developed and can be used in the near term. Others, such as high-temperature thermochemical water-splitting, biological, and photo-electrochemical, are in early stages of laboratory development and considered potential pathways for the long term, but will not be available any time soon (USDOE 2006).

Storage

Hydrogen storage will be required onboard vehicles and at hydrogen production sites, hydrogen refueling stations, and stationary power sites. Developing safe, reliable, compact, and cost-effective hydrogen storage technologies is one of the most technically challenging barriers to widespread use of hydrogen as a form of energy. Possible approaches to storing hydrogen include:

• Physical storage of compressed hydrogen gas in high pressure tanks
• Physical storage of cryogenic hydrogen in insulated tanks
• Storage in advanced materials—within the structure or on the surface of certain materials, as well as in the form of chemical compounds that undergo a chemical reaction to release hydrogen. Hydrogen can be stored on the surfaces of solids by adsorption, in which hydrogen associates with the surface of a material either as hydrogen molecules or hydrogen atoms. (USDOE 2011b)

Hydrogen has physical characteristics that make it difficult to store in large quantities without taking up a significant amount of space. On a weight basis, hydrogen has nearly three times the energy content of gasoline. On a volume basis, however, the situation is reversed, with gasoline having nearly four times the energy content of hydrogen. This makes hydrogen a challenge to store, particularly within the size and weight constraints of a vehicle (USDOE 2011b).

To be competitive with conventional vehicles, hydrogen-powered cars must be able to travel more than 300 miles between fills, which is generally regarded as the minimum for widespread public acceptance. A typical light-duty fuel cell vehicle will need to carry 4 to 10 kilograms of hydrogen, depending on the size and type of vehicle, to allow a driving range of more than 300 miles (~483 kilometers), the DOE performance goal. Drivers must also be able to refuel at a speed comparable to the rate of refueling today's gasoline vehicles. Using currently available high-pressure tank storage technology, placing a sufficient quantity of hydrogen onboard a vehicle to provide a 300-mile driving range would require a very large tank—larger than the trunk of a typical automobile. Aside from loss of cargo space, there would also be the added weight of the tank, which would probably reduce fuel economy. To acheive the 300-mile driving range, new low-cost materials and components for hydrogen storage systems are needed, along with low-cost, high-volume manufacturing methods for those materials and components. Hydrogen storage research is focused primarily on technologies and systems used onboard a vehicle. Efforts are being made to improve the weight, volume, and cost of current hydrogen storage systems and to identify and develop new technologies that can achieve similar performance, at a similar cost, to gasoline fuel storage systems (USDOE 2011b). Although automakers have recently demonstrated progress with some prototype vehicles traveling more than 300 miles on a single fill, this driving range must be achievable across different vehicle models and without compromising space, performance, or cost.

Compressed Gas and Liquid Hydrogen Tanks

Traditional compressed hydrogen gas tanks are much larger and heavier than what is needed for light-duty vehicles. Light-weight, safe, composite materials are needed that can reduce the weight and volume of compressed gas storage systems. Liquefied hydrogen is denser than gaseous hydrogen and thus contains more energy in a given volume. Similar sized liquid hydrogen tanks can store more hydrogen than compressed gas tanks, but it requires about 30 to 40 percent of the energy content of the hydrogen to liquefy it (Armaroli and Balzani 2011, 288). Tank insulation required to prevent hydrogen loss adds to the weight, volume, and costs of liquid hydrogen tanks. A hybrid tank concept is being evaluated that can store high-pressure hydrogen gas under cryogenic conditions (cooled to –120 to –196°C); these "cryo-compressed" tanks may allow relatively lighter weight and more compact storage (USDOE 2011b). Gasoline tanks used in cars and trucks today may be shaped to take maximum advantage of available vehicle space. Compressed hydrogen tanks have to be cylindrical to ensure their integrity under high pressure (Armaroli and Balzani 2011, 288). High-pressure hydrogen tanks that may be shaped to available space are being evaluated as an alternative to cylindrical tanks, which do not package well in a vehicle (USDOE 2011b).

Materials-Based Storage

Hydrogen atoms or molecules bound tightly with other elements in a compound, or potential storage material, may make it possible to store larger quantities of hydrogen in smaller volumes. Several different kinds of materials are under investigation, including metal hydrides, adsorbent materials, and chemical hydrides, in addition to identifying new materials with potential for favorable hydrogen storage attributes. Hydrogen storage in materials offers great promise, but additional research is required to better understand the mechanism of hydrogen storage in materials under practical operating conditions and to overcome critical challenges related to capacity, the uptake and release of hydrogen, management of heat during refueling, cost, and life cycle impacts (USDOE 2011b). In 2004 the U.S. Department of Energy stopped funding research and development for onboard reforming of conventional fuels into hydrogen, shifting attention toward improved onboard storage of hydrogen as a compressed gas, a liquid, or in other materials (Wald 2009; Ekins, Hawkins, and Hughes 2010, 29–30).

Transportation

Most of the hydrogen used in the United States today is produced at or near where it is used—typically at large industrial sites. As a result, an efficient means of transporting large quantities of hydrogen fuel over long distances and at low cost does not yet exist. Before hydrogen can become a mainstream energy source, the infrastructure (i.e., miles of transmission and distribution pipelines, bulk storage vessels, and refueling stations) must be built.

Suppliers currently transport hydrogen by pipeline or over roadways using tube trailers or cryogenic liquid hydrogen tankers. In some cases, liquefied hydrogen is transported by barge. Hydrogen can also be moved by barge or truck using chemical carriers, which are substances composed of substantial amounts of hydrogen and other elements: for example, ethanol (C_2H_5OH) and ammonia (NH_3).

Transmission by pipeline is the least expensive way to transport large amounts of hydrogen; several lines have been built in the United States, near large petroleum refineries and chemical plants in Illinois, California, and along the Gulf Coast. However, in comparison with the more than 1 million miles of natural gas pipelines, the current hydrogen pipeline infrastructure in the United States is very small, less than 1,200 miles in length (USDOE 2010). Moreover, natural gas pipelines are not suited for hydrogen transport because high-pressure hydrogen leaks easily through the smallest of holes and embrittles the mild steel used for gas pipeline construction. Pipelines for hydrogen require different materials, welding procedures, and designs for valves, compressors, sensors, and safety devices than those used for natural gas (Armaroli and Balzani 2011, 290).

Compressed hydrogen can be transported over highways in high-pressure tube trailers. This option is used primarily to move modest amounts of hydrogen over relatively short distances. It tends to become cost prohibitive for distances greater than about 200 miles from the location of production (USDOE 2010). By comparison, for a given volume, liquefied hydrogen that has been cooled to −253°C is denser and contains greater energy content than gaseous hydrogen. In the absence of an existing pipeline, shipping liquefied hydrogen is a preferred method of transporting hydrogen over long distances because a tanker truck can carry more than a tube truck, at lower cost (Ekins, Hawkins, and Hughes 2010, 44). However, liquefaction is costly because it requires a substantial amount of energy. Nonetheless, due to the limited amount of pipeline available, hydrogen is often transported as a liquid in superinsulated, cryogenic tank trucks and later vaporized for use at the receiving site (USDOE 2010).

For a given volume, hydrogen contains a smaller amount of usable energy than other fuels such as natural gas and gasoline. Because of its low volumetric energy density, hydrogen is comparatively more costly to transport and store. Principally, this is due to the large initial capital investment required to construct a new pipeline infrastructure. There are also a number of technical concerns with pipeline transmission of hydrogen over long distances, including the potential for hydrogen embrittlement of steel and welds used for pipeline construction, the need for lower-cost, higher-reliability hydrogen compression technology, and the desire to prevent hydrogen permeation and leakage from pipeline and other containment materials (USDOE 2010). No ship tankers exist yet for liquefied hydrogen, but presumably could be built similar to those for liquefied natural gas (Ekins, Hawkins, and Hughes 2010, 43).

The method by which hydrogen is produced also affects the cost and method of transportation. Distributed production at the point of use, such as directly at refueling stations or at stationary power sites, eliminates long-distance transportation costs. Conversely, production in large central plants results in lower production costs due to greater economies of scale, but requires long-distance transport that increases transportation costs. Consequently, the costs of hydrogen production and transportation must be analyzed together (USDOE 2010).

Efforts are being made to better understand the options and trade-offs for hydrogen transportation from central and decentralized production sites under various delivery scenarios. In the United States, research is also focused on developing:

• Lower-cost, more reliable hydrogen compression technology
• More cost-effective bulk hydrogen storage technology
• New materials for lower-cost hydrogen pipelines
• More energy-efficient and lower-cost hydrogen liquefaction processes
• Integrated production, delivery, and end-use technologies

Building a national hydrogen delivery infrastructure will be a significant challenge. It will take time to develop and will probably include various combinations of technologies. Infrastructure needs and resources will vary by region and by type of market (e.g., urban, interstate, or rural), and infrastructure options (or the delivery mix) will continue to evolve as the demand for hydrogen grows and as delivery technologies mature (USDOE 2010).

Distribution

A delivery infrastructure for hydrogen will include land dedicated to the pipelines, truck storage, storage facilities, compressors, and dispensers involved in delivering fuel to end-users. To date, most hydrogen fueling stations have been constructed to support demonstration projects. As the hydrogen market increases, it is expected that existing fueling stations will expand to meet the demand, offering hydrogen pumps in addition to gasoline or natural gas pumps. Other hydrogen fueling stations will be stand-alone operations, some with self-service pumps (USDOE 2009).

By 2011 only a few states and the District of Columbia had announced plans to construct the refueling and maintenance stations needed to support hydrogen vehicles. California had progressed furthest, with thirty-one installed hydrogen refueling stations, about half of the United States total, and a few private maintenance facilities. As of 2007 there were a total of sixty-three hydrogen demonstration refueling stations in the United States. Two-thirds of the existing refueling stations are capable of self-producing hydrogen, and the remaining one-third are stationary or mobile refueling stations that rely on deliveries of liquid or gaseous hydrogen for their operation. Currently, there are no home refueling stations except those located at manufacturers' research facilities. California hosts the nation's only hydrogen refueling station connected to a hydrogen pipeline and a centralized production plant (USEIA 2008b).

Utilization

Fuels cells are the key to greater future utilization of hydrogen. A fuel cell is a technology that allows energy stored in hydrogen to be converted into electrical energy for end use. Stationary fuel cells can be used as backup power for critical facilities during emergencies, power generation, power for remote locations, and cogeneration, in which excess heat released during electricity generation is used for other applications. Fuel cell vehicles can be used for transportation of people and goods in small or large quantities. Fuel cells can power almost any portable application that uses batteries, from hand-held devices to portable generators. They can also power transportation, including personal vehicles, trucks, buses, and marine vessels, as well as provide auxiliary power to traditional transportation technologies. Hydrogen can play a particularly important role in the future by replacing some imported petroleum currently used in cars and trucks.

Although fuel cells can use a variety of fuels, including gasoline, hydrogen is usually preferred because of the ease with which it can be converted to electricity and its ability to combine with oxygen to emit only pure water and potentially useful heat as the only by-products. Fuel cells look and function very similar to batteries. A fuel cell continues to convert chemical energy to electricity as long as fresh hydrogen is fed into it (USEIA 2008b). Hydrogen-powered fuel cells are not only pollution-free, but have two to three times the efficiency of traditional combustion technologies. A conventional combustion-based power plant typically generates electricity at efficiencies of 33 to 35 percent, while fuel cell systems can generate electricity at efficiencies up to 60 percent—and if by-product heat is used in cogeneration, the overall efficiency can approach 90 percent. Under normal driving conditions, the gasoline engine in a conventional car is less

Figure 12.2 **Hydrogen Fuel Cell**

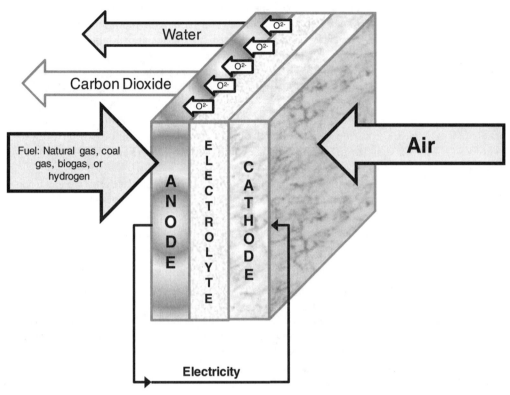

Source: USDOE 2011a.

than 20 percent efficient at converting chemical energy in gasoline into power that moves the vehicle. Hydrogen fuel cell vehicles, which use electric motors, are more energy-efficient, using 40 to 60 percent of the fuel's energy—corresponding to more than a 50 percent reduction in fuel consumption, compared to a conventional vehicle with a gasoline internal combustion engine. Fuel cells operate quietly and have fewer moving parts that may need maintenance or repair (USDOE 2011a). Their size, flexibility, and corresponding electrical output make fuel cells ideal for a wide variety of applications, from a few kilowatts to power a laptop computer to several megawatts at a central power generation facility (USEIA 2008b).

A single fuel cell consists of an electrolyte sandwiched between two electrodes, an anode and a cathode, as illustrated in Figure 12.2. Bipolar plates on either side of the cell help distribute gases and serve as current collectors. In a polymer electrolyte membrane (PEM) fuel cell, which is widely regarded as the most promising for light-duty transportation, hydrogen gas flows through channels to the anode, where a catalyst causes the hydrogen molecules to separate into protons and electrons. The membrane allows only protons to pass through it. While protons are conducted through a membrane to the other side of the cell, a stream of negatively charged electrons follows an external circuit to a cathode. This flow of electrons is electricity that can be used to do work, such as power a motor (USDOE 2011a).

On the other side of the cell, oxygen gas, typically drawn from outside air, flows through channels to the cathode. When electrons return from doing work, they react with oxygen and hydrogen protons, which have moved through the membrane, at the cathode to form water. This union generates heat that can be used outside the fuel cell (USDOE 2011a).

The power produced by a fuel cell depends on several factors, including the fuel cell type, size, temperature at which it operates, and pressure at which gases are supplied. A single fuel cell produces approximately one volt or less—barely enough electricity for even the smallest applications. To increase the amount of electricity generated, individual fuel cells are combined in series to form a "stack" (the term is often used to refer to the entire stack, as well as to an individual cell) (Nice and Strickland 2011). Depending on the application, a fuel cell stack may contain only a few or as many as hundreds of individual cells layered together. This scalability makes fuel cells ideal for a wide variety of applications, from laptop computers (50–100 watts) to homes (1–5 kWe), vehicles (50–125 kWe), and central power station generation (1–200 MWe or more) (USDOE 2011a).

In general, all fuel cells have the same basic configuration, an electrolyte and two electrodes. But there are different types of fuel cells, classified primarily by the kind of electrolyte used. The electrolyte determines the chemical reactions that take place in the fuel cell, the temperature range of operation, and other factors that determine its most suitable applications. Fuel cells are classified by their electrolyte and operational characteristics:

- The polymer electrolyte membrane fuel cell is lightweight and has a low operating temperature. PEM fuel cells operate on hydrogen and oxygen from air. Other fuels can be used, but must be reformed on-site, which can reduce fueling cost but also drives up the purchase price and maintenance costs and results in CO_2 emissions. PEM systems are typically designed to serve in seventy- to 120-kilowatt transportation applications and may be usable as uninterruptible power supplies in special commercial applications. Current PEM stack life is typically around 1,350 hours, as used in automotive applications.
- Alkaline fuel cells (AFCs) are one of the most mature fuel cell technologies. AFCs have a combined electricity and heat efficiency of 60 percent and were used for production of electrical power and heated water on the Gemini and Apollo spacecraft. They are often used in military applications. However, their short operating time renders them less than cost-effective in commercial applications. Their susceptibility to contamination by even a small amount of CO_2 in the air also requires purification of the hydrogen feed.
- The direct methanol fuel cell (DMFC) uses pure methanol mixed with steam. Liquid methanol has a higher energy density than hydrogen, and an existing infrastructure for transport and supply of methanol can be utilized.
- Phosphoric acid fuel cells (PAFCs) are commercially available today for stationary power applications, and over 200 units have been placed in operation. They are less efficient than other fuel cell designs and tend to be large, heavy and expensive, but they have been used in emergency backup power and remote power applications.
- Molten carbonate fuel cells (MCFCs) and solid oxide fuel cells (SOFC) are high-temperature designs that promise high operating efficiencies and have been used by electric utilities in large central station generation.
- The newest fuel cell technology is the unitized regenerative fuel cell (URFC), which can produce electricity from hydrogen and oxygen while generating heat and water. It is lighter than a separate electrolyzer and generator, making it desirable for weight-sensitive applications. (USEIA 2008b)

Reducing cost and improving durability are the two most significant challenges to fuel cell commercialization. Fuel cell systems must be cost-competitive with, and perform as well as or better than, traditional power technologies over the life of the system. Ongoing research is focused on identifying and developing new materials to reduce the cost and extend the life of fuel cell stack components, including membranes, catalysts, bipolar plates, and membrane-electrode assemblies. Low-cost, high-volume manufacturing processes will also help to make fuel cell systems cost-competitive with traditional technologies (USDOE 2011a).

A multibillion-dollar hydrogen industry exists in the United States, serving diverse hydrogen end-use applications. About 99 percent of hydrogen produced is used in chemical and petrochemical applications. Of the end uses, the largest consumers are oil refineries, ammonia plants, chloralkali plants, and methanol plants. Examples of current hydrogen end uses include:

- Petroleum refining, to remove sulfur from crude oil as well as to convert heavy crude oil to lighter products
- Chemical processing, to manufacture ammonia, methanol, chlorine, caustic soda, and hydrogenated nonedible oils for soaps, insulation, plastics, ointments, and other chemicals
- Pharmaceuticals, to produce sorbitol, which is used in cosmetics, adhesives, surfactants, and vitamins
- Metal production and fabrication, to create a protective atmosphere in high-temperature operations, such as stainless steel manufacturing
- Food processing, to hydrogenate oils, such as soybean, fish, cottonseed, and corn oil
- Laboratory research, to conduct experimentation concerning supercriticality
- Electronics, to create a special atmosphere for production of semiconductor circuits
- Glass manufacturing, to create a protective atmosphere for float glass production
- Power generation, to cool turbo-generators and to protect piping in nuclear reactors (USEIA 2008b)

Stationary power generation and the transportation sector are widely viewed as two sectors where there may be opportunities to greatly expand future uses of hydrogen.

STATIONARY USES OF HYDROGEN

Comprehensive data on U.S. stationary fuel cell installations are not available, but large cogeneration, uninterruptible power supply systems, and home energy stations are in production or under development. Cogeneration (combined heat and power) systems are being manufactured for large commercial buildings or industrial sites that require significant amounts of electricity, water heating, space heating, or process heat. Fuel cells combined with a heat recovery system can meet some or all of these needs, as well as providing a source of purified water. Small, stand-alone cogeneration systems currently are viable in some areas where the high cost of transmitting power justifies the added cost of a fuel cell. Currently, U.S. companies such as Plug Power manufacture fuel cell systems able to produce up to five kilowatts of electricity and nine kilowatts of thermal energy. Excess heat can be used for water or space heating to further reduce a site's electrical energy use (USEIA 2008b). This would be adequate for modest residential use.

Uninterruptible power supply systems, in which fuel cells are used as backup power supplies if a primary power system fails, are one of the fastest growth areas for stationary fuel cell technologies. Uninterruptible power supply systems often are used in telecommunications, banking, hospitals, and military applications. Battery systems have been used for many years to provide backup power to essential services, but battery output time is relatively short. Fuel cells with refillable fuel storage systems can provide power for as long as required during a blackout (USEIA 2008b).

Home energy stations are another variant of small, stand-alone cogeneration systems. They use either reformers or electrolyzers to produce hydrogen fuel for personal vehicles, and they also incorporate a hydrogen fuel cell that can provide heat and electricity for a home. One advantage of these stations is they offer enhanced utilization of hydrogen gas and therefore help to defray some of the overall cost of the hydrogen refueling station. Appliance-sized home energy stations are being developed by several automobile manufacturers as a potential alternative to commercial refueling stations (USEIA 2008b).

There continues to be a lack of basic knowledge and information concerning failure rates for components of the hydrogen infrastructure and especially for hydrogen tankers involved in transport accidents. A salient and underexplored issue is leakage in enclosed structures, such as garages in homes and commercial establishments. Hydrogen's explosion behavior following high-pressure releases, and the related likelihood of occurrence, are poorly understood. Widely accepted standards, methodologies, mitigation techniques, and regulations are not yet available. "Accumulated experience with hydrogen is presently limited to a number of industrial applications whose scale and proximity to the general public are small" (Ricci, Bellaby, and Flynn 2010, 222–223). Many hydrogen and fuel cell safety codes and standards in effect today are based on existing practices from the chemical and aerospace industries. Efforts are under way by code and standards organizations to develop new, more appropriate codes and standards that will ensure the safe use of hydrogen for transportation and stationary applications. Many of these new applications are in the retail environment; new codes and standards reflect this transition from industrial to retail hydrogen applications (USDOE 2011a). Improved hydrogen and fuel cell safety codes and standards are needed before widespread adoption of hydrogen technologies by the general public.

FUEL CELL VEHICLES

Fuel cell vehicles, powered by hydrogen, have the potential to revolutionize our transportation system. They are more efficient than conventional internal combustion engine vehicles and produce no harmful tailpipe exhaust—their only emission is water. However, this exhaust water freezes at low temperatures (Kawai 2004, 66), limiting the ability of fuel cell vehicles to start and operate in cold seasons or climates. Fuel cell vehicles and the hydrogen infrastructure to fuel them are in early stages of development. Fuel cell vehicles use electricity to power motors located near the vehicle's wheels. In contrast to electric vehicles, which generally use electricity produced off the vehicle to charge onboard batteries, fuel cell vehicles produce their electricity onboard using a fuel cell. The fuel cell is powered by hydrogen from an onboard fuel tank (USDOE 2007).

Fuel cell vehicles can be fueled with pure hydrogen gas stored directly on the vehicle or extracted from a secondary fuel—such as methanol, ethanol, or natural gas—that carries hydrogen. These secondary fuels must first be converted into hydrogen gas by an onboard device called a reformer. Fuel cell vehicles fueled with pure hydrogen emit no pollutants, only water and heat. Vehicles that use secondary fuels and a reformer produce small amounts of carbon dioxide, a greenhouse gas. Due to its simplicity and weight-saving advantages, liquid hydrogen remains the most convenient way to power hydrogen vehicles (Armaroli and Balzani 2011, 296). Fuel cell vehicles can be equipped with other advanced technologies to increase efficiency, such as regenerative braking systems often used today on electric vehicles, which capture the energy lost during braking and store it in a large battery (USDOE 2007).

From 2000 to 2005, ninety-five light-duty fuel cell vehicles were placed in California and traveled more than 220,000 miles on that state's roads and highways. These cars are still being tested and are available to a few fleets and consumers (California Energy Commission 2011). Much of the industry's fuel cell research and development information remains proprietary. In 2005, General Motors and Daimler Chrysler acknowledged expenditures of more than $1 billion in fuel cell vehicle development. General Motors began market testing a hundred Chevrolet Equinox fuel cell sport utility vehicles. Daimler started leasing its Mercedes Benz B-Class fuel cell vehicle in California in 2010 (Shenhar 2012). Other automobile manufacturers, including Toyota, Ford, and Volkswagen, have developed fuel cell concept cars (USEIA 2008b).

Honda introduced its first fuel cell vehicle, called the FCX, in 1999 and in 2007 unveiled the first production model of the FCX Clarity. Limited marketing of the FCX Clarity began in 2008 in the United States and Japan. In 2011 the FCX Clarity was available in the United States only in the Los Angeles area, where sixteen hydrogen filling stations are available; as of July 2009, ten drivers had leased the Clarity for US$600 a month. Honda, which had 200 vehicles available for lease, stated it could start mass-producing vehicles based on the FCX concept by the year 2020 (*Washington Times* 2009). In 2010 Lotus Cars announced it was developing a fleet of hydrogen taxis in London (Jha 2010). Heavy-duty fuel cell vehicles in testing and preproduction include fuel cell buses manufactured by Van Hool and New Flyer and an electric/hydrogen fuel cell hybrid semi-tractor produced by Vision Motor Corporation (USDOE 2007). In 2005 fuel cell buses began testing at Sun Line Transit in Thousand Palms, Alameda-Contra Costa Transit, and Santa Clara Valley Transportation Authority (California Energy Commission 2011). Buses have also been tested at Sacramento Municipal Utility District and the University of California at Davis (Unnasch and Browning 2000).

All fuel cell vehicle concepts currently under development use electric motors to power the wheels, typically accomplished through combination of an electric battery storage system and an onboard hydrogen fuel cell. Depending on the degree of hybridization, a battery may provide pure "plug-in" electricity to drive a vehicle some distance, after which the fuel cell takes over. A battery system may be complemented by a hydrogen storage system and a fuel cell, in order to extend driving range to 300 miles.

The primary impediments to deployment of hydrogen fuel cell vehicles include cost, fuel cell durability, and restricted operational temperature range of the cell. The costs of current fuel cell vehicles are high as a result of high component costs and the fact that the vehicles are either custom-built or produced in limited quantities. Also of concern is achieving the necessary minimum range for consumer acceptance (USEIA 2008b). The primary cost component of the fuel cell vehicle is the fuel cell itself (Ekins, Hawkins, and Hughes 2010, 51), which has a life expectancy about half that of an internal combustion engine. Thus, consumers would have to replace the fuel cell in order to achieve a vehicle operating lifetime equivalent to that of a traditional engine. Other features of fuel cell vehicles are reasonably well understood at this time and have been commercialized to some extent in the current generation of hybrid vehicles (USEIA 2008b).

Hydrogen can also be used to power vehicles with internal combustion engines, or fuel cells on electric vehicles. The hydrogen internal combustion engine is a slightly modified version of the familiar gasoline-powered engine. However, intransigent problems of consumer acceptance have plagued this type of vehicle due to difficulties in injecting highly flammable hydrogen through a hot intake manifold without producing periodic loud reports comparable to gunfire, as the hydrogen ignites prematurely and backfires. Consumers apparently are not fond of the sensation of being shot at while driving down the street.

COSTS OF HYDROGEN UTILIZATION

Environmental Costs of Utilizing Hydrogen Technologies

As discussed above, potential environmental costs of using hydrogen technologies include dedication of land to its production, distribution, and use, and safety issues in production and distribution facilities. Another issue to consider is the effect of hydrogen emissions on the atmosphere.

Waste Heat Disposal

Any hydrogen production or utilization technology that has a potential cogeneration use generates significant heat that is not consumed directly in that process. This can be a benefit, unless there is no convenient use of the heat, in which case it becomes waste and must be dealt with appropriately using cooling towers or some other cooling mechanism. Merely venting heat to the atmosphere is not acceptable under air quality regulations in effect in the United States today. This issue affects only a few of the technologies described above and would normally be taken into consideration during selection of the production or utilization technology for a particular end use.

A group of researchers at California Institute of Technology in 2003 suggested future hydrogen emissions produced by increased use of fuel cell technology could substantially damage the ozone layer. In a large-scale hydrogen production and utilization system, approximately 10 to 20 percent of the hydrogen would escape into the atmosphere. If hydrogen fuel cells replaced all of today's oil- and gas-based combustion technologies, such losses would double or even triple the total hydrogen emitted into the atmosphere at the earth's surface. Hydrogen would be oxidized when it reached the stratosphere, cooling it and creating more clouds. This cooling would make holes in the ozone layer larger and longer lasting. The extra hydrogen would lead to a 5 to 8 percent rise in ozone depletion at the North Pole and between 3 and 7 percent at the South Pole (Tromp et al. 2003). However, although it may be possible to produce enough hydrogen to reduce imports of foreign oil and perhaps even the influence of foreign countries on world oil supplies, it seems unlikely it will ever be feasible to produce enough hydrogen to replace total daily U.S. gasoline demand (Armaroli and Balzani 2011, 282, 284).

Dollar Costs of Utilizing Hydrogen Technologies

The market cost at $17 to $21 per kilogram for 20.1 million metric tons of hydrogen energy delivered to consumers in calendar year 2010 is estimated at $342.1 to $422.5 billion (calculated from Lipman 2011, 12, and USDOE 2012). Market cost to consumers is difficult to estimate because the U.S. Department of Energy does not regularly publish consumption, price, or cost data for hydrogen, and about 95 percent of total demand is captive; that is, hydrogen is produced at the site of consumption either by the consumer or by contractors producing it directly for the consumer. The remainder is produced as "merchant" hydrogen for resale, and price data is proprietary for almost all of it. Federal subsidies and tax expenditures for hydrogen energy not used to generate electricity were estimated at $230 million for FY2007 (USEIA 2008a, xviii). To reduce the costs of producing hydrogen, efforts are being made to reduce capital equipment, operations, and maintenance costs and to improve the efficiency of hydrogen production technologies. Related efforts include developing new hydrogen delivery methods and infrastructure, improving carbon sequestration technology to ensure that coal-based hydrogen production releases almost no greenhouse gas emissions, and improving biomass growth, harvesting, and handling to reduce the cost of biomass resources used in hydrogen production (USDOE 2006).

The greatest challenge to hydrogen production is cost reduction. For cost-competitive transportation, hydrogen must be comparable to conventional fuels and technologies on a per-mile basis in order to succeed in the commercial marketplace. This means that the cost of hydrogen, including the cost of delivery—regardless of the production technology—must be in the range of $2 to $4 per gallon gasoline equivalent, not counting taxes. The appropriate match between a fuel cell technology and the intended application depends on the magnitude and duration of power needed; the cost, performance, and durability of fuel cells; and operating temperature range.

All fuel cells produce some by-product heat, but the temperature of by-product heat can vary dramatically, from about 180°F for PEM fuels to more than 1,200° for molten carbonate fuel cells. Fuel cells that produce high-temperature by-product heat with over 250 kilowatts of capacity are suitable for combined heat and power generation applications in industrial and large commercial settings. Those that produce low-temperature by-product heat are suitable for both mobile uses, such as light-duty vehicles and forklifts, and residential applications providing electricity plus space and water heating (USEIA 2008b).

The installed capital cost of phosphoric acid fuel cells in the commercial sector varies according to size. For 200-kilowatt systems, the cost quoted by United Technologies Corporation for the PureCell 200 ranged from $6,000 to $7,750 per kilowatt, and for the PureCell 400 system the installed cost ranged from $3,625 to $4,500 per kilowatt in 2008. The first generation of commercial molten carbonate fuel cells in 2010 cost about $6,200 per kilowatt. Molten carbonate fuel cells use high operating temperatures of the fuel cell to reform methane and steam to produce hydrogen. The CO_2 produced is recycled to restore the chemical used to generate electricity. Efficiencies for production of only electricity can approach 50 percent, and overall efficiencies (electricity plus by-product heat) are about 70 percent when both products are fully used (USEIA 2008b).

If research succeeds in lowering installed capital costs of molten carbonate fuel cells below $2,500 per kilowatt, the technology could satisfy a significant percentage of new demand for combined heat and power in industrial and commercial markets. The resulting market penetration, once cost reductions are achieved, may be slow because industrial and commercial boilers are long-lived and are rarely replaced before they fail. Consequently, fuel cell technology is unlikely to replace existing boilers or existing cogeneration equipment before it fails. Market potential in the commercial sector is better but does not promise rapid growth. Commercial electricity and heat demands are expected to grow more quickly than in the industrial sector. Nevertheless, it appears unlikely the capital costs and performance of molten carbonate fuel cells will improve to levels needed for substantial penetration of this new market (USEIA 2008b).

With only about 1,350 hours between stack and catalyst replacement, PEM fuel cells are not sufficiently durable to penetrate most markets in large numbers. The electricity generation efficiency of a PEM fuel cell is projected to increase to 36 percent by 2030, while combined efficiency for electricity and by-product heat is expected to range between 50 and 65 percent if all electricity and heat are used. At a delivered hydrogen cost of $2 to $3 per kilogram ($17.54 to $26.32 per million Btu), the fuel component of the cost of electricity generation is expected to range between 14 and 21 cents per kilowatt-hour, which would not be competitive with projected central-station delivered electricity prices of 10.5 cents per kilowatt-hour in 2030. Because construction costs for hydrogen pipelines to all homes would be extremely expensive, a more likely option might use the existing natural gas infrastructure and on-site natural gas steam reforming. The cost of that option is currently considered too high, at up to $40 per million Btu; additional research and development of small-scale steam methane reforming will be required to bring delivered fuel cost under $2 per kilogram of hydrogen (USEIA 2008b).

The U.S. Department of Energy estimates the cost of a fuel cell system would have to be in the range of $30 to $45 per kilowatt for it to be competitive with internal combustion engines, a substantial cost reduction, most of which is expected to be achieved through mass production on the order of 500,000 vehicles per year (Ekins, Hawkins, and Hughes 2010, 51). One study from 2002 suggested the cost of a complete hydrogen fuel cell vehicle in 2007 would be $36,500. The range of costs for 2015 to 2030 has been estimated at $18,000 to $34,000, with some vehicles cost-competitive and others costing 15 to 20 percent more than comparable internal combustion engine vehicles. These estimates were based on fuel cell costs of $35 to $75 per kilowatt and apparently assumed mass production or a substantial technical development, or both (Ekins, Hawkins, and Hughes 2010, 51). Honda Motor Company, which began marketing its Clarity FCX fuel cell vehicle in the United States in 2008 for lease, but not for sale, is not saying how much it cost to build, but others have estimated that the car, which is not mass-produced, may cost $120,000 to $140,000 per vehicle (Ohnsman 2008). In fairness to Honda, the Clarity FCX is a prototype test vehicle, designed to secure operating data in the hands of consumers, and should not be expected to compete for price with other vehicles in the marketplace.

Production of hydrogen using renewable resources is significantly more expensive than using fossil fuels. One estimate suggests that production of hydrogen using partial oxidation of oil or coal gasification is about twice as expensive as reforming natural gas, the least expensive method; water electrolysis is about five times as expensive; electrolysis powered by wind or photovoltaics is at best six times as expensive as reforming natural gas; and it is unlikely there will be any significant production using thermochemical conversion or biochemical or photo-electrochemical processes before 2030 (Infield 2004, 77). Absent a major technological breakthrough, the prospect for production of hydrogen at competitive dollar cost without significant increase of greenhouse gases seems unlikely in the interim.

National Security Costs of Utilizing Hydrogen Technologies

Hydrogen is a domestic resource. No country or group of countries is able to control supplies or determine price for fuel or materials to construct hydrogen fuel cells. Hydrogen energy technologies produce no carbon emissions or greenhouse gases other than the small amount created during the manufacture of equipment. Consequently, utilizing hydrogen technologies will not contribute much to climate change or a rise in sea level. Hydrogen technologies do not produce toxic waste that must be isolated from the human environment for millennia, or other materials useful to terrorists. Consequently, the national security costs of utilizing hydrogen energy technologies are negligible. Like solar energy, utilization of hydrogen technologies can be conceptualized as having net national security benefits.

SUMMARY OF COSTS

The costs of utilizing hydrogen technologies are summarized in Figure 12.3. Hydrogen use does not pollute the air like combustion of fossil fuels such as coal or natural gas, produces negligible greenhouse gases, and will not produce atmospheric emissions that cause acid rain. These are substantial environmental benefits of hydrogen use that should make it attractive to a significant part of the domestic population. The environmental costs for producing and using hydrogen technologies are incurred mostly during manufacture of equipment and facilities, and during hydrogen production using fossil fuels, such that the environmental costs of utilizing hydrogen must be considered "low" compared to most conventional fuel technologies in use today.

Dollar costs for use of stationary hydrogen technologies generating electricity are not competitive today with conventional fuels for most applications, and must be considered "high." Dollar costs for use of hydrogen in fuel cell vehicles are "high" but coming down, with some light-duty utility vehicles and buses beginning to enter the marketplace. The primary impediments to widespread use of hydrogen are the high cost of fuel cells and the high cost of producing hydrogen. Fuel cell technology is underdeveloped, compared to other conventional transportation fuels (Kawai 2004, 66), and it is reasonable to expect continued improvements in efficiencies of production

Figure 12.3 **The Costs of Hydrogen Technologies**

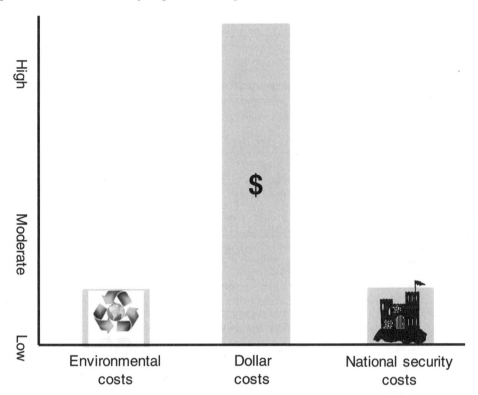

and operation, including the inconvenient fact that exhaust water freezes at low temperatures. National security costs for hydrogen technologies are very "low" or negligible because materials for producing them and the hydrogen they utilize are available in the United States. This is a very significant advantage hydrogen technologies hold over other energy technologies used for transportation that may be acquired from foreign sources, contribute to global climate change, or leave a legacy of long-term waste products that are attractive to terrorists. Energy sources of the future will have to be cleaner, more secure, and more efficient than current sources. Fuel cells fulfill these requirements.

REFERENCES

Armaroli, Nicola, and Vincenzo Balzani. 2011. *Energy for a Sustainable World*. Weinheim, Germany: Wiley-VCH Verlag.

California Energy Commission. 2011. "Fuel Cell Vehicles." www.consumerenergycenter.org/transportation/fuelcell/index.html.

Ekins, Paul, Sam Hawkins, and Nick Hughes. 2010. "Hydrogen Technologies and Costs." In *Hydrogen Energy: Economic and Social Challenges*, ed. Paul Ekins, 29–58. Washington, DC: Earthscan.

Infield, D. 2004. "Hydrogen from Renewable Energy Resources." In *Fuel Cells for Automotive Applications*, ed. R.H. Thring, 75–88. New York: American Society of Mechanical Engineers.

Jha, Alok. 2010. "Hydrogen Taxi Cabs to Serve London by 2012 Olympics." *The Guardian*, February 22.

Kawai, Taiyo. 2004. "Fuel Cell Hybrid Vehicles: The Challenge for the Future." In *The Hydrogen Energy Transition: Moving Toward the Post Petroleum Age in Transportation*, ed. Daniel Sperling and James S. Cannon, 59–72. Boston: Elsevier.

Lipman, Timothy. 2011. *An Overview of Hydrogen Production and Storage Systems with Renewable Hydrogen Case Studies*. Montpelier, VT: Clean Energy States Alliance.

Nice, Karim, and Jonathan Strickland. 2011. "How Fuel Cells Work." How Stuff Works. http://auto.howstuffworks.com/fuel-efficiency/alternative-fuels/fuel-cell.htm.

Ogden, Joan. 2004. "Where Will the Hydrogen Come from? System Considerations and Hydrogen Supply." In *The Hydrogen Energy Transition: Moving Toward the Post Petroleum Age in Transportation*, ed. Daniel Sperling and James S. Cannon, 73–92. Boston: Elsevier.

Ohnsman, Alan. 2008. "Honda to Deliver 200 Fuel-Cell Autos Through 2011 (Update 2)." Bloomberg.com, May 21. www.bloomberg.com/apps/news?pid=newsarchive&sid=a693eL42oJHo.

Rand, D.A.J., and R.M. Dell. 2008. *Hydrogen Energy: Challenges and Prospects*. Cambridge, UK: Royal Society of Chemistry.

Ricci, Miriam, Paul Bellaby, and Rob Flynn. 2010. "Hydrogen Risks: A Critical Analysis of Expert Knowledge and Expectations." In *Hydrogen Energy: Economic and Social Challenges*, ed. Paul Ekins, 217–240. Washington, DC: Earthscan.

Shenhar, Gabe. 2012. "Mercedes-Benz B-Class Fuel-Cell-Powered Car Shows Progress." May 8, 2012. http://news.consumerreports.org/cars/2012/05/mercedes-benz-b-class-fuel-cell-powered-car-shows-progress.html.

Tromp, Tracey K., Run-Lie Shia, Mark Allen, John M. Eiler, and Y.L. Yung. 2003. "Potential Environmental Impact of a Hydrogen Economy on the Stratosphere." *Science* 300 (June 13): 1740–1743.

Unnasch, Stefan, and Louis Browning. 2000. *Fuel Cycle Energy Conversion Efficiency Analysis: Status Report*. Mountain View, CA: ARCADIS Geraghty & Miller.

U.S. Department of Energy (DOE). 2006. "Hydrogen Production." Fact sheet, October. Washington, DC: U.S. Government Printing Office. www.hydrogen.energy.gov/pdfs/doe_h2_production.pdf.

———. 2007. *Validation of Hydrogen Fuel Cell Vehicle and Infrastructure Technology*. Golden, CO: National Renewable Energy Laboratory. www.afdc.energy.gov/afdc/pdfs/42284.pdf.

———. 2009. *Hydrogen Fueling: Coming Soon to a Station Near You*. Washington, DC: U.S. Government Printing Office.

———. 2010. "Hydrogen Distribution and Delivery Infrastructure Basics." Washington, DC: U.S. Government Printing Office. www1.eere.energy.gov/hydrogenandfuelcells/education/basics_delivery.html.

———. 2011a. "Future Fuel Cells R&D." October 3. www.fossil.energy.gov/programs/powersystems/fuelcells/index.html.

———. 2011b. "Hydrogen Storage." January. Washington, DC: U.S. Government Printing Office. www.hydrogen.energy.gov/pdfs/doe_h2_storage.pdf.

———. 2012. "Hydrogen Production." In *Hydrogen Data Book*. Washington, DC: U.S. Government Printing Office. http://hydrogen.pnl.gov/cocoon/morf/hydrogen/article/706.

U.S. Energy Information Administration (USEIA). 2008a. *Federal Financial Interventions and Subsidies in Energy Markets 2007*. Washington, DC: U.S. Government Printing Office.

———. 2008b. *The Impact of Increased Use of Hydrogen on Petroleum Consumption and Carbon Dioxide Emissions*. Washington, DC: U.S. Energy Information Administration.

———. 2011. *Annual Energy Review 2010*. Washington, DC: U.S. Government Printing Office.

Wald, Matthew L. 2009. "U.S. Drops Research into Fuel Cells for Cars." *New York Times*, May 8.

Washington Times. 2009. "Hydrogen-Powered Vehicles on Horizon." August 24.

White, C., B. Strazier, E. Granite, J. Hofman, and H. Pennline. 2003. "Separation and Capture of CO_2 from Large Stationary Sources and Sequestration in Geological Formations: Coal Beds and Deep Saline Aquifers." *Journal of the Air & Water Waste Management Association* 53 (June): 645.

13

Transportation and Electricity Transmission

There is no separate fuel cycle for fuels used in transportation or for electricity transmission. Transportation and electricity transmission are part of several fuel cycles for energy technologies described in previous chapters. The environmental, dollar, and national security costs of transportation of fuels and electric power transmission must be considered as additional to the costs of utilizing each energy fuel technology. That is, transportation and transmission costs are in addition to generation costs for each energy technology that involves conversion of a fuel to electricity and each fuel that requires transportation from its location of production to its location of end use. Transportation of energy fuels to the point of their end use adds dollar costs to the price of each fuel, compared to what it would be priced at for consumption at the point of production. Consumption of energy fuels near their point of origin would be less expensive.

TRANSPORTATION

Transportation deserves special treatment because mobility imposes limitations on what fuels can be used for it. Many fuels cannot be used for transportation until they are converted to another form, such as a storable liquid or electricity. For example, coal was used to power trains and ships at one time and could still be used now, but it is not used in that manner today because diesel fuel is easier to handle. Synthetic liquid fuels from coal could be used in transportation vehicles today, but they are more expensive than petroleum fuels. The principal limiting factor concerning energy use in transportation is that the energy source must be amenable to storage onboard the conveyance in sufficient quantities to get to the next fueling station, at a competitive price. Nuclear, solar, wind, geothermal, hydro, and ocean energy technologies cannot be used for transportation unless converted to electricity, and then their energy must be stored in batteries carried on each vehicle.

Petroleum, natural gas, and liquids or gases from renewable resources are the principal fuels used in transportation. Seventy-one percent of the petroleum consumed in the United States in 2010 was used in transportation by automobiles and motorcycles, light-duty trucks (minivans, pickup trucks, sport utility vehicles), heavy-duty trucks, and buses. Petroleum accounted for 94 percent of all energy used in transportation, with 2 percent coming from natural gas and 4 percent from renewable energy sources, principally biomass fuels such as ethanol blended with gasoline (Davis, Diegel, and Boundy 2011, Figure 2.0).

In the United States there are over 4 million miles of public roads (USDOT 2011, Table 1.11), and energy fuels are transported over many of them in bulk every day. Over 254 million cars, buses, and trucks traveling U.S. roads (USDOT 2011, Table 1.11) are the main reason for the country's reliance on foreign oil (Sperling and Cannon 2004, 1). Although there has been discussion for many years about the utility of electric vehicles, and 2012 will see the Chevrolet Volt, the first commercially available all-electric car since they went out of fashion in the 1930s (Bellis 2011), electric cars and electricity currently provide a minuscule portion of our transportation needs.

Figure 13.1 **Role of Transmission System**

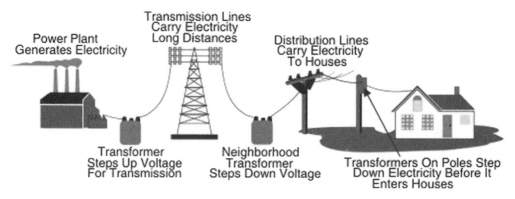

Source: USEIA 2011d.

TRANSMISSION

Most of the energy fuel technologies currently in use, to the extent that they rely upon central-station generation, also rely on high-voltage transmission of electric power to remote locations or lower-voltage distribution to consumers. Only electricity used at the location where it is generated, and energy fuels that require no transmission (e.g., fuel in cars and trucks), avoid these costs. The role of transmission and distribution lines is illustrated in Figure 13.1.

Because large quantities of electricity cannot be stored effectively, it must be produced at the same time it is used. High-voltage transmission lines are used to carry electricity from power-generating stations to places it is needed. Before arriving at the point of use, high-voltage electricity must be stepped down to a lower voltage using transformers so it can be used safely (USEIA 2011a), as illustrated in Figure 13.1. In 2010, 3.889 trillion megawatt-hours (MWh) of electricity (USEIA 2011b, Table 7.2) were consumed by residential, commercial, and industrial customers in the United States. Most of this electricity was transported over high-voltage transmission lines (NERC 2011c). Alternating current transmitted at high-voltage loses some of its energy to heat due to resistance of the conductor (Brown and Sedano 2004, 35). Thus, less energy is received than the amount transmitted, and the difference is described as transmission losses. The higher the voltage of transmission lines, the more efficient they are at transmitting electricity, resulting in lower transmission losses. At the national level, transmission losses are generally estimated as the difference between what was produced and what was consumed. Total transmission losses in the United States were about 5.7 percent in 2010, or 236,013 MWh (calculated from USEIA 2011b, Table ES1). Revenues lost due to transmission loses were worth $1.6 to $2.7 billion in 2010, depending on whether the electricity would have been sold to residential or industrial consumers at average retail prices (calculated from USEIA 2011b, Table ES1). These revenues might not have been lost if the electricity had been generated nearer to consumers and did not require long-distance, high-voltage transmission to get to markets.

SOURCES OF ELECTRICITY

The portion of net electric generating capacity available from each fuel source in the United States during summer 2010 is illustrated in Figure 13.2. Summer is when maximum simultaneous demand

Figure 13.2 **Summer Electric Generating Capacity by Fuel Source, 2010**

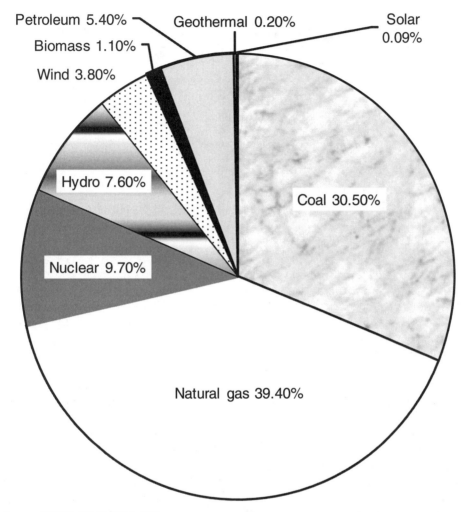

Petroleum 5.40% Geothermal 0.20% Solar 0.09%
Biomass 1.10%
Wind 3.80%
Hydro 7.60%
Coal 30.50%
Nuclear 9.70%
Natural gas 39.40%

Source: USEIA 2011b, Table ES1.

for electricity generally occurs in the United States. Total electric generating capacity available in the United States in 2010 was slightly more than 1 million (1,039,137) megawatts (MWe), with almost two-fifths (39.4 percent) from natural gas and nearly one-third (30.5 percent) from coal. Nuclear capacity was 9.7 percent and oil 5.4 percent of total generating capacity available. About 12.8 percent of total generating capacity was provided by all renewable sources together.

The portion of electricity actually produced in the United States by each fuel source in 2010 is illustrated in Figure 13.3. Total electricity generated in 2010 was a bit over 4 trillion (4,125,060,000) MWh, with 44.8 percent generated using coal, 24.0 percent from natural gas, less than one (0.9) percent from petroleum products, and 19.6 percent from nuclear plants. Renewable sources together generated about 10.4 percent of total electric power, the largest portion produced using hydroelectric facilities at 6.3 percent, then wind at 2.3 percent, biomass at 1.4 percent, geothermal

Figure 13.3 **Sources of U.S. Electricity Generation, 2010**

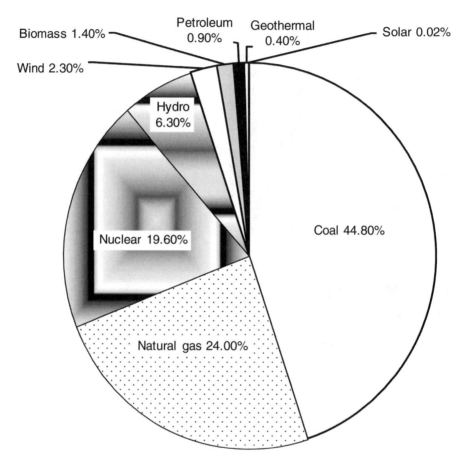

Source: USEIA 2011b, Table ES1.

at 0.4 percent, and solar (thermal electric and photovoltaic) at 0.02 percent of total U.S. electricity generated in 2010.

The portion of electricity produced by renewable sources is increasing rapidly, but is still small. The trend in recent years in the electric utility industry for construction of new capacity has been overwhelmingly in favor of natural gas, and away from oil and coal, with renewable sources of energy only beginning to make inroads. Boilers at many former oil-fired plants were converted to natural gas in the previous twenty years. Wind energy has been the fastest growing segment of renewable sources since 1999.

At the beginning of the twentieth century, there were over 4,000 individual electric utilities, each operating in isolation. Almost all of them used low-voltage connections from nearby power plants to distribute electricity to local customers. As the demand for electricity grew after World War II, electric utilities interconnected their transmission systems. Coordination over a wide area may minimize operating costs and capital expenditures for plant construction, enhance system stability and recovery capabilities during emergency operating conditions, and provide opportunities for reducing total construction, thereby enabling siting of facilities so as to produce the required amount of power with minimum adverse environmental impact (Hamilton 1980, 44–45; 1979, 127).

Interconnection meant electric utilities might share the perceived benefits of building larger, often jointly owned generators to serve their combined electricity demand. Interconnection also reduced the amount of extra capacity or "reserve margin" each utility had to maintain to assure reliable service. With growing demand for new power plants came a need for higher voltage interconnections to transport additional power over longer distances. In the western states, the U.S. Bureau of Reclamation and Bonneville Power Administration played major roles in development of larger interconnected systems by linking their own power-generating facilities and by exercising leadership in a series of studies with private electric utilities during the 1950s and 1960s (Hamilton 1980, 42–45). Over time, three large interconnected systems evolved in the United States (USEIA 2011a).

Transmission and distribution lines owned by an individual utility are no longer resources that can be used only by that firm. Firms routinely transmit electric energy over lines owned by other firms, paying for the service. Buyers and sellers of electricity may be geographically widely separated. Consequently, close oversight of operations within the three power grids is needed to keep the various components operating smoothly and linked together (NERC 2011c). The interconnected systems now include over 3,200 electric distribution utilities, over 10,000 generating units, over 334 million customers (USEIA 2011a), and about 394,549 miles of transmission and distribution lines with greater than 100kV capacity (NERC 2011a, 34).

Originally, each generating company was responsible for maintaining its own electrical system safely and planning for the future needs of its customers. Later, voluntary standards were developed by the electric utility industry to ensure coordination for linked interconnection operations. These voluntary standards were instituted after a major blackout in 1965 that darkened New York, a large portion of the East Coast, and parts of Canada (USEIA 2011a; Hamilton 1979, 128). Now, planning is done in a somewhat more coordinated manner to achieve adequacy of supply, to establish and oversee formal operational standards for running the bulk power systems, and to address security concerns for critical electrical infrastructures. All of this coordination is administered under mandatory procedures set up by the electric power industry's electricity reliability organization pursuant to the Energy Policy Act of 2005 (16 USC §8240), with oversight provided by the Federal Energy Regulatory Commission and the U.S. Department of Energy.

Yet interconnection and integration are incomplete. There is no national power grid. As noted above, there are actually three power grids operating in the forty-eight contiguous states: (1) the Eastern Interconnected System (for states east of the Rocky Mountains) with about 692,658 MWe generating capacity, (2) the Western Interconnected System (from the Pacific Ocean to the Rocky Mountain States) with about 158,407 MWe generating capacity, and (3) the Texas Interconnected System with about 73,857 MWe generating capacity in 2010. Together, these systems had about 924,922 MWe generating capacity in 2010, but they generally operated independently of each other, with limited links between them (USEIA 2011b, Table 4.2.A). The Texas system is not synchronously connected to the Eastern or Western Interconnection but can exchange about 860 MWe with neighboring states and Mexico through direct-current links. Interregional transfer capabilities are not generally relied upon to maintain transmission reliability or address capacity shortages, although emergency support arrangements are in place that provide for mutual support over asynchronous ties or through block load transfers (NERC 2011a, 176). Electric utilities in Texas have long avoided interstate interconnections in order to avoid regulation of wholesale sales of electricity by the Federal Energy Regulatory Commission. Despite the absence of any insurmountable technical barrier, and despite a long history of feasibility studies by a variety of federal government agencies that have encouraged electric utilities to do so (USDOE 2002; Hamilton 1980, 42–56; USDOE 1979, esp. vol. II, note 2 at 4), they have steadfastly resisted integration of their facilities into a single national power grid. Yet major areas in Canada are interconnected with the Western and Eastern power grids, which have limited direct-current interties with each other, while small parts of Mexico have limited connections with Texas and the Western power grid (USEIA 2011a). Electric utilities are simply unwilling to make the investments in transmission facilities that would make operation of the entire grid possible, even though such investments would be profitable.

Most of the electrical transmission components have been in existence for many years. It is generally agreed that some replacement and upgrading of current lines are needed, and there is growing evidence that the U.S. transmission system is in urgent need of modernization.

The system has become congested because growth in electricity demand and investment in new generation facilities have not been matched by investment in new transmission facilities. Transmission problems have been compounded by incomplete transition to fair and efficient competitive wholesale electricity markets. Because the existing transmission system was not designed to meet present demand, daily transmission constraints or "bottlenecks" increase electricity costs to consumers and increase the risk of blackouts.

Eliminating transmission constraints or bottlenecks is essential to ensuring reliable and affordable electricity now and in the future. According to an assessment by the Department of Energy, the U.S. transmission system facilitates wholesale electricity markets that lower consumers' electricity bills by nearly $13 billion annually, but despite these overall savings, interregional transmission congestion costs consumers hundreds of millions of dollars annually. Relieving bottlenecks in four U.S. regions (California, the Pennsylvania-New Jersey-Maryland interconnection, New York, and New England) could save consumers about $500 million annually. Savings might be even greater because the analysis did not capture all of the factors, such as impacts on reliability, that result from bottlenecks (USDOE 2002).

According to DOE, there are four significant challenges to improving the transmission power grid infrastructure:

- Siting new transmission lines (obtaining approvals of a new route and needed land) when there is local opposition to construction
- Determining an equitable approach for recovering construction costs of a transmission line built within one state when it provides economic and system operation benefits to out-of-state customers
- Ensuring the network of long-distance transmission lines reaches sites where high-quality renewable resources are located, often distant from areas where demand for electricity is concentrated
- Determining who is responsible for paying for new transmission lines. Uncertainty over who is responsible affects the private sector's willingness to build and its ability to raise money to construct new transmission lines (USDOE 2002)

COSTS OF ELECTRIC POWER UTILIZATION

Environmental Costs of Utilizing Electric Power

Environmental costs of electric power transmission accrue mostly from construction of an interconnected high-voltage grid system. Transmission structures are constructed by using a standard drill rig to bore a hole for a stable foundation for a transmission tower. If water is encountered, pumps will be used to move the water to either adjacent upland areas or to waiting tanker trucks for proper disposal. When bedrock is close to the surface or when subsoils primarily consist of large boulders and cobbles, blasting may be required. Heavy trucks carry concrete to boreholes to construct foundations for transmission structures. Cranes then erect towers on the foundations. Finally a transmission wire is strung between towers using large pulleys. After construction is completed, the right-of-way is graded, and agricultural soils are decompacted. New transmission lines are built with a grounded shield wire placed along the top of the poles, above the conductors. Typically, the shield wire is bonded to ground at each transmission structure. This protects the transmission line from lightning. Transmission poles, like trees or other tall objects, are more likely to intercept lightning strikes than other structures, but do not attract lightning. Lightning is not more likely to strike houses or cars near a transmission line. Short objects under or very near a line may actually receive some protection from lightning strikes (PSC Wisconsin 2011) if transmission poles are taller.

Protected Species

Construction and maintenance of transmission lines may destroy endangered or threatened plants and animals or may alter their habitat so it becomes unsuitable for them. Trees used by rare birds for nesting may be cut down or soil erosion may degrade rivers and wetlands that provide required habitat. Impacts of new transmission lines on wildlife include bird kills from collisions with wires where previously there were none. Transmission towers make attractive nesting locations for some larger species of birds, and many are killed each year by making connections between two or more wires. Some newer designs of transmission towers discourage bird landings to minimize this occurrence. Impacts on small wildlife stem primarily from disturbing land surface. Some impacts are short-term and confined to the location of transmission towers; others may have far-reaching, long-term effects. The most direct effect on small wildlife is destruction or displacement of species in areas excavated for towers. Mobile wildlife species like game animals, birds, and predators leave these areas. More sedentary animals like invertebrates, many reptiles, burrowing rodents, and small mammals may be directly destroyed. If streams, lakes, ponds, or marshes are filled, drained, or damaged, fish, aquatic invertebrates, and amphibians are destroyed. Food supplies for predators are reduced by destruction of these species. Animal populations displaced or destroyed may eventually be replaced from populations in surrounding ranges, provided habitat is restored. An exception could be extinction of resident endangered species.

Many wildlife species are highly dependent on vegetation growing in natural drainages that may need to be traversed by transmission lines. Vegetation provides essential food, nesting sites, and cover for escape from predators. Any activity that destroys vegetation near ponds, reservoirs, marshes, and wetlands reduces the quality and quantity of habitat essential for waterfowl, shore birds, and many terrestrial species. Small mammals and birds may be harmed by damage to hedgerows between farm fields. The habitat requirements of many animal species do not permit them to adjust to changes created by land disturbance that reduce living space. Some species tolerate very little disturbance. In instances where a particularly critical habitat is restricted, such as a pond or primary breeding area, a species could be rendered extinct.

If preliminary research and field assessments indicate rare species or natural communities may be present in a project area, the utility should conduct field surveys prior to construction. If a protected or rare species is likely to be in the project area, impacts can usually be avoided or minimized by redesigning or relocating the transmission line, using special construction techniques, or limiting the time of construction to specific seasons. In some limited cases, right-of-ways can be managed to provide habitat for endangered or threatened species, such as osprey nesting platforms built on top of transmission poles where wires are far enough apart to avoid contact (PSC Wisconsin 2011).

Water Resources

Construction and operation of transmission lines across creeks, streams, rivers, and lakes may have both short-term and long-term effects. Water quality can be impacted by work within a lake or river and by nearby land clearing and construction activities. Removal of nearby vegetation can cause water temperatures to rise and negatively affect aquatic habitats. It can also increase erosion of adjacent soils, causing sediment to be deposited into a water body, especially during rainfall. Construction often requires building temporary bridges across small channels, which if improperly installed may damage banks and cause erosion. Overhead transmission lines across major rivers, streams, or lakes may have a visual impact on users and pose a potential collision hazard for waterfowl and other large birds, especially when located in a migratory corridor (PSC Wisconsin 2011).

Some waters are characterized as being valuable or unique for various features including fisheries, hydrology, geology, and recreation. Regulations require that these shall not be degraded in quality without good justification. By assigning these classifications to specific streams, high-quality waters receive additional protection from point source pollution. Degradation of trout habitat is caused by siltation from erosion and drained wetlands, among other factors. Impacts to surface waters can be avoided by rerouting a transmission line away from a water body, adjusting pole placements to span the water resource overhead, boring a line under a water resource, or constructing temporary bridge structures across it. Methods to minimize impacts include avoiding pole placements adjacent to water, using approved erosion control methods, using alternative construction methods such as helicopter construction, landscaping to screen poles from the view of river users, and maintaining shaded stream cover (PSC Wisconsin 2011).

Several methods and cable types are available for constructing a transmission line under a water resource. Directional boring of holes under waterways for lower-voltage transmission and distribution lines is common. High-voltage lines are rarely constructed underground due to substantial engineering, dollar costs, and operational hurdles that would need to be overcome for underground construction to be a feasible alternative to overhead construction. Constructing a line underground minimizes construction and esthetic impacts to a water resource. However, it does require potentially large construction entrance and exit pits on either side of a water body. There is also potential for contamination by drilling fluids into a water body and subsurface environment (PSC Wisconsin 2011).

Use of properly designed temporary bridge structures avoids driving construction equipment through streams. Temporary bridges may consist of timber mats that allow heavy construction equipment to cross streams, creeks, and other drainage features without damaging the banks or increasing the potential for soil erosion. Temporary bridges should be located to avoid unique or sensitive portions of waterways, like riffles, pools, and spawning beds. Proper erosion control is necessary for all construction activities, especially those that may affect water resources (PSC Wisconsin 2011).

Woodlands and shrub or scrub areas along streams are a valuable buffer between farm fields and corridors of natural habitats. Vegetation maintains soil moisture levels in stream banks, helps stabilize banks, and encourages diversity of wildlife habitats. Removal of vegetative buffers from stream corridors may raise the water temperature above what is necessary for good trout stream habitat. Existing vegetative buffers should be left undisturbed or minimally disturbed. Where construction impacts cannot be avoided, low-growing native tree and shrub buffers should be replanted to maintain preconstruction quality of stream water (PSC Wisconsin 2011).

Wetlands

Wetlands occur in many different forms and serve vital functions including storing runoff, regenerating groundwater, filtering sediments and pollutants, and providing habitat for aquatic species and wildlife. Construction and maintenance of transmission lines can seriously damage wetlands. Heavy machinery can crush wetland soils and vegetation. Wetland soils, especially very peaty soils, can be easily compacted, increasing runoff, blocking flows, and greatly reducing the wetland's water-holding capacity. Construction of access roads can change the quantity or direction of water flow, causing permanent damage to wetland soils and vegetation. Construction and maintenance equipment that crosses wetlands can stir up sediments, endangering fish and other aquatic life. Transmission lines can be collision obstacles for waterfowl and other large water birds. Clearing forested wetlands can expose a wetland to invasive and shrubby plants, thus removing habitat for species in the forest interior. Vehicles and construction equipment can introduce exotic plant species such as purple loosestrife. With few natural controls, these species may outcompete high-quality native vegetation, destroying valuable wildlife habitat. Any of these activities can impair or limit wetland functions. Organic soils consist of layers of decomposed plant material that formed very slowly. Disturbed wetland soils are not easily repaired. Severe soil disturbances may permanently alter wetland hydrology. A secondary effect of disturbance is the opportunistic spread of invasive weedy species that provide little food and habitat for wildlife (PSC Wisconsin 2011).

Local, state, and federal laws regulate certain activities in wetlands. When fill material is proposed to be placed in a federal wetland, a permit is required from the U.S. Army Corps of Engineers under the Clean Water Act, Section 404 (33 USC §1344). When a Section 404 permit is required, a state agency must determine if the proposed activity is in compliance with applicable state water quality standards. If a proposal is found to be in compliance with state standards, the agency will permit the activity.

To minimize potential impacts to wetlands, a utility can avoid placing transmission lines through them; adjust pole placements to span wetlands or limit the number of poles located in them; limit construction to winter months when soil and water are more likely to be frozen and vegetation is dormant; and use mats and wide-track vehicles to spread the distribution of equipment weight when crossing wetlands during the growing season or when they are not frozen. A utility may use alternative construction equipment such as helicopters or marsh buggies for construction within wetlands; clean construction equipment after working in areas infested by purple loosestrife or other known invasive, exotic species; and place markers on the top shield wire to make lines more visible to birds if collision potential is high (PSC Wisconsin 2011).

Woodlands

Forests provide recreational opportunities, wildlife and plant habitats, and timber. Building a transmission line through woodlands requires that all trees and brush be cleared from the right-of-way. One mile of 100-foot right-of-way through a forest results in loss of approximately twelve acres of trees. Transmission construction impacts include forest fragmentation and the loss and degradation of wooded habitat, aesthetic enjoyment of the resource, and loss of income. Different machines and techniques are used to remove trees from a transmission right-of-way depending on whether woodlands consist of mature trees, have large quantities of understory trees, or are in sensitive environments such as a wooded wetland. These machines and techniques can range from large whole-tree processors, which can cause rutting and compaction of the forest floor, to hand-clearing with chainsaws in more sensitive environments. Timber removed for construction of a high-voltage transmission line remains the property of the landowner. Small-diameter limbs and branches are often chipped or burned. Wood chips may be spread on the right-of-way, piled to allow transport by the landowner to specific locations, or chipped directly into a truck and hauled off the right-of-way (PSC Wisconsin 2011).

A transmission line right-of-way can fragment a large forest into smaller tracts. Fragmentation makes interior forest species more vulnerable to predators, parasites, competition from edge species, and catastrophic events such as blowdown during a storm. Continued fragmentation of a forest can cause a permanent reduction in species diversity and suitable habitat. Loss of forested habitat increases the number of common (edge) plants and animals that can encroach into what were forest interiors. This encroachment can have impacts on the number, health, and survival of interior forest species, many of which are rare. Edge species that can encroach into forest interiors via transmission right-of-ways include raccoons, cowbirds, crows, deer, and box elder trees. Interior forest species include songbirds, wolves, and hemlock trees (PSC Wisconsin 2011).

Construction vehicles may inadvertently bring into forest interiors invasive or nonnative plant species. The opening of the forest floor to sunlight through tree-clearing of a right-of-way can further encourage these aggressive, invasive species to proliferate. Problematic invasive species include buckthorn, honeysuckle, purple loosestrife, and garlic mustard. Invasive species, once introduced, have few local natural controls on their reproduction so they can easily spread. Their spread can alter the ecology of a forest as they outcompete native species for sunlight and nutrients, further reducing suitable habitat and food sources for local wildlife. A cleared right-of-way increases human access into a forest, which may lead to trespassing and vandalism. It can also provide recreation opportunities such as access for hunting, hiking, and snowmobiling. Impacts to woodlands from transmission line construction can be minimized by avoiding routes that fragment major forest blocks; adjusting pole placement and span length to minimize the need for tree removal and trimming along forest edges; allowing tree and shrub species that reach heights of twelve to fifteen feet to grow within a right-of-way; and following state guidelines for preventing the spread of exotic invasive plant species and diseases (PSC Wisconsin 2011).

Archeological and Historical Resources

Archeological and historical sites are protected resources that are important and increasingly rare tools for learning about the past. They may also have religious significance. Transmission line construction and maintenance can damage sites by digging, crushing artifacts with heavy equipment, uprooting trees, exposing sites to erosion or the elements, or making sites more accessible to vandals. Impacts can occur wherever soils will be disturbed, at pole locations, or where heavy equipment is used (PSC Wisconsin 2011).

State historical societies often have primary responsibility for protecting archeological and historical resources. They manage records of all known sites that are updated as new information becomes available. The database must be searched for any sites that might be located along any proposed transmission routes. Route changes are seldom necessary. Judicious transmission pole placement can often be used to span resources and avoid impacts to archeological and historical sites. If during construction an archeological site is encountered, construction at the site must be stopped and authorities notified by the utility. The authorities then make recommendations on how construction should proceed in order to manage or minimize impacts to the resource (PSC Wisconsin 2011).

Noise and Light Impacts

During each phase of construction of a transmission line, noise will be generated by construction equipment. Initially, vegetation in the right-of-way is cut using mowers, whole tree processors, or chainsaws. Brush and logs may be chipped or burned in the right-of-way. Trucks are used to haul away material that cannot be stockpiled or disposed of on-site and to bring in necessary construction materials. Typical construction vehicles include bucket trucks, cranes or digger derricks, backhoes, pulling machines, pole trailers, and dumpsters. Once transmission lines are built, vibration or humming noise can be noticeable; it is, however, most often associated with older transmission lines. It is usually the result of conductor mounting hardware that has loosened slightly over the years and can be easily identified and repaired as part of line maintenance. Other sounds caused by transmission lines are sizzles, crackles, or hissing noises that occur during periods of high humidity. These are usually associated with high-voltage transmission lines and are weather dependent, caused by ionization of electricity in moist air near the wires. Though this noise is audible to those very close to transmission lines, it quickly dissipates with distance and is easily drowned out by typical background noises. Ionization in foggy conditions can also cause a corona, which is a luminous blue discharge of light usually where wires connect to the insulators. Residential properties located in close proximity to a substation may be affected by noise and light associated with operation of a new or enlarged substation (PSC Wisconsin 2011).

Aesthetics

The overall aesthetic appearance of a transmission line is often unpleasant to many people, especially where proposed lines would cross natural landscapes and private properties. Tall or wide structures may seem out of proportion and incompatible with agricultural landscapes or residential neighborhoods. At fifty to 180 feet in height (Minnesota Electric Transmission Planning 2011), transmission towers are visible for substantial distances. Landowners who have chosen to bury electric distribution lines on their property may find transmission lines bordering their property particularly disruptive to scenic views. Yet some people do not notice transmission lines or do not find them objectionable from an aesthetic perspective.

Aesthetic impacts depend on the physical relationship of the viewer and the transmission line (distance and sight line); the activity of the viewer (e.g., living in the area, driving through, or sightseeing); and contrast between transmission structures and the surrounding environment, such as whether a line stands out or blends in. A transmission line can affect aesthetics by removing a resource, such as clearing fencerows or forest; intruding on the view of a landscape and degrading the surrounding environment; or changing the context of a view area and evoking an image of industrialization in a previously rural area (PSC Wisconsin 2011).

Electric transmission lines may be routed to avoid areas considered scenic. Routes can be chosen that pass through commercial or industrial areas or along land use boundaries. The form, color, or texture of a line can be modified to somewhat minimize aesthetic impacts. Planting vegetative screens to block views of a transmission line, leaving a right-of-way in a natural state at road crossings, and piling brush from a cleared right-of-way so it provides wildlife habitat can mitigate visual impacts of transmission lines. Aesthetics are to a great extent based on individual perceptions. Siting, design, construction materials, and right-of-way management can mitigate some adverse aesthetic effects of a line, but perhaps not others (PSC Wisconsin 2011).

Electromagnetic Fields

Health concerns over exposure to electric and magnetic fields (EMF) are often raised when a new transmission line is proposed. Exposure to electric and magnetic fields caused by transmission lines has been studied since the late 1970s. These fields occur whenever electricity is used. A magnetic field is created when electric current flows through any device, including the electric wiring in a home. Every day we are exposed to many small sources of EMF from vacuum cleaners, microwaves, computers, and fluorescent lights. Research to date has uncovered only weak and inconsistent associations between exposures and human health. Magnetic fields can be measured with a gauss meter. The magnitude of the magnetic field is related to current flow, not line voltage. A 69 kV line can have a higher magnetic field than a 345 kV line. Magnetic fields quickly dissipate with distance from transmission lines. A common method to reduce EMF is to bring lines closer together. This causes the fields created by each of three conductors to interfere with each other and produce a reduced total magnetic field. Consequently, magnetic fields generated by double-circuit lines are less than those generated by single-circuit lines because they interact and produce a lower total magnetic field. In addition, double circuit poles are often taller, resulting in less of a magnetic field at ground level (PSC Wisconsin 2011).

Pacemakers and implantable cardioverter defibrillators (ICDs) have been associated with problems arising from interference caused by EMF. This electromagnetic interference (EMI) can cause inappropriate triggering of a device or inhibit a device from functioning properly. Sources of EMI documented by medical personnel include radio-controlled model cars, car engines, digital cellular phones, antitheft security systems, and high-voltage transmission lines (PSC Wisconsin 2011). ICD manufacturers' recommended thresholds for modulated magnetic fields are five to ten times greater than the magnetic field likely to be produced by a high-voltage transmission line. Research shows a wide range of responses for the threshold at which ICDs and pacemakers responded to an external EMI source. The results for each unit depended on the make and model of the device and the patient's height, build, and physical orientation with respect to the electric field. Pacemaker and ICD patients are informed about potential problems associated with exposure to EMI and must adjust their behavior accordingly. Avoiding sources of EMI is a standard response; patients can shield themselves from EMI with a car, a building, or the enclosed cab of a truck (PSC Wisconsin 2011).

In some areas of the United States, exposure of people to transmission lines is quite common. Federal government approvals of right-of-ways for transmission lines across public lands often comprised 35 percent of all permits required, in a study of twenty-four new electric generation and transmission projects in the southwestern states. The average number of permits required per project was thirty-two (Hamilton 1989; Hamilton and Wengert 1980, 74). This study was completed before deregulation of the electric utility industry severed ownership of most generation facilities from that of transmission facilities. It is unknown how many approvals may be required today for construction of new transmission lines, which are now often built separately from generation projects. Exposure to electromagnetic fields from electric transmission lines increases as new lines are built. Securing transmission line right-of-ways remains a significant source of environmental and dollar costs for transmission projects in the United States.

Dollar Costs of Utilizing Electric Power

The bulk electric power system in the United States represents more than $1 trillion worth of generating and transmission assets (NERC 2011b). Transmission lines are expensive to build, with double-circuit high-voltage lines costing about $369,000 to $1.9 million per mile on flat land in rural settings (Ng 2009, 4; Colorado Long-Range Transmission Planning Group 2004, Appendix F) and 345kV lines costing about $615,000 to $2.6 million per mile in dollars adjusted to 2010 (Long-Range Transmission Planning Group 2004, Appendix F; American Electric Power 2008). A single transmission tower may cost upwards of $30,000, and a corner tower $50,000. Transmission corridors built on hilly, forested, suburban, or urban terrain cost significantly more per mile than those built on flat, unforested, or uninhabited land. Even removal of transmission lines is expensive, often costing $468,000 or more per mile in 2010 dollars for double-circuit high-voltage lines (American Electric Power 2008). Generating facilities located adjacent to consumers avoid these costs. Federal subsidies and tax expenditures for improvements to electricity transmission were estimated at $971 million for FY2010, reduced from almost $1.1 billion in FY2007 (USEIA 2011a, xiii, xviii).

Blackouts, discussed below as an indicator of vulnerability of the transmission system and a national security cost, are also an expensive drain on the economy. The total direct and indirect cost to the national economy of the major blackout in eight northeastern states and two Canadian provinces in 2003 was estimated at US$6.8 to US$10.3 billion (ICF Consulting 2003). Some estimate the costs of electric power outages at $26 billion per year in the United States (Casazza and Delea 2003), while others estimate that blackouts cost the nation about $80 billion annually (Lawrence Berkeley National Laboratory 2005). The Electric Power Research Institute estimates that power outages and low power quality cost the economy over $119 billion per year (EPRI 2001).

National Security Costs of Electric Power

Alternating current flows one direction and then reverses direction and flows the opposite way, while direct current flows in only one direction. The nature of alternating-current electrical technologies used in a U.S. bulk electric power system makes it peculiarly susceptible to sabotage:

> Throughout the grid, the alternating electric current must change its direction of flow back and forth at an essentially constant rate, which in North America is sixty cycles per second: this constancy is called "frequency stability." Stability of voltage—the amount of electrical "pressure" in the line (as opposed to current, the amount of electrical flow)—is vital to avoid damage to equipment. Power is transmitted over three parallel lines, each bearing a precise time relationship to the others—somewhat akin to singing a three-part round. The "phase stability" among these different lines, and between voltage and current, must also be maintained. And these exacting relationships must be kept in step with each other in all parts of the grid at once ("synchronization"). (Lovins and Lovins 1982, 123)

When adding new generating capacity to an existing grid, care must be taken to configure connections and other features of the grid to preserve frequency stability, phase stability, and synchronization. Sometimes this requires building transmission lines between other parts of the grid besides those lines that connect new capacity directly to it.

Moreover, in an interconnected electric grid, everything happens very fast. If frequency stability, phase stability, or synchronization is disrupted, control response is often required in thousandths of a second, not in minutes or hours (Lovins and Lovins 1982, 124), and several responses in rapid succession may be required. Human reasoning and reflexes are usually inadequate to this task, so there is heavy reliance on computerized assistance using programmed responses to discrete stimuli.

Several characteristics of contemporary bulk electric power supply transmission grids make them vulnerable to sabotage, including centralization of power supplies, long transmission distances, continuity and synchronism in grids, high capital intensity, and long lead times (Lovins and Lovins 1982, 34–46). Increasing geographic separation over time between major energy facilities and their customers concentrated most generating resources in very large capacity facilities in relatively small areas remote from population concentrations they serve, made interconnected systems more vulnerable to disruptions, and made the connecting transmission links between them longer and more tenuous, exposing them to mishaps over greater distances. Facilities concentrated into small areas make large targets. Long connecting links mean transmission lines were often built in rural areas where they are difficult to keep under constant observation. Long transmission distances impose additional capital and operating costs on bulk electric transmission systems, in addition to transmission losses, while increasing vulnerability to all types of natural and unnatural hazards and increasing response times for repair of damaged equipment. Because electricity cannot be easily stored, centralized supply of electricity requires a continuous, direct connection from producer to consumer, and interruptions of supply are instantaneously disruptive. "The grid exposes large flows of energy to interruption by single acts at single points, and there is only limited freedom to reroute the flow around the damage" (Lovins and Lovins 1982, 38). Electrical grids require continuous, meticulous management because their operation must be kept synchronous. Departures from synchronism can seriously damage expensive equipment and cause a whole grid to break down. This exacting requirement of synchronism raises serious problems for grid stability (Lovins and Lovins 1982, 39).

The electric power industry is the most capital-intensive industry in the United States, and a central power station is the most capital-intensive single facility in all industries (Edison Electric Institute 1992). Capital intensity reflects the degree to which a project commits scarce resources, and indirectly measures the difficulty of building or rebuilding it with limited resources. Capital-intensive plants need to run almost continuously to pay interest on capital, thus placing a high premium on the correctness of engineering expectations that they will prove reliable. External interference can produce massive financial penalties as well as disrupting energy supplies. High capital intensity commonly reflects a degree of complexity that hampers diagnosis and repair of faults and limits available stocks of costly spare parts. Another result of high capital intensity is limited ability to adapt to fluctuating demands. High demand may require new capacity which a supplier cannot afford, while lower demand reduces revenues needed to keep paying off high capital charges (Lovins and Lovins 1982, 43–45).

Long lead times required to build major energy facilities contribute to high capital cost and investment risk. Uncertainties of forecasting future demand increase with longer lead times, thereby increasing risk (Lovins and Lovins 1982, 45). Typical lead times reported by electric utilities in the western United States for construction of additional thermal generating capacity increased significantly after 1967, running 10 to 15 years for nuclear plants, 6 to 11 years for coal-fired plants, 4 to 8 years for combined cycle plants, and 3 to 7 years for combustion turbines in 1978 (Hamilton and Wengert 1980, 69) before demand for new plants evaporated. Such long lead times require foreknowledge of demand, technology, and financial costs further into the future, when forecasts are likely to be more uncertain. Certainty is the first casualty of time in forecasting.

Electric transmission networks are large, complex, and difficult to operate successfully. They link very large generating units, are highly centralized, and are vulnerable to outages cause by weather, seismic disturbances, and human actions. Local distribution networks are often disrupted by automobile accidents involving collisions between motor vehicles and power poles, generally affecting small geographic areas. However, the larger regional high-voltage bulk electric power networks are also vulnerable to local disruptions involving equipment failure, human error, or intentional acts of sabotage. Unfortunately, transmission networks are so vast, complicated, and fragile that local disruptions may have multistate regional ramifications.

The desirability of increased interdependence that accompanies interconnection of facilities was dramatically put in question by the Northeast power failure of November 9, 1965 (Hamilton 1979, 128), when an incorrect setting on a backup protective relay disconnected a high-voltage 230kV transmission line in Ontario, Canada, triggering a series of events on the interconnected transmission grid that resulted in loss of electric service to about 30 million customers over 80,000 square miles in six northeastern states (New York, Connecticut, Massachusetts, Rhode Island, Pennsylvania, and New Jersey) and substantial portions of Ontario for up to thirteen hours (USFPC 1967). On that date the United States found out how vulnerable it is to large-scale disruptions of the electric transmission system. Brief, local disruptions had occurred frequently in the past, but this was the first time several states were blacked out for many hours, and the effect on the industry was profound. An extensive report on this first major regional blackout published by the Federal Power Commission (FPC) in 1967 suggested ways of increasing the reliability of the nation's transmission systems. Shortly thereafter the FPC called on the electric power industry to establish national and regional coordinating bodies (Hamilton 1980, 46). The industry responded by setting up nine regional and one national coordinating council, the National Electric Reliability Council, "which subsequently dealt primarily with transmission reliability and not with the economic aspects of coordination" (Breyer and MacAvoy 1974, 112). "Reliability" in this context meant maintaining the capability to deliver electricity to consumers without significant or widespread interruption (Hamilton 1980, 42).

The council was created in 1968 as a voluntary association of nine regional reliability councils that together blanketed the United States, most of Canada, and small portions of northern Mexico; it was incorporated in 1975 as a not-for-profit corporation in New Jersey (National Electric Reliability Council 1976, 2). With the vivid and frightening memory of the Northeastern blackout still fresh, the emphasis at that time was on *reliability* of the transmission network in order to avoid future power blackouts. However, emphasis soon shifted to the *adequacy* of bulk power supply (National Electric Reliability Council 1976, 3) to meet demand for electric power.

Each of the regional councils established a planning coordination committee to accumulate data relevant to the interconnected systems in their regions, to perform regional studies, and to formulate reports and recommendations for their respective councils. These committees studied the performance of interconnected systems within their regions and recommended system design criteria for adding new generating and transmission capacity to interconnected systems. They compiled and shared information pertaining to planned generator additions and performed regional studies to assess actual and potential performance problems of the growing interconnected grids. This oversight involved maintenance of regional data banks and small technical staffs and use of computer simulations of existing and planned load-flows of electricity within regional interconnected systems under normal and disturbed conditions.

Although it continued to be the responsibility of each individual utility to plan facilities and resources to meet its future load demands, regional planning coordination committees were involved in early stages of planning new facilities or increases in generating capacity of existing facilities, well before cost analysis of such plans had begun. Based on technical consideration of additional generating capacity at a proposed geographical location, these committees used sophisticated computer simulation models of existing regional interconnected grids to advise utilities about what equipment might be necessary for effective and efficient interconnection of additional generating or transmission capacity to each system. As new facilities were built, they were added to simulation models (Hamilton 1980, 47). The exact number is unknown, but presumably hundreds of individuals had access to and participated in these modeling simulations using numerous versions of the modeling software over the ensuing years, in exercises designed to reveal operational weaknesses and bottlenecks of regional interconnected transmission grids—precisely what a terrorist would want to know to cause the most widespread disruption. Widespread availability of this modeling software, and the large number of individuals who learned how to use it, constitute a major unsung vulnerability of bulk electric power transmission systems in the United States in 2012.

When it became evident that operation of the major bulk electric power systems on the continent had extended beyond the borders of the United States, the National Electric Reliability Council was expanded to include electric utilities in Canada and Mexico and renamed the North American Electric Reliability Council.

However, increased efforts at coordination were not sufficient to prevent more blackouts. In the West, major disruptions recurred on July 2, 1996, leaving 2 million people without electric service in parts of fourteen states, two Canadian provinces, and northern Mexico for several hours; on August 10, 1996, leaving 7.5 million customers in the dark in parts of the same fourteen states, two Canadian provinces, and northern Mexico for up to nine hours; and on June 25, 1998, cutting electric service to 152,000 customers in five states and three Canadian provinces for up to nineteen hours (NERC 2011c).

In the East, on July 13, 1977, a lightning strike on two 345kV lines on a common tower in northern Westchester County, New York, separated them from the interconnected system, resulting in electrical isolation of the entire Consolidated Edison system from the surrounding electrical grid, triggering a cascading blackout that left about 9 million customers in New York City without electric service for up to twenty-six hours. Sloppy maintenance, flawed design of safety equipment, improper settings of emergency relays, human error, communications failures, equipment malfunctions, and unexpected behavior of operating systems during restoration of service all played roles in this catastrophe (Lovins and Lovins 1982, 51–58). Again on August 14, 2003, electric service was severed to over 50 million people in eight northeastern states and two Canadian provinces for up to thirty hours, in an event eerily similar to the 1965 blackout and in roughly the same area (Hilt 2006, 3).

In response, the Energy Policy Act of 2005 created a national Electric Reliability Organization (ERO), an independent, self-regulating entity that enforces mandatory electric reliability rules on all users, owners, and operators of the nation's transmission system (16 USC §8240). The North American Electric Reliability Council changed its name to the North American Electric Reliability Corporation (keeping the acronym NERC) in 2007, when the U.S. Federal Energy Regulatory Commission (FERC) granted NERC the legal authority to enforce reliability standards with all U.S. users, owners, and operators of the bulk electric power system and made compliance with those standards mandatory and enforceable. NERC has been granted similar authority by provincial governments in Canada. Thus, NERC is now an international regulatory authority established to regulate reliability of the bulk power system in North America. NERC develops and enforces reliability standards; assesses reliability annually via a ten-year assessment and winter and summer seasonal assessments; monitors the bulk power system; and trains and certifies industry operating personnel. NERC is the Electric Reliability Organization for North America, subject to oversight by FERC and governmental authorities in Canada. However, NERC cannot order construction of generation or transmission facilities or adopt enforceable standards having that effect (NERC 2011c).

Minor disruptions are not uncommon in the three grids that make up the U.S. bulk electric power supply system, but most are so brief they may go unnoticed by the public. In 2009 there were a total of 128 disturbances across the United States reported by regional reliability councils to the North American Electric Reliability Corporation. More than half were caused by weather-related factors, about 17 percent by equipment failure, and less than 1 percent by human error. However, reports of equipment failures did not explain why the equipment failed; causes of four outages were unknown, and one was caused by a software virus (NERC 2010). The number of disturbances per year increased steadily from 2004 to 2009, with the greatest increases in 2007 and 2009 (no report was prepared for 2008). This suggests grid stability and control issues are worsening, not improving. An industry review of the causes of major blackouts concluded that "system operators have been at the center of every blackout investigation since the 1965 Northeast blackout, which was the catalyst for the formation of NERC. In almost every instance, had system operators taken appropriate actions, these blackouts would not have occurred" (NERC 2004, 3).

It is possible for the human mind to conceive of technology so sophisticated and complex that we are able to build it but unable to understand or control it after it is built. "There is a good deal about the operation of modern large-scale power grids that able engineers are hard pressed to anticipate even in normal operation. In abnormal operation, as Con Ed found, grids can be complex enough to defy prior analysis. This is in itself a source of vulnerability" (Lovins and Lovins 1982, 139).

No long-term blackouts have been caused in the United States by sabotage to bulk electric power facilities. But electric power system components have been targets of numerous isolated acts of sabotage in this country, and several incidents have resulted in multimillion-dollar repair bills. Some terrorist groups hostile to the United States clearly have the capability of causing massive damage (U.S. Congress, Office of Technology Assessment 1990, 14).

It has been estimated that an average of thirty-nine attacks per year took place on U.S. energy assets during the 1980s (U.S. Congress, Office of Technology Assessment 1990, 15). Between 1970 and mid-1980 there were at least 174 incidents of sabotage or terrorism against energy facilities in the United States (Lovins and Lovins 1982, 83–84). More than half of those in the United States were against power lines, power stations, or substations, almost one-third of them against power lines alone. A manual on how to attack power lines and electrical equipment was published and widely distributed some years ago (Foreman and Haywood 1987). "If foreign terrorist groups wish to attack the United States, they can probably find assistance here in obtaining target information and in camouflaging their activities" (Alexander 1982).

The resources necessary to conduct successful attacks against electric transmission facilities are readily available to those who might wish to do so. Mortars, bazookas, rocket-propelled grenades, shoulder-fired precision-guided rockets, poison gas, explosives, aircraft, ships and small submersible vessels, tanks, and similar vehicles "are sufficiently available at National Guard and Army bases, where a wide variety of other sizable weapons have been stolen in the past" (Lovins and Lovins 1982, 79–82). Some equipment is available legally over the counter to determined terrorists. In 1977 a U.S. Department of the Interior official testified in Congress that "a relatively small group of dedicated, knowledgeable individuals . . . could bring down [the power grid supplying] almost any section of the country" or could black out "a widespread network" if more widely coordinated (U.S. Congress, Joint Committee 1977, 87). It seems clear that "the United States has reached the point where a few people could probably black out most of the country" (Lovins and Lovins 1982, 1).

The Pacific Northwest-Southwest Intertie is a complicated assembly of several 230, 345, and 500 kV alternating-current, and 750 and 1,000 kV direct-current high-voltage transmission lines running from Celilo, Oregon, at the Washington border, to Sylmar, California, near Los Angeles. These lines allow Northwest utilities in California to sell Canada's share of Columbia River Treaty energy while it continues to be surplus to Canadian and Northwest needs. Canada agreed to sell and Northwest utilities agreed to buy this energy, initially about 1.4 million kilowatts per year. Benefits were expected to exceed costs by a ratio of 2.5 to one, with direct dollar benefits to Northwest utilities of $1 billion, to California utilities of $869 million, and to Arizona and Nevada utilities of $724 million (Lindseth 1966, 7–8). Completed in 1993, several of these lines often run parallel with each other in the same transmission corridor, intersecting with other transmission lines of comparable voltage. Interruption of one or two of these lines is sufficient to destabilize the grid in California and cause widespread blackouts, especially on a hot summer day when the network is already stressed by peak air conditioning loads.

In 1967 a large construction crane was driven into three large transmission line towers to destroy them in Louisiana, and a crucial 1,000 kV direct-current line on the Pacific Intertie suffered at least three attacks near Lovelock, Nevada, in 1970 (Lovins and Lovins 1982, 82). In 1979 and 1980, conservative Minnesota farmers known as "bolt weevils" toppled fifteen towers and caused $7 million dollars' damage to a direct-current high-voltage line using only a few people and hand tools. An outbreak of "insulator disease," commonly ascribed to rifles (or even to sophisticated slingshots), littered the ground with the remains of more than 8,000 fragile glass insulators. The aluminum wires, an inch and a half in diameter, proved vulnerable to rifle fire (Casper and Wellstone 1981, 277, 284, 285). In 1987 guy wires were cut and a transmission line tower was toppled on a 1,800 MWe, 1,000kV DC Pacific Intertie in California. It took about four days to repair the damage (U.S. Congress, Office of Technology Assessment 1990, 15). Previous terrorist attacks on the electric grid have used all available civilian and military firearms up to and including heavy machine guns, twenty-millimeter cannons, antitank guns, and recoilless rifles. Catalogs of equipment useful to terrorists have been published, much of it available illegally in the United States (Lovins and Lovins 1982, 79–82).

Electric utilities have long suffered the expense of repairing insulators, transmission lines, and substations vandalized by frustrated or bored hunters. A trained sniper, armed with any one of several sniper rifles available (Bushmaster 2011; CZ 2011; Remington 2011) with a good scope could probably bring down a high-voltage transmission line or two from a single perch and be gone before law enforcement could arrive. Designed for and used by the U.S. military, these rifles have a daylight range of 800 yards, nearly half a mile, and are available online, in gun shops, and at gun shows nationwide. Any of the hundreds of personnel trained as military snipers in the past ten years would be able to get to a hidden perch, hit a 1,240- to 5,000-millimeter-long high-voltage transmission line insulator, and get away without being observed. If either snipers or their spotters (snipers generally work in pairs) (Masterson 2011) had access to a computer simulation model of a regional transmission grid and could figure out where the weak points are in the transmission system, they might be able to cause a widespread blackout by knocking out a key transmission line or substation. They would have adequate time for several shots if the target was located in a rural area, as are substantial portions of the Pacific Northwest-Southwest Intertie in California and Nevada and other major lines throughout the country. Potential targets are numerous on high-voltage bulk electric power networks throughout the United States. This point cannot be made too forcefully: the situation described is not "someday, maybe" but today, now. It bears repeating that, as stated above, the United States has *already* reached the point where a few people can probably black out most of the country (Lovins and Lovins 1982, 1).

Figure 13.4 **The Added Costs of Electricity Technologies**

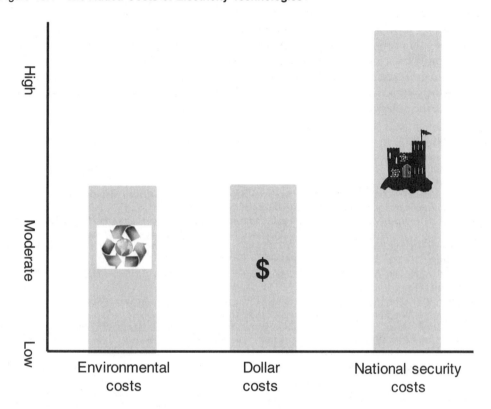

SUMMARY OF COSTS

The costs of electric power transmission technologies are summarized in Figure 13.4. Transmission of electricity is not a fuel technology in itself, but a bundle of related technologies that adds significant costs to the use of generating technologies discussed above to the extent that they rely upon central-station generation, high-voltage transmission of electric power to remote locations, or lower-voltage distribution to consumers. Electricity used at the location where it is generated, and energy fuels that require no transmission over wires (e.g., fuel in cars and trucks), do not entail the additional risks and costs of electric power transmission.

Transmission of electricity does not add much pollution to the air except during manufacturing of wires, towers, substations, and insulators, where hazardous materials and considerable heat from use of fossil fuels may be used to fabricate transmission equipment. Combustion of fossil fuels produces considerably more air pollution and greenhouse gases than transmission of electricity. Bulk electric power transmission will not produce atmospheric emissions that cause acid rain. Construction and use of transmission lines does involve some disruption of the environment in the form of unsightly transmission towers in rural areas and the impact of transmission networks upon wildlife, especially birds, so the additional environmental costs must be considered "moderate."

Dollar costs for the use of electric transmission technologies are always in addition to the dollar costs incurred by use of any fuel technology. Energy technologies that do not use electric transmission are not required to include the dollar costs of producing, operating, and maintaining them in pricing. Consequently, the dollar costs for utilizing electric transmission must be considered "moderate" and added to the other costs of using a fuel technology that requires high-voltage transmission. Although the materials for producing them are all available in the United States, the national security costs for utilizing bulk electric power transmission networks must be considered "high" due to their great vulnerability and attractiveness to terrorist attack. Transmission facilities make extremely attractive targets for terrorists because their destruction could cause widespread disruption of the American society and economy.

REFERENCES

Alexander, Yonah. 1982. "International Network of Terrorism." In *Political Terrorism and Energy*, ed. Yonah Alexander and Charles K. Ebinger. New York: Praeger.

American Electric Power. 2008. "Transmission Facts." Columbus, OH: American Electric Power. www.aep. com/about/transmission/docs/transmission-facts.pdf.

Bellis, Mary. 2011. *History of Electric Vehicles: Decline and Rise of Electric Cars from 1930 to 1990*. About. com: Inventors. http://inventors.about.com/od/estartinventions/a/Electric-Vehicles.htm.

Breyer, Steven G., and Paul W. MacAvoy. 1974. *Energy Regulation by the Federal Power Commission*. Washington, DC: Brookings Institution Press.

Brown, Matthew H., and Richard P. Sedano. 2004. *Electricity Transmission: A Primer*. Denver, CO: National Council on Electric Policy.

Bushmaster. 2011. "Stainless Varmint Special Rifle." *SniperWorld*. www.sniperworld.com/item/768_Bushmaster_Rifles_Shotguns_Bushmaster_PCWVMS24-9SS_V.aspx.

Casazza, J., and F. Delea. 2003. *Understanding Electric Power Systems*. Hoboken, NJ: Wiley.

Casper, B.M., and P.D. Wellstone. 1981. *Powerline: The First Battle of America's Energy War*. Amherst: University of Massachusetts Press.

Clark, W., and J. Page. 1981. *Energy, Vulnerability, and War: Alternatives for America*. New York: W.W. Norton.

Colorado Long-Range Transmission Planning Group. 2004. *Colorado Long Range Transmission Planning Study*. Golden, CO: Excel Energy. www.rmao.com/wtpp/Clrtpg/AF_TSGT_CostEstimation_Guide. pdf.

CZ. 2011. "CZ 750 Tactical Sniper Rifle." SniperWorld. www.sniperworld.com/item/44539_CZ_Rifles_Shotguns_CZ_750_TACTICAL_308WIN_26_HB_SYN.aspx.

Davis, Stacy C., Susan W. Diegel, and Robert G. Boundy. 2011. *Transportation Energy Data Book*, 30th ed. Washington, DC: U.S. Government Printing Office.

Edison Electric Institute Inc. 1992. "The Nation's Most Capital-Intensive Industry." *Electric Perspectives* 16 (July/August): 52.

Electric Power Research Institute (EPRI). 2001. *The Cost of Power Disturbances to Industrial & Digital Economy Companies*. Palo Alto, CA: Electric Power Research Institute.

Foreman, Dave, and Bill Haywood, eds. 1987. *Ecodefense: A Field Guide to Monkey Wrenching*, 2nd ed. Tucson, AZ: Ned Ludd Books.

Goodman, James E. 2003. *Blackout*. New York: North Point Press.

Hamilton, Michael S. 1979. "Bulk Power Supply Reliability and Proposals for a National Grid: Road Signs in What Direction?" In *New Dimensions to Energy Policy*, ed. Robert M. Lawrence, 125–144. Lexington, MA: Lexington Books.

———. 1980. "Regional Interconnections: The Western Systems Coordinating Council, Regional Reliability, Economy and Efficiency." In *Regional Factors in Siting and Planning Energy Facilities in the Eleven Western States: A Report to the Western Interstate Nuclear Board*, ed. Norman Wengert and Robert M. Lawrence, 41–60. Fort Collins: Colorado State University Experiment Station.

———. 1989. "Relationships Between Electric Power Project Characteristics and Regulatory System Structure." *Energy Systems and Policy* 12: 179–89.

Hamilton, Michael S., and Norman Wengert. 1980. *Environmental, Legal and Political Constraints on Power Plant Siting in the Southwestern United States*. A Report to the Los Alamos Scientific Laboratory. Fort Collins: Colorado State University Experiment Station, 1980.

Hilt, David W. 2006. "Impacts and Actions Resulting from the August 14, 2003 Blackout." PowerPoint presentation, July 29. Princeton, NJ: North American Electric Reliability Council.

ICF Consulting. 2003. "The Economic Cost of the Blackout." Issue paper. Fairfax, VA: ICF Consulting.

Lawrence Berkeley National Laboratory. 2005. "Berkeley Lab Study Estimates $80 Billion Annual Cost of Power Interruptions." Press release, February 2. Berkeley, CA: Lawrence Berkeley National Laboratory. www.lbl.gov/Science-Articles/Archive/EETD-power-interruptions.html.

Lindseth, E.V. 1966. "The Pacific Northwest-Southwest Intertie." Presented at the Water Resources Engineering Conference of the American Society of Civil Engineers, Denver, CO, May 20.

Lovins, Amory B., E. Kyle Datta, Thomas Feiler, Karl R. Rábago, Joel N. Swisher, André Lehmann, and Ken Wicker. 2002. *Small Is Profitable*. Snowmass, CO: Rocky Mountain Institute.

Lovins, Amory B., and L. Hunter Lovins. 1982. *Brittle Power: Energy Strategy for National Security*. Andover, MA: Brick House.

Masterson, Jason. 2011. "The Sniper." Sniperworld. www.sniperworld.com/Article.aspx?AKey=The_Sniper.

Mims, Natalie, Mathias Bell, and Stephen Doig. 2009. *Assessing the Electric Productivity Gap and the U.S. Efficiency Opportunity*. Boulder: Rocky Mountain Institute.

Minnesota Electric Transmission Planning. 2011. *How the Electric Transmission System Works*. www.minnelectrans.com/transmission-system.html

National Electric Reliability Council. 1976. *1975 Annual Report*. Princeton, NJ: National Electric Reliability Council.

National Research Council (NRC). 2010. *Hidden Costs of Energy: Unpriced Consequences of Energy Production and Use*. Washington, DC: National Academies Press.

Ng, Peter. 2009. "Draft Unit Cost Guide for Transmission Lines." Presented at a Stakeholder Meeting, Folsom, CA, February 26. San Francisco, CA: Pacific Gas & Electric Company.

North American Electric Reliability Corporation (NERC). 2004. *A Review of System Operations Leading Up to the Blackout of August 14, 2003*. Princeton, NJ: North American Electric Reliability Corporation.

———. 2010. *2009 System Disturbances*. Princeton, NJ: North American Electric Reliability Corporation.

———. 2011a. *2011 Long-Term Reliability Assessment*. Report, November. Princeton, NJ: North American Electric Reliability Corporation.

———. 2011b. "Company Overview: Fast Facts." www.nerc.com/page.php?cid=1|7|10.

———. 2011c. "Examples of Major Bulk Electric System Power Outages." Table, March 18. Princeton, NJ: North American Electric Reliability Corporation. www.nerc.com/docs/docs/blackout/BlackoutTable.pdf.

Public Service Commission of Wisconsin (PSC Wisconsin). 2011. *Environmental Impacts of Transmission Lines*. Report. Madison: Public Service Commission of Wisconsin.

Remington. 2011. "Remington M24 Sniper Weapon System." www.remingtonle.com/rifles/m24.htm.

Rocky Mountain Area OASIS. 2004. "Colorado Long Range Transmission Planning Cost Estimates." April. www.rmao.com/wtpp/Clrtpg/AF_TSGT_CostEstimation_Guide.pdf.

Sperling, Daniel, and James S. Cannon. 2004. "Introduction and Overview." In *The Hydrogen Energy Transition: Moving Toward the Post Petroleum Age in Transportation*, ed. Daniel Sperling and James S. Cannon. Boston: Elsevier.

U.S. Congress, Joint Committee on Defense Production. 1977. *Emergency Preparedness in the Electric Power Industry and the Implications of the New York Blackout for Emergency Planning*. Hearings before the Joint Committee on Defense Production, 95th Cong, 1st sess., August 10–11.

U.S. Congress, Office of Technology Assessment. 1990. Physical Vulnerability of Electric System to Natural Disasters and Sabotage. Washington, DC: U.S. Government Printing Office.

U.S. Department of Energy (USDOE). 1979. National Power Grid Study. Washington, DC: U.S. Government Printing Office.

———. 2002. National Transmission Grid Study. Washington, DC: U.S. Government Printing Office.

U.S. Department of Transportation (USDOT). 2011. National Transportation Statistics. Washington, DC: U.S. Government Printing Office.

———. 2011a. Direct Federal Financial Interventions and Subsidies in Energy Markets 2010. Washington, DC: U.S. Government Printing Office.

U.S. Energy Information Administration (USEIA). 2011b. Electric Power Annual 2010. Washington, DC: U.S. Government Printing Office. www.eia.gov/electricity/annual/.

———. 2011c. "Electricity Explained: Electricity in the United States." www.eia.gov/energyexplained/index.cfm?page=electricity_in_the_united_states.

———. 2011d. "Electricity Explained: How Electricity is Delivered to Consumers." www.eia.gov/energyexplained/index.cfm?page=electricity_delivery.

U.S. Federal Power Commission (USFPC). 1967. Prevention of Power Failures. Washington, DC: U.S. Government Printing Office.

14

Conclusion

National energy policy choices in the United States are constrained by three primary costs of continued high energy use: higher energy prices, greater environmental degradation, and increased security risk. A conceptual framework is presented here for analysis of various conventional and renewable energy fuel technologies in terms of their respective dollar costs, environmental costs, and national security costs to the nation. The focus here is on analysis of technological options for formulating a coherent national energy policy for the United States.

A systematic examination of the various energy fuel technologies in terms of their environmental, dollar, and national security costs, assigning simple numerical weights to them (high = 3, moderate = 2, low = 1) produces a rough ranking from lowest overall costs to highest costs as follows:

1. Conservation and efficiency
1. Geothermal heat pump
1. Solar energy
2. Beneficial biomass
3. Hydroelectric energy
4. Hydrogen
4. Harmful biomass
5. Wind
5. Ocean
6. Natural gas
6. Geothermal power plants
7. Electricity
8. Coal
8. Petroleum
9. Nuclear energy

On the basis of this analysis, technologies at the top of the list are the most desirable for the United States to emphasize in national energy policy in the immediate future. Several tie scores are apparent in this ranking, which must be considered imprecise, but sufficient for ordinal data. What is significant about it is the position of each energy fuel technology in the ranking relative to the others, not the interval between them.

Moreover, because electricity is not really an energy fuel technology, but merely a transportation technology, the environmental, dollar, and national security costs of utilizing the several fuels requiring bulk electric power transmission must be adjusted upward to reflect the additional costs of high-voltage transmission to energy end users. Of paramount concern in making these calculations is the vulnerability to sabotage and higher national security costs in an increasingly unstable political world. Not all energy fuel technologies require a transmission grid, and a few could make use of bulk electric power transmission or not, depending on the specific mode of an energy technology used.

Fuel technologies requiring a transmission grid include nuclear, petroleum, coal, geothermal power plants, natural gas, ocean, wind, hydroelectric, and solar energy fuel technologies, altering the ranking between them and producing an adjusted ranking from lowest aggregate costs to highest costs as follows:

1. Conservation and efficiency
1. Geothermal heat pump
1. Beneficial biomass
2. Hydrogen
2. Harmful biomass
3. Solar energy
4. Hydroelectric energy
5. Wind
5. Ocean
6. Natural gas
6. Geothermal power plants
7. Coal
7. Petroleum
8. Nuclear energy

Realistically, four of these energy fuel technologies—ocean, geothermal power plants, hydroelectric, and wind—are limited geographically by their nature to specific portions of the country. Although they may make significant contributions to energy use in restricted locales, they cannot be considered likely to make substantial new contributions to national energy consumption, even with a high-voltage transmission grid. Ocean thermal energy conversion may someday dominate electricity production in Hawaii, displacing some diesel and natural gas capacity, but cannot be transmitted or produced on the U.S. mainland. Tidal energy technologies have considerable promise for the long term, but will be limited to coastal areas and perhaps a few river locations. Geothermal power plants are already approaching their maximum potential in California and may make small contributions in a few other states, but are not expected to expand greatly and are limited by dollar costs and available transmission capacity. All the large hydro sites available in the United States are currently in use, and small hydro plants are decreasing in number, as they are decommissioned to allow free run of migratory fish species. That trend might be reversed, but it seems unlikely, given the substantial time and effort required to secure licenses for new hydroelectric facilities. Although wind generators are aesthetically disadvantaged, they remain the most likely option of this bunch to increase total capacity significantly, but only as long as government subsidies continue to attract capital, if only in areas with strong, steady winds. Because such areas are often found in scenic and coastal areas, public opposition to new wind generators is increasing and likely to slow the growth of this energy supply option, which is further limited by the availability of high-voltage transmission capacity and attitudes within the electric power industry that frown on variable-rate generating sources that sit idle much of the time. Thus, a list of energy fuel technologies that have potential for significant increases in capacity to supply future demand, ranked from lowest overall costs to highest costs, looks like the following:

1. Conservation and efficiency
1. Geothermal heat pump
1. Beneficial biomass
2. Hydrogen
2. Harmful biomass
3. Solar energy
4. Natural gas
5. Coal
5. Petroleum
6. Nuclear energy

To formulate new national energy policy, this is what we have to work with, and it is not a bad crop of energy fuel technologies. The list includes only technologies that are currently in use or on the threshold of commercial development on a large scale and amenable to rapid expansion with or without subsidies. It includes energy fuel technologies useful in both transportation and stationary applications, most of which have aggregate costs lower than technologies currently in widespread use.

Unfortunately, the three energy fuels currently in widest use are the ones with the highest mix of environmental, dollar, and national security costs: nuclear, petroleum, and coal. Use of these energy technologies will probably continue in the short term, but should be deemphasized in national energy policy. The five energy technologies with the lowest mix of costs are the ones we should favor in national energy policy: conservation and efficiency improvements, geothermal heat pumps, beneficial biomass, hydrogen, and solar energy. An easy policy choice can be made to eliminate harmful biomass from the list on the grounds it produces exactly the same products as beneficial biomass for higher aggregate costs, and using food crops for energy production would be detrimental to agriculture and food supplies, as discussed in Chapter 9. Greater use of energy fuels with the lowest mix of costs will also encourage development of technologies that minimize demand for high-voltage electric transmission services by building energy supplies closer to their end-use locations, which seems desirable for national security reasons.

CONSERVATION AND EFFICIENCY

Everything eventually wears out and can be replaced with something more energy-efficient. Opportunities for improving energy efficiency and increasing energy conservation are so numerous in the American economy that they are actually increasing with the pace of technological innovation. This is true for all types of appliances currently in use, as well as housing stock, factory buildings and processes, commercial establishments, automobiles, trucks and buses, and other energy-using devices. Corporate average fuel economy (CAFE) standards and greenhouse gas emission standards have increased the energy efficiency of motor vehicles by boosting fuel economy and hold promise for further improvements. Market adoption of advanced technologies in conventional vehicles is expected to improve fuel economy through model year 2020 and reduce fuel costs thereafter, due in part to greater penetration of unconventionally fueled (electric, hybrid, natural gas, hydrogen) vehicles and in part to the addition of new technologies in conventional vehicles (USEIA 2011), as discussed in Chapter 10. Using evolving conventional technologies, automakers could produce a fleet of cars and light trucks that achieve over thirty-five miles per gallon by 2020. Hybrid, fuel cell, and other advanced technologies make vehicles even more efficient (UCS 2007b).

U.S. homes on average are already becoming more energy-efficient, due in part to building code and appliance standards with strict efficiency requirements. Energy use per household continues to decline, and use of energy-efficient, multipane windows is increasing, especially in new homes. Home owners continue to use caulking and weather-stripping to seal cracks and air leakages, add insulation, and replace incandescent light bulbs with more energy-efficient compact fluorescent or light-emitting diode lights. New models of appliances (refrigerators, freezers, ovens, stoves, dishwashers, clothes washers, and clothes dryers) and heating and cooling equipment continue to use less energy than previous models. Better insulation and construction design have become the hallmark of energy efficiency in new housing construction (USEIA 2011). These trends may be expected to continue.

Efficiency of commercial buildings continues to improve, especially in space cooling, refrigeration, and lighting, due to efficiency standards and development of more efficient technologies (USEIA 2011). Replacement of incandescent lamps with compact fluorescent lamps has only just begun in commercial buildings, where there are opportunities for more efficient lighting and elimination of overillumination to reduce lighting energy use by about 50 percent (USEIA 2011). Advanced dynamic window technologies hold great potential for reducing energy used to heat and cool a building (Risser 2011).

Many opportunities have been identified where industry might conserve energy or improve energy efficiency (Lovins et al. 2002, 107–309). Fuel used by manufacturing facilities to make steam can be reduced 20 percent by insulating steam and condensate return lines, stopping steam leakage, and maintaining steam traps. Use of variable-speed electric motors can achieve energy savings ranging from 3 to 60 percent, depending on how a motor is used. Motor coils made of superconducting materials can also reduce energy losses. Installing variable-speed drives, along with preventive maintenance to detect and fix air leaks, can improve industrial energy efficiency of pumps and compressors 20 to 50 percent (EESI 2006, 1).

The U.S. economy has the potential to reduce annual nontransportation energy consumption by roughly 23 percent by 2020, eliminating more than $1.2 trillion in waste—well beyond the $520 billion up-front investment that would be required. This reduction in energy use would result in abatement of 1.1 gigatons of greenhouse gas emissions annually—the equivalent of taking the entire U.S. fleet of passenger vehicles and light trucks off the roads. Turning off or switching to standby mode of all computers in U.S. office buildings at night, sealing heating and cooling ducts to reduce air leaks, and replacing old appliances are some of the most cost-efficient measures to reduce emissions of greenhouse gases (Granade et al. 2009), as discussed in Chapter 10.

Some analysts argue that renewable energy fuel technologies work better than oil and coal and can compete purely on the basis of price in 2012. They argue the United States can have an economy 158 percent larger in 2050 than in 2010 without relying on oil, coal, or nuclear electric generation, and using one-third less natural gas than in 2010. Moreover, they argue this transition would cost $5 trillion less than business-as-usual, require no new federal taxes, subsidies, mandates, or laws, and is already under way (Lovins and Rocky Mountain Institute 2011). Whether this is accurate remains to be seen, but it certainly seems plausible in 2012. Continuous efforts to increase energy conservation and improve energy efficiency should be favored in public policy as the most cost-effective way to reduce our national dependency on fossil fuels, avoid unnecessary environmental costs, and increase national security. Such efforts will also maintain existing jobs and produce new ones.

GEOTHERMAL HEAT PUMPS

The most promising future applications of geothermal energy in the United States involve heat pumps using shallow ground energy to heat and cool school, residential, commercial, and industrial buildings in any location (UCS 2009). Geothermal heat pump technology is widely available commercially in 2012, with potential savings of 30 to 70 percent over conventional heating options, and 20 to 50 percent over other cooling systems (ClimateMaster 2011; Excel Energy Solutions 2011; Smithfield Construction 2011). This technology is now competitive with other conventional heating and cooling systems for residential, commercial, and industrial buildings. High-efficiency geothermal heat pump systems are on average 48 percent more efficient than the best gas furnaces and more than 75 percent more efficient than oil furnaces (L'Ecuyer, Zoi, and Hoffman 1993).

The U.S. Department of Energy found that geothermal heat pumps can save a typical home hundreds of dollars in energy costs each year, with the system typically paying for itself in eight to twelve years. Tax credits and other incentives can reduce the payback period to five years or less (Hughes 2008). Installing geothermal heat pumps during new building construction is the most effective and efficient way to use them, because it avoids digging up areas around existing buildings. Geothermal heat pumps are highly reliable, require little maintenance, and are built to last for decades. They add considerably to the value of homes (GeoExchange 2011). Public policy should favor geothermal heat pumps in new and retrofitted residential, commercial, and industrial buildings for space heating and cooling, to displace consumption of electricity, fuel oil, and other fossil fuels wherever possible.

BENEFICIAL BIOMASS

Energy crops that do not compete with food crops for land, leftover portions of crop residues such as wheat straw or corn stover, sustainably harvested wood and forest residues, and clean municipal and industrial wastes constitute beneficial biomass (Tilman et al. 2009), which can be processed in a variety of ways to produce solid, gaseous, or liquid fuels to generate electricity. Liquids can be further processed to make synthetic liquid biofuels or other useful chemicals (UCS 2010), which have great potential to help supply our transportation needs (Luque et al. 2008). Use of cellulosic ethanol, a beneficial biomass product made from woody plants, may reduce greenhouse gas emissions more than 85 percent (UCS 2007a), as discussed in Chapter 9.

Generation of electricity using beneficial biomass is price competitive with other conventional fuels in 2012. Ethanol production from cellulosic feedstocks such as agricultural wastes, grasses, and wood is nearly price-competitive with ethanol produced from other agricultural feedstocks such as corn in some areas, and ethanol-blended fuel is competitive in the transportation marketplace. Biofuels derived from many resources can play a role in reducing pollution contributing to climate change, while providing domestic substitutes for petroleum feedstocks and fuels obtained from foreign sources. Based on current estimates, about 300 million tons of biomass annually can be obtained from waste products such as agricultural residues, forestry residues, and municipal and construction waste (Perlack et al. 2005), without reliance on cultivation of food crops for energy crops or exploitation of new energy crops other than cellulosic biomass like switchgrass. Any significant expansion beyond this level, however, must be based on a scientific determination that the required volume of biomass can be produced in a sustainable manner. Greater demand for biofuels will have to be balanced with demand for electric power generation, biogas and chemical production, and traditional agricultural uses such as food, feed, and fiber. Still, beneficial biomass has great potential in the short term for increasing production of liquid fuels that will help displace consumption of petroleum, and even greater potential for small-scale stationary industrial applications that may sell electricity to the grid, but are able to operate without depending on a grid connection.

HYDROGEN

Stationary power generation and transportation are two areas where use of hydrogen may be greatly expanded in the short term. Stationary facilities for large cogeneration plants, uninterruptible power supply systems, and home energy stations are in production or will be soon, providing opportunities to reduce reliance on the high-voltage transmission grid and displace some fossil-fueled electricity generation. Emergency diesel generators for hospitals and other critical uses may also be displaced by hydrogen fuel cells currently available, and the availability of home energy stations will support expanded use of hydrogen fuel cell vehicles.

Fuel cell vehicles, powered by hydrogen, have the potential to revolutionize our transportation system, as discussed in Chapter 12. The greatest near-term potential for hydrogen fuel cells is in fleets of large buses and trucks with predominantly local passenger and freight delivery or service uses, resulting in displacement of petroleum fuel consumption. As costs come down, wider use by the public of fuel cell vehicles now being tested by consumers in California will further displace consumption of petroleum fuels.

Public policy should provide financial incentives to reduce the cost of fuel cells and support development of a hydrogen distribution system nationwide, based either on multifuel fueling stations or expansion of existing industrial gas distribution facilities. In the 1960s, American Honda Motor Corporation established a national network of dealerships to introduce its motorcycles to U.S. consumers in five years, including vehicle sales, service by factory-trained mechanics, and local spare parts inventories (Prahalad and Hamel 1990; Hamel and Prahalad 1989). If Honda could do that, surely the United States can figure out how to build a national distribution system for hydrogen fuel over five years.

SOLAR

Solar photovoltaics are cost-competitive with central-station generation of electricity today and are being installed at an increasing rate on commercial, industrial, and residential buildings. They do not require connection to an electric grid, but may be more affordable if they are connected so their owners can sell surplus energy. State net-metering laws that require electric utilities to credit homeowners for any excess power they generate from solar technologies on their homes have proven particularly useful in encouraging homeowners to purchase photovoltaic equipment. Net metering has made it possible for electric utilities to offer rebate programs encouraging on-site consumers of electricity to install significant amounts of solar photovoltaics, which have enabled utilities to meet electricity demand without construction of new, environmentally disruptive central-station generating facilities (Black Hills Energy 2011).

Installation of a photovoltaic system immediately adds resale value to a residence. Homes equipped with solar photovoltaics have lower operating costs in the form of monthly electric bills than do comparable nonsolar homes, and a photovoltaic system allows homeowners to fix their costs for electricity at the cost of installation of the system, providing protection against future electric rate increases. On new homes, these costs can be included in the mortgage, typically providing a 10 to 20 percent average annual return on the initial investment. Moreover, use of innovative financial instruments such as long-term power purchase agreements will make photovoltaics available to more users, as discussed in Chapter 5.

Solar photovoltaic systems or flat-plate thermal collectors can be installed on most of the 14,333 square miles of underutilized roof space scattered across the United States, making it unnecessary and wasteful to construct solar collectors on undeveloped open land. If only one-third of the existing underutilized rooftop space in the United States was used for photovoltaic collectors, it would be enough to generate all of the nonpeak-load electricity consumed in the country in 2011. This calls into serious question the need to build new electric generating stations of any kind, solar or otherwise, on undeveloped land such as public lands in the desert Southwest. Better utilization of existing developed building sites would be better policy and provide a new revenue stream for existing building owners. Utilizing existing roof space for location of solar facilities would avoid potential impacts on existing land uses, archeological resources, wildlife habitat, and ecosystems, perhaps reducing the need for changing land uses to zero for photovoltaic collectors and nonconcentrating thermal collectors (USDOE 2004).

Solar technologies are ranked third in the list of technologies for greater utilization in the future only because solar power plant technologies have high national security costs when the additional costs of bulk electric power transmission are added in. If consideration of large-scale solar electric power technologies is eliminated, solar technologies move to a four-way tie for the highest rank in the list, along with conservation and efficiency, geothermal heat pumps, and beneficial biomass. Construction of solar power towers and fields full of photovoltaic collectors not yet built should be abandoned as unnecessarily destructive of land that might be productively used for something else and as increasing the national security costs of solar power by making it reliant on bulk electric power transmission networks. In addition, if solar power towers became numerous and provided substantial contributions to energy supplies, they would constitute attractive targets for terrorists. Use of high-voltage electric transmission networks is unnecessary if solar photovoltaics are constructed near their end use, as they would be if rooftops were more frequently utilized.

FEASIBILITY OF RENEWABLES

Our current national reliance on conventional energy sources will not change overnight, but it is already changing. Continued emphasis on finding new opportunities for energy conservation and improving energy efficiency should be our highest national priority, because they have the lowest environmental, dollar, and national security costs and tend to provide the most employment and value added of all the alternatives. A continuous process of reevaluating our existing stocks of buildings and machinery should be instituted, to identify opportunities for improvements in energy conservation and efficiency. Every new building constructed in the future should have ground-source geothermal heat pumps for space heating and cooling, passive solar design to conserve energy, and solar photovoltaics for electricity, thus ensuring affordable energy supplies that are not dependent on vulnerable bulk electric power transmission in a politically unstable world. Large new commercial buildings can also take advantage of the human heat sources within by utilizing sophisticated ventilation with heat exchangers for space heating (Hinchey 2011).

Germany has had great success simulating rapid expansion of renewable energy fuel technologies to displace a heavy reliance on nuclear capacity since its Renewable Energy Act (Erneurbare-Energien-Gesetz, or EEG) became effective in 2000. The portion of electricity produced from renewable energy in Germany in 2010 was 101.7 billion kilowatt-hours, increased from 6.3 percent of the national total in 2000 to over 20 percent at the beginning of 2011. In 2011 about 17 percent of electricity, 8 percent of heat, and 6 percent of fuel used in Germany were generated from renewable sources, reducing Germany's energy imports. CO_2 emissions were reduced 110 million metric tons due to use of renewable energy supplies during 2010. Employment in the renewable energy sector increased about 8 percent in 2009 over the previous year, mostly in small and medium-sized companies. About two-thirds of these jobs were attributed to the Renewable Energy Act (German Renewable Energies Agency 2011).

The EEG provides guaranteed feed-in tariffs and mandatory connection to the electric grid for producers of electricity using renewable fuel technologies. Every kilowatt-hour generated from renewable energy facilities receives a fixed feed-in tariff. If the transmission grid is overloaded, network operators must feed this electricity into the grid preferentially to electricity generated by conventional sources (nuclear power, coal, and gas). Renewable energy generators receive a twenty-year, technology-specific, guaranteed payment for their electricity. Small and medium-sized independent power producers now have access to the interconnected electricity market, along with private land owners. Anyone who produces renewable energy can sell it for a twenty-year fixed price (Lauber and Mez 2004).

EEG remuneration rates reveal what electricity from wind, hydro, solar, bio, and geothermal energy actually costs to produce in Germany. Remuneration rates are paid by consumers through their electricity bills, not by taxpayer subsidies. The "polluter pays principle" distributes increased costs directly to the consumer: whoever consumes more energy pays more. Rates of remuneration for new sources are reduced 1 percent per year, exerting pressure on producers to become more efficient and less costly. Because the feed-in tariff provides financial certainty, the EEG has been found to be more cost-effective and less bureaucratic than other support schemes such as investment or production tax credits, quota-based renewable portfolio standards, and auction mechanisms. The net benefit of the EEG exceeded costs of initial investment by about US$4.97 billion in 2005. The feed-in tariff generates more competition, more jobs, and more rapid deployment of renewable energy technologies for manufacturing, and it does not pick technological winners, such as more mature technology versus solar photovoltaics technology (Butler and Neuhoff 2008; Morris 2007; EC 2005). Public policy favoring renewable energy fuel technologies while deemphasizing fossil fuels and nuclear energy has produced dramatic results in Germany, a modern industrialized country, and might do so in the United States as well.

The U.S. electric utility industry marketplace has for many years moved away from nuclear electric generating stations and oil-fired power plants and, in the absence of some ill-advised massive federal government initiative at the expense of the taxpayer, seems poised to continue to do so. Future national energy policy should place heavy reliance on decentralized development of solar photovoltaic technology for our electric needs, supplemented by continued reliance on hydroelectric, geothermal, beneficial biomass, and wind resources for small, increasingly local portions of our electricity needs during a transition period.

NATURAL GAS

Transportation needs in the United States will continue to be met for some years with petroleum products, which must be viewed increasingly as transition fuels and conserved for use as feedstocks for manufactured goods while we develop greater reliance on beneficial biomass and hydrogen fuel cell technologies for liquid fuels. Greater use of natural gas should be encouraged during a transition away from reliance on petroleum, especially for fleets of large buses and trucks delivering people and goods over long distances. As long as natural gas is plentiful in the United States, it is less expensive, contributes less greenhouse gases, and is less environmentally disruptive and has lower national security costs than petroleum. Use of petroleum products should be reduced due to their higher environmental, dollar, and national security costs as compared to natural gas, beneficial biomass, and hydrogen, but the latter two fuels should be used instead of natural gas whenever possible.

COAL

Implementation of new air quality rules for toxic air pollutants in January 2012 has had and will continue to have significant effects on the use of coal in the United States, stimulating overdue retirement of many ancient coal-fired power plants (USEPA 2011a, 2011b) that should have been decommissioned many years ago. Although electric utility executives may be expected to complain about this a great deal, these plants are so old—most of them predating passage of the Clean Air Act of 1970, some of them over fifty years old—they have already paid for themselves in profits and amortization and are the dirtiest power plants in the United States (perhaps in the world) because many of them have long operated without any significant air pollution controls (USOSM 1993, 10–14).

Damage estimates for various external effects of utilizing coal, oil, and natural gas added up to more than $120 billion per year by 2005, principally from emissions of nitrogen oxides, sulfur dioxide, and particulate matter (NRC 2010, 21). Climate-related damages per ton of carbon dioxide equivalent are expected to be 50 to 80 percent worse in 2030 than in 2005 (NRC 2010, 19). These estimates substantially understate the actual damages because they do not include the cost of impacts from criteria air pollutants on ecosystem services or nongrain agricultural crops, effects attributable to emissions of hazardous air pollutants, or many other kinds of damages that could not be quantified (NRC 2010, 5, 21).

Executives in the electric utility industry who complain about the dollar costs of regulations imposed upon their businesses while they report record annual profits need to be reminded periodically that laws that impose regulatory restrictions on human behavior exist for a reason. Those laws were not created out of whimsy or idle speculation or fantastic imagination. Laws that impose regulatory restrictions on human behavior are usually a direct response to real events that actually happened in the past or real possibilities that seem likely in the near future.

The profit motive is so strong in the United States that some people need to be reminded periodically it is not socially acceptable to cause death or injury to others just to make a profit. Our libraries are full of descriptions of death and injury to others, and destruction of their property, for the sake of profit—historical events have actually occurred and would probably happen again in the absence of such laws. In fact, behavior that causes such events continues today in some quarters, which is why we occasionally hear on the evening news about successful law enforcement proceedings against major corporations charged with violating those same regulations. ENRON, a major energy trader that caused significant damage to the economy of the State of California, as well as to its own stockholders, comes immediately to mind. Law enforcement actions prove the need for regulatory restrictions on human behavior. New rules to reduce toxic air pollutants are a case in point. With retirement of highly polluting coal-fired power plants, other sources of power will be needed to fill demand. Renewables are available to meet the need with lower overall costs than so-called clean coal or new coal plant construction.

PETROLEUM

The chemical industry uses liquid petroleum as feedstock for production of plastics, polyurethane, solvents, asphalt, and hundreds of other products (USEIA 2010) with high added value to the economy and to human life. Petroleum use for such a low-grade economic activity as transportation seems profligate and short-sighted, considering that petroleum is a finite resource and there are other energy fuel technologies available for transportation, requiring only the continued development and adoption of innovations already under way (Lovins and Rocky Mountain Institute 2011, 16–75). Increased use of unconventionally fueled (electric, hybrid, fuel cell) vehicles has already begun and should be encouraged as an act of patriotism, as well as economic self-interest.

NUCLEAR

It should be obvious to anyone concerned about energy policy (or human health and safety) that the once noble experiment of using nuclear electric generating technology safely is beyond human capability, that it is simply too risky, and the stakes too high, for it to be in the public interest, as distinct from the private interests of its proponents. No fair evaluation of the costs of using nuclear energy technology has ever taken full account of the costs of radioactive waste disposal and concluded that the benefits exceed the costs. Previous efforts to identify permanent high-level radioactive waste disposal technology produced safety and site selection criteria that are conceptually flawed to the point of intellectual dishonesty. The desire to use nuclear technology has simply outstripped the human capacity for reason in the search for technological solutions to apparently unsolvable difficulties. Excluding foreseeable costs from the analysis because they are unknown, or minimizing them because it is convenient, or imposing them on the general public whatever they may be, is simply not intellectually or morally defensible. When foreseeable natural disasters can render entire landscapes permanently uninhabitable because of the presence of a nuclear reactor, it is clear that we can and must make sounder energy choices.

FURTHER RESEARCH

This book provides a conceptual framework for analysis of energy policy choices, but it is only a start. Future academic research may fruitfully examine whether informed individuals find the analytical framework useful by providing opportunities for a number of respondents to read the material in each chapter and then apply a scoring instrument to verify results of the admittedly subjective, but informed, scoring system used here. Respondents might be asked to read summaries of the chapters here and then score each energy fuel technology on the basis of a five-point Likert scale (high, moderately high, moderate, moderately low, low), applying a modified Delphi technique to validate the results of this analysis. With a sufficient number of respondents, statistical measures could then be applied to the results to determine if the overall assessment here reflects the reasoning of a wider segment of the population.

There is no assurance this conceptual framework would produce similar results for other nation-states. Broader research might be attempted using this conceptual framework to evaluate energy policy choices for another nation-state, or a comparative evaluation of several nation-states might be undertaken to determine if their differing economic, environmental, and national security situations produce similar or different results. What seems appropriate for one nation-state is not automatically appropriate for another, and it would be illuminating to examine similarities and differences.

With some modifications, the conceptual framework might be applied to subnational state energy policy decision making in the United States. Each state in the United States should have an energy policy tailored to its climatic, natural resource, and economic circumstances within the context of the nation as a whole. What is appropriate for California may not be appropriate (or economically feasible) for North Dakota or New Jersey, yet each state has something to contribute to our national energy future. Some energy fuel technologies might be emphasized more in one state than in another in order to move the entire country in a desirable direction. State by state policy comparisons would also be of potential interest in advancing our knowledge of public policy and perhaps even federalism and intergovernmental relations. The large number of national government energy-related programs should be fertile ground for exploration of those issues.

OBSERVATIONS

It should be obvious by now to anyone who is paying attention that climate change is here and our profligate combustion of fossil fuels is the principal cause. We need to slow it down, rethink what we do, shift to less harmful technologies, and act to leave a better world for our children. If polar bears become extinct in the wild, the blame will fall squarely on everyone who drives a car or uses electricity generated with fossil fuels, and especially on the oil and coal company executives who have gotten wealthy encouraging greater use of fossil fuels while denying their own culpability. It is difficult to imagine anything more sad and senseless.

Movement toward a less centralized pattern of energy use to make our energy supplies less vulnerable and less attractive to terrorists is possible. Lower-cost or at least fixed-cost energy choices for residential and commercial energy users are available. Industrial users have strong incentives for self-generation of energy supplies in the prospects of a new revenue stream for excess energy generated and more secure energy supplies than are currently supplied by interconnected power grids.

A quiet concrete home to withstand more frequent storms, electrified by solar photovoltaics, heated and cooled by geothermal heat pumps, with household water heated by solar thermal collectors and a hybrid or fuel cell car in the garage—this is not an impossible dream. It is within reach, if we want it. The important question is, do we want it? We have the technology and the ingenuity. Do we have the will?

The focus here has been to establish a beginning for development of a conceptual framework for analysis of technological options useful in formulating a coherent national energy policy for the United States. If this book has advanced the discussion of relevant issues that must be addressed during the formation of energy policy, it has served its purpose.

REFERENCES

Black Hills Energy. 2011. *Black Hills Energy 2010 Renewable Energy Compliance Report*. Hearing before the Public Utilities Commission of the State of Colorado, Docket No. 09A-494E. In the Matter of the Application of Black Hills/Colorado Electric Utility Company LP, for an Order Approving Its 2010 Qualifying Retail Utility Compliance Plan. Attachment A. 1 June, Denver, CO. Available from Colorado Public Utilities Commission, 1560 Broadway, Suite 250, Denver, CO 80202.

Butler, L., and K. Neuhoff. 2008. "Comparison of Feed-In Tariff, Quota and Auction Mechanisms to Support Wind Power Development." *Renewable Energy* 33: 1854–1867.

ClimateMaster. 2011. "Geothermal Applications." www.climatemaster.com/commercial-geothermal.

Commission of the European Communities (EC). 2005. *Communication from the Commission: The Support of Electricity from Renewable Energy Sources {SEC(2005) 1571}*. Brussels: Commission of the European Communities.

Environmental and Energy Study Institute (EESI). 2006. "Industrial Energy Efficiency: Using New Technologies to Reduce Energy Use in Industry and Manufacturing." Washington, DC: Environmental and Energy Study Institute.

Excel Energy Solutions Inc. 2011. "Geothermal Heating and Cooling: Introduction to Geothermal." www.excelenergysolutions.com/geothermal-heating-cooling-main.html.

GeoExchange. 2011. "Geothermal Heat Pumps." www.geoexchange.org/index.php?option=com_content&view=article&id=48:geothermal-heat-pumps&catid=375:geothermal-hvac&Itemid=32.

German Renewable Energies Agency. 2011. "Politik: Ausbauziele und Förderung Erneuerbarer Energien" (Politics: targets and promotion of renewable energy). www.unendlich-viel-energie.de/de/politik/10-jahre-eeg.html.

Granade, Hannah Choi, Jon Creyts, Anton Derkach, Philip Farese, Scott Nyquist, and Ken Ostrowski. 2009. *Unlocking Energy Efficiency in the U.S. Economy*. Atlanta, GA: McKinsey.

Hamel, Gary, and C.K. Prahalad. 1989. "Strategic Intent." *Harvard Business Review* (May–June): 63–76.

Hinchey, Xanthe. 2011. "Harvesting Energy: Body Heat to Warm Buildings." BBC News, January 9. www.bbc.co.uk/news/business-12137680.

Hughes, Patrick J. 2008. *Geothermal (Ground-Source) Heat Pumps: Market Status, Barriers to Adoption, and Actions to Overcome Barriers*. Oak Ridge: Oak Ridge National Laboratory. www1.eere.energy.gov/geothermal/pdfs/ornl_ghp_study.pdf.

Lauber, Volkmar, and Lutz Mez. 2004. "Three Decades of Renewable Electricity Policies in Germany." *Energy and Environment* 15: 599–623.

L'Ecuyer, Michael, Cathy Zoi, and John S. Hoffman. 1993. *Space Conditioning: The Next Frontier*. Washington, DC: U.S. Environmental Protection Agency.

Lovins, Amory B., E. Kyle Datta, Thomas Feiler, Karl R. Rábago, Joel N. Swisher, André Lehmann, and Ken Wicker. 2002. *Small Is Profitable*. Snowmass, CO: Rocky Mountain Institute.

Lovins, Amory B., and Rocky Mountain Institute. 2011. *Reinventing Fire: Bold Business Solutions for the New Energy Era*. White River Junction, VT: Chelsea Green.

Luque, Rafael, Lorenzo Herrero-Davila, Juan M. Campelo, James H. Clark, Jose M. Hidalgo, Diego Luna, Jose M. Marinas, and Antonio A. Romero. 2008. "Biofuels: A Technological Perspective." *Energy and Environmental Science* 1: 542–564.

Morris, C. 2007. "The Irony of U.S. and UK Renewable Policies: What Prevents These Two Countries from Accepting Germany's Success?" *Renewable Energy World*, June 25.

National Research Council (NRC). 2010. *Hidden Costs of Energy: Unpriced Consequences of Energy Production and Use*. Washington, DC: National Academies Press.

Perlack, Robert D., Lynn L. Wright, Anthony F. Turhollow, Robin L. Graham, Bryce J. Stokes, and Donald C. Erbach. 2005. *Biomass as Feedstock for a Bioenergy and Bioproducts Industry: The Technical Feasibility of a Billion-Ton Annual Supply*. Springfield, VA: U.S. Department of Commerce.

Prahalad, C.K., and Gary Hamel. 1990. "The Core Competence of the Corporation." *Harvard Business Review* (May–June): 79–91.

Risser, Roland. 2011. "Making Smart Windows Smarter." Energy.gov, April 5. http://energy.gov/articles/making-smart-windows-smarter.

Smithfield Construction. 2011. "Earth Power . . ." www.smithfieldconstruction.com/geothermal.htm.

Tilman, David, Robert Socolow, Jonathan A. Foley, Jason Hill, Eric Larson, Lee Lynd, Stephen Pacala, John Reilly, Tim Searchinger, Chris Somerville, and Robert Williams. 2009. "Beneficial Biofuels: The Food, Energy and Environment Trilemma." *Science* 325 (July 17): 270–271.

Union of Concerned Scientists (UCS). 2007a. *Biofuels: An Important Part of a Low-Carbon Diet*. Cambridge, MA: Union of Concerned Scientists.

———. 2007b. "Fuel Economy Basics." November 26. www.ucsusa.org/clean_vehicles/solutions/cleaner_cars_pickups_and_suvs/fuel-economy-basics.html.

———. 2009. "How Geothermal Energy Works." December 16. www.ucsusa.org/clean_energy/technology_and_impacts/energy_technologies/how-geothermal-energy-works.html.

———. 2010. "How Biomass Energy Works." October 29. www.ucsusa.org/clean_energy/technology_and_impacts/energy_technologies/how-biomass-energy-works.html.

U.S. Department of Energy (USDOE). 2004. "How Much Land Will PV Need to Supply Our Electricity?" *PV FAQs*, February (revised). www.nrel.gov/docs/fy04osti/35097.pdf.

U.S. Energy Information Administration (USEIA). 2010. "Oil: Crude and Petroleum Products Explained. Use of Oil: Basics." www.eia.doe.gov/energyexplained/index.cfm?page=oil_use.

———. 2011. *Annual Energy Outlook 2011*. Washington, DC: U.S. Government Printing Office.

U.S. Environmental Protection Agency (USEPA). 2011a. "EPA Issues First National Standards for Mercury Pollution from Power Plants." Press Release, December 21. Washington, DC: U.S. Environmental Protection Agency.

———. 2011b. "EPA Reduces Smokestack Pollution, Protecting Americans' Health from Soot and Smog." Press Release, July 7. Washington, DC: U.S. Environmental Protection Agency.

U.S. Office of Surface Mining Reclamation and Enforcement (USOSM). 1993. *Impact of Acid Rain Controls on Surface Mining Reclamation and Enforcement: Programs and Workload*. Washington, DC: U.S. Department of the Interior, Office of Surface Mining Reclamation and Enforcement.

Index

~~~~~~~~~~~~~~~~~

About the Author

~~~~~~~~~~~~~~~~~~~~

Michael S. Hamilton (PhD 1984, Colorado State University) is emeritus professor of political science at the University of Southern Maine, specializing in environmental and natural resources policy and administration. He has served in various capacities in local, state, and national government. In 2006 his scholarly book, *Mining Environmental Policy: Comparing Indonesia and the USA*, was named by the American Society for Public Administration as the Best Book of Public Administration Scholarship published in 2004 and 2005. His most recent book, *The Dynamics of Law*, 4th ed. (with George W. Spiro) was published by M.E. Sharpe in 2008.